LOVE IS DEEPER THAN WORDS

KEY LESSONS FROM THE PROPHETS

Fadwa Wazwaz

Copyright © 2023 Fadwa Wazwaz. All rights reserved.

No part of this book may be reproduced, or stored in a retrieval system, or transmitted in any form or by any means, electronic, mechanical, photocopying, recording, or otherwise, without express written permission of the publisher.

Cover design by: bookcoverzone.com

ISBN-13: 978-1-7347975-2-7

ISBN-10: 97817347975-3-4 (ebook)

Library of Congress Control Number: 2022905969

Printed in the United States of America

Little Wonders Publishing
Brooklyn Park, Minnesota 55443

In loving memory of those who are forever in our hearts.

To Prophet Muhammad, upon him peace and blessings, God's Chosen One, and also to Amenah Abdel Jawwad Wazwaz, my beloved mother, who loved him tremendously. She raised us under very difficult circumstances, with very little support and few resources, working hard to teach us the faith through her resilience and character in the face of life's challenges and difficult health struggles. In loving memory of my father, Muhammad Abdur Rahman Wazwaz; my paternal grandfather, Abdur Rahman Ibrahim Ali Wazwaz; my maternal grandfather, Abdel Jawwad Ibrahim Ali Wazwaz; my paternal grandmother, Sabriya Abdul Khaliq Abu Turki; and my maternal grandmother, Hamdeh Muhammad al Jamal, without whom I would not exist. Also to all the Prophets of God all the way to Prophet Adam, upon them peace. Finally, to Maryam Laid, my beautiful daughter who I hope will find this book beneficial and write her own book and share her wisdom.

Table of Contents

Why Do Bad Things Happen To Good People? 1

Where Is God: Can I Tell You about Al Fattah? 29

Love Is Deeper Than Words 79

Contemplation and Little Wonders 91

The Covenant 121

Muhammad: The Gates of Heaven Are Open 139

Ego (*Nafs*) versus Faith 171

Learning from Charlatans 195

Trauma, Abuse, Pain, and Suffering 205

Handling Uncertainty: Harness the Wind 221

Abraham: Unless My Lord Guides Me 241

Boundaries and Transgressors 283

Hope versus Obligation 295

What Is Security, and How Do We Find It? 305

Toward Reconciliation and Healing 327

Allahu Akbar: We Love Life 349

The Strong Rope 363

References 381

Acknowledgments 383

About the Author 385

Introduction

*If your eyes saw of Our Beauty that which they saw,
You would not turn away from Us to other ones.*

*And if your ears heard the Beauty of Our Speech,
You would take off the cloak of pride and come to Us.*

*And if you tasted of (Our) Love even a little
You would excuse those who died of Our Love.*

*And if only a breeze from near Us blew to you,
You would die of alienation and eagerness to Our Nearness.*

I begin the book by a set of lines, that I found in the analysis of God al Aziz by Dr. Rateb al Nabulsi (An-Nabulsi). I want to thank you for reading or purchasing this book. I look forward to your feedback and review. Love has been used to nurture society as well as to manipulate people. The title of the book came from questions about where love is in the Quran and why Islam teaches hatred. I used to answer the questions by showing such references in the Quran, but the questioner would return with "problem verses." I invited national speakers to respond, then realized that people are treating God as a human being and asking Him human-related questions. This is the seed of their confusion.

Many search for love in all the wrong places, and some have it close by and cannot recognize it. The epitome of love is love of God, and that is a gift to seek and pray for. This book will help you reflect on the meaning of love, the beauty of God Al-Wadud, and the beauty of His Love.

Parts of this book address reflections on why bad things happen to good people; some of the Beautiful Names of God; the covenant, and faith lessons on love, ego, boundaries, security, healing, and psychological suffering.

There is a need for physicians for people facing trauma, abuse, pain, and psychological problems. The reflections in this book do not undermine the experts. The reflections are outside the scope of medical diagnosis and necessary medical treatment.

This book is not aimed at refuting the narratives of other faiths. Rather, it is meant to share the narrative of the prophets' stories in the Quran. In that spirit, I see those who share the narrative of their faith as loving, kind, and generous. In the past, I was involved in interfaith events at mosques and churches, where each religion got a chance to share its narrative and meanings of normative life experiences. A case in point: two sweet ladies who said they were Jehovah's Witnesses knocked on my door. They wanted to share their message. I thanked them for their kind gesture and intention.

I explained I am Muslim and that if they would like to share their message, they were welcome to come to the mosque, where we invite members of other faiths, and each can speak to the audience. They can also invite Muslims to church, and each party can share what they hold to be true.

They started to share passages from the Bible, and I explained that I used to be involved with interfaith programs and am very familiar with the Christian faith, although out of respect, I do not speak on their behalf. I might share the work of some Christians who share our understanding of some issues, but I do not speak for other faiths.

They continued to share their understanding of the Day of Judgment. I thanked them again for their kindness and wishing for my salvation and asked them to join me in prayer, as God is Witness.

May God guide us to the truth and path of guidance to Him. Amen. They agreed and kindly left, after sharing their card.

Why Do Bad Things Happen To Good People?

> *Do men think that they will be left alone on saying, "We believe", and that they will not be tested? We did test those before them, and Allah will certainly know those who are true from those who are false. (Quran 29:2-3)*

Why bad things happen to good people is a classic question that many have explored throughout the ages. There is a book with the title by Harold Kushner. If you search online, the question is asked in various faiths and circles by people suffering or watching their loved ones suffer. Often, the question is raised in an accusatory way toward God. One reviewer of the book said clearly:

> *Harold Kushner rationalizes suffering by assuming God either cannot or won't intervene to stop it, perhaps with more emphasis on the "cannot." The book builds up to a very good analysis of the Book of Job, where God says that Man cannot understand His work, and perhaps the book should simply have ended here. Instead, the author provides an alternative to Job's analysis, by venturing that God is simply too weak or uncaring to intervene in Man's day to day problems. In Kushner's eyes, religion simply becomes a way of meeting people who can support you in your suffering, but other than that, God really can't help much! This is Atheism-Lite: Just a little bit of God allowed, but not too much. For those seeking a deeper theological (and less hopeless) understanding of suffering, there are many better texts—starting with Thomas Aquinas' analysis of the Book of Job. (reviewer)*

Let us first explore their questions to help us understand.

Does Islam Permit Abortion?

I wanted to share a talk that I heard by Shaykh Rateb al-Nabulsi. You can reflect on it and, as you do, note your thoughts. Shaykh al-

Nabulsi tells a story about another shaykh who had a dream. In the dream, he sees Prophet Muhammad, upon him peace and blessings, who tells him to send greetings to a person in town and give him glad tidings that he is his neighbor in paradise.

The shaykh wondered what this man had done to reach such a station compared to himself, who was working hard to teach and spread the religion. So, he went to give the man the glad tidings but requested that he tell him what deeds he had done to reach such a station. In confidence, the man in question said to him that he was once married to a woman who gave birth four months into their marriage, meaning she was pregnant without his knowledge by someone else. He could have divorced her, in which case she would have been shamed, ostracized, and possibly faced "honor killing," given the town's social reality at the time.

He took the baby while still asleep and went to the mosque. He hid the baby in his thobe (a traditional, long dress). As people entered the mosque, he placed the baby near the door and entered to pray. No one saw him put the baby there. After the prayer, the baby started crying, and some people praying rushed to see what was happening. They wondered who had left the baby there and who would take care of it. The man raised his hand to adopt the baby, leading people to believe that he was unaware of the baby beforehand and that he was just doing a kind act by offering to adopt it. In this way, he covered the woman's sins from everyone in town, including her family and her child, and made her appear as a righteous woman raising a child left at the mosque door out of the kindness of her heart. He did not divorce her but saw God using him to nurture her back to God with grace and make it easy on her soul to repent and grow in faith and purity sincerely.

This story aims not to shame or obligate someone into accepting a relationship in which someone deceived them about taking a child who was not their own. However, if we spent the time and money now used to fight abortion to care for these women and children in dire need, we would be faithfully against abortion according to the spirit of the law. How much time and money are spent fighting abortion, and how much are spent on faithfully giving women opportunities for forgiveness, grace, and a new chapter in their lives?

"I Heard a Rumor..."

Social media has been used to connect people and exchange ideas. Unfortunately, it has also been used to spread lies and false rumors.

People blame social media for many things. I want to give an example to illustrate how, at times, we blame the media instead of looking into our own hearts, which will use whatever means available to manifest what is within it.

Around twenty-plus years ago, an argument took place among a group of women. One of the women involved left the scene of the argument and went straight to the deli, a twenty-minute drive. Social media and cell phones were not around then. Email was mainly used by college students and educational institutes. It was so absurd it needed someone to intervene to resolve the dispute. A mob formed, egging each other to pressure the Shaykh to side with them.

His name was Shaykh Ayman. He was from Jordan and studying for his Ph.D. I met his wife, Sanaa, at college and instantly liked her. We bonded very well. Although she was not a scholar, she was graceful and knowledgeable.

When he entered, the mob took turns pushing their version of the narrative. After they finished, they gave him a letter to sign to support them and judge on their behalf. They wanted him to judge they were right without any evidence. The bandwagon fallacy is not evidence. The woman provided sufficient evidence of a history of abuse by the individuals. He discarded their letter and even threw the pen away. He would not be pressured, he said, to support injustice.

He was the sort of person who, when rumors reached him, they died. He firmly explained the issues with their narratives and the injustice they were asking him to support. He was brief and concise. When he had finished, he stood up and left.

Let us go back even further in time to the early 1900s and another social culture in a small, rural Arab village. A fight broke out between a couple, and the fight escalated to such a degree that it turned into a battle between two families. The rumors and provocation got so bad that some men were pressured by the women of the family to "man up," to prove their virility by putting the men in the other family in their place.

Well, one man got a gun, went to the other family's home, and started shooting. He was targeting one person but mistakenly ended up shooting an innocent man who was not involved in the feud and who was fasting at the time. When people tried to save the victim by giving him water, he refused to break his fast, saying he wanted to die while fasting. He passed away.

God might use him as a witness against everyone involved. Although he was not a female child, it is insightful to reflect on the question the following verse raises:

> When the female [infant], buried alive, is questioned: For what crime she was killed?

—Quran 81:8–9

Over the years, I have met many people of faith who were very noble. They were often not supported because they would not succumb to a mob's social pressure or emotional blackmail or just blindly do the government's bidding.

Slippery Slope

However, it is not just governments that steal or rob the poor. If we're being honest, at times, we ourselves use our skills to bargain down and cheat gullible or vulnerable people.

Many poor villages were destroyed by tourists who came to make a quick buck by exploiting the labor of poor people, people who were not protected by labor laws.

We need to respect the sweat and struggle of the local villagers who labored to produce the goods. Often, we see these as small injustices, and we comfort ourselves that at least we did not rob a bank.

However, if we're not mindful, small steps toward bad behavior can allow us to drift away from our values without our brains ever noticing. This is incrementalism, the "slippery slope," a process whereby we lower our ethical standards or compromise our values, slowly and gradually, until eventually we become unaware of just how much we are contributing to the oppression of others.

Blame It on Politicians

We listen to loud voices but fail to look at actions that have more impact on our lives.

For example, we made a loud noise against Representative Ilhan Omar's reference to 9/11 while trying to explain the mistreatment of Muslims in the aftermath of the attack. Her choice of words was not the best. However, her talk was about the impact 9/11 had on Muslims in the United States.

We overlooked the fact that Representative Omar was among the cosponsors of a bill to reauthorize the 9/11 Victim Compensation

Fund. Yet many politicians were absent during the congressional hearings when this was taking place.

What lessons can we extract from those who yell "Patriotism!" loudly yet disappear in moments like this?

Blame It on Religion

I remember this case like it was yesterday. Three innocent youths killed execution style by a neighbor who clearly hated them.

On February 10, 2015, Deah Shaddy Barakat, Yusor Mohammad Abu-Salha, and Razan Mohammad Abu-Salha were murdered in Chapel Hill, North Carolina. Over four years later, on June 12, 2019, their killer finally pleaded guilty in court to three counts of murder and one count of discharging a firearm into an occupied building. He accepted three consecutive life sentences without the possibility of parole.

At the strike of the calamity, I recall the words of one of the family members, words that I saved:

> *It doesn't makes sense, and for that I rely on the Most Wise. It hurts and for that I know that God will not burden me more than I can handle. I know my brother, his wife, and his sister-in-law are together as ultimate winners. This life was only ever a test and they have passed with flying colors. They have won, and for that I rejoice. I am sincerely happy for each of them. I pray God grants the rest of us the patience to accept this. We live as Muslims to die as Muslims. May Allah enter them to the highest of Paradise. May we be reunited with them...God is great. God is greater. (Barakat)*

The words were full of faith, surrendering to God in grace and acceptance of His decree in the face of a calamity full of pain and suffering. Hopefully, their sharing of this horrible story will help others who are struggling with similar pain and atrocities.

Many headlines, including one in the *New York Times*, asked if Craig Hicks, the murderer, had committed a hate crime. This was not a hate crime; it was an act of domestic terrorism and should have been tried as such.

Stories

Stories help us reflect on our own lives and extract meaning and understanding. There are a few stories in the eighteenth chapter of the Quran, titled "The Kahf" or "The Cave." Just simple information is shared, and the reader is left to explore the questions, conversations, and interactions of the characters with God.

One of these stories is about two men: one successful in the material sense and another not so. Sometimes we deem ourselves good people because we do not do anything terrible per se. But we are deluded. And our internal state is such that we have these thought processes that God is aware of, and life experiences come to teach us lessons or nurture within us genuine faith. God knows what our inner stories and thoughts are, and we do as well. In our clash with others, we might spill them out, and it might become evident if we are faithful or deluded.

Who are you in such conversations? Have you ever clashed with someone in a similar conversation? What were your thoughts? Did a calamity hit you after hard work and success, even though you never harmed anyone, but your thoughts and view of yourself and others were akin to the successful person in this passage?

Parable of Two Men

Let us read and reflect on Chapter 18 of the Holy Quran, or "The Kahf," Verses 32–44:

> *Set forth to them the parable of two men: for one of them We provided two gardens of grape-vines and surrounded them with date palms; in between the two We placed corn-fields. Each of those gardens brought forth its produce, and failed not in the least therein: in the midst of them We caused a river to flow. [Abundant] was the produce this man had: he said to his companion, in the course of a mutual argument: "more wealth have I than you, and more honor and power in [my following of] men."*
>
> *He went into his garden in a state [of mind] unjust to his soul: He said, "I deem not that this will ever perish, "Nor do I deem that the Hour [of Judgment] will [ever] come: Even if I am brought back to my Lord, I shall surely find [there] something better in exchange." His companion said to him, in the course of the argument with him: "Dost thou deny Him Who created thee out of dust, then out of a sperm-drop, then fashioned thee into a man?*
>
> *"But [I think] for my part that He is Allah, My Lord, and none shall I associate with my Lord.*

> "Why didst thou not, as thou wentest into thy garden, say: 'Allah's will [be done]! There is no power but with Allah!' If thou dost see me less than thee in wealth and sons, "It may be that my Lord will give me something better than thy garden, and that He will send on thy garden thunderbolts [by way of reckoning] from heaven, making it [but] slippery sand! Or the water of the garden will run off underground so that thou wilt never be able to find it." So his fruits [and enjoyment] were encompassed [with ruin], and he remained twisting and turning his hands over what he had spent on his property, which had [now] tumbled to pieces to its very foundations, and he could only say, "Woe is me! Would I had never ascribed partners to my Lord and Cherisher!" Nor had he numbers to help him against Allah, nor was he able to deliver himself. There, the [only] protection comes from Allah, the True One. He is the Best to reward, and the Best to give success.

We may have credited our success to our hard work, but we neglected to recognize our privilege and bountiful resources, and we claimed credit for our success rather than being grateful to God for such blessings and sharing them with others. This challenge can help one understand that knowledge.

My Body, My Business

> And the messengers whom We sent before thee were all [men] who ate food and walked through the streets: We have made some of you as a trial for others: will ye have patience? for Allah is One Who sees [all things].
>
> —Quran 25:20

At times, we have arguments. However, while we sell it to others for ourselves, we eliminate God from such an argument. A case in point: "my body is my business. No one should tell me what choice or decision to make with my body."

If you ask this same person on a different occasion, do you believe God has the right to make whatever decisions He wants with His creation, His heaven, His hellfire, and His universe? It is His property, and His business.

I have never met one person who believes "my body is my business" who replied yes. The point I wish to raise is not to argue with this understanding but rather that you cannot sell an argument to others if, deep within, you do not believe it or accept it for others.

In this case, God. Hence, the question of why bad things happen to good people stems from having a bad opinion and judgment of God. Chapter 21, Verse 23 of the Holy Quran teaches us "He cannot be questioned for His acts, but they will be questioned [for theirs]."

We are invited to surrender to this revelation and seek wisdom and understanding. What we can extract from the argument "My body, my business" is how it feels to be controlled by others and not to treat God in such a manner that He owes us an explanation for His actions. Hence, as Muslims, when we see disturbing things, we say, "To God we belong, to God is our final return."

Other Stories

As we learned with COVID-19, our actions do not just impact us but other innocent people too. For example, we practice social distancing, wear masks, and wash our hands to protect ourselves and others. Hence, the laws have more to do with public concern and protecting innocent people from harm, rather than controlling others.

A young woman in Florida got married, then divorced. The individual didn't give her the agreed-upon *mahr* or dowry—sort of like a gift that the spouse has to pay. The problem did not end there. She became sick and found out she had AIDS. I am not sure what happened to her, but I recall the case, and there are others like it.

A woman with four kids went to the doctor for a checkup as she was pregnant. She did not speak English well, so she did not understand when the doctor explained she had AIDS. They brought in a translator who explained it to her. She was shocked, given that she was living a very traditional and socially conservative lifestyle. Her husband had violated that relationship without her knowledge. Both she and her husband passed away, leaving all four kids. I am not sure what happened to the fifth child she was carrying.

I am sure we have all heard similar stories in which one party's actions transgressing and violating moral values bring harm to many innocents. Often, when one speaks against sexual promiscuity, people respond with the following:

1. My body is not sinful.
2. Sex is not sinful.

3. Women and men should embrace their sexuality.

I'd like to pose the following question: If we use our bodies in ways that can significantly injure innocent individuals without their knowledge, authorization, or consent, are our decisions about our bodies purely "our business"?

We all wish to call out instances in which individuals in power cross lines and hurt the environment, such as falsehoods that lead to war, buildings that break the rules, and countless other types of injustice and tyranny. Remember the aftermath of COVID-19, when individuals exploited their freedom to behave carelessly, with little regard for how their actions might negatively or tragically affect the lives of others. We must acknowledge that AIDS and sexually transmitted illnesses are a worldwide issue.

Our body is our business if the impact of our choices and decisions is exclusively on us and any consenting adult. When they affect innocent others outside that circle, their consultation and demands for protection from such harm are reasonable.

Lessons in Compassion

Sometimes things happen to teach us compassion and mercy. An example of that would be a child or a loved one who develops a terminal disease. As we take care of them, we ourselves are nurtured in compassion and mercy.

Sometimes such individual carers will learn from these experiences to help others in similar cases, like social activism for the blind, the deaf, and orphans.

Prophet Muhammad, upon him peace and blessings, grew up as an orphan. Except for His daughter Fatima, He watched all his children pass before him. Sometimes, trials are the means to nurture such understanding within us.

Lessons on Justice

> *The word of thy Lord doth find its fulfilment in truth and in justice: None can change His words: for He is the one who heareth and knoweth all. Wert thou to follow the common run of those on earth, they will lead thee away from the way of Allah. They follow nothing but conjecture: they do nothing but lie. Thy Lord knoweth best who strayeth from His way: He knoweth best who they are that receive His guidance.*

—Quran 6:115–117

Unfortunately, only a few people are truthful in their perceptions, narrations of events, or relationships with others. Sometimes difficulties come our way to teach us knowledge and help us discern between the real and the false, the just and the oppressor.

We see in the story of Prophet Solomon, upon him peace, that the Queen of Sheba first had to deal with bad kings who ruled with tyranny over their people. From this experience, she learned what not to do and gained wisdom and respect such that she ruled over her people through consultation and wisdom. Prophet Solomon, upon him peace, was informed by one of his birds, the hoopoe, a woman ruling over the people, and has been given many blessings and has a mighty throne, are worshiping the sun instead of Allah. Prophet Solomon, upon him peace, decided to send a message to the Queen, whose name was Bilqis, inviting her and her people to worship God:

When faced with a letter from Prophet Solomon, upon him peace, she could have responded by turning the army against him and fighting until death. She could have acted threatened and insecure and started to spread hate, given her experiences of bad kings. She could have started conjecturing all sorts of falsehoods.

Instead, she responded with truth and justice. She consulted her chiefs and declined to energize her army into war. She went to engage Prophet Solomon, upon him peace.

Queen Bilqis was wise and tested Prophet Solomon by sending him gifts to see his reaction. In this way, she would know if Prophet Solomon, upon him peace, was only interested in wealth or true in his call to God. Prophet Solomon responded with: Will ye give me abundance in wealth? But that which Allah has given me is better than that which He has given you! (Quran, 27:36)

The Queen of Sheba was impressed and traveled to meet the one who had sent a message to her. The sad part is that many of us do not learn from such negative experiences what not to do. We give speeches, conjecture, make assumptions, and lie.

Instead of assuming we are closer to unjust rulers and learning how to be just, we assume we are just rulers. Instead of starting with "I do not know," we begin with conjecture and lies and demand that others accept them as truth.

Being just and true is no easy matter. It is no mean feat for the common folk to do. It is something we should strive for and is well rewarded by God Most High.

It has been narrated on the authority of 'Abdullah b. 'Amr that the Messenger of Allah, upon him peace and blessings, said: "Behold! the Dispensers of justice will be seated on the pulpits of Light beside God, on the right side of the Merciful, Exalted and Glorious. Either side of the Being is the right side, both being equally meritorious. [The Dispensers of justice are] those who do justice in their rules, in matters relating to their families and in all that they undertake to do." (Muslim 1827)

Nurturing a World Leader

A world leader needs to be sharp and able to deal with threats to their country and have a strong commander-in-chief personality that can bring their country or people together.

Although both Moses and Aaron were brothers and prophets, upon them peace, God chose Moses, upon him peace, to lead his people. He learned strong leadership skills while being raised in the house of the Pharaoh.

The Pharaoh used his leadership skills for oppression and domination. However, these skills can be purified and used for good. When Moses, upon him peace, was exiled from Egypt, these skills were fine-tuned under a prophet. Working as a shepherd, he was able to learn patience, mercy, and forbearance. Then, he was sent back to Egypt to become a world leader.

Lessons on Truth

In the past, I argued that the "obvious truths" are based on many layers of self-deception that hinder our understanding of ourselves and, thus, others.

A case in point: in the hours following a shooting that left a Canadian soldier dead, Bill Maher, a comedian, and yapping commentator on everything had this to say: "Turns out the attacker was Islamic—what are the odds, huh? It's almost like there's an elephant in the room." (Ghabra)

Whenever a Muslim is the offender, Sam Harris and Richard Dawkins argue likewise. Dawkins and Harris are atheists and scientists who love to engage in political and social controversies based on fallacies and prejudice.

The problem with this format is that no one asks who created the room. And how and why is there an elephant in the room? The room is usually the psychological and social construction of those with power and voice, while the elephant in the room is always the little people or people who are unprotected and voiceless. It is somewhat dishonest to argue, "It's almost like there's an elephant in the room."

Truth is not as obvious as societal ills—and psychological constructions bury the reality of things and people.

To get to this lesson's point: sometimes we do not understand the wisdom behind events. Moses, upon him peace, did not know he was being trained and nurtured as a prophet, messenger, and world leader. Years later, God explained His wisdom behind events happening to him. Likewise for Prophet Muhammad, upon Him peace and blessings.

The processing of these situations came later as they needed to grow in certitude and faith to understand the wisdom. Some trauma psychologists argue against facing trauma and processing immediately. Rather, they argue that it is better to strengthen the wellbeing of the survivor, and when the survivor indicates that they are ready, to help them face the trauma.

> *Recovery requires a significant amount of rebuilding of the self and renewing a sense of connection to the foundations of life. The goal in rebuilding and renewing cannot be to throw out everything from the past or try to get back to things the way they used to be. Rather it must be to reclaim familiar and enduring elements of the past and reframe them in a new configuration of purpose and meaning. (Odelya Gertel Kraybill Ph.D.)*

We learn from this that the best way to receive or embrace trials and tribulations is to surrender, not to people but to God. What does it mean to surrender? It means to accept and not deny reality. We don't have to like it, but we should turn to God and seek His help and guidance in dealing with it.

God told Prophet Muhammad, upon him peace and blessings, it is not you the enemies are against but the truth. The elevation of truth can destroy the psychological and social constructs or the room, enabling racism, xenophobia, and other forms of oppression.

At times, in engaging in the "elephant in the room" conversations, there is an invisible social agreement that does not accept everyone. As we saw in the Charlie Hebdo affair, there were double standards regarding free speech that mocks people with power and those without influence and power. What value is speech or discussion in which others are treated as objects and interrogated, psychoanalyzed, and judged—but not engaged with as human beings?

Charlie Hebdo is a French satirical weekly magazine featuring cartoons, reports, polemics, and jokes. They regularly produce racist cartoons of immigrants, the poor, and Prophet Muhammad, upon him peace and blessings. In 2015, twelve people were massacred after racist and inflammatory depictions of Prophet Muhammad, upon him peace and blessings were published. There was global outrage at the violence. However, the international outrage was in denial of France's colonialism. France's 1830 invasion of Algeria began a 130-year quest of murder, expropriation, racism, exploitation, and misrule that only ended after a vicious anti-colonial struggle costing well over one million Algerian lives. Why are we not discussing this elephant?

"The elephant in the room," we want to discuss are attempts to erase from our psyche the injustices we committed against others. It is not our differences or fear of our differences that nurtures hatred among us, but rather acts of injustice. If these acts of oppression are not rectified, and we have the power and voice to do so, then the hatred brews and festers.

One of God's Names is *An-Nur*, or the Light. The word for oppression in Arabic is *dhulm*, which means darkness. Hence, one understanding of *dhulm* or oppression is disconnection from God, the Light. Some tribulations can happen to connect us to the Light, become a means to connect our communities to the Light, or destroy the social and psychological constructs that prevent the Light from entering the room, making us see an elephant conjecture instead of facts.

Lessons on Wisdom

Moses, upon him peace, met with a man of the elect, Al Khidr, of those who were given special knowledge. It is important to note that he was not running after Moses, upon him peace. Rather, Moses wanted to meet him and follow him to learn wisdom.

He also had certain rules of engagement and spreading knowledge. It is important to note this, given the numerous spiritual gurus who create cults and harm people. The *Associated Press* had an article about a spiritual guru. (Hays)

I mention cases like this a lot to help people differentiate between a spiritual teacher and a fraud as there are people out there making such claims that seek people out to manipulate and harm them.

The relationship between Moses, upon him peace, and Al Khidr was strictly student and teacher. When Moses could not meet the guidelines, he and the teacher parted ways in peace. He explained his actions based on his knowledge of the spiritual world to help us understand some of life's blows:

> *He answered: "This is the parting between me and thee: now will I tell thee the interpretation of [those things] over which thou wast unable to hold patience.*
>
> *As for the boat, it belonged to certain men in dire want: they plied on the water: I but wished to render it unserviceable, for there was after them a certain king who seized on every boat by force...*
>
> —Quran 18:78-79
>
> *I did it not of my own accord. Such is the interpretation of [those things] over which thou wast unable to hold patience.*
>
> —Quran 18:82

At times, a bad thing happens to us to protect us from a worst atrocity that was going to harm us. Once, my car struggled to start when the traffic light turned green. A car ran the red light, leading to a car hitting another car before we crossed the intersection.

Lessons on Support

Suppose your faith is such that you can turn to God for support, help, and faith to deal with your trials. You lost a child or spouse, have personal financial problems, et cetera, and prayed to God to grant you patience and reward you with something better.

Now let us play with the dials and the settings. It is recommended to fast throughout the year, optional fasting. Few can fast—or do so. However, during Ramadan, with group support and motivation, even the weakest members manage to join the fast.

Trials and tribulations are the same. Sometimes we can handle a trial if others struggle in the same trials, and we motivate each other for strength in faith.

Lessons on Unfairness

However, what if the issue is not the trial but the fact that someone like us in faith and work ethic is given more than we are or rewarded differently?

Two best friends both got married, and each had a child. One lost her husband in an accident, and her child was severely injured and required lots of care. The other is having a happy married life and raising their child.

Sometimes the trial is not what happened to you as much as what happened to you versus what happened to another with the same level of faith and work ethics.

Let us go back to the question I asked before. Does God have a right to make decisions with His universe and His creation?

> *Say, "O Allah, Owner of Sovereignty, You give sovereignty to whom You will and You take sovereignty away from whom You will. You honor whom You will and You humble whom You will. In Your hand is [all] good. Indeed, You are over all things competent. You cause the night to enter the day, and You cause the day to enter the night; and You bring the living out of the dead, and You bring the dead out of the living. And You give provision to whom You will without account."*
>
> —Quran 3:26–27

It is natural for us to struggle and get piqued at unfairness. A scientific study by primatologist Frans de Waal showed that capuchin monkeys "get" unfairness. In the filmed experiment, one of the monkeys was originally quite satisfied with a cucumber reward for carrying out a task. But the animal quickly becomes piqued when a second monkey was given a vastly preferable grape reward for carrying out the same task. As human beings, we reject unfairness.

I want to add that this is not condoning economic slavery or inequality, but rather expressing how we will accept receiving a cucumber, meaning our nature is such that we can handle a trial. However, if someone else gets a grape, we start to protest. Hence, it is not sufficient to test one with a trial that will not shake their nature and force them to struggle.

God knows our nature, and at times, to make a trial a true test, it comes in such a way that shakes us. Hence, we are forced to turn to God to pass the trial, which is the aim of the trial anyway. If we can pass by turning to ourselves or our kind, gentle, easygoing nature, then the trial did not serve its purpose, and we were not tested fairly or challenged to our inner depths.

The trial might be a means to push labor laws or better pay or remove economic injustices. In the case of the two women, it might be to assess and reframe their perception of life.

Lessons in Patience

To continue from the previous lesson, let us play with the dials and settings some more.

This time, we have people. Some are given to mischief and others are, well … angelic in nature. An example of this would be two people, one innocent and one guilty, waiting for a trial.

The innocent one is found guilty, and the guilty one is found innocent, and all charges dropped.

You probably comforted your soul with God when they were both standing trial, but when this result came, it might have pushed you to question God, not in an understanding way but in an accusatory way.

Joseph, upon him peace, was innocent in prison. Another man in prison was freed after standing trial. He also forgot to relay a message to the king on behalf of Joseph. In such situations, God is testing your faith to a higher degree and intensity than before and rewarding you with more closeness and reliance on Him. Peoples' levels of faith are not all at the same degree. Sometimes God invites you to higher stages and greater closeness to Him.

You can question God, or you can open your heart to the invitation before you. This does not mean you do not use the means available to you to fight oppression but that you do not accuse God and blame Him.

"Our greatest export today is our entertainment, and it is our culture," Ta-Nehisi Coates told *Democracy Now!* in June 2019, a day after he testified to Congress about the need for reparations.

> *It is impossible to imagine American culture without jazz, without the blues, without hip-hop. It's impossible to imagine American cinema without, regrettably, Birth of a Nation. It's impossible to imagine American literature at this point without James Baldwin, without Toni Morrison. All of these are the primary, secondary, tertiary fruits of slavery. And so, if you strip slavery out of America, if you strip black people out of America, you really don't have an America.*

Oppression teaches us things and higher realities that privilege never will. Read a book by someone oppressed and read another by a person who lived a life of privilege. Which one will have more gems of wisdom and beneficial understandings?

I prefer the books and writings of Toni Morrison to those of Ivanka Trump. Again, you are not supposed to develop Stockholm syndrome or attachment to abuse and suffering. Joseph, upon him peace, wanted out of prison. You are invited to receive higher understandings of faith while fighting oppression. These understandings will be shared with humanity through you and will be of benefit.

Lessons on Fighting Oppression

Sometimes God uses you to discipline people and to bear witness to His protection, criterion, and aid. At times, we must face our enemies in battle and remove the chains of oppression.

> *O ye who believe! if ye fear Allah, He will grant you a criterion [to judge between right and wrong], remove from you [all] evil [that may afflict] you, and forgive you: for Allah is the Lord of grace unbounded. Remember how the Unbelievers plotted against thee, to keep thee in bonds, or slay thee, or get thee out [of thy home]. They plot and plan, and Allah too plans; but the best of planners is Allah.*
>
> *When Our Signs are rehearsed to them, they say: "We have heard this [before]: if we wished, we could say [words] like these: these are nothing but tales of the ancients."*
>
> —Quran 8:29–31

Lessons on Treachery

I wanted to combine the lessons on inequity between two like people and the next one: the innocent and the one given to mischief. Let us play with the dial and settings some more. This time, someone who is given a grape stands up for someone given a cucumber, then is backstabbed.

We often find or assume that only people who are oppressed will stand for the oppressed. Or we assume those who are living lives of privilege will not take a stand. And if they do, at times, they find they are backstabbed, or it backfires in their faces.

An example of this would be Moses, upon him peace, who was walking in the city and saw two men fighting. One was a fellow Israelite and the other an Egyptian. The Israelite recognized Moses, upon him peace, and asked for his help.

Moses, upon him peace, wanted to help and, not realizing his strength and power, struck the Egyptian one blow to push him away. The Egyptian died. Moses, upon him peace, felt remorse as that was never his intention.

> *And he entered the city at a time when its people were not watching: and he found there two men fighting—one of his own religion, and the other, of his foes. Now the man of his own religion appealed to him against his foe, and Moses struck him with his fist and made an end of him. He said: "This is a work of Evil [Satan]: for he is an enemy that manifestly misleads!" He prayed: "O my Lord! I have indeed wronged my soul! Do Thou then forgive me!" So [Allah] forgave him: for He is the Oft-Forgiving, Most Merciful. He said: "O my Lord! For that Thou hast bestowed Thy Grace on me, never shall I be a help to those who sin!"*

—Quran 28:15-17

The next day, Moses saw the same man involved in yet another fight. He felt this man was a troublesome person. No one knew what had happened the previous day, except Moses and his fellow Israelite.

> *So he saw the morning in the city, looking about, in a state of fear, when behold, the man who had, the day before, sought his help called aloud for his help [again]. Moses said to him: "Thou art truly, it is clear, a quarrelsome fellow!" Then he tried to help him, but the fellow Israelite projects his reality unto Moses, putting his life in danger by mentioning what happened yesterday, with no regard to Moses.*

> *And when he wanted to strike the one who was an enemy to both of them, he said, "O Moses, do you intend to kill me as you killed someone yesterday? You only want to be a tyrant in the land and do not want to be of the amenders."*

—Quran 28:18–19

The Egyptian heard this remark and rushed to report Moses to the authorities.

> *And a man came from the farthest end of the city, running. He said, "O Moses, indeed the eminent ones are conferring over you [intending] to kill you, so leave [the city]; indeed, I am to you of the sincere advisors." So he left it, fearful and anticipating [apprehension]. He said, "My Lord, save me from the wrongdoing people. Then, when he turned his face towards [the land of] Madyan, he said: "I do hope that my Lord will show me the smooth and straight Path."*
>
> —Quran 28:20–22

What lessons can one extract from this trial?

Moses, upon him peace, was being trained to become a prophet and learn wisdom in fighting oppression and helping people. He had to learn the power of his strength but also that among the oppressed are wrongdoers. While he was sacrificing his privilege and life for his fellow Israelite, the latter was willing to sacrifice Moses's life to become a tyrant and project his inner reality onto Moses while doing so.

> *When he reached full age, and was firmly established [in life], We bestowed on him wisdom and knowledge: for thus do We reward those who do good.*
>
> —Quran 28:14

I am about to wrap up the theme for this chapter. I want to pause and bring us to a conversation in Chapter 18 of the Quran.

> *And [warn of] the Day when We will remove the mountains and you will see the earth prominent, and We will gather them and not leave behind from them anyone. And they will be presented before your Lord in rows, [and He will say], "You have certainly come to Us just as We created you the first time. But you claimed that We would never make for you an appointment." And the record [of deeds] will be placed [open], and you will see the criminals fearful of that within it, and they will say, "Oh, Woe to us! What is this book that leaves nothing small or great except that it has enumerated it?" And they will find what they did present [before them].*
>
> *And your Lord does injustice to no one.*
>
> *And [mention] when We said to the angels, "Prostrate to Adam," and they prostrated, except for Iblees. He was of the jinn and departed from the command of his*

> *Lord. Then will you take him and his descendants as allies other than Me while they are enemies to you? Wretched it is for the wrongdoers as an exchange. I did not make them witness to the creation of the heavens and the earth or to the creation of themselves, and I would not have taken the misguiders as assistants.*
>
> —Quran 18:47–51

This passage serves as a powerful reminder to those who have been wronged that justice will eventually prevail. No matter how big or small the action, all of our deeds are recorded, and oppressors will have to answer for their actions. This assurance helps increase our faith and confidence in pursuing justice, even when faced with additional injustice. Furthermore, it serves as a warning to those who may consider oppressing others, as they will face the consequences of their actions. Despite the challenges and obstacles that may arise, the words of God offer reassurance that justice will always prevail.

If God lets them go in this world, it is because He did not see good in them. If God saw good in them, He would have disciplined them, nurtured them, trained them, purified them, et cetera.

Iblees or Satan is such a person. So are the Pharaoh and those who follow them in their actions and plotting and planning. We see people get away with many crimes and face justice after decades, likewise, on the Day of Judgment. People who thought they had escaped justice will face their book of deeds.

Another lesson in this passage is that while some start to blame God during trials and tribulations and hold a bad opinion of Him, God has a good opinion of humanity—by creating human beings, bestowing on us His divine breath, and inviting us to turn to Him, a door at the ranks of the angels or higher was opened by knowing God through these trials and tribulations at an intimate level that the angels could not.

It also teaches us that love is deeper than words. What may appear as double standards might be God protecting you from criminal behavior or preventing you from engaging or enabling injustice. He saw goodness in you, and out of His Love for you, He rewarded you by preventing you from committing the actions of criminals.

You will find many examples of God shedding light on bad things happening to good people. Ultimately, we are invited to realize that the universe and everything within it belong to God, Most High.

In fact, during a calamity or a trial, Muslims will comfort each other with the saying, "To God we belong, and to God is our final return."

In summary, it's crucial to remember that our understanding of God, ourselves, and love may be flawed when faced with trying circumstances. By seeking the truth about our existence and the hereafter, we strengthen our faith in the face of challenges. This will expand our hearts to higher realities, where such questions are no longer logical to consider due to this wisdom and inner insight.

His Universe, His Property, and His Business

> *They have not estimated Allah His Rightful Estimate. Verily, Allah is All-Strong, All-Mighty.*
>
> —Quran 22:74

God is not a human being. People try to human-explain God's actions. If we reflect on His Names and Attributes - we can stop placing God on the witness stand and asking accusatory questions that make sense to ask of another human being, but not of God. We don't ask human-related questions of fish or bees, so why of God?

There is nothing wrong with turning to God to comfort one's soul and seek guidance and wisdom in one's trial. We go wrong when we bring God, Most High, to our station, put Him on a witness stand, and prosecute Him for His decisions and actions. That is pure arrogance.

You have heard of the term *mansplaining*, an explanation of something by a man, typically to a woman, in a manner regarded as condescending or patronizing. There is also "human-explaining," an accusation of God by humans in a way considered to be condescending or patronizing.

> *They made not a just estimate of Allah such as is due to Him. And on the Day of Resurrection the whole of the earth will be grasped by His Hand and the heavens will be rolled up in His Right Hand. Glorified be He, and High be He above all that they associate as partners with Him!*
>
> —Quran 39:67

The experiences we have among each other should help us reflect on our behavior toward God. We should take a step back and ask ourselves if we engage toward God in ways that we dislike from others toward us. If we can accept "My body, my business," why do we struggle with "His universe, His business"?

As you reflect on why bad things happen to good people while reading the Quran, you will come to Chapter 56, titled *"Al Waqi'ah"* or "The Big Event." It refers to the Day of Judgment. It can refer to any event or misfortune that shakes you to your core and puts you in dire need. This chapter is between the chapters *"Ar-Rahman"* and *"Al-Hadid."* I like to think that the chapter *"Al Hadid,"* or "The Iron," references misfortunes or bad things happening via an event that brings us to *Ar-Rahman*.

Ar-Rahman is one of God's most referenced names in the Quran. We begin every activity, including our five daily prayers, by calling on His name *Ar-Rahman*, which means "The Most Lovingly Beneficent, The Most Kind and Giving, The Most Gracious, The Infinitely Good.

> Imagine there's heaven, hell, and a Sacred Law
> Imagine with certainty standing before God answering for our deeds.
> Imagine every evil we do; we will face true accountability.
> Imagine every good we do; we shall be rewarded.
> Imagine no one will treated with injustice
> and no one will escape justice. . .

How would we treat each other if we knew there were consequences and a Day of Judgment? Knowing we are human, would we call on *Ar-Rahman* as often as possible in every event and activity because we desire His Mercy, Kindness, and Beneficence to help us weather our flaws and shortcomings and the consequences to our actions?

Trials and tribulations bring us to our most basic human need: His Guidance and Mercy. Moses came to this junction after he was forced to flee the Pharaoh. He said: "O, my Lord! truly am I in [desperate] need of any good that Thou dost send me!" (Quran 28:24)

He made this prayer after helping women in need of his strength to water their flock. His helping without asking for anything in return illustrates that his heart was still full of hope and goodness, instead of despair.

The Danger of Conjecture: Answer the Call

Who should tell the definitive story of humanity, the Creator or created?

> *[His father] said, "Have you no desire for my gods, O Abraham? If you do not desist, I will surely stone you, so avoid me a prolonged time."*
>
> *[Abraham] said, "Peace will be upon you. I will ask forgiveness for you of my Lord. Indeed, He is ever gracious to me. And I will leave you and those you invoke other than Allah and will invoke my Lord. I expect that I will not be in invocation to my Lord unhappy."*
>
> *So when he had left them and those they worshipped other than Allah, We gave him Isaac and Jacob, and each [of them] We made a prophet. And We gave them of Our mercy, and we made for them a reputation of high honor.*
>
> *And mention in the Book, Moses. Indeed, he was chosen, and he was a messenger and a prophet. And We called him from the side of the mount at [his] right and brought him near, confiding [to him].*
>
> *And We gave him out of Our mercy his brother Aaron as a prophet.*
>
> *And mention in the Book, Ishmael. Indeed, he was true to his promise, and he was a messenger and a prophet. And he used to enjoin on his people prayer and zakah and was to his Lord pleasing.*
>
> *And mention in the Book, Idrees. Indeed, he was a man of truth and a prophet. And We raised him to a high station.*
>
> *Those were some of the prophets on whom Allah did bestow His Grace, of the posterity of Adam, and of those who We carried (in the Ark) with Noah, and of the posterity of Abraham and Israel of those whom We guided and chose. Whenever the Signs of (Allah) Most Gracious were rehearsed to them, they would fall down in prostrate adoration and in tears.*
>
> —Quran 19:46–58

24-Love Is Deeper Than Words

Borrowing from Nigerian novelist Chimamanda Adichie's TED talk: The danger of a single story.

It is impossible to talk about faith without talking about power. One of the Names of God is *Ad-Daarr*. Whenever I think about the world's power structures, I think about this name.

Imam Ghazali said, do not suppose that poison kills or harms by itself ... or that kings or men or Satan, or any creature, are capable of good or evil, benefit or harm, by themselves. For all of these are subservient causes from which nothing proceeds except that for which they were utilized.

We begin each morning and evening with these supplications:

> *I seek refuge in the Perfect Words of Allah from the evil of what He has created.*
>
> *In the Name of Allah, with Whose Name nothing on the earth or in the heaven can cause harm, and He is the All-Hearing, the All-Knowing.*
>
> *There is none worthy of worship except Allah alone. He has no partners. To Him belongs the Dominion, to Him belongs all praise and He is capable over all things (Riyad as-Salihin).*

God's attributes *Ad-Daarr* and *An-Nafi'* often acknowledge how balance and harmony are established and maintained in our world.

An-Nafi' (creator of good) is the opposite of *Ad-Daarr* (distresser). These opposing attributes teach us that what is the sweetest nectar to one person may be bitter poison to another.

Such opposites help make us aware of who is in power and that we are all subservient to the All-Knowing hand of Allah, through whom balance and harmony are created and maintained even if we don't understand.

There is a Divine Plan beyond our human comprehension, and these pairs of opposites remind us to constantly focus our attention on His Glory, regardless of whether the situation is smooth and easy or rough and challenging.

Abu Hashim Madani said, "There is only one virtue and one sin for a soul on the path: virtue when he is conscious of God and sin when he is not."

Listening to just one definitive story—one story about people of faith, the Prophet Muhammad, and Moses—risks a critical misunderstanding. The Nigerian novelist Chimamanda Adichie argued in her powerful TED talk that our lives and cultures are composed of many overlapping stories. She is correct that stories are dependent on power. How they are told, who tells them, when they're told, and how many stories are told depend on power. Power is the ability not just to tell stories but to make them the absolute and definitive reality of humanity.

Palestinian poet Mourid Barghouti writes that if you want to dispossess a people, the simplest way to do it is to tell their story and start with "secondly." Start the story with the trial or tribulation, the fall, and not with the Divine Breath into Adam; you have an entirely different story. Start the story with evil and human suffering, and not with our turning away from God, and you have an altogether different story.

But it would never have occurred to me to think that just because I had read a novel in which a character was a spiritual abuser, he was somehow representative of all people of faith. This is not because I am a better person than liberals but because of the Quran's cultural and powerful stories; I had many stories of people who represented God faithfully. I had many stories of the Prophets and the righteous people. I read about Adam, Noah, Abraham, Jesus, Moses, and Muhammad, upon them peace and blessings. I have read about Mary, Asiya, Fatima, Khadijah, Sarah, and Hajar, upon them peace. I did not have a single story of people calling to God faithfully.

Some years ago, I learned that people of God were expected to have a large following to be successful. Then, the stories of Abraham and Noah, upon them peace, and the many Prophets who did not have large followings centered me.

These stories teach us lessons about resolve, patience, sincerity, and truthfulness. Righteous people faced significant trials while connected to God throughout. And most of all, they met a kind of normalized political fear that invaded their lives then and invades our lives now.

These stories were the means to nurture and train the final Messenger, Prophet Muhammad, upon him peace and blessings. Yet they not only developed him but also built stories of faith during his lifetime experience and nurtured and built the companions who surrounded him. Stories of conjecture contribute to social, mental, emotional, and psychological illnesses, and the problem with these illnesses is not that they are untrue but that they are incomplete.

Of course, trials, tribulations, evil, and human suffering exist. But other stories are not about catastrophe, and it is vital—it is just as important—to talk about them.

I've always felt that it was impossible to engage properly with a place or person without engaging with all of that place's or person's stories. The consequence of conjecture is this: it disconnects people from God. This results in the spread of disinformation and misinformation. It makes our awareness and consciousness of God difficult. It emphasizes human suffering and evil rather than God's many blessings.

So, what if we learned about the life experiences of Prophet Abraham and his family and how they lived their faith? What if we kept reviewing the life of Prophet Muhammad, upon him peace and blessings, and his companions? What if we had a network that broadcast the diverse Prophetic stories worldwide—what the Nigerian writer Chinua Achebe calls "a balance of stories"? What if people knew about Hajar, a strong and remarkable African woman who raised her child in the desert? Now, conventional wisdom is that people don't read such stories. But there was no one in the desert of Mecca when God told Abraham to call. Let God take care of bringing people to read and listen to the stories, and you call to them.

I often mention that the Prophets' stories helped correct my perception of the world and strengthened my faith. I do believe they are also a source of healing.

What if our children knew about the Prophets' stories more than contemporary musicians, talented people singing in English and Korean pop, Arabic and Spanish, and Ijo, mixing influences from Jay Z to Fela to Bob Marley to their grandfathers?

What if they knew about how Asiya protected Prophet Moses, upon him peace, within the kingdom of the Pharaoh? What if we learned about the many companions in the battle of Badr, full of faith, fighting oppression in the face of insurmountable odds? What if the story of Maryam, the mother of Jesus, became prevalent to our girls growing up? Or Joseph to our young boys in the face of hypersexualization?

Whenever I am home, I am reminded of the usual sources of pain for most Muslims: our failed infrastructure, our failed governments, and the incredible resilience of people who thrive despite the government rather than because of it. I began to share lessons from the Prophets' stories and reflect on God's Most Beautiful Names, and I saw those lessons trickle through.

Stories matter. Many stories matter. Stories have been used to dispossess and malign, but stories can also be used to nurture and ease our journey to God. Stories can break the dignity of a people, but stories can also repair that broken dignity and reconnect us to God.

Prophet Muhammad, upon him peace and blessings, endured great hardship to receive the Quran from God, listen to it, practice it, and teach it to his companions. He put the Quran into practice to the point where he was called the "walking Quran." He nurtured his companions with its teachings and wisdom, listening to and applying its teachings. I'd like to conclude with this thought: when we reject conjecture, listen to the one calling us to faith, and respond to that call, we are led to the path that leads to paradise.

Where Is God: Can I Tell You about Al Fattah?

> *"And to Allah belong the Most Beautiful Names, so invoke Him by them. And leave [the company of] those who practice deviation concerning His names. They will be recompensed for what they have been doing. And among those We created is a community which guides by truth and thereby establishes justice." (Quran 7:180–181)*

God is often described as an extension of ourselves and our tribe. We regularly speak for Him, obligate, oppose, and challenge Him. We question His presence when He fails to satisfy our desires or trials outside our control and influence. We seldom pause to evaluate if our understanding of God reflects our egoism, cravings for power, lordship, and avoidance of accountability. When some speak for God, they describe Him as a superhuman deity granted permission by us to fulfill our requests, and we can fire Him if our wants and demands are unmet. He cannot speak outside our master-slave narrative of which we are the masters.

We don't get to know Him or seek to know Him. We don't understand His speech, what pleases or angers Him. His words are absent from our lives until we want to control others or steal their homeland, at which point we quote Him. We are told stories that He hopes we believe in Him, begging and pleading as though He needs our attention and love. So, although He created us and the universe, which we interpret in ways that stoke our ego, we give Him permission to speak to us in ways uncommon for domestic workers.

How can we become aware of His Lordship? How can we become aware of who He is and bear witness to His Lordship and Majesty? Is it feasible to uncover the meaning of His speech from other humans?

The Master-Slave narrative contends that each regards the other as a danger to its existence. Some relegate God to nonexistence because we see Him as a danger to our existence. We want to be lords and the ultimate measure of everything. Our sentiments, desires, powers, and so forth serve as the objective standard by which everything experienced must be assessed. On the other hand, the presence of a being that can speak with a new accurate measure on our feelings, needs, thoughts, and capacities of each self-consciousness is threatening.

This assertion of God as Lord of the Universe, not just ourselves, creates a battle among some unaware of their boundaries. This inner battle with all its power manifests outwardly by dominating others or denying the existence of God, seen as a threat. Although the individual is aware of their perspective, they are threatened with the knowledge of the Prophets. Such individuals attempt to promote their god-like measure of truth and silence or kill the prophets.

The Prophets are His chosen representatives who share His words, guidance, and what He knows, loves, and hates, opening the door for us to know Him as Lord of the Worlds, as He wants to be known. They invite us to recognize His Majesty, which is possible when we know ourselves as human beings, not lords. Their eyes saw His Beauty that which they saw, and they never turned away from Him to other ones. They endured trials and tribulations with Him, by Him, and for Him, forcing us to reconsider our narratives and the false relationship with Him we created in our minds, reflecting our egoism.

Begin with the End in Mind

> *In the name of Allah, Most Gracious, Most Merciful. Praise be to Allah, the Cherisher and Sustainer of the worlds; Most Gracious, Most Merciful; Master of the Day of Judgment. Thee do we worship, and Thine aid we seek. Show us the straight way, the way of those on whom Thou hast bestowed Thy Grace, those whose (portion) is not wrath, and who go not astray.*
>
> —Quran 1:1-7

At least seventeen times a day, it is obligatory to remind ourselves of this reality in prayer. "Al-Fatiha" is the first chapter of the Quran, the key or opening. The chapter begins with the first words of Prophet Adam, upon him peace, a reminder to our origin, and emphasizes the human need for His Mercy and Guidance. The chapter also emphasizes the covenant and taking of God as Lord, Master of the Day of Judgment, and our need to show resolve for the straight path.

Prophet Muhammad, upon him peace and blessings, refers to it as a light. We want to know how to engage each other, and this chapter begins the discussion and connection between ourselves and God.

The entire Quran is 114 chapters and 6,000 verses. The aim is not to rush through the reading but to connect to the central figures within the reading.

It is encouraged to read the entire Quran and listen to God at least once a month. This might be difficult at first, but if you do not judge yourself, wait for the right feelings to manifest, and just do it regardless the mood or feelings, over time, you will develop a love of listening to the Quran and listening to the meanings of the verses.

I have found reading the first chapter of the Quran very beneficial. Reading this all the time, with reflection, seeking guidance, helps me walk in the right path. Reading about the daily sufferings can make one wonder if God is with them or not.

If God protected you from oppressing others or yourself, that is a clear sign that God is with you. If God opened the doors for you to oppress others, that is a clear sign that God is not with you.

In places where suffering is great and people are very insecure and unprotected, it can be difficult to swallow this and feel content. However, it is essential that we protect our hearts and minds during such moments, to protect our mental and spiritual health.

Al Quran: A Message From The Divine

An invitation to listen to the Beauty of His Speech, and take off the cloak of pride and turn to Him.

God does not leave us in the dark, but rather introduces Himself to us. We would rejoice if we got a letter from a human King or Queen, and Al-Fatiha and the Quran are messages from the Lord of the Worlds to humanity. Prophet Muhammad, upon him peace and blessings, said:

> *I ask You by every name belonging to You which You named Yourself with, or You taught to any of Your creation, or revealed in Your Book, or You have*

> *preserved in the knowledge of the unseen with You, that You make the Quran the life of my heart and the light of my breast, and a departure for my sorrow and a release for my anxiety, Allah will remove his anxiety and sadness and replace it with happiness.*
>
> —Ahmad 3704

Take the Quran as your companion. I like reading or listening to people tell their stories. However, I have not seen or heard stories as beautifully described as the stories in the Quran. The arguments used are reflective and engaging. The details are just enough to make you think and reflect. There isn't any sensationalism, drama, or unnecessary information.

> *So when the Qur'an is recited, then listen to it and pay attention that you may receive mercy.*
>
> —Quran 7:204

First, be still and listen. After years in the land of Midian, Moses, upon him peace, was called, and God explained the wisdom behind his life experiences.

What Does It Mean to Listen?

Most of us will read the Quran looking for ways or verses to win an argument. Most of my blogs or writings were reflections from years ago that I started to polish and share when I became a blogger for the *Star Tribune*. As I mentioned in the blog, layer by layer, the Quran unfolds its wisdom. Try not to read the Quran looking for cool quotes or memes. There is a time to share what you learned. However, open the Quran to learn and seek guidance. It is a different journey if you are coming to Quran to listen attentively with humility.

Initially, years ago, reading the Quran was difficult. At times, certain passages disturbed me. However, as time flew and I continued to listen, the beauty in the passages and the light in its wisdom started to unfold layer by layer. Now, listening to various scholars discuss the verses of Quran is something that I enjoy. And the conversations within the Quran help me not just understand life but nurture within myself love of the Prophets and God.

It is OK to say, "I don't understand" but listen. The understanding will come to you at the right moment after serious study, and you will develop a relationship with the Author as you struggle to know Him.

The words will no longer be words on a page or thoughts in one's mind or an analysis—but a connection—to oneself, to the prophets and believers, and, more importantly, to God. The prophets are described as upon hearing the verses of God, fall down in prostration and tears of adoration. May we reach that state of love of God that the Prophets reached: "Whenever the Signs of (Allah) Most Gracious were rehearsed to them, they would fall down in prostrate adoration and in tears" (Quran 19:58).

The Prophets were known to be the most beneficial to humanity and divinely protected from error and sin. However, they still relied on God's Mercy to enter Heaven and asked Him to make them in the company of the righteous. Righteous people pray for the ability to do good deeds and the company of people who are sincere and true to God, as though they are not among them. Hence, when they are engaged in such deeds, they see them as gifts from His Mercy, and not from them.

> *[Solomon prayed,] "O my Lord! so enable me that I may be grateful for Thy favours, which thou hast bestowed on me and my parents, and that I may work the righteousness that will please Thee: And admit me, by Thy Grace, to the ranks of Thy righteous Servants."*

—Quran 27:19

One can find many examples of His Mercy, but I will end this here with the best for last.

> *Indeed, in this [Quran] is notification for a worshiping people. And We have not sent you, [O Muhammad], except as a Mercy to the worlds.*

—Quran 21:106–107

The prophets and messengers were sent as a mercy to their tribe and people. Prophet Muhammad, upon him peace and blessings, was sent as a Mercy from the Most Merciful of those who show Mercy to nurture humanity to a higher understanding of themselves and deliver the message, the Quran.

***Ar-Rahman*:** All Merciful

"My mercy covers everything" (Quran 7:156).

One of God's Most Beautiful Names is *Ar-Rahman*. Often, we do not recognize His Mercy and Love, given the lens through which we see the world. A scholar said that the angels keep saying *Ar Rahman* when God is angry. They pray for believers:

> *Those who sustain the Throne (of Allah) and those around it Sing Glory and Praise to their Lord; believe in Him; and implore Forgiveness for those who believe: "Our Lord! Thy Reach is over all things, in Mercy and Knowledge. Forgive, then, those who turn in Repentance, and follow Thy Path; and preserve them from the Penalty of the Blazing Fire!"*

—Quran 40:7

The Quran has shared ways to communicate our needs with God using His Beautiful Names. In communication classes, they teach various types of communication, and when speaking with people of high social rank, you must respect their station. People called out a representative who yelled, "Liar!" at former president Barack Obama during a public session. They also reprimanded Judge Brett Kavanaugh when he responded rudely to Senator Amy Klobuchar during a hearing regarding Christine Blasey Ford.

Likewise, when we communicate with God regarding our needs, the Prophets teach us how to address God as Lord, the Most Merciful of those who show Mercy, not as our buddy. We address Him using His Most Beautiful Names, which He taught us to use via His prophets.

Some examples follow Prophets using His Name *Ar-Rahman* (Most Merciful, Most Gracious, Infinitely Good, Most Beneficent). The Prophet Muhammad, upon him peace and blessings, taught Muslims to turn to God with the opening chapter.

> *[Abraham] Our Lord! make of us Muslims, bowing to Thy (Will), and of our progeny a people Muslim, bowing to Thy (will); and show us our place for the celebration of (due) rites; and turn unto us (in Mercy); for Thou art the Oft-Returning, Most Merciful.*

—Quran 2:128

> Moses prayed, "O my Lord! forgive me and my brother! Admit us to Thy mercy! For Thou art the Most Merciful of those who show mercy!"
>
> —Quran 7:151

> [Jacob] said: "Shall I trust you with him with any result other than when I trusted you with his brother aforetime? But Allah is the best to take care (of him), and He is the Most Merciful of those who show mercy!"
>
> —Quran 12:64

> [Joseph] said: "This day let no reproach be (cast) on you: Allah will forgive you, and He is the Most Merciful of those who show mercy!"
>
> —Quran 12:92

> Behold, the youths betook themselves to the Cave: they said, "Our Lord! bestow on us Mercy from Thyself and dispose of our affair for us in the right way!"
>
> —Quran 18:10

> And (remember) Job, when He cried to his Lord, "Truly distress has seized me, but Thou art the Most Merciful of those that are merciful."
>
> —Quran 21:83

At times, we use His Name by acknowledging that without His Mercy, we would be lost. Instead of saying, "You are Most Merciful," we would say, "We would be lost without Your Mercy," an acknowledgment that the source of Mercy is Him.

> [Adam and Eve prayed.] They said: "Our Lord! We have wronged our own souls: If thou forgive us not and bestow not upon us Thy Mercy, we shall certainly be lost."
>
> —Quran 7:23

> Noah said: "O my Lord! I do seek refuge with Thee, lest I ask Thee for that of which I have no knowledge. And unless thou forgive me and have mercy on me, I should indeed be lost!"
>
> —Quran 11:47

Ar-Rahim: Especially Merciful

> *And those who came after them say: "Our Lord! Forgive us and our brethren who came before us into the faith, and leave not, in our hearts, rancour (or sense of injury) against those who have believed. Our Lord! Thou art indeed Full of Kindness, Most Merciful."*
>
> —Quran 59:10

One of God's names is Ar-Rahim. It comes from the same root word as Ar-Rahman. Prophet Muhammad, upon him peace and blessings, said God's Name Al-Rahman or the Most Merciful, whose love and Mercy are manifested to all his creation, and Ar-Rahim is the Most Merciful, whose love and Mercy are manifested to believers who are merciful on earth.

Hence, He is the One who bestows even more grace and reward to those striving to practice the faith. This Beautiful Name is reserved for showing Mercy to merciful believers, using God's bounties in a good way.

Rahman conveys the idea of fullness and extensiveness, indicating the excellent quality of love and Mercy that engulfs all creation without any effort or request on our part, while *Rahim* conveys the idea of constant renewal and giving liberal reward to those acting according to His Will.

Ar-Rahman is the Beneficent One whose endless outpouring of love and Mercy are continually showered upon all of creation, while *Ar-Rahim* is the Merciful One whose love and Mercy are manifested as that which is received as the consequence of one's deeds.

In Muhammad Ali's translation of the Quran, *Rahman* and *Rahim* are both derived from the root signifying tenderness requiring the exercise of beneficence and kindness, comprising the ideas of Love and Mercy. Thus, *Rahman* is expressive of the utmost degree of love and generosity and *Rahim* of unbounded and constant favor and Mercy.

Al 'Azhim: The Magnificent

> *"Then celebrate with praises the name of thy Lord, the Supreme!" (Quran 56:74).*

I remember the day like yesterday; we were listening to speaker after speaker, one more dynamic than the next. I cannot recall their speeches, just the audience's reaction: much laughter, very well attended, and yelling *Takbeer* (the call of Muslims to remember and cry out the name Allah, the Greatest) or *Allahu Akbar* (Allah, the Greatest).

Then a middle-aged man took the stage. It appeared he feared public speaking as he made no eye contact with anyone in the audience. He was so nervous that you could not make out the introduction of his speech; hence, the audience started to chat and did not pay much attention to him. For some reason, this speaker caught my attention. He kept fumbling with his pages and glasses as he continued.

Then he started to read some verses from the Quran, and I realized I had heard these verses before but could not recall the *surah*. For whatever reason, this time, they were so loud and present in the room, despite the speaker's nervousness and the audience ignoring him.

I turned to the woman chatting next to me and asked her if she could recall the chapter. She said, "*Al Waqiah*," or "The Big Event."

> *It is We Who have created you: why will ye not witness the Truth? Do ye then see? The (human Seed) that ye throw out, Is it ye who create it, or are We the Creators? We have decreed Death to be your common lot, and We are not to be frustrated from changing your Forms and creating you (again) in (forms) that ye know not. And ye certainly know already the first form of creation: why then do ye not celebrate His praises? See ye the seed that ye sow in the ground? Is it ye that cause it to grow, or are We the Cause? Were it Our Will, We could crumble it to dry powder, and ye would be left in wonderment, (Saying), "We are indeed left with debts (for nothing): Indeed are we shut out (of the fruits of our labour)." See ye the water which ye drink? Do ye bring it down (in rain) from the cloud or do We? Were it Our Will, We could make it salt (and unpalatable): then why do ye not give thanks? See ye the Fire which ye kindle? Is it ye who grow the tree which feeds the fire, or do We grow it? We have made it a memorial (of Our handiwork) and an article of comfort and convenience for the denizens of deserts. Then celebrate with praises the name of thy Lord, the Supreme!*

—Quran 57–74

He is Most Merciful and Most Powerful. A person who has no power and treats you with mercy does so out of selfish desires or compulsion. One who is Most Powerful and can destroy you but treats you with Mercy acts out of genuine love and kindness toward you.

To appreciate His Name, *Al 'Azhim* (the Most Supreme in Glory or Most Powerful), one can reflect on this passage in the Quran, which is recommended to recite after each prayer for protection from harm.

> *Allah! There is no god but He the Living, the Self-subsisting, Eternal. No slumber can seize Him nor sleep. His are all things in the heavens and on earth. Who is there can intercede in His presence except as He permitteth? He knoweth what (appeareth to His creatures as) before or after or behind them. Nor shall they compass aught of His knowledge except as He willeth. His Throne doth extend over the heavens and the earth, and He feeleth no fatigue in guarding and preserving them for He is the Most High, the Supreme (in glory).*

—Quran 255

By reflecting on His Attribute, *Al 'Azhim*, we can now communicate with God as Lord, who's full of Supreme Glory and Mighty Splendor. His Greatness is in Rank, Most Revered, Most Magnificent, Most Dignified, and Most Honored.

It is with this realization that one must address Him. His Supremacy in Glory can be witnessed in our daily lives and this day and age, with microscopes that can discover amazing creatures and life-forms in the sea and amazing galaxies in the sky. One can appreciate Him when trying to multitask: how forgetful we become, how distracted due to stress, and how sleep overtakes us when we are exhausted. When we think of someone being Supreme, we do not think of their needs, just an image of what they appear to be. In reality, they have needs. We all have needs, and as we age, the needs grow, and our ability to function well decreases. Just watching our children make us fatigued, and how many parents fall asleep trying to take care of their hyperactive child? We start to misplace our keys, forget appointments, and make so many mistakes because of the exhaustion of caring for one or more children. Now imagine or contemplate how God, *Al Azhim*, runs the entire universe without any fatigue or slumber.

When we go to people for protection, they are all human and have needs. They are prone to mistakes and exhaustion. They also have limited power; as the magicians told the Pharaoh, you have power over us in this temporal world. He had no power over their souls, conscience, hearts, or will.

Dhul Jalali wal-Ikhram: Lord of Majesty and Bounty

> "Recite frequently: 'Ya Dhal-Jalali wal-Ikram! [O You, Possessor of Majesty and Honor]." (Messenger of Allah, upon him peace and blessings)

To fully appreciate God's Mercy, one has to understand His Name of Majesty and Honor. His Mercy is bestowed to humanity out of His Generosity and Majesty, not out of any need or obligation. It is difficult to appreciate His Mercy and receive it as a gift when we have in our mind that God is like Mother Teresa or some nice person who has no Majestic Glory or is not known for His Infinite Generosity.

So, if one imagines someone like a Mother Teresa being kind and merciful to us and the Creator of the whole universe and all its glory manifesting His Mercy to us, those are not the same. Our appreciation of these gifts is also not the same. This helps us address God and seek His Mercy at His station, not our own.

Every person we can think of as majestic is majestic because people make them great. In addition, such a person has needs. They also die. God's attribute of being *Dhul Jalali wal-Ikram*, or Lord of Majesty and Bounty is not dependent on anyone or anything for Him to be Majestic. Everything would perish except for "the Face of your Lord, Owner of Majesty and Honor" (Quran 55:27).

It was quite amazing to notice that when He mentions this attribute of Majesty, it is coupled with everyone, and everything will perish. He does not need you or me to be Majestic.

Everyone wants to be royalty or near royalty. We all want honor. It is a natural human motive to seek honor and royalty. However, in whose eyes do you seek it? And from whom do you seek it? And why do you seek it? These are important questions to sit and review.

> [Abraham]Grant me honourable mention on the tongue of truth among the latest (generations); Make me one of the inheritors of the Garden of Bliss; Forgive my father, for that he is among those astray; And let me not be in disgrace on the Day when (men) will be raised up; The

> *Day whereon neither wealth nor sons will avail, But only he (will prosper) that brings to Allah a sound heart.*
>
> —Quran 26:84–89

Abraham, upon him peace, is known as the father of the prophets. Calling his father to God brought upon him persecution and oppression from his father and his father's clan. Despite the oppression he faced, his heart was full of genuine concern for his father, and like Noah, he tried to appeal to God on his behalf. This is genuine love. He made this prayer in private to God.

What are you doing in private: praying for people's guidance or plotting and planning to harm people?

As God addressed Noah, upon him peace, Abraham was also told to stop. When God chooses a guide, it is because they will desire that people go to heaven. Their heart is full of a genuine love of God and a desire for people to be saved. Salvation is different from control. People who control others are oppressors whose concern is their image in people's eyes. If they are oppressed, they will pray that the people who reject them go to hell. In reality, they use God to call people to them. Salvation is about nurturing others to turn to God with a clean heart. Even when people reject them, they pray to God for their salvation.

He is a prophet, yet he prays that he is not disgraced on the day of resurrection. After everything perishes, everyone will be resurrected before the true Majesty, where all face reality. It will become very clear at that time that disgrace invokes no station with God.

Ash-Shakur: The Most Appreciative

> *Verily this is a Reward for you, and your Endeavour is accepted and recognised. (Quran 76:22)*

One of God's Most Beautiful Names is *Ash-Shakur*, who appreciates the good you do for His sake. The most minor thing you do for His sake, He rewards you for and notes. It is a commerce or a transaction that never fails. Sometimes our trials and tribulations are the means and carry the lessons that teach us to be appreciative and grateful; however, we do not have a holistic view of gratitude.

> *Allah does not intend to make difficulty for you, but He intends to purify you and complete His favor upon you*

> *that you may be grateful. And call in remembrance the favour of Allah unto you, and His covenant, which He ratified with you, when ye said: "We hear and we obey": And fear Allah, for Allah knoweth well the secrets of.*
>
> —*Quran: 5:6–7*

Positive (and Negative) Attitudes Toward Gratitude

When it comes to our relationship with God, we will never be able to express "enough" gratitude. A gratitude toward God is both pure and infinite. Yet we aren't grateful because God benefits from our gratitude or because our thanks somehow put God in our debt. We express gratitude because it purifies our hearts and brings us closer to God.

Just as we express thanks to God, we should also express gratitude to our fellow humans. Yet sometimes, when gratitude comes between people, it loses its essential purity. It becomes twisted up in other desires.

At some point or another, all of us have probably felt unappreciated—as though we were working hard for someone, but that other person didn't recognize our efforts. Other people's gratitude can also make us feel good, and it's only human to enjoy when others express thanks to us. But it's important not to expect gratitude. It's especially important not to try to squeeze it out of others. If we are feeling unappreciated, that's when we need to turn to God.

The archetype of bad gratitude is Satan, who was grateful to God only in the moments when there was some benefit to him. Satan wanted God to be forever grateful and for his actions to put God forever in his debt. As soon as Satan was no longer feeling God's gratitude—as soon as he was feeling God's anger instead—he forgot all the good God had done for him.

After that, Satan projected his own state of mind when he told God, "You will find humanity ungrateful." Instead of seeing and grappling with his own ingratitude, Satan started working to prove others were ungrateful. It's important that we not follow that path.

42-Love Is Deeper Than Words

Why Didn't They Thank Me?

Sometimes, when we sacrifice ourselves for others, we see little gratitude in return. As Richard A. Grossman writes in his *Little Voices*, we might feel underappreciated by demanding and unappreciative elderly parents, who make us feel trapped. Or it could be difficult children, a spouse, or someone else who makes us feel trapped or invisible, someone who has pushed us into being a "little voice."

Any time we feel angry, invisible, and unappreciated, we need to take a step back and examine our rights and responsibilities. That's when it's time to take a time-out and have a conversation with God, and we can even call God's name—Ya Shakur—the one who is appreciative of good deeds. Even when no one else is there to appreciate us, God will be.

It's said that, as-Samiri lost his mother at a young age, the Angel Gabriel raised him and took care of him. The story has a hidden question and a point of reflection, particularly for parents.

Moses, upon him peace, was separated from his mother and raised by the Pharaoh, just as-Samiri lost his mother and was raised by the Angel Gabriel. The former becomes a prophet and the latter a wrongdoer and unbeliever.

Sometimes, we rely on good company or on angelic parents and don't make an effort to turn to God. Others of us, who had bad parents or parents with bad parenting skills, might feel angry toward God, blaming God for their bad guidance. Such a person might think, had you given me good parents, I wouldn't have turned out like this. So it's your fault I went astray.

It's true that the environment leaves an impact on each of our actions. For instance, Moses was driven to accidentally kill a man. However, we also know that God came to Moses at that moment as the Oft Forgiving, and Moses immediately repented without rationalizing his actions. He also accepted the consequences, and God opened the door for him to be nurtured by a Prophet.

> "O you who have attained to faith! Respond to the call of God and the Apostle whenever he calls you unto that which will give you life; and know that God intervenes between man and [the desires of] his heart, and that unto Him you shall be gathered."

—Quran, 8:24

Years later, he was told to return to the Pharaoh and share the message of faith with him. Moses, upon him peace, did not desire to go to the Pharaoh and was worried about the man who was accidentally killed. When he delivered the message openly and transparently, here is how the Pharaoh responded:

> [But when Moses had delivered his message, Pharaoh] said: Did we not bring thee up among us when thou wert a child? And didst thou not spend among us years of thy [later] life? And yet thou didst commit that [heinous] deed of thine, and [hast thus shown that] thou art one of the ingrate!
>
> —Quran, 26:18–19

There are several lessons to take from this. One is that if we are good parents, we should thank God and pray for our children. Yet there's still the possibility they might turn out like as-Samiri. We shouldn't look down on bad parents or parents with bad parenting skills and think that we're better; we don't know what resources and parenting support they had.

And sometimes, God nurtures a tyrant with a child. Moses, upon him peace, was still a loving child in the house of the Pharaoh. Asiya fell in love with Moses, upon him peace, instantaneously. He was the way God was able to come between the Pharaoh and his heart. As an adult, Moses does not deny that he received nurturing, and he does not deny the accidental death of the Egyptian. Yet he became a mirror for the Pharaoh, who denied God's nurturing as well as his own transgressions against the Israelites.

Ultimately, when we thank anyone, we are really thanking God for using that person to benefit us. And when we help anyone, we should never entertain the thought that without our help, this person would be nothing. In truth, without God, we would all be lost. We must rely on God and keep turning to God in private. He is already aware of everything in our hearts. If you have bad parents or parents with bad parenting skills, then turn to God. He will give you secret nurturing and guide you as He guided Moses, upon him peace. If you have good parents, then turn to God and do not be deluded. Thank God for the gift of good parents and their nurturing.

Gratitude as Yoke

You probably also know someone who uses gratitude as a cudgel. This person might have bought you a cup of coffee or a gift or have helped you out when times were tough. Instead of accepting your thanks and moving on, they—like Satan—want to hold you to this debt forever. They keep reminding you, repeatedly, about whatever they have done. This insistence on your gratitude can also be disempowering. It can steal your confidence and rewrite your story.

Sometimes people who become obsessed with gratitude are less interested in doing good than in making their image look good. Sometimes they do good acts with the intention—conscious or unconscious—of making others submissive to their needs.

Meeting people with unhealthy attitudes toward gratitude can teach us an important lesson: we should never ask people to be grateful to us. When we do good for others, our hope should be for a reward from God. When we do good, we should not be expecting something in return from other people. Gratitude can become an addiction, and we need to be mindful of that. Satan was one such gratitude addict: he was addicted to praise and appreciation, and he thought that made God indebted to him. When he did wrong, instead of being concerned about his relationship with God, Satan's main concern was with his own status and image.

If you find yourself seeking gratitude from others, then the best way to help yourself is to turn toward God. If you do something for another person, they may not be appreciative! You shouldn't try to prove their ingratitude—that is between them and God. Instead, turn to God for comfort.

Remember that when the prophets came to humanity, they didn't come seeking reward from their fellow humans. They focused on the good opinion of God. We should never make a "career" of doing good to climb a ladder of social standing, as the Quran tells us in chapter 18, verses 103 to 105:

> *Say: "Shall we tell you of those who lose most in respect of their deeds? Those whose efforts have been wasted in this life, while they thought that they were acquiring good by their works? They are those who deny the Signs of their Lord and the fact of their having to meet Him (in the Hereafter): vain will be their works, nor shall We, on the Day of Judgment, give them any weight."*

The Pitfalls of Showing Gratitude

We should show gratitude when others do us a kindness. But that doesn't mean people will always appreciate our expressions of gratitude. Sometimes people will have bad associations with gratitude. Sometimes people will misunderstand our expressions of gratitude. We should be mindful that not everyone can accept our expressions.

Sometimes we should express our gratitude directly to God in prayer. After all, whoever did the kindness to us or benefited us was ultimately sent by God.

Gratitude and Balance

Another important aspect of gratitude is balance. When we look at the world, we should always be looking with both eyes open.

We shouldn't close our eyes to the evil going on around us. I sometimes speak out about oppressive US foreign and domestic policies. But this doesn't mean I don't also recognize the benefits I've received growing up and living in the US. Sometimes people close both eyes to avoid looking at the world around them. Sometimes people close one eye: they see only the positives or only the negatives.

It's important to speak the truth about oppression. But it's also important to seek out the positives. Looking for good in the world is part of being grateful.

For instance, we should call out sexism when we see it. But we should also see that there are men who speak up for women and work against misogyny. Gratitude isn't about denying that there are bad things going on. It's also about acknowledging the positive.

The same happens in individual relationships. It's easy to be grateful to another person when they are directly benefiting you—when they are kind and supportive. But if you have a falling out or a misunderstanding, or if the person is unkind, then it becomes difficult to remain grateful for the positive things they did do. We should always look at others with both eyes open and seek to find the positives. This passage from the Quran is instructive:

> *Seest thou not that Allah sends down rain from the sky? With it We then bring out produce of various colours. And in the mountains are tracts white and red, of various*

> *shades of colour, and black intense in hue. And so amongst men and crawling creatures and cattle, are they of various colours. Those truly fear Allah, among His Servants, who have knowledge: for Allah is Exalted in Might, Oft-Forgiving. Those who rehearse the Book of Allah, establish regular Prayer, and spend (in Charity) out of what We have provided for them, secretly and openly, hope for a commerce that will never fail:*
>
> *For He will pay them their needs, nay, He will give them (even) more out of His Bounty: for He is Oft-Forgiving, Most Ready to appreciate (service).*
>
> *That which We have revealed to thee of the Book is the Truth, confirming what was (revealed) before it: for Allah is assuredly—with respect to His Servants—well acquainted and Fully Observant.*
>
> *Then We have given the Book for inheritance to such of Our Servants as We have chosen: but there are among them some who wrong their own souls; some who follow a middle course; and some who are, by Allah's leave, foremost in good deeds; that is the highest Grace. Gardens of Eternity will they enter: therein will they be adorned with bracelets of gold and pearls; and their garments there will be of silk. And they will say:*
>
> *Praise be to Allah, Who has removed from us (all) sorrow: for our Lord is indeed Oft-Forgiving Ready to appreciate (service):*
>
> *Who has, out of His Bounty, settled us in a Home that will last: no toil nor sense of weariness shall touch us therein.*
>
> —Quran, 35:27–35

This passage reminds us that we will face trouble, sadness, and toil. But even if we are in difficulty now, we should believe that something good can happen. This doesn't deny trouble; it asks us to also believe that something good is coming.

When we hope for "a commerce that will never fail," we need to remember that's not going to come from other people. The relationship that will never fail us—in which we can always and unfailingly express our gratitude—is our relationship with God.

As-Sami': The All-Hearing

> *When you elevate the All-Hearing above changes which happen to Him when audible sounds occur, and exalt Him above hearing by ears, you will realize that His hearing is an attribute by which the perfection of the qualities of things heard is disclosed. Whoever does not take care in considering this matter will inevitably fall into mere anthropomorphism. So, be wary, and be precise when you consider it.*
>
> —Imam al-Ghazali

One of God's Names is As-Sami' or the All-Hearing.

It is important to mention that we do not speak to God to inform Him of anything He doesn't know, hear, or understand about us. In fact, He knows us more than we know ourselves. We speak to God to listen to ourselves and know ourselves, not so that He can hear us. Talking to God at His station, not ours, promotes healing.

What does it mean to speak to God at His station?

Don't speak for Him or His Intentions or prosecute Him. Speak for yourself: your needs, feelings, struggles, actions, and thoughts. Use His Names or Attributes. We don't like mansplaining or fill-in-the-blank-splaining, so don't human-explain His actions.

I mentioned disassociation, which is part of the trauma. We allow the disassociation to melt as water dripping over an extended period or a river whirling on a rock that can break through the stone. We can process our feelings, emotions, and thoughts by speaking to God.

Despite their trials, the Prophets are described as excellent servants who were ever turning to God. This continual turning to God protected their hearts from trauma of trials and tribulations.

Ash-Shaheed or the Witness

> *"Him to Whom belongs the dominion of the heavens and the earth! And Allah is Witness to all things"*
>
> —Quran 85:9

The importance of a witness during a major trial or tribulation cannot be emphasized - but what does one do if they cannot find one?

One of God's names is *ash-Shaheed*, the Omniscient Witness, the Certifier, or the Testifier. The word shaheed in Arabic also means *martyr* as, both in English and in Arabic, part of the essence of martyrdom is witnessing in life and witnessing on the Day of Judgment.

The One who directly and ever presently observes everything in creation. The One from whose knowledge nothing is hidden.

The One who witnesses both that which is seen and that which is unseen. The One who has knowledge of all that always happens everywhere. Most importantly, the one who we can turn to and be present with.

So, what does it mean to take God as a witness? It doesn't mean you go before the public and say, "Hey, God's on my side; He's my witness!" God isn't going to appear in court to be your witness, and you certainly can't obligate God to your point of view.

When you're suffering and being abused, you must find an empathetic witness somewhere in your life. First and foremost, turn to God. We should turn to God always, and if someone else appropriate is there, then take that means also. If there isn't another person who can stand as your witness, then God is sufficient. When Prophet Muhammad, upon him peace and blessings, took God as his witness, he added those who know the book. "The Unbelievers say: 'No messenger art thou.' Say: 'Enough for a witness between me and you is Allah, and such as have knowledge of the Book'" (Quran 13:43).

Those who had knowledge of the scripture recognized him as a Messenger and Prophet.

Surviving Abuse

Just as with the Prophet Joseph, peace upon him, the abuser in your life could be someone very close to you. It could be a father, a brother, or a husband, and you may not have any empathetic witness at all. To the outside world, your abuser might seem like a nice guy, just as an authoritarian or apartheid regime can sometimes excel at PR.

At times, the abused can start to wonder if they're crazy, if their feelings are real or not. And this is where it's critical to have a witness. I discuss gaslighting and emotional abuse in a later section.

Trauma therapist Peter A. Levine has said that trauma is not what happens to us but what we hold inside in the absence of an empathetic witness. The young Malala Yousafzai was shot in the head, for instance, and had the force of the Taliban against her. Externally, she was hurt very badly. But internally, she had a family who witnessed for her and helped her stand up again: they became her wings.

For this reason, it seems—at least to the outside observer—that Malala's trial and tribulation did not turn into trauma.

People become traumatized when they don't have that empathetic witness. For instance, with domestic violence, some people are able to come out of it, and others aren't. One of the critical factors is whether a person has an empathetic witness: family, friends, coworkers, a therapist, or someone else.

A woman might survive an acid attack and, with the help of her very loving father, go on to rebuild her life. A person might suffer much less than this, but with no empathetic witness, their trials turn into trauma. In this case, a traumatized person often goes on to harm themselves or others.

The Quran give us many cases in which people suffer trials and abuse, and God is the empathetic witness. But how to connect to God as Witness?

Reaching Out to God as a Witness

Having God as a witness isn't about speaking for God or on behalf of God. It's about speaking to God and speaking to oneself, so that—when trials and tribulations hit you—you don't absorb them and become traumatized, suffering more than it was meant for you to suffer, so traumatized that you can't heal.

We have examples of this in the Quran in the story of Prophets Jacob and Joseph, upon them peace, who both took God as an empathetic witness. Because they did so, even in their darkest times, God carried part of their suffering and turned it into wisdom and light.

Joseph suffered when his brothers put him down a well and then sold him into slavery, and Jacob suffered when he lost his beloved son. The Quran tells us:

> *So they did take him away, and they all agreed to throw him down to the bottom of the well: and We put into his heart (this Message): "Of a surety thou shalt (one day) tell them the truth of this their affair while they know (thee) not."*

—Quran, 12:15

So Joseph knew that one day the truth would be revealed, and he was not traumatized. He was also comforted by the fact that Allah informed him that he would prevail over his brothers such that one day, he would be able to recount to them their wicked deeds under circumstances so different from his condition at the time that they would not even recognize him.

When you take God as a witness, you allow God to protect your soul and heart from trauma, just as Joseph did. One of the very first things you want to do in faith and in healing is to protect your soul. Joseph was the heart and soul of his family, and if Joseph's brothers had killed him instead of putting him down the well and selling him, they would've killed their own consciences and innocence.

However, some goodness remained in Joseph's brothers, and they didn't kill him. Instead of destroying the voice of conscience and innocence, they just pushed it away. Joseph is thus a symbol of what they did to themselves: they silenced their consciences and their connections to God. Just so, the abuser is disconnected from themselves, from their conscience, and from God.

In his time of need, Joseph was able to turn to God for protection with the following prayer: "Unless Thou turn away their snare from me, I should (in my youthful folly) feel inclined towards them and join the ranks of the ignorant" (12:33).

Jacob also was constantly longing for and feeling grief for his son Joseph. He was mentally and emotionally abused by his other sons, who were exasperated by his continual longing for Joseph and out of touch with their own consciences. Sometimes, Jacob was overtaken by sadness. Yet he turned to God, and his suffering did not turn into trauma.

He said: "I only complain of my distraction and anguish to Allah, and I know from Allah that which ye know not" (12:86).

And he was not swayed from missing his son Joseph: "O my sons! go ye and enquire about Joseph and his brother, and never give up hope of Allah's Soothing Mercy: truly no one despairs of Allah's Soothing Mercy, except those who have no faith" (12:87).

At the physical level, Jacob is in pain and misery, but he's neither traumatized nor broken.

Taking God as your witness, as Joseph did, doesn't mean you can prevent trials. But you can prevent yourself from absorbing them such that they destroy your soul. But how?

First, it's important not to be ashamed of your weakness, as Joseph and Jacob were not ashamed of their weaknesses. We are sometimes helpless, powerless, voiceless, bewildered, and shocked. Sometimes we can't understand what's happening. Don't be ashamed of that! We're human beings, and that is our humanity. Instead of holding that inside, we need to turn to God with our vulnerability and weakness, not to people. As Jacob said, "I complain of my pain and my sadness to God."

We can turn over that pain, suffering, and uncertainty to God as Joseph did, sheltering under God's protection.

Surviving Trauma

On February 10, 2015, the three young Muslims—Deah, Yusor, and Razan—were murdered in their North Carolina home. In response, their family has built what they call a "love army" to combat Islamophobia.

The family doesn't pretend the loss doesn't hurt. But they share it with God and the community as empathetic witnesses. In the words of family member Farris Barakat:

> *It doesn't makes sense, and for that I rely on the Most Wise. It hurts and for that I know that God will not burden me more than I can handle. I know my brother, his wife, and his sister-in-law are together as ultimate winners. . . .. Please pray for them, their friends, and the family. I haven't even begun to fully comprehend what has happened. But I know for sure those three together have done so much we are all proud of. No reason to stop being proud now. God is great. God is greater.*

It's essential to have witnesses to our pain so we don't end up becoming an abuser and an oppressor, beginning the cycle with someone else. This doesn't mean we don't stand up for ourselves. It doesn't mean you just take it!

Jacob said talk to God, complain to God, and allow Him to comfort your heart and soul so that you feel his soothing mercy. This doesn't mean you don't fight back or attempt to remove harm. But it does mean you do that in a way that doesn't destroy your soul.

We shouldn't just be patient and wait and do nothing. That's not what this is about! But while we are trying to remove the harm, it's also important that we don't destroy our own conscience and our souls.

Sometimes, abuse can be widespread and systematic, and it requires tremendous healing at a societal and systemic level. When we ask God to be our witness, this doesn't mean we don't also act to remove the harm. But it does mean we do it with acceptance. We recognize what's happened, but we don't become so angry that we refuse to accept the reality surrounding us.

Throughout, we must invite God to be our empathetic witness and our supporter and aid. In doing so, we must win the struggle with our ego so we are true in our request.

As-Salaam: The Source of Peace

Many seek peace by struggling, battling, and trying to impose their will on others, yet external peace will only prevail as a reflection of inner peace. The only path to outer peace is awareness of the tranquil depths of inner peace, and the only source of such inner peace is the One known as *As-Salaam*.

Islam and *salaam* share the same s-l-m root, which means to surrender to God's will and enter into peace or wholeness. Upon reflection, Islam means to be at peace with or reconciled with the ways and commands of Allah and is often described as self-resignation, surrender, or submission to the will of Allah.

The prophets demonstrated and lived this surrender well. Prophet Muhammad, upon him peace and blessings, nurtured his community during his lifetime such that they went from being at war with each other to building communities of peace with each other and with other communities of faith.

If you have tried to make peace between people, you might have encountered many difficulties or a dead end. In learning about the prophets' lives, we know to turn to God and pray to be instruments of peace. Without His guidance and surrendering our will to Him, we will continue to be at war within ourselves and each other. I quoted a *hadith* on leaders by Prophet Muhammad, upon him peace and blessings. The worst leaders are those who anger you and whom you anger. They curse you, and you curse them. At first, I understood it as if you hated a leader, that meant the person was a bad leader.

A Vicious Cycle of Hate and Anger

When words fail, the prophets teach us to turn the matter over to God and pray. A good fight does not mean we do not act. It just means that as we take action, we do not fight with hatred and a mindset that condemns people; instead, we offer people doors to forgiveness from God and reparation.

And if words fail, we turn to the Source of Peace, *As-Salaam*, and pray as His Vision and Knowledge of all matters is best. If you find it hard to pray, it might indicate that either you absorbed the spirit of the oppressor or you're fighting with hatred, and your ego is driving you. If you continue, you become a reflection of the oppressor or fight, disconnected from the Source of Peace.

If you cannot pray for others, at least pray for yourself. Ask God that you not be oppressed or oppress others: "O Allah, O As-Salaam, I seek refuge that I should oppress or be oppressed."

There is a difference between Zen and peace. Zen depends on the self, whereas peace, or *salaam*, relies on God, the Source of Peace. Many are unaware that when the first revelation was sent to the Prophet, upon him peace and blessings, it traumatized him so much that he considered throwing himself off a mountaintop. Some see this as a sign of him being crazy. Others read it with the whole story and realize that the trauma indicates something out of his control, thought, preparation, or anticipation.

Zen, as people talk about inner peace nowadays, is about control and being in control. *Salaam* or Peace is about surrendering to God. Here are some examples of Zen prayers from Tai Sheridan's *Zen Prayers For Repairing Your Life*:

- Prayer for Embodiment: I open myself to loving my body as the miracle of my own life and as the ground of my integrity and spiritual life.
- I am ready to delight in all of my bodily senses as a means of connecting to nature and humanity.
- I am ready to care for and nourish my body so it is vital and of benefit to all life.
- I am ready to rid myself of all shame and guilt that I have accumulated about my appearance and my body.
- I open myself to loving my body as the miracle of my own life and as the ground of my integrity and spiritual life.

Here are some examples of prayers by Prophet Muhammad, upon him Peace and blessings:

- O, Allah! I beseech You for guidance, piety, chastity, and contentment.
- O, Allah! Forgive me, have mercy on me, guide me, guard me against harm and provide me with sustenance and salvation.
- Allah, make my religion easy for me by virtue of which my affairs are protected, set right for me my world where my life exists, make good for me my Hereafter which is my resort to which I have to return, and make my life prone to perform all types of good, and make death a comfort for me from every evil.
- O, Allah! I have considerably wronged myself. There is none to forgive the sins but You. So grant me pardon and have mercy on me. You are the Most Forgiving, the Most Compassionate.
- O, Allah! I seek refuge in You from hunger; indeed, it is the worst companion. And I seek refuge in You from treachery; indeed, it is a bad inner trait.

Al-'Aziz: The Victorious One

> *Glory to thy Lord, the Lord of Honour and Power! (He is free) from what they ascribe (to Him)!*
>
> —Quran 37:180

The Divine Name *Al-'Aziz* is used throughout the Quran and has many beautiful meanings that can connect a person to the nearness of Allah. People question God's power and strength and accuse Him of being incompetent to punish tyrants or people who disobey Him. Some might ask Him, "Why don't you punish these people since they are defying You?" We learn from Jesus, upon him peace, in the following verse how to reconcile our feelings: "If You should punish them—indeed they are Your servants; but if You forgive them—indeed it is You who is the Exalted in Might, the Wise" (Quran 5:118).

We learn from this verse to focus on God, the Wise, when we do not comprehend His actions and to not human-explain. God explains Himself in the following verses:

> *To Allah belongs the dominion of the heavens and the earth and whatever is within them. And He is over all things competent.*
>
> —Quran 5:120
>
> *To Him be glory throughout the heavens and the earth: and He is Exalted in Power, Full of Wisdom!*
>
> —Quran 45:37
>
> *They say, "If we return to Medina, surely the more honorable (element) will expel therefrom the meaner." But honor belongs to Allah and His Messenger, and the Believers, but the Hypocrites know not.*
>
> —Quran 63:8
>
> *[Satan] said, "By your might, I will surely mislead them all."*
>
> —Quran 38:82

Even Satan knew that he could not do anything without God's power, meaning he could not overpower or overcome Him. Yet some humans think that they can overpower or overcome God. As humans, some of us might enjoy dignity, royalty, or power. We might have VIP status. However, *Al-'Aziz* is unique to God. His Might is Majestic and embedded with Dignity, Honor, and Power.

Al-'Aziz has complete mastery over all His creation. As the verses above show, none can take that away from Him. We learn that if you are made to feel small in the eyes of others, to seek the

One who is above His creation. The One who is the only source of all strength, power, and might.

Al-'Aziz is Unique, and nothing is like Him. This Name is attributed only to Allah, the One and Only, the like of Whom there is none equal. Al-'Aziz is the Victorious One Who overpowers and is never overpowered. If a person is overcome, he is by no means 'aziz, but relatively weak and humble. In addition, a person can dominate others one day and be overpowered by others another day. For example, a human being is overcome by sleep or illness, but nothing can Overpower God, Al-'Aziz.

The word 'azza means to make stronger or more powerful. If someone is weak, we cannot make them stronger or more powerful since we are not the source of Might and Power. Even the Prophets could not strengthen themselves with strong and committed companions. However, Al-'Aziz is the Mighty and Forceful. In Chapter 36, Verse 14: "When We sent to them two, but they denied them, so We strengthened them with a third, and they said, 'Indeed, we are messengers to you.'"

> Say, "O Allah, Owner of Sovereignty, You give sovereignty to whom You will, and You take sovereignty away from whom You will. You honor whom You will and You humble whom You will. In Your hand is [all] good. Indeed, You are over all things competent."
>
> —Quran 3:26

The verse above helps us understand that if we see someone held with honor, might, or power, God Al-'Aziz gave this position as a gift and test. If we are honored, it is not due to our ability to provide ourselves with such a position but because God grants such people this power and honor. If the person misuses this position, this honor and strength can be stripped from them, and they will be disgraced by the same people who honored them.

Reflect on the story of Joseph, upon him peace, and the prime minister's wife who put him in prison and made him the lowest of the low. She had temporal nobility and power, but she lacked dignity and self-respect. Joseph, upon him peace, was overpowered by her, but he was full of honor and dignity, "and if he will not do what I order him, he will surely be imprisoned and will be of those debased" (Quran 12:32).

If you believe that only Allah is the One Who grants you honor and dignity, then you believe that even if all mankind gathers to raise you up in rank, without His Divine Leave, they will never be able to do so. And you believe that if Allah, All-Mighty, raises you up in position, none could ever degrade or humiliate you, you would never ask anyone but Allah to grant you honor and dignity. You would turn to Him with true love and sincere devotion by showing complete obedience.

God strengthened Joseph, upon him peace, and made him rise above her in the land and the entire kingdom in need of him. This can only come from *Al-'Aziz*. Moses, upon him peace, was still in a station of honor when he left Egypt as a fugitive to the land of Midian. When God placed him under Prophet Shuy'ab, upon him peace, Moses, upon him peace, did not go there as a beggar, but through invitation and their need of his strength. The Pharaoh was hated in people's hearts even though he was tested with temporary power. The people did not need the Pharoah.

All the Prophets and Messengers are mighty and honorable because Allah has made them the gates to His Divine Mercy, Grace, Bounty, and Light. That is why when you attain the Prophet's pleasure, you attain Allah's Pleasure, and that is why Allah, Most Gracious, associated His Prophet's name with His own Name. Therefore, the holy Prophet, upon him peace and blessings, is *'Aziz* (mighty and honorable) because all people need him for both their secular and religious affairs.

Gh, F, R: The Roots of Forgiveness

Repentance is about growth, wisdom, love, and respect. Let me give an example from literature and the arts to help us understand this.

In *Pride and Prejudice*, Jane Austen introduces her readers to several characters and marriages. The characters' stories help us better understand the social reality and time. Marriages help us understand the mission, purpose, motive, and commonality between the partners.

In the book, there are a few stories on marriage and love. The main story introduces love between two characters, Mr. Darcy and Lizzie, who both have flaws and shortcomings but can challenge each other and grow.

Repentance is like that: a means to nurture the soul and strengthen it to connect to God sincerely and truthfully.

Initially, Mr. Darcy professes love to Lizzie in a way that insults her and her family, yet he is proud of his social position and rank, expecting her to jump for joy.

She politely turns him down, and he wants an explanation. Think of her family as God's other creation.

As in the movie *Beauty and the Beast*, Mr. Darcy had to go through a character transformation process to understand what love and personal development are and become a nobleman in the end.

At times, we worship God like that. We insult His other creation and profess our love for Him most ardently. And those other creations might be akin to Lizzie's family, full of flaws and shortcomings.

We learn that our love was a form of emotional blackmail: obligation, to be precise. Through repentance, we open our hearts to understand and receive nurturing that teaches us the difference between love and emotional blackmail.

> *And O my people, ask forgiveness of your Lord and then repent to Him. He will send [rain from] the sky upon you in showers and increase you in strength [added] to your strength. And do not turn away, [being] criminals.*

—Quran 11:52

Without repentance, our hearts are like stone, unable to receive the rain or benefit. Hence, nothing grows within or outside us.

A sign of hope. A door opens after the actions of a meddler. Mr. Darcy tries again, this time without emotional blackmail.

Instead of expecting her to jump for joy at his second marriage proposal while insulting her and disrespecting her family, he learns to respect her family, respect her right not to want to marry him, and help her family without her knowledge out of genuine love.

Another character, Mr. Wickham, did not wish to grow; neither did Lydia. Other characters retained their agreeable dispositions, yet experienced no growth or significant transformation. No repentance means no growth, and usually, such individuals become the town gossips.

Mr. Darcy's first marriage proposal reminds us of Satan's love of God. I love you, but your other creation must go. They're beneath me. Satan also obligated God to accept such love.

Satan said, "Because You have put me in error, I will surely sit in wait for them on Your straight path." It is vengeful, selfish, and vindictive.

Mr. Darcy's second attempt at a marriage proposal was akin to Adam, upon him peace, and his love of God: open to growth, nurturing, and personal development. "How can I make amends?" asks Mr. Darcy. He was full of hope yet divorced of obligation. Hence, he received the spiritual rain to strengthen him and benefit those around him.

Likewise, Prophet Adam, upon him peace: "Our Lord, we have wronged ourselves, and if You do not forgive us and have mercy upon us, we will surely be among the losers" (Quran 7:23).

Adam was focused on his relationship with God and his own wrongdoing, not Satan's wrongdoings or disbelief. He was not vengeful, selfish, or vindictive.

At times, our love for God is like that. We might say to God, "We love you most ardently," but we obligate God to a result. It lacks awe and respect for His Station and Majesty. We disrespect His other creation, like Satan scorned Adam, upon him peace.

However, we must be willing to go through a character transformation that beautifies and further ennobles us to receive God's love.

The months before Ramadan help prepare our hearts to receive the blessings and gifts that Ramadan will shower upon us and God's love, which our pride and arrogance often repel.

Israa and Miraj demonstrated the true servanthood of Prophet Muhammad, upon him peace and blessings. They also manifested his genuine and true love of God and respect for His Majesty and creation. In reward, he ascended to the heavens and was given the gift of the five daily prayers to share with God's creation. When someone loves you, they want to remain connected with you. And that is what the prayers are: a Divine connection. The message these prayers give is that we can face life's struggles and hardships with patience and prayer. They teach us to rely on God, not our egos or other people.

When we think about Ramadan, the first thing that comes to mind is often the act of fasting from dawn to dusk. Fasting certainly is the most visible part of Ramadan observance. But there is more beyond the visible, beyond giving up daytime eating and struggling to be a better person. At its core, Ramadan is about dropping the walls we keep around us, making ourselves vulnerable, and approaching God *Al Ghafir, Al Ghaffar,* and *Al Ghafur.*

The Arabic letters *gh, f,* and *r* are the roots of these three beautiful names of God. As Shaykh Tosun Bayrak al-Jerrahi al-Halveti writes in *The Most Beautiful Names of God,*

> *"Al-Ghafir"* means that God hides our faults from other people, the name *"Al-Ghafur"* means that he keeps knowledge of our fault from the angels, and the name *"Al-Ghaffar"* means that God relieves us of continual suffering by veiling many of our faults from our own eyes.

All this comes from a great compassion. After all, it's toxic to live in constant fear of making a mistake, and we can't grow while being hypersensitive or hypercritical.

God's forgiveness is a central part of His message to us. Scholar Juan Cole has found 262 places in the Quran where words with the letters *gh, f,* and *r*—the root of forgiving—are used. Ramadan is a time when we reflect on this forgiveness. It's a time to reflect on our need both to be forgiven and to forgive. We must learn from God *Al-Ghafir, Al-Ghaffar,* and *Al- Ghafur* to approach Him in all vulnerability and be guided by Him. But we must also learn to overlook minor shortcomings in ourselves and others.

God Al-Ghaffar and Al-Ghafur

A large part of Ramadan is finding forgiveness. A true search for forgiveness doesn't mean approaching the people around us, who might feel pressured into forgiving us our misdeeds. Instead, it means approaching God in a vulnerable state. It means a silent and vulnerable prostration, in which only God can see or hear us.

Why ask God for forgiveness if it's other people we wronged?

Sometimes, instead of approaching God for forgiveness, we might turn instead to the public. Instead of approaching God in all humility, we seek validation from other people. This might seem, on its face, like the right thing to do. And sometimes, a public acknowledgement of wrongdoing could be part of repairing a harm. But often, publicly admitting our mistakes is a way not of repairing the harm but of normalizing our wrongdoing.

Former president Donald Trump is, for instance, very open about types of wrongdoing. But this has not made him rethink his behavior or repair the harm. Instead, it has normalized the harm for others. Trump has been quite honest about how he demeans women, but this has not made him vulnerable. Instead, it has given a license to others to behave in similar ways.

Asking others for forgiveness is often a performance more than an act of holistic, repentant vulnerability. Instead of addressing the harm, it can promote social acceptance of the abuse.

When we have done harm, the first thing we need to do is not talk about it publicly or go person to person, gathering supporters. We need to lower our defenses and approach God.

Nurturing Ourselves, Nurturing Others

What does it mean to follow the example of God Al-Ghafir? Those of us who have children know that, when you're raising a child, you have to overlook small faults in order to nurture your child toward being better. If a parent were to point out every tiny thing that's wrong with their child, then the two of them, parent and child, wouldn't be able to live together, much less depend on each other.

The same is true of other family members. There are always tensions in a family. Even in the Prophet's own family, upon them peace and blessings, there were conflicts. Tension, instability, and rivalries exist within families as they do within larger communities. That's part of what it means to be human.

God Al-Ghafir shields many of our faults and sins from others in our community. Many times, when a public figure we admire is revealed to have acted badly, we wonder, *why didn't I know?* We didn't know because God was shielding that person's sins from the world to give that person a chance to be nurtured toward growth.

When we understand this attribute of *God Al-Ghafir*, we understand what God wants from us. We, too, must learn to overlook some faults.

There is a vast difference between faults and harm! Overlooking someone's faults doesn't mean you should ever overlook the harm they do. It certainly doesn't mean you should stay in a violent or abusive relationship. Rather, it means that shortcomings shouldn't be exaggerated, and that people should be allowed to repair the damage that they've done and move on without being constantly reminded of past errors.

When Moses returned to Egypt, the first thing Pharaoh did was immediately remind him of his past wrongdoing. In our own era, people troll social media, looking for missteps or unkind words from years before, repeatedly throwing them back at people. People from marginalized communities are particularly vulnerable. They often aren't allowed to make a misstep without being raked over the coals for it repeatedly.

Our daily news coverage often goes looking for faults, brokenness, and things to sensationalize in marginalized communities, particularly among Muslims, African Americans, and Native communities. We should follow the lesson of God *Al-Ghafir*. We should not shame others for past acts, nor should we ever define communities by terrible acts done by fringe members. A shaming mentality is not healthy for any society, and bullying trickles down, all the way down to children in school.

We should never shame people, which condemns them to hating themselves for mistakes they have made. Sometimes the shame doesn't even belong to the person being shamed; it belongs to the person who threw it at them. Shame is not the path God *Al-Ghafir* has shown us.

Hidden from Ourselves

It is human to remember, but it is even more human to forget. None of us has a perfect memory. Often, we must forget painful things so we can grow and return to them later. It is the mercy of God *Al-Ghaffar* that allows us to forget certain things we have done. After all, if we constantly thought about every bad thing we have ever done, we would not be able to move forward. Often, we need to become stronger before we can review the past. Moses had to leave Egypt and regain his strength before he was able to grapple with his past.

Forgetting Is One of God's Mercies

God doesn't want us to walk around constantly fretting and angry, ashamed of ourselves, thinking that we are sinners. Yes, we are weak. So we should remember that we are weak and vulnerable, and we should remember that we need to turn to God with that vulnerability. Only He can give us forgiveness. As Shaykh al-Halveti writes in *The Most Beautiful Names of God*:

> *A sinner is like a poor fellow who has fallen into a sewer. What is the first thing that he must do? He cannot face others in that state, nor can he stand himself. He must wash and cleanse himself, unless he is insane, not realizing his offensive state. The soap and water with which to wash one's interior is repentance. Woe to those who do not see nor smell the dirty stench filling their interiors!*

That is, it does no good to stand in our offensive state before the public. What we need to do is repent to God.

A person I know once said that the antidote to being ashamed of ourselves is empathy for others. While I respect the feeling behind this, and empathy is certainly important, it will not bring us relief. Instead, the antidote to shame is repentance. If we come close to God, then God will guide us to repair harm that we have done even as He veils small transgressions from our eyes. God will inspire us.

Hidden Even from the Angels

The Quran tells us that the angels didn't see Satan's faults. This is because God hides people's faults and gives them the space to repent. He hides our faults even from angels. It was not the angels who outed Satan; it was Satan himself who openly declared war on God. This space of complete privacy allows us to become vulnerable before God, confess, and repent.

Vulnerability is not a performance in front of other people. It is about lowering the defensive walls that surround us, trusting God, and coming close to God. God hides your sins to such an extent that, if you come to Him, He even sometimes turns a sin into a good deed.

During the month of Ramadan, we need to promote forgiveness. Part of doing this is overlooking the faults of others and allowing them to make themselves vulnerable before God. We're all vulnerable because we're all human beings. As we fast together, we need to recognize our common weaknesses. Sometimes we need to look away to give someone the space and courage to make themselves vulnerable before God.

Between Pardon and Repentance

> *O ye who believe! Avoid suspicion as much (as possible): for suspicion in some cases is a sin: And spy not on each other behind their backs. Would any of you like to eat the flesh of his dead brother? Nay, ye would abhor it . . . But fear Allah: For Allah is Oft-Returning, Most Merciful.*
>
> —Quran 49:12

God's names *Al-Ghaffar* and *Al-Ghafur* tell us about how God is constantly forgiving us. These names mean that God is covering our flaws so that He hides them from our own eyes, the eyes of others, and even from the angels. This act of generosity allows us to go about our lives without being paralyzed by anxiety.

God *Al-Ghaffar* and God *Al-Ghafur* offer us a spiritual "safe space," a place where we can feel we are among allies. Here, we are safe from the critical gaze of those who would attack us for minor mishaps, as the marginalized are so often attacked and shamed by the larger community. This is particularly true when the marginalized stand up for their rights.

In the safe space of *Al-Ghaffar* and *Al-Ghafur*, God gives us a place to be shaded from the constantly critical gaze of others. Yet it isn't simply a space for us to relax, shielded from judgment. It's meant to allow us space to grow, to dig deep within ourselves, find the causes of harm, and transform. After this, approaching God *at-Tawwab* is that next step. This is the stage when we are not just seeking a safe space away from the world, but we are turning to God for strength and faith and to work on our repentance.

God at-Tawwab

When we allow ourself to be shielded by God *Al-Ghaffar* and *Al-Ghafur*, we are in a state of retreat. But when we approach God *at-Tawwab*, we are turning toward God with repentance or in a state of *tawbah*. In doing this, we are growing, transforming, and returning to our essential state of purity.

As Shaykh al-Halveti writes in *The Most Beautiful Names of God*, repentance is "not simply seeing the wrong and ugliness of one's actions, regretting having done bad things and wishing not to repeat them," and it's not just about fearing God's punishment and hoping for mercy. That would be, in al-Halveti's words, like cutting off the tops of the weeds but leaving the roots. Repentance is akin to digging out the roots and trying to eliminate the *cause* of one's sins, the ways in which one has transgressed against others. That is, God is promising us not just His mercy and forgiveness but His help with our inner cleansing, facilitating our full repentance.

We can see this process in action clearly in the story of when Moses, upon him peace, left Egypt after he accidentally killed an Egyptian solider. First, he left the environment where he was under attack, pulling back into a spiritual safe space where he could be sheltered and nurtured by God.

This was not punishment, as what Prophet Moses did was not a sin. Moses had used his best judgment to protect a fellow Jew, but he had miscalculated in killing the soldier. Even though he had broken no Sacred Law or commandment, he knew, between himself and God, that he had done something wrong. So immediately, to cleanse his heart, Moses approached God *at-Tawwab*, Turning to God with a heart full of repentance.

The same is true for us. When we turn to God *at-Tawwab*, then He opens a door for what we need in that moment. It could be nurturing, it could be strengthening, or it could be cleansing. For Moses, God opened the door for him to leave Egypt, go to the land of Midian, and be nurtured under the Prophet Shuy'ab. If we turn to God and repent, then He will inspire us or create an opportunity for us to change.

Tawbah, or seeking forgiveness from God, is an active process. You can't just say, "I seek forgiveness from God, *astaghfirullah*." It must involve action, although that is different for each person. Once, there was a man who had killed ninety-nine people. The killer asked a man who was known to be a saint whether he could be forgiven, and the saint said he didn't think so. The man killed this saint. After that, he went to a learned man, who told him, yes, the killer could find repentance, but first he needed to travel to another town.

The man who had killed ninety-nine people died on the way to that new town. Angels came to measure the distance; they wanted to see whether the man was closer to the town of his crimes or the town of his repentance. God intervened and stretched the distance, so that the man was closer to town of repentance. This was the man's *tawbah*, because he died while making a sincere effort to repent. He had struggled, and he had failed, but only God knew what was in the man's heart.

Yet for each of us, *tawbah*—or the act of approaching God *at-Tawwab*—means making an effort. If, many years ago, you borrowed money and still owe it, you cannot simply ask God's forgiveness. You must actively look for the person to whom you owe money. If you can't find them, then the next step is giving to a charity in their name. You must try to repair the harm, not just ask for forgiveness. Being forgiven by God doesn't mean you won't face punishment. But God will know how to intervene and whether you need to be strengthened, nurtured, or purified from within.

God al-Afuw

Perhaps we are not prepared to seek God *at-Tawwab*, or perhaps we aren't even sure what we have done wrong. It is always the right time to approach God *Al-Afuw*, who pardons us and obliterates our sins.

We might seek God's pardon for any number of reasons. God *Al-Afuw* means that God not only forgives us but also completely erases our sin, removing it and allowing it to die. He removes the penalty so we can be at peace. God *Al-Afuw* gives us a clean slate. Why? This might help jump-start someone who has been in difficult circumstances and who, for whatever reason, has done evil. Sometimes, the more evil a person does, the harder it is to break out and do good. So God gives them a chance to obliterate all their sins.

Sometimes, we can see from the outside that God is not punishing a person's sin, as God did not immediately punish Pharaoh. That doesn't mean He won't respond. It means that, for now, He is being God *al-Afuw*. He is giving space, a clean slate, and a chance for someone to start over. Sometimes, as with Pharaoh, the person doesn't take their opportunity. Sometimes, as with the magicians, they do.

But it is not only those who are weighed down with sin who should approach God *al-Afuw*. We should always turn to God to pardon us. After all, none of us should ever feel certain that we have done no wrong.

Perhaps we don't even know that we have harmed others. Often, we do not. When we know we have done harm, we can approach God *at-Tawwab*. But there are a thousand micro-harms we cannot perceive. We cannot know the impact of many of our small daily interactions on others. Perhaps we were curt in line with a grocery store clerk or on the phone. Perhaps our bag knocked into someone and, thinking about our own troubles, we failed to notice.

Perhaps it was something else. For instance, we often don't see how our privilege affects others. Our privilege—because of our abilities, an accident of birth, systems of power, or other reasons—can be part of societal imbalances. This privilege can be part of a system that harms others.

Turning to God Al-Afuw means a clean slate. But it doesn't mean that we should close our eyes and feel our work is done. Once we have that clean slate, we should take the new energy and build society. Turning to God Al-Afuw keeps us conscious of the fact that we need to constantly purify ourselves and listen to others who we may have harmed. We need to *always* be open to listening to how we're affecting others. This is not so that we can punish ourselves or so we can ask God to punish us. It's so we can build society.

It's human nature to see the good we've done, rather than all the things we've been given. This sometimes blinds us to how we're affecting others. That blindness doesn't mean we should constantly castigate or punish ourselves. That won't help society either. It means we should turn to God al-Afuw and then turn back to our society, humbly, and see what we can do to repair and build.

When we can, and when we know what we've done wrong, we should approach God al-Tawwab. But we should also seek God Al-Afuw to remove the sins we cannot carry. Once God has obliterated these sins, it's up to us to act in gratitude, to build society, and do something in return. Now that we're starting with a clean slate, we can build not with a heart filled with entitlement, but one filled with gratitude.

Erasing the Sins of Zihar

During Muhammad's time, there was a woman named Khaulah bint-Thalabah, who was married to a man named Aus bin Samit Ansari. At the time, there was a practice called *zihar*, by which a man could divorce his partner with a simple verbal declaration, saying she was like a mother to him. After this, the woman received nothing, and reconciliation was impossible.

Khaulah bint-Thalabah went to Prophet Muhammad, upon him peace and blessings, to ask for help. By the standards of the time, she was already an old woman with many children, and providing for these children alone was going to be a hardship. Yet the Prophet Muhammad, upon him peace and blessings, was unable to help her, as *zihar* was the customary law of the time, and there was no law of God that contradicted it. So Khaulah bint-Thalabah took her complaint to God.

After this, God sent a revelation to the Prophet Muhammad that condemned and forbade *zihar*, which became a sin, and any man who used it was to be punished. After this, God went a step further, helping erase the sin and reconciling Khaulah bint-Thalabah and Aus bin Samit Ansari. The impact of his words disappeared, and the family was reunited.

What this story shows us is that *Al-Afuw* isn't just about erasing the sin; it's also about erasing the conditions that underpinned and facilitated the sin. You can't fight domestic violence, for instance, without dealing with misogyny. If society looks at women as less than men, then that underlying attitude is going to enable domestic violence. Aus bin Samit Ansari caused harm to Khaulah bint-Thalabah, and it was not enough for him to say he was sorry to repair the harm. To remove the impact, God also had to remove the social condition that enabled it. Without this step, Aus bin Samit Ansari could have fallen back into the same bad patterns, as happens with domestic violence. God *al-Afuw* didn't erase only the sin but the conditions that led to it.

It's Hard to Be Grateful

Most of us, by our nature, are ungrateful. Yet knowing this, we can appreciate God *Al-Afuw* even more.

Some of those who lived in ancient Egypt worshiped the calf even after they were saved from the Pharaoh and after they watched him and his soldiers drown. God Most High God Most High tells us:

> "...and when We appointed for Moses forty nights [on Mount Sinai], and in his absence, you took to worshipping the [golden] calf, and thus became evildoers: yet, even after that, We blotted out your sin, so that you might have cause to be grateful."
>
> —Quran 2:51-52

It's always good to try to be grateful; after all, God's doors are always open to the ones who choose to enter. But, in the final days of Ramadan, it's particularly important to turn to God and ask to be pardoned. As we are seeking forgiveness from God in these last ten days of Ramadan, we should realize that if we have violated others, they will also come before God, seeking their rights. We should never be intoxicated by our own good deeds such that we overlook the harm we may have done others.

It's possible that they raise a petition before God, and all our good deeds transfer to them to compensate for some wrong we have done them. Indeed, it might be that all their bad deeds transfer to us, depending on the severity of our wrongdoing and how much or how little we have done to repair the harm. People of faith do not deny their wrongdoings but keep trying to repent, seek forgiveness, and repair the harm. We should listen to those who say we have harmed them even when we don't, at first, believe we have done anything wrong.

The final ten days of Ramadan are the best time to appeal to God for forgiveness, not only for ourselves but also for our families and everyone struggling in faith, including those who are ungrateful. After all, none of us are sufficiently grateful for all we have, and the Prophets and Righteous people prayed for help being grateful instead of assuming they already were.

That doesn't mean we should force repentance, gratitude, or patience on others. Once, there was a woman who was grieving over the death of her brother. Prophet Muhammad, upon him peace and blessings, called on her to be patient, as he practiced patience. She told him to go away. Instead of arguing, or telling her that she was wrong, he listened and went away.

Once this woman realized that he was Prophet Muhammad, upon him peace and blessings, she ran after him to apologize. He reminded her again to be patient, and this time she accepted his advice.

On the last day of Ramadan, we should be grateful and love the moment, asking for a pardon regardless of what we think are our sins, as there is so much, we cannot see. Hopefully, as we exit Ramadan, so we exit our lives.

An-Nafi' and Ad-Daarr

> "And if Allah should touch you with adversity, there is no remover of it except Him. And if He touches you with good – then He is over all things competent."
>
> —Quran 6:17

Why Muhammad Fled to God

There are two names of God, often spoken together, that show the balance of our world. They are *An-Nafi'* and *Ad Daarr*.

The name *An-Nafi'* means God is the one who helps and confers all advantages, who creates all that produces benefit for us, from our wealth to our charms to our intelligence. It is God who gives us moments of genuine and healthy laughter and who comforts our souls.

The name *Ad Daarr* means God is the one who, in His wisdom, also allows adversity or distress. God does not set out to punish us. But He has given us free will, and he allows things that hurt us to exist. Adversity and distress are not necessarily punishments just as ease and comfort aren't necessarily rewards. Allah Most High Allah Most High creates ease and adversity to test, reward, punish, or any combination thereof. He is the doer, and He wills all of it. God is not pleased by adversity, distress, or punishment.

These two names fit together, and together they show how benefit and harm are part of a cycle, like circling around the Ka'aba. These apparent opposites make us aware that every action is part of a larger balance, even when the whole pattern is not visible to us.

When we receive benefits, we should turn to God. And when harm falls to us, we should also turn to God. We may turn to other people in both cases as well as a means by which we turn to God— to be grateful or to seek help. But the prophets show us that turning to God can give us a sense of empowerment. God will use people as a means to respond and aid us. This way, we will never be humiliated by seeking help that doesn't come. We will always have God.

How to Keep the Faith

Everyone eventually finds obstacles in their path. All of us, eventually, find people who will hurt us, whether these people are close or distant. These trials can help us find ourselves. Indeed, these trials can be a mercy. After all, people who know only an echo chamber of praise often are unable to listen—as Satan was unable to listen—and they often take the wrong path.

Sometimes we can turn to others to help us. But sometimes, as when Joseph was alone or when Asiya was alone with Pharaoh, there is nothing to do but flee to God.

Satan refused to flee to God. He was obsessed with God's command, and yet he didn't understand or worship God. So when the command changed and he needed to be flexible and listen, Satan was unable.

Laws change over time: even the qibla itself changed. God gave the command to face Jerusalem, and Muhammad, upon him peace and blessings, faced Jerusalem. Then God said to face Mecca, and Muhammad changed directions. So laws shifted even during Muhammad's time. The important thing is not to worship God's command, but to worship God.

Muhammad also understood that Islam could come with many different cultural flowerings. The important thing was the core of Islam, not the outward cultural trappings. Certainly, Muhammad didn't expect to see everyone practice Islam as a Qurayshi would.

Now, Indonesia's practice of Islam is different from that in China, and in Nigeria. The aim of religious law should be to keep us respecting our rights and fulfilling our responsibilities and to bring us to God. Our aim should not be to worship the law.

Muhammad, upon him peace and blessings, went from one place to the next, and he allowed and encouraged variant cultural practices, as long as they did not bring harm to the people. The only time he touched on cultural issues was when they brought harm to the people, such as with alcohol, which was an agreed-upon harm. It is important to note that the Messenger of Allah, upon him peace and blessings, did not legislate of his own volition or desire and only by consensus.

Why Would God Allow Good People to Be Harmed?

There are many reasons God might allow harm. We don't know these reasons and should never try to act on God's behalf, to teach others through harming them. Yet harm can help us learn many things.

All the prophets were attacked and hurt, and the Prophet Muhammad was harmed the most of all. After each of these harmful experiences, the prophets fled to God and turned to Him, and thus they witnessed that He was the one who could guide, help, aid, and protect. Perhaps none of us can understand God by sitting down on a couch and reading about Him on a weekend afternoon. Even the prophets had to experience pain and suffering.

Indeed, the prophets were constantly being attacked, not just physically but emotionally, mentally, and psychologically.

Once, the Prophet Muhammad, upon him peace and blessings, went to pray near Mecca. Relatives and some of the community members threw trash over his head while he was bowing. They were laughing at him and mocking him, trying to humiliate him in front of everyone.

One of his aunts used to put thorns on the ground so that when Muhammad walked, they would hurt his feet. She also made-up songs to taunt him. Once, when the Prophet went to Ta'if, a youth chased him with stones and ridiculed and mocked him.

Two of the Prophet's married daughters were divorced, just to cause the Prophet harm. Yet he welcomed his daughters home and treated them with dignity and respect. Whatever others did to humiliate him, he turned to God for help, and he bore it all with patience.

Muhammad also experienced all types of character assassination, both from family members and from outsiders. They called him crazy, a liar, a magician, and a breaker of family ties. And yet he was able to overcome all this by turning to God for help and solace.

The prophets attempted to nurture society despite being attacked, abused, and mocked. They did this with tremendous character, and it helps us see the road we need to travel.

What then?

People came from many directions to set upon the Prophet and his companions. The Prophet, upon him peace and blessings, would flee to God and call for help and aid. In this way, he experienced and witnessed God.

We, too, can follow this path. We can turn to God, such that He comes to our aid, stands by us, and helps us. This can help build our strength and our emotional and spiritual muscles.

The prophets relied on God and aid from God. For them, the door to God was always open.

If you had the choice, should you live without harm? The prophet was given a choice: Would you like to live in wealth, as some of your companions do? Would you like to be protected from all harm? Muhammad was asked this question by the angels, and his answer was an unequivocal *no*. After all, if Muhammad was to be guiding people, then he had to know the people's reality. He had to experience it and to keep faith alongside them. It's exceptionally hard—if it's possible at all—to live separately, in a mansion, and preach to the poor.

Muhammad knew what other people suffered since he was being persecuted while they were being persecuted. Indeed, the prophets all experienced human suffering.

Thus, God filled Muhammad's heart with mercy. Muhammad was the first among the Muslims to face oppression from family and community, as well as from outsiders. He was the first to be forced into exile, to be mocked and ridiculed, and to face war and hardships. His wisdom was to learn patience and humility and to rely on God.

There were many who did evil turns to Muhammad, such as Hind, who had Muhammad's beloved Uncle Hamza killed and mutilated. Yet Hind was later welcomed into the community of Muslims. Muhammad had to struggle with the idea of engaging her. But with God's help, he did.

Why Me?

Sometimes, when we are faced with trials and tribulations, we ask, "Why me?" Sometimes, we say, "I am good person, so this shouldn't happen to me!" And yet the Prophet was sinless, and still he experienced trials. At each moment, Muhammad fled to God.

We must entertain the idea that we have sinned. Yet, even if you are sinless, repent anyway. Repenting is different from feeling guilt as we discussed earlier. It's an internal state of correction, learning, and coming closer to God.

It's only the arrogant and egotistical person who does not repent or flee to God during a trial. Adam fled to God and sought repentance, as did every prophet. It is only those like Satan or

Pharaoh who refused, who thought fleeing to God was a form of humiliation.

Flee to God

When people hurt you, God uses these trials to push you to Him. People usually run to more powerful people for help and victory. However, if the person harming you is the most powerful or influential in the town, and no one will respond to their oppression and push them back within their boundaries, then who does this person go to? The person turns to God.

God wants you to turn to Him and connect to Him. That is the wisdom behind the problem. He found you heedless and not mindful of your values and faith.

Every person finds someone who is an obstacle in their path or someone who will hurt them. No one can escape that. God allows these obstacles and hurts so you do not rely on them. Work with people, but do not rely on them. Engage them, but do not rely on them. Benefit them, but take your complaints to God.

Why does God allow people who are Muslims to hurt other Muslims? God has made some of you a trial for others; will you be patient? This means some people are a source of pain, a trial or tribulation to hurt others, so people do not attach themselves to them or seek comfort in them.

Understand that An-Nafi' and Ad-Daarr Are Allah

At times, the wisdom is you are not abiding by the boundaries of Islam, and God wants to discipline you to teach you to be aware and to be mindful. Or you sinned, and God wants to purify you from sin. Or people are praising you, and this praise is going to harm you, and God wants to protect you from this praise so you do not become intoxicated. On the outside, it is painful, but internally, it is a form of Mercy to protect you from a bad state that afflicted Satan.

A lot of people view the religion as rules and laws and are unmindful of servitude to God, and God has placed them on this earth in two ways: Gratitude in good times, not just in words but to share the gifts to benefit people, and Patience in bad times. Patience is a form of servitude, including persisting with goodness while remaining within the boundaries of Allah in adversity.

So God will send people to hurt you with their tongues to protect you from arrogance and egoism, to expect reward from God, and to turn to God for help and protection.

Don't ask why or question His wisdom. Have a good opinion of God always. God requires from you patience in bad times and gratitude in good times.

Why did God allow bad people to harm the Prophet and his companions? So they would turn to Him and witness that He is the one who will guide, help, aid, and protect. He could not witness this by sitting down on a couch and reading it. Even the Prophet had to experience this, even though he was sinless.

What did the Prophet used to pray for? Many people in many directions were set upon the Prophet and his companions. The Prophet, upon him peace and blessings, would flee to God and cry for help and aid, so one does not find comfort from them, and one experiences and witnesses God in truth helping Him and aiding Him.

He relied on God and the aid and victory from God. His patience and responding according to his values and patiently beseeching God for help opened the door for help from God. Since they lost hope in everyone and anyone helping them, they only had hope in God.

You Are in Our Eyes

The Prophet did not have constant happy days. He was given the choice to live like his companions or live protected from any harm. He chose to live like his companions so he could be a living guide, showing them that, like them, he was facing harm, pain, and all types of oppression and persecution so they could learn and know how to use their faith to face these trials and oppressions.

What would Satan say to the companions if the Prophet did not experience the oppression they experienced? He would tell them, "He is calling you to be patient, yet he is living like a king. He is preaching to you to do what he is not experiencing." Who would listen if he lived in a mansion while those he called to were in hunger and pain?

God filled his heart with His Mercy for His creation. And he was the first of the Muslims to face and taste oppression from family, community, and outside. He was the first to be kicked out in exile, and mocked and ridiculed, faced war, et cetera.

This is a reality that needs to be embraced by all, privileged or unprivileged. The wisdom is to learn patience and humility and to rely on God. Like all the prophets fled to God during a trial. He is the Powerful One, the Strong, the One who can Abase your oppressors or guide them.

The Prophet turned and fled to God, sought His help and aid, and relied only on God. Sometimes trial and tribulation occur because one is away from prayers. The aim is not to be perfect or sinless but that the person is continuously and perpetually fleeing to God—not a once or in an isolated moment, but always turning to Him. The problem or trouble is the trial and tribulation come, and the person says, "I am a good person. Why did this happen to me?" They don't understand the wisdom, which is to turn and flee to God. If you sinned, repent. If you did not, still turn and flee to God. The Prophet was sinless and fled to God and turned to Him. You are a servant of God, and you need to experience this servitude by constantly turning to Him. You cannot just intellectually learn this; you must experience it.

All of us commit sin, and God is Oft-Forgiving. However, the aim is not to feel bad but to turn to God and experience His Forgiveness, His reality, and His presence. The aim is to turn to God while experiencing total helplessness, powerlessness, and no hope for help from anyone except God and seek His help and victory.

We all sin, but how often we turn to God and repent and repair the harm is the question we need to focus on. How often? In an isolated moment?

The Muslim leaders of the past, the righteous ones—yes, they had problems, but ask how often they repented and fled to God? How many times did they cry and seek His Forgiveness. Not as an act, but genuinely feeling the wrong and feeling remorseful. Asking God for help and aid and Forgiveness. The people God loves are not the sinless, but if you count the times they repent, it is perpetual and continuous.

The arrogant and egotistical person does not repent or flee to God during a trial. Adam fled and sought repentance, and so did every prophet. Yet Satan and Pharaoh would not. Satan was a worshipping slave but did not like the feeling of being humiliated, whereas as Adam accepted it and turned and fled to God, seeking forgiveness and mercy.

Some would get angry and say, "God, why did you do this to me? I am a good person and doing good deeds." They lose sight of the wisdom that the Prophets were sinless and were persecuted the most, yet they accepted their trials and tribulations with patience, fleeing and beseeching God for help, aid, and victory. Again, this is an ongoing and circular process, not a one-time event. It was faced by the sinless and the best of creation, and as humans, we, too, will face trials and tribulations.

Al-Hayy and Al-Qayyum

Prophet Muhammad, upon him peace and blessings, taught to say:

> *Ya Hayyu Ya Qayyum, [O Living! O Sustainer!] I call upon Your Mercy for assistance, and from Your punishment I seek refuge! Make good all my affairs and do not entrust me to myself or any of Your creation even for the blink of an eye.!*

This prayer or supplication connects us to two Beautiful Names of God.

When we feel distress, emotionally, mentally, and spiritually dead for whatever reason we should reach out and connect to The Living or *Al-Hayy*. He will pump life into us emotionally, mentally, and spiritually, for He is the One who alone has absolute, independent life.

We should also connect to The Eternal Sustainer, or *Al-Qayyum*, who is the One who alone needs none to sustain Him and who always sustains all things, in every way.

We want relief. So we must reject suicide and homicide and seek relief and assistance from Him when we are in danger or distress.

The end of the prayer is: O Allah, Your mercy I am hopeful for, so do not leave me to myself for the blink of an eye, and put all my affairs in order, there is no god but You.

It is said that the ego is a treacherous companion, and whenever God leaves a person to their ego, even in the blink of an eye, the ego is bound to hurt them in various ways. When feeling down, we should reach out to God and ask for His Mercy with this prayer. We must reject the ego as a companion even for the blink of an eye, as it will lead us to places such as suicide as a solution. Instead, we must seek His companionship and ask for His Assistance to rectify our affairs. In life, we will all face danger and distress, stumble and face our weaknesses. It is challenging to meet our needs and our human condition. We can hate that reality or connect to God and seek His relief to help us through whatever distress we are facing.

Love Is Deeper Than Words

On those who believe and work deeds of righteousness, will (Allah) Most Gracious bestow love. (Quran 19:96)

Some scholars mention two extremes that cause people to go astray: justice and love. And there is a spectrum in between the extremes. Hence, in reading *Al-Fatiha*, the opening and first chapter of the Quran, we seek protection and guidance from both extremes: "Show us the straight way, The way of those on whom Thou hast bestowed Thy Grace, those whose (portion) is not wrath, and who go not astray" (Quran 1:6–7).

The first book, *God Intervenes Between A Person And Their Heart*, discusses the spirit of the law concerning justice, and the second book, *Love Is Deeper Than Words*, discusses the spirit of the law with respect to love. I do not touch on what is permissible and impermissible since such knowledge is in the domain of jurists and scholars qualified to speak on such matters.

> *But say not for any false thing that your tongues may put forth, "This is lawful, and this is forbidden," so as to ascribe false things to Allah. For those who ascribe false things to Allah, will never prosper.*
>
> —Quran 16:116

Case example: When my mother had a major stroke during her back surgery, I argued with the neurosurgeon that my mother had a stroke three days before security was called. I explained that I was with my mom during every hospital visit, and that I knew how she recovered post-surgery or anesthesia, and this was not a normal recovery. An agreement was reached to give her a CAT scan. The results came back, and the neurosurgeon tried to backpedal, claiming it was a minor stroke. I told him, "I do not want to discuss anything with you. I need to speak to the chief surgeon." He reviewed the test results and said, "Your mother had a major stroke. There is no hope of recovery." Now, I know my mother's medical history and can argue with a doctor about medical procedures. However, I do not know how to do neurosurgery. My discovery that my mother had a stroke and proving the neurosurgeon with decades of experience wrong does not make me a neurosurgeon.

Likewise, with matters of faith, one can argue with jurists on issues that they know, given their experiences in a field or history. Jurists with decades of experience and knowledge can be dead wrong, but this does not make the one arguing with them a jurist. We do not worship our jurists. However, we do not take the matter or specialization of being a jurist lightly.

In other words, given the example above, although I was right, no one would trust me to perform surgery on their loved ones. I just knew that the neurosurgeon refused to consider my mother had a stroke. Likewise, some jurists become arrogant and refuse to listen to the knowledge of those living in situations that require them to think outside the box and out of autopilot mode.

I listen to and respect many teachers from various schools of thought. However, I relied heavily on the teachings of Dr. Muhammad Said Ramadan al-Bouti and Shaykh Muhammad Metwalli al-Sha'rawi in gathering my ideas.

Why Is the Theme "Love Is Deeper than Words"?

From a lesson by Dr. Ramadan al-Bouti: Love is a powerful force, such that whatever a person loves enslaves and drives them. God wants us to love Him more than anything else. This isn't because He needs our love, but because God loves us. The key point he makes is do *not* compare God to human beings. God is not a human being, so sometimes our questions are not just rationalizing but foolish.

Al Ghani: God, The Rich One

God is *Al Ghani*. He is free of want and need. He is Self-Sufficient. If all humanity lovingly worshipped God, this would not benefit Him in the least. And all of humanity choosing disobedience would not bring Him the slightest harm.

He wants us to love Him more than anyone and anything else to protect us from being enslaved to any person or object, including our ego. His love for us is protective and nurturing.

Then why not compel us to love Him? Since He has power over us, God can compel us. We are His universe, His property, and His creation.

Because His love invites with beautiful wisdom but does not compel or force. Instead, we are free to choose out of love and conviction to know, obey, and seek Him. God gives us the power and choice to disobey Him, yet many lovingly choose to obey.

> *Say thou: "This is my way: I do invite unto Allah, on evidence clear as the seeing with one's eyes I and whoever follows me. Glory to Allah! and never will I join gods with Allah!"*
>
> *Nor did We send before thee (as messengers) any but men, whom we did inspire, (men) living in human habitations. Do they not travel through the earth, and see what was the end of those before them? But the home of the hereafter is best, for those who do right. Will ye not then understand?*
>
> *(Respite will be granted) until, when the messengers give up hope (of their people) and (come to) think that they were treated as liars, there reaches them Our help, and those whom We will are delivered into safety. But never will be warded off our punishment from those who are in sin.*
>
> —Quran 12:108–110

Al-Hameed: God, The Most Praiseworthy

Allah is the Most Worthy of Praise. He is the one who is praised by all of existence. Praising means worshiping the Lord of the Worlds, who bestows endless blessings with reverence and gratitude. Everyone that exists praises Allah through their mouths, deeds, or simply by being. *Al-Hameed* is the only one deserving devotion, respect, thanksgiving, and honor. How can one laud someone other than Him in His presence when all comes from Him? He is the giver of all gifts and the source of all excellence.

He has created and formed us in beautiful shapes, granting us gifts of strength, intelligence, language, and so on. He has given us food, water, and oxygen and subjugated His other creatures to us. These gifts glorify Allah; those who brought them worship Allah; should we not accept these gifts and praise Allah as well?

Adam, upon him peace, responded with "*Alhamdulillah*" or "All Praise be to God." So what is in Adam's heart? *Hamd* or Praising God, an act of respect and gratitude.

On the outside, the Angels knew of God's Majesty, and so did Satan. However, Satan hid his reality from the Angels and himself, but not God. In his heart, there was no awe of God, but the awe of himself. So how could he know God, if he didn't know himself?

Adam was in heaven, enjoying life and Utopia, including a companion, Eve. All these gifts came to Adam without him asking for them or God breaking him or Eve. God did not break Satan, who openly declared that he would use all his power to turn creation against God. Satan misled Adam and Eve, upon them peace.

God forgave Adam and Eve, upon them peace. He deprived Satan of His Mercy and Forgiveness. No one can provoke God to act. When the punishment comes, it is always at an appointed time that is hidden with God.

So why are we on earth? Divine Plan. Being on earth helps us know ourselves and our innate nature and helps us know God and Praise Him with awe, respect, and gratitude for the many gifts including the Divine Breath.

> *It is He Who hath made you (His) agents, inheritors of the earth: He hath raised you in ranks, some above others: that He may try you in the gifts He hath given you: for thy Lord is quick in punishment: yet He is indeed Oft-forgiving, Most Merciful.*

> —Quran 6:165

As-Sitteer. God, The Concealer

> *Listen to the reed and the tale it tells, how it sings of separation.*

> —Rumi

Although not in the Quran but as a *hadith*, Allah is known as *As-Sitteer*, similar to *Al-Haleem*, or the Forbearing. He conceals or covers the faults and shortcomings of His creation.

While we disobey Him and depend on Him, He conceals our sins and is independent of all His creation. However, these sins affect our souls and can lead us further away from God. In response, God calls us to return repeatedly.

He descends to the lowest heaven in the last third of every night, when everyone is sleeping, and invites us to His door to speak with Him privately.

Our human condition is just the means to know ourselves and an invitation to know God more than the angels and bring us closer to Him. Abu Hurairah reported that The Messenger of Allah, upon him peace and blessings, said, Our Lord Most High descends to the lowest heaven in the last third of every night, saying:

1. Who is calling upon Me that I may answer him?
2. Who is asking from Me that I may give him?
3. Who is seeking My forgiveness that I may forgive him? (al-Bukhari 1145)

There is another saying by the Prophet Muhammad, upon him peace and blessings, that when God loves a servant, this love leads to the angels and people loving them, a gift from God to His sincere and true servants.

I hear this saying misconstrued by many influencers with many followers as they use their large following to showcase God's love for them. In several chapters of this book, I focus on the ego and Pharaoh, the archetypal character that best represents a defiant and rebellious ego that fears no one. One can distance oneself from such actions or reflect on his story so they do not meet a similar fate

According to the Quran, before we were born, our souls met before God:

> *When your Lord drew forth from the Children of Adam, from their loins, their descendants, and made them testify concerning themselves, (saying) "Am I not your Lord?" They said: "Yea! We do testify."*

—Quran 7:172

Awe and Respect

> *[So mention] when your Lord said to the angels, "Indeed, I am going to create a human being from clay. So when I have proportioned him and breathed into him of My [created] soul, then fall down to him in prostration." So the angels prostrated—all of them entirely. Except Iblees; he was arrogant and became among the disbelievers.*

—Quran 38:71–74

We often accuse God of our reality. I want to call us further to reflect on this verse. God does not pit Prophet Adam, upon him peace, against Satan. God honors Adam, upon him peace, with His Divine Breath and calls the Angels to prostrate, a prostration of respect.

The angels prostrated in respect to Adam, upon him peace. God honored Adam and his progeny. Adam, upon him peace, says *"Alhamdulillah"* or "All praise belongs to God." The greatest of God's creations is not the stars or galaxies but the human being.

"Except Iblees; he was arrogant and became among the disbelievers."

Without this breath, we are just intelligent apes. With it, we can do great wonders and great evil, depending on how we receive this gift and the state of our hearts, as mentioned previously. Our ability to love, build beautiful things, show compassion and kindness, and serve creation are signs of this gift. Everything we see in creation inclines to its source, its roots. Hence, the longing of our *ruh*, or soul, is for God.

When disconnected, we mistake this longing for substitutes, thinking we will find peace and contentment. Then we face disillusionment or disappointment. That longing within us remains. Is it a search for meaning, or could it be the *ruh*, or soul, searching for its beloved, its Creator—namely, God?

Maybe it is our testification to the covenant before God subconsciously probing our conscience. Remember when? Could it be a search for one's true self divorced from the world's influence and pollution?

Maybe the pain or the echo reflects our separation, our *ruh* calling us to make a U-turn or take the next exit and reconnect with God.

Here is an example that best expresses this reality. A man was married to a woman who treated him very well and gave him respect and honor. However, he left her for someone else. The new person mistreated him. He realized his mistake, and his conscience bothered him as he faced his ingratitude.

Was he ungrateful to his wife, or was this experience possibly a means to call him to the higher reality of his ingratitude to God? This example is how I interpret Prophet Muhammad, upon him peace and blessings, saying, "Whoever does not thank people has not thanked Allah."

We probably experienced something similar, possibly from a spouse or maybe in other relations. Such experiences call us to reflect on how we responded to God, Most High, first and foremost, when He honored us, gifted us with His Divine Breath, and commanded the angels to prostrate to Adam, upon him peace, out of respect. Do we respond with gratitude to this tremendous generosity, respect, and honor?

When we look at mammals or apes, have we ever thought to thank God for being recipients of His Divine Breath? Being human instead of apes? When we ignore or turn away, are we any different than the man in the case in point example I gave?

As we reflect on these experiences, I want to share the following: Mu'adh, a companion of the Prophet Muhammad, upon him peace and blessings, narrates that the Prophet said, "O Mu'adh! By Allah, I love you, so I advise you never to forget to recite after every prayer: 'O Allah, help me remember You, to be grateful to You, and to worship You in an excellent manner.'"

Angels

Although the angels did not understand why Adam, upon him peace, was made a vicegerent on earth, they prostrated out of respect. They were appointed as sincere advisers and more. God has given each person two angels to guard them and two others to record their deeds.

While God told Adam, upon him peace, to stay away from Satan, He commanded the angels to accompany each person from their birth to their grave.

> *He is the Irresistible (Supreme), over His slaves, and He sends guardians (angels guarding and writing all of one's good and bad deeds) over you, until when death approaches one of you, Our messengers (angel of death and his assistants) take his soul, and they never neglect their duty.*
>
> —Quran 6:61

A man said to 'Ali ibn Abi Talib (may Allah be pleased with him): "A group from (the tribe of) Murad wanted to kill you." 'Ali (may Allah be pleased with him) said, "With every man, there are two angels who protect him from everything that is not decreed;

when the decree comes, they withdraw and do not stand between him and it. A man's decreed lifespan is his protection." We read this in the Quran as well:

> *It is the same (to Him) whether any of you conceals his speech or declares it openly, whether he be hid by night or goes forth freely by day.*
>
> *For him (each person), there are angels in succession, before and behind him. They guard him by the command of Allah.*
>
> —Quran 13:10–11

God *Al-Wadud*, or Most Loving

The small reflections are meant to answer questions I have received over time, which usually begin with "How can a loving God …?" Also "Where in the Quran does it say, 'God is Loving'? I don't see 'God is Love' in the Quran," and so on. My answer has always been "Love is deeper than words."

When someone genuinely loves you, they invite you to know them at a level that others cannot. However, you must know yourself to know anyone: hence, our temporary stop on earth.

That invitation to know God more intimately was granted to Adam and his progeny, more intimately than the angels themselves could know God. This is also a sign of His Love for His creation.

If our human weakness, the human condition, and mistakes were meant to disgrace and shame us into faith, then God would not veil us when He corrects, disciplines, and nurtures us.

One of God's Most Beautiful Names is *Al-Wadud* or the Most Loving. One of the greatest gifts that God can bestow on His servants is a love of Him. You can turn to God today and seek that gift. It is embedded in our *ruh*, or soul, which allows us to give and receive compassion and love. How do we begin to receive it? First, we can be grateful that we are recipients of the Divine Breath: "[A]nd when I have formed him fully and breathed into him of My spirit, fall down before him in prostration!" (Quran 15:29).

God honored Adam, upon him peace, when He created him and asked the entirety of the angels' kingdom to prostrate to him out of respect.

He also assigned angels who respect him and his progeny to guard him and record his deeds. We can appreciate this as we listen to cases of bias and prejudice and how, over time, people confess to colluding with others to undermine one's security or discredit them.

For example, a New York police officer confessed to a link between the NYPD, the FBI, and the killing of Malcolm X.

The angels who were commanded to guard and record our actions were not full of prejudice, envy, malice, or spitefulness or "under duress and fear of retaliation." They were pure souls. Hence, their testimony and witness of our deeds cannot be challenged. They did not have internal shame to project onto Adam, and they did not hesitate to prostrate to him out of respect.

They were not full of envy either. They questioned God's decision, seeking to understand, not to argue, debate, and reject like Satan.

> *Behold, thy Lord said to the angels: "I will create a vicegerent on earth." They said: "Wilt Thou place therein one who will make mischief therein and shed blood? Whilst we do celebrate Thy praises and glorify Thy holy (name)?" He said: "I know what ye know not."*

—Quran 2:30

The angels trusted God and His decision. They replied: "Limitless art Thou in Thy glory! No knowledge have we save that which Thou hast imparted unto us. Verily, Thou alone art all-knowing, truly wise (Quran 2:32)" They fulfilled their role to guard Adam, upon him peace, as commanded. This is also an act of love from God toward Adam and his progeny.

We appreciate things when we experience their opposites. Imagine if the people bearing witness against you were people who wished to harm, discredit, and shame you in order to feel good about themselves? They want to keep you down because they feel threatened by you. Why? They cannot control you or your will, given your strength, wisdom, dignity, ethics, principles, and self-respect.

What would they record? What would they hear? What would they understand? Can you trust them to protect you when your life is in danger? Would they encourage you to do good or evil? Would they present evidence to prove their case or manufacture it? An excerpt from the article for reflection:

> *"My job was to infiltrate civil rights organizations throughout New York City, to find evidence of criminal activity, so the FBI could discredit and arrest its*

> leaders," Wood stated in the letter. "Under the direction of my handlers, I was told to encourage leaders and members of civil rights groups to commit felonious acts."
>
> It is He Who creates from the very beginning, and He can restore (life). And He is the Oft-Forgiving, Full of Loving-Kindness, Lord of the Throne of Glory, Doer (without let) of all that He intends.
>
> —Quran 85:13–16

To repent or turn to God, we must first acknowledge or realize our ingratitude to Him. And more so our lack of remembrance and praise for a Most Loving God.

If you had a diamond and lost it, you would frantically search for it. You might lose sleep trying to find it. If someone took it, you would go after them. You would not give up trying to find it, knowing its value. However, if you lose a worthless coin, a penny, you will probably just go on with life without a second thought. In this book, I emphasize that the disgrace is not in the slip of Adam, upon him peace, and his exit from heaven as that was predestined. The disgrace was in Satan, who failed to return.

And He taught Adam, upon him peace, the names all things. Then He showed them to the angels and said: "Inform Me of the names of these, if you are truthful. They said, "Exalted are You; we have no knowledge except what You have taught us. Indeed, it is You who is the Knowing, the Wise." (Quran 2:32)

God is All-Knowing and All-Wise. While the Angels asked to understand, Satan debated God's decision and knowledge.

> [Satan] said, "Because You have put me in error, I will surely sit in wait for them on Your straight path. Then I will come to them from before them and from behind them and on their right and on their left, and You will not find most of them grateful [to You]." [Allah] said, "Get out of Paradise, reproached and expelled. Whoever follows you among them - I will surely fill Hell with you, all together."
>
> —Quran 7:16-19

Although the Angels responded to God with humility, praise, reverence, and surrender, Satan begins by accusing and questioning God's wisdom, "You have put me in error," and then claims he will scheme and plan to put humans in the wrong. Eventually, at the pinnacle of self-deception, he casts his ingratitude onto humanity. Are Satan's plans an expression of his appreciation or ingratitude toward God?

In a special event, discussed in Chapter 17 of the Quran, "*Al-Israa* and *Al-Mi'raj*," God reveals to us the reality of Prophet Muhammad, upon him peace and blessings, in His eyes. The world did not know his secret or station. This event teaches us that our aim is to focus on God's gaze and knowledge of us.

This station was given to him after he faced the worst of trials from family and external forces, as neither could see his true reality. After such individuals return to our Lord, their love remains in the hearts of humanity and spreads far and wide, thousands of years later, without any marketing or schemes. Though in their lifetimes, they faced persecution and insults.

Reflect on the stories of the prophets and the elect, the number of followers, and the psychological warfare they faced for God's sake, and look at how many people honor and love them although they never met them.

I have never met Dr. Ramadan al-Bouti or Imam al-Sha'rawi, yet I love their teachings and hold them in high regard. No one told me or shamed me into liking them. I just listened to their teachings and found the love for their teachings in my heart.

Contemplation and Little Wonders

Indeed, in the creation of the heavens and the earth, and the alternation of the night and the day, and the [great] ships which sail through the sea with that which benefits people, and what Allah has sent down from the heavens of rain, giving life thereby to the earth after its lifelessness and dispersing therein every [kind of] moving creature, and [His] directing of the winds and the clouds controlled between the heaven and earth are signs for a people who use reason. (Quran 2:164)

The Quran calls us to look at the natural world and other creations and reflect. In 2020, we experienced a pandemic and COVID fatigue. I felt that a pause to reflect on nature might help us deal with anxiety and fatigue. Maybe we cannot be social now, but there are many beautiful sunrises, sunsets, water sounds, and chirping birds to connect with.

Some people among us may be blind, but they do not lose out on connecting with nature. The sounds of ocean waves are known to help with focus and relaxation. Try to listen to the waves as you read, write, study, or work to help you maintain focus. You can also use them as white noise to help you or your child go to sleep. As you listen, you can make *dhikr*, or remembrance of God.

Even if you are deaf and cannot hear, you can smell the roses or other flowers. Some have a scent that is incredibly beautiful. The flowers attract bees. There is a chapter in the Quran titled "The Bees" or "*An-Nahl*." It mentions the benefits of bees and the blessings they give to humankind. So we taste delicious and sweet food that is nutritious and beneficial. There is also touch. Have you heard of grounding?

Nature Puts You Back in Touch with the Ground

Grounding or earthing is an emerging field of study that explores the beneficial effects on your system of connecting to the earth. When you make direct physical contact with the earth through your bare feet or by lying in the grass, you reconnect electrically to the battery of the planet. This contact helps to balance the flow of energy in your physiology and has been shown to reduce inflammation, reduce stress and anxiety as well as improve circulatory function, sleeping rhythms, and mood. These benefits appear to be clear indicators that the human body is designed to be in direct contact with the earth.

Just as the earth grounds us, the mountains ground or stabilize the earth. I love to look at the mountains as they remind me of the strength of faith in a storm or conviction in the face of strong winds. There are mountains that stand firm and volcanoes that tell another story. The blessing of rain, which is every farmer's delight. Of course, climate change has had many impacts such that there are places dealing with drought and praying for rain and others with floods.

> *Set forth to them the similitude of the life of this world: It is like the rain which we send down from the skies: the earth's vegetation absorbs it, but soon it becomes dry stubble, which the winds do scatter: it is (only) Allah who prevails over all things.*
>
> —Quran 18:45

We are healed, comforted, and amazed by nature and all the benefits it provides. However, we are reminded that nature, like everything else, is a means that God can use to benefit us or turn us to Him in hope and fear. There are also the galaxies.

> *And thus, did We show Abraham the realm of the heavens and the earth that he would be among the certain [in faith]. When the night covered him over, He saw a star: He said: "This is my Lord." But when it set, He said: "I love not those that set." When he saw the moon rising in splendour, he said: "This is my Lord." But when the moon set, He said: "unless my Lord guide me, I shall surely be among those who go astray." When he saw the sun rising in splendour, he said: "This is my Lord; this is the greatest (of all)." But when the sun set, he said: "O my people! I am indeed free from your (guilt) of giving partners to Allah. "For me, I have set my face, firmly and*

> truly, towards Him Who created the heavens and the earth, and never shall I give partners to Allah."
>
> —Quran 6:75–79

There are chapters in the Quran titled "The Stars," "The Moon," and "The Sun." I will share some verses from each chapter. The following verses are from "*An-Najm,*" or "The Stars":

> *By the Star when it goes down, Your Companion is neither astray nor being misled. Nor does he say (aught) of (his own) Desire. It is no less than inspiration sent down to him: He was taught by one Mighty in Power, Endued with Wisdom: for he appeared (in stately form); While he was in the highest part of the horizon: Then he approached and came closer, And was at a distance of but two bow-lengths or (even) nearer; So did (Allah) convey the inspiration to His Servant (conveyed) what He (meant) to convey. The (Prophet's) (mind and) heart in no way falsified that which he saw. Will ye then dispute with him concerning what he saw?*
>
> —Quran 53:1–12

Chapter 54 of the Holy Quran is titled "*Al-Qamar,*" or "The Moon." Surprisingly, the chapter speaks less to the beauty of the moon and more to reminders of how humanity rejected the Messengers, calls to faith, and beneficial admonitions of the Day of Judgment. Then it raises the question, after each reminder: "And We have indeed made the Quran easy to understand and remember: then is there any that will receive admonition?"

In another chapter, the moon is described: "[A]nd [in] the moon, for which We have determined phases [which it must traverse] till it becomes like an old date-stalk, dried-up and curved" (Quran 36:39).

What do the moon and its cycle and phases mean to you? The moon's cycle and phases may represent the impermanence of life and the constant change we all experience. It reminds us to embrace the present moment and appreciate the beauty in each phase of our lives.

> *[And] neither may the sun overtake the moon, nor can the night usurp the time of day, since all of them float through space [in accordance with Our laws].*
>
> —Quran 36:40

This reminds me of the conversation between Prophet Abraham, upon him peace, and the tyrant of his time: "God causes the sun to rise in the east, so you cause it to come up from the west. Thus was the disbeliever absolutely defeated. And God guides not wrongdoing folk" (Quran 2:258).

There are many chapters in the Holy Quran such as "The Moon"; "The Stars"; "*Al-Fajr*," or "The Dawnbreak and the Night"; and many more. There is also a chapter titled "The Sun."

> *By the Sun and his (glorious) splendour; By the Moon as she follows him; By the Day as it shows up (the Sun's) glory; By the Night as it conceals it; By the Firmament and its (wonderful) structure; By the Earth and its (wide) expanse: By the Soul, and the proportion and order given to it; And its enlightenment as to its wrong and its right; Truly he succeeds that purifies it, And he fails that corrupts it!*
>
> —Quran 91:1–10

The natural world is described in the Quran as a never-ending source of revealing proofs of Allah's greatness and power in its intricate forms and phenomena. The Quran advises people to look at nature as a reminder of Allah's incredible power, even when debating with powerful people. In fact, it motivates people to research and comprehend Allah's clear messages worldwide.

I watched a video of an atheist who struggled to search for God and was considering Islam. In the video, he shares his communication with God. He says he is giving God a chance while considering becoming Muslim. He wanted a special sign, of a magical sense, like a house falling down. There were many false assumptions in his communication with God. He assumed God was begging him to believe in him, possibly needing his worship and acknowledgment. He continued to plead with God that he was giving Him a chance. Nothing happens. "Absolutely nothing," he concludes. He picks up the Quran to read where he left off. The next verse speaks directly to him. It is the verse that begins this chapter (Quran 2:164). I discuss this video further in the section on the contemplation of God's creation. (Reuben)

Why Nature?

I heard it from one teacher who said the god you believe doesn't exist; we believe doesn't exist. People ascribe false attributes to God. How can you know Him, if you are looking for false attributes of Him? I do not have the recording to share, so I am going by my notes and will not mention the name in case I misquoted the person. Often, when people look to scripture or to understand faith and seek to know God, they have this idea of a god in their mind and engage that false idea.

Prophet Abraham, upon him peace, guided his community through reasoning exercises. He began that the star is god. However, he reasoned with them it is just a heavenly body, like other celestial bodies, and cannot be a god. There must be one that directs all these heavenly bodies. To communicate emotions, feelings, and inner thoughts and realities, people use poetry, music, and the arts. They are also used to nurture affection, love, human bonding, and intimacy.

But, our relationship with one another as humans is not what we are encouraged to cultivate while interacting with God. This error is not limited to atheists. This was evident in Paula White's preaching. I mentioned the dialogue with God in the atheist's video. This is how most people interact with their concept of God. A wizard with magical abilities, to whom they give a chance in the same way that one gives another human being a chance to build a relationship or emotional attachment.

Thus, we treat God as a human being and engage Him accordingly. We test Him as we test other human beings or test the boundaries as we do with parents, friends, and relatives. We begin answering our questions, failing to realize that in doing so, we are engaging in rationalization, not knowledge. The beautiful part of this raw and open storytelling of the atheist sharing his conversation with God, is that God does not answer this person confirming his idea of a god or his rationalizations but instead brings him to Himself, nurturing him to a higher understanding and asking him to look at the set of data with a new set of eyes.

After examining the same data with a fresh perspective, he came to a realization that had been previously obscured. Our relationship with God should be characterized by a feeling of "awe." This realization of reverence and wonder arises from recognizing

God's Greatness and Majesty. It inspires us to be humble and grateful for all we have received. When we approach God with awe, we acknowledge His Power and Sovereignty over everything and recognize our own poverty and weakness compared to Him. This reverence can help us receive guidance from God and trust in His commands. It can also motivate us to live our lives in a way that is pleasing to Him, striving to glorify Him in all that we do.

> *They have not appraised Allah with true appraisal. Indeed, Allah is Powerful and Exalted in Might. Allah chooses from the angels messengers and from the people. Indeed, Allah is Hearing and Seeing. He knows what is [presently] before them and what will be after them. And to Allah will be returned [all] matters. O you who have believed, bow and prostrate and worship your Lord and do good that you may succeed.*
>
> —Quran 22:74–77

And the best way to communicate such feelings and nurture such awe in one's heart and mind is reflecting on nature. It leaves you stunned, amazed, and bewildered. People interpret what they observe based on the light that dominates their hearts. Most often, their observations of others are mere projections or rationalizations. Hence, you can't answer your own questions; rather you must grow within to receive the answer.

God gives you and me a chance or an invitation to accept ourselves and receive guidance, not the other way around. Now look at the heavenly bodies and nature again.

Malik ul Mulk

A brief definition of *Malik ul Mulk* is "the Master of the Kingdom, The Owner of All Sovereignty, and the Lord of Absolute Ruling Power." We crave to know and understand. Allah opens doors for us to discover knowledge, reflect upon it, and realize that

> *Allah is the only Ruler of the entire Universe, visible and invisible, and of all creation, from before the beginning and after the end. There is none like Him because He is the creator of His kingdom, which He created from nothing. Only He knows the size of His kingdom, the number of its population, and the strength of its armies. Only His will, His rule, and His justice exist.*
>
> —Shaykh Tosun Bayrak al-Jerrahi al-Halveti, *The Name and the Named*

The Universe is a whole with harmonious parts, created for a purpose and realizing and fulfilling this purpose: worshiping God: "O you who have believed, bow and prostrate and worship your Lord and do good that you may succeed."

Allah says, "I was a hidden treasure, I wished to be known; therefore, I created creation." Thus, the purpose and function of the creation are to know, seek guidance, and worship the Creator. All the scientific discoveries and knowledge seeking have a purpose: to increase us in faith and certitude, not distract us into fruitless debates.

Despite the beauty of nature and the Universe, humanity is the supreme creation and the deputy of Allah. Some scholars comment that therefore, Allah bestows upon some of His servants, for an appointed time, kingdoms, land, property, and wealth and grants them power over them.

> *Say, "O Allah, Owner of Sovereignty, You give sovereignty to whom You will and You take sovereignty away from whom You will. You honor whom You will and You humble whom You will. In Your hand is [all] good. Indeed, You are over all things competent."*
>
> —Quran, 3:26

We observe how, when celestial bodies operate according to His laws, they operate harmoniously. Our egos pollute this harmony that we observe throughout the Universe. Whatever is given to humanity is a trust. If a society uses this according to laws conveyed via the angels and messengers, they are rewarded. Otherwise, they will be taken to account. Certain people are granted knowledge of how to govern, nurture society, and even purify our souls and humble our egos. Through angels and messengers, God forbids us to follow our egos, which can lead us to abuse this knowledge and power.

Historically and now, we have not followed God's laws but used war to solve our problems. Despite our social evolution, interfaith programs, numerous universities filled with studies, research, psychologists, strategists, social and political scientists, human relations professionals, humanities, and arts, our response to complex issues is merely reaching for war, xenophobia, apartheid, colonialism, and manmade laws that elevate one people and dehumanize others.

The harmony we observe, we must admit we cannot fulfill among ourselves. Which is to be expected and is a sign of our need of God to direct and guide our lives as He directs the Universe. Imagine if we had to rule the Universe and share power in doing so. If we had control over the sun, moon, and stars, would any of us be alive today?

We can clearly observe the tremendous Milky Way and universe and the multitude of creatures within soil, sea, land, and heavens. He is the Owner of this whole kingdom. Our discovery of this creation and these creatures is the answer to our questions, not a distraction from God. Signs of His Greatness, Power, Strength, and Ruling Power. It is God giving us a chance to think and reflect on our discoveries. They are signs directing us to the Creator and Master of what we are discovering.

We know everything on this earth will perish; scientific theories make such claims, and so does the Quran: "Everyone upon the earth will perish, And there will remain the Face of your Lord, Owner of Majesty and Honor" (55:26–27).

Some commentators said the earth will be destroyed; others mentioned that those who do not obey God's laws will perish. We are witnessing how our actions on earth are affecting the environment and climate. This is also a motivation.

The Beautiful Name of God *Al-Malik Al-Mulk*—Allah is the Majestic One in His Kingdom as He wishes. He has no need of this kingdom or universe. The kingdom and universe need Him to operate harmoniously as we observe and struggle to do as humankind on earth. His wisdom has no limit, nor is there any subsequent order or harmony after His. So have humility as you observe the signs and ask God to increase you in certitude and faith.

If you are still struggling after all these signs around you, ask God to polish the mirror of your heart and to help you see the signs with His Light and Wisdom, not your own.

Once we understand our true relationship with God, as with all relationships, we cannot take that relationship for granted. Our relationship with God is one of Creator, or *Malik ul-Mulk*, and His creation. Hence, our prayer is an act of surrender and acceptance that we believe in God, and this helps nurture the true relationship between ourselves and God as one between the *Malik ul Mulk* and His creation and not two human beings. It is not just a declaration onstage like cheerleading.

We go out of our way to guard and protect our VIP relationships; in that spirit, our relationship with God must be protected and nurtured to a much higher degree. A relationship that is taken for granted eventually dies. We must guard this relationship according to appointed times, just like the way the sun and moon swim in their orbits according to law, not our desire.

This relationship should also help us "do good" as the bees give back honey for humanity's benefit; we must further confirm that relationship with our property by giving charity for the benefit of others. *Sadaqah*, or voluntary charity, is a means to confirm this relationship, a financial act of surrender, and a responsibility to govern justly and ethically on earth.

> *HAST THOU ever considered [the kind of man] who gives the lie to all Divine Moral Law?*
>
> *Behold, it is this [kind of man] that thrusts the orphan away, and feels no urge to feed the needy.*
>
> *Woe, then, unto those praying ones whose hearts from their prayer are neglectful those who want only to be seen and praised, and, withal, deny all assistance [to their fellow men]!*
>
> —Quran, 107:1-7

The best way to show reverence is to revere and respect the message He sent you, reflect on it, seek guidance and understanding, and then struggle to put it into practice.

Relationships and human bonding require healthy engagement with ourselves, with God, and with our fellow human beings. It is important to understand psychological manipulation, which helps us understand the importance of having pure hearts in communication and engagement with others. I appreciated Prophet Muhammad, upon him peace and blessings, and his purity of heart and wondered if the message was sent to someone without a sound heart or mind, what would happen to it?

It would have been destroyed, corrupted, and polluted. What does this have to do with nature? Nature teaches us that every darkness eventually melts into a slow-emerging beautiful sunrise. It is good to watch it daily as it nurtures hope.

Yet every solar zenith eventually sets. This humbles our expectations of life and our fellow human beings. We accept that this is a place of trials and tribulations, not utopia, as we watch the sunset.

The sunset teaches patience as we watch the emerging darkness. It is recommended to increase one's prayer during the darkest parts of the night, which also reminds us of how to face trials and tribulations.

The stars remind us to look to the great who passed such trials and tribulations; as humans, we all struggle to put our faith and values into practice. And their teachings and practice help us walk through such difficult times. Their light and spirit shine through the darkest hours.

> *Behold! in the creation of the heavens and the earth; in the alternation of the night and the day; in the sailing of the ships through the ocean for the profit of mankind; in the rain which Allah sends down from the skies, and the life which He gives therewith to an earth that is dead; in the beasts of all kinds that He scatters through the earth; in the change of the winds, and the clouds which they Trail like their slaves between the sky and the earth; (Here) indeed are Signs for a people that are wise.*
>
> —Quran 2:164

I began this theme with the verse above and tried to call us to reflect on the many signs that direct us to God. Ibn 'Ata Allah Iskandari said, "When was He ever absent so that He would be found? And when was He ever distant so that Signs are needed to lead to Him?"

There is nothing wrong with admitting our humanity and recognizing that the issue or our need for signs reflects our disconnection with ourselves, or we could be in an environment that is divorced from God, distracts us from God, distorts the message of God or misapplies it, et cetera.

In such a case, God opens doors for us to separate from such environments and to help us break free from the psychological manipulations that affect our hearts, minds, and understanding of God. We see this in the stories of Noah, Moses, Abraham, and even Prophet Muhammad, upon them peace and blessings.

In current-day reality, we saw this in the lives of Nelson Mandela and even Malcolm X, who wanted to break free from psychological manipulation. It is protection from becoming psychological slaves to abusers.

Ships are an indication of such a reality of our lives, as well as the wonders of the sea. When we look at the great ships we have built over the years, we see all the necessary environmental factors that made it possible for us to sail through the seas discovering other lands, resources, or a new life.

However, the ships, like our hearts, were also used to bring slaves and invaders to our lands. And we come to realize these are all means that God can use to benefit us, refine us, or punish us.

Ships are not always used for noble means. Every ship we are invited to is not the ship that Noah built. Some people were forced on ships as slaves and abused. When we obsess over storms or assume to know God's intention behind His plans, we lose sight of this reality.

Nature teaches us how a seed takes time to sprout and how things can be growing internally without any visible signs externally. This is important to reflect on as the message is meant to be internalized and realized, not an overpowering argument, show and tell, or psychological manipulations.

> *Allah has revealed (from time to time) the most beautiful Message in the form of a Book, consistent with itself, (yet) repeating (its teaching in various aspects): the skins of those who fear their Lord tremble thereat; then their skins and their hearts do soften to the celebration of Allah's praises. Such is the guidance of Allah: He guides therewith whom He pleases, but such as Allah leaves to stray, can have none to guide.*
>
> —Quran 39:23

We come to acknowledge God as *Malik ul-Mulk*, and our acceptance of ourselves and worship of Him nurture us to witness a Subhan Allah or Glory be to God moment.

Unbelievable beauty with colors blending in the water in a reflective way. It was quite depressing listening to all the news on what is happening all around the world. It can make one blind to the beauty that is around us. If one looks, one sees the beautiful order. As God says in the Quran, the night does not outstrip the day or the day outstrip the night. The sun and moon each swim in their own orbit.

Lessons from Contemplation by Malik Badri

> *Men of knowledge have been resorting to thought with the remembrance of God (dhikr), and to remembrance of God with thought, imploring the hearts to speak, until the hearts responded with wisdom.*
>
> —Hasan Al-Basri

I will share some insights from the book, Contemplation: An Islamic Psycho-spiritual Study by Malik Badri (Badri). I learned of the author early on via Islamonline, which is no longer available. I purchased his book and found his writings beneficial. I have an old edition, published in 2000. I checked, and there is a new edition that is longer and published in 2018. I intend to purchase it and would encourage you as well.

Scientists tell us that we barely discovered 4% of the surface in outer space. The rest are largely unknown. Of the oceans: "It might be shocking to find out, but only 5% of the ocean has been explored and charted by humans. The rest, especially its depths, are still unknown." (Fava)

> *Say: "I do admonish you on one point: that ye do stand up before Allah,- (It may be) in pairs, or (it may be) singly,- and reflect (within yourselves): your Companion is not possessed: he is no less than a warner to you, in face of a terrible Penalty."*
>
> —Quran 34:46

Just like we barely studied the visible heavens and ocean and got carried with that bit of knowledge based on observable animal behavior, we got carried away with theories about the internal reality of humans - which is vast - as the oceans and outer space. Possibly, more so.

The author of Contemplation, Malik Badri - discourages Muslims from following behaviorism, as this field of psychology treats human beings like machines, instruments, or animals and instead promotes the field of psychology: Cognitive Psychology.

I have been pushing this field instead of behaviorism, so I was delighted to run across Badri's works. I fully support his work and recommendations. Behaviorism aims at controlling and brainwashing people. They present human beings as devoid of human consciousness, mental or spiritual essence.

The author argues that the Muslim world needs to focus on developing its own ideas and values based on the Quran rather than blindly accepting those of the West, emphasizing the importance of the soul and critical thinking in shaping a society that is not easily swayed by external influences.

> *(Allah) Most Gracious! It is He Who has taught the Qur'an. He has created man: He has taught him speech (and intelligence). The sun and the moon follow courses (exactly) computed;*
>
> —Quran 55:1-5

On the PHILO-notes channel, one of their YouTube videos, Behaviorism vs. Cognitivism, discusses the significant difference between behaviorism and cognitive psychology as some of the essential psychological foundations of education. (Behaviorism vs Cognitivism)

We learned about behaviorism by studying animals. Cognition is through the brain. All cognitive has to be done on human beings. Behaviors are the end result. What happens before that behaviorists are not concerned. In cognitive psychology, how you get to the correct answer is important. The process and the product are critical. *How did you get to the product? Explain the process.* Activation of prior knowledge in behaviorism is irrelevant. However, it is essential under cognitive psychology because thinking does not happen from scratch. Behaviorists provide stimuli to get the proper behavior. In cognitive psychology, you must prepare the environment, you must have the material, and you must have the activities to be able to think and reason.

And that is what earth is, the environment to facilitate our learning about ourselves, each other, and God.

Some of the difficulties of speaking about Islamic beliefs come from the difficulty in translating some words into other languages. In this case, the phrase *tafakkur* or *tadabbur* has been translated superficially as meditate or contemplate.

Malik Badri explains in his book Contemplation that while *taffakkur* or *tadabbur* carry meanings of reflecting, meditating, or thinking - the aim is spiritual. *Tafakkur* is a form of worship and praising God, recognizing the universe He created, and we inherited it as a gift from Him. In other religions or new age thinking, contemplation, or *tafakkur* is about reaching inner peace, nirvana, a higher state of consciousness, Zen, sober, et cetera. It is divorced from worshiping God or Praising God.

Badri explains further, "the meditative procedures of Eastern religions tend to sacrifice conscious sober thinking in order to obtain altered states of consciousness, whereas *tafakkur* as an Islamic form of worship is a cognitive spiritual activity in which the rational mind, emotion and spirit must be combined." Hence, he used contemplation expanding his translation to an Islamic psycho-spiritual study. I agree with Badri but used the terminology, reflections of faith.

The aim of reflection is to worship God. The earth and heaven were created and prepared for us, an environment of learning as the chosen vicegerents to enable our understanding of ourselves, His creation, and the universe toward worshiping our Creator.

In fact, the animal kingdom was subjugated to us and is surprised when we turn away or our distracted from worshiping God.

For example, the Hoopoe bird was shocked that the Queen of Saba was worshiping the Sun instead of the Creator of the Sun.

> *But the Hoopoe tarried not far: he (came up and) said: "I have compassed (territory) which thou hast not compassed, and I have come to thee from Saba with tidings true.*
>
> *"I found (there) a woman ruling over them and provided with every requisite; and she has a magnificent throne.*
>
> *"I found her and her people worshipping the sun besides Allah: Satan has made their deeds seem pleasing in their eyes, and has kept them away from the Path,- so they receive no guidance,*
>
> *"(Kept them away from the Path), that they should not worship Allah, Who brings to light what is hidden in the heavens and the earth, and knows what ye hide and what ye reveal.*
>
> *"Allah! there is no god but He!- Lord of the Throne Supreme!"*

—Quran 27:22-26

Lessons from Science and Faith by Mustafa Mahmoud

In a scholarly commentary video, Dr. Mahmoud discusses various scientific discoveries demonstrating evidence of human-bird communication. The Quran reveals what people are discovering now. Creatures and animals communicate uniquely; some humans have been gifted to understand animal communication. Although the video is in Arabic, I encourage you to watch the video with someone who understands Arabic and can translate the content for you. There is intelligent communication taking place between animals and human beings. (D. M. Mahmoud)

When we understand behaviorism, conditioning, stimulus, and response, of which brainwashing is a branch, we can appreciate Ramadan as a gift from God. Often, people emphasize that Ramadan, the month of fasting, is about feeling for the poor. However, the poor are also required to fast. The Quran clearly mentions that Ramadan is about learning restraint.

Why?

To protect us from being manipulated, conditioned, brainwashed, and turning away from God in a stimulus and response manner. It is a protective gift from Our Lord, Creator, *Al-Waali*, or the Protecting Friend. *The only self-work we are asked to do is discipline and restrain the self.* Remembrance of God will repel Satan. However, the self requires training in restraint and discipline, so it does not respond to whatever stimulus in a mindless and brainless manner.

Remembrance of God is the backbone for positive change. I have not read Al-Hikmah fi Makhluqat Allah (The Wisdom Behind God's Creation) by al-Ghazali. However, Badri references the book and quotes al-Ghazali on remembrance of God, and contemplation is critical to every good deed: "The way to a cognizance of God is to glorify Him in His creation, to contemplate His wonderful works, to understand the wisdom in His various inventions...It is a means to strengthen certainty and happiness...The Almighty created the minds and perfected them with revelation, ordering men with such minds to think of His creatures, to *contemplate and learn a lesson from what wonders He has entrusted in His creation.*"

Contemplation activates all the cognitive activities a human being employs so that the response is based on knowledge, cognition, faith, restraint, and not a stimulus.

The Stages

Dr. Badri mentions several stages that a believer is invited to when contemplating the creation of God.

1. Perception: see, hear, feel, smell, taste, even indirectly, such as imagination
2. Wonder: beauty, excellence, precision, harmony, vastness, flawlessness, miraculous appearance
3. *Subhan Allah*: connection, realization, amazement, appreciation
4. *Shuhud* or Witnessing: spiritual cognition. "Our Lord, You did not create this in vain; praise be to You; then protect us from the punishment of the Fire" (Quran 3:191).

Believers and unbelievers recognize the first two stages alike. It is primitive contemplation or usage of our senses and faculties that do not go beyond the stimulus and response stage. The following two stages invite believers to connect their reflection with cognition into an act of worship.

Throughout the Quran, you will notice God engaging us in the process, or the stages, connecting our perception, emotion, and cognition to our spiritual heart, et cetera. A case in point are the images from the James Webb Telescope revealed by NASA in 2022. Go to the NASA website and search for images of the Universe. This is just the nearest observable heaven.

The images captured by the James Webb Telescope provide us with a glimpse of the vastness and complexity of the universe, reminding us of our small place in it and our connection to something greater. They inspire awe and wonder, encouraging us to contemplate the mysteries of creation and our spiritual journey.

> *[And] who created seven heavens in layers. You do not see in the creation of the Most Merciful any inconsistency. So return [your] vision [to the sky]; do you see any breaks? Then return [your] vision twice again. [Your] vision will return to you humbled while it is dazzled. And We have certainly beautified the nearest heaven with stars...*
>
> —Quran 67:3-4

Emotional, rational, or holistic?

"I would like to weave one of the lessons by Dr. Mahmoud on sound and the lessons in chapter three of the book, Contemplation by Malik Badri. (D. M. Mahmoud)

In the video series on science and religion, Dr. Mahmoud discusses the scientific analysis and discoveries of sounds based on science. There are sounds that we cannot hear. However, they have a significant effect on us. Sounds that can destroy kidney stones, and sounds, and some that can cause major destruction. He cites verses from the Quran on sounds that reconcile with scientific discoveries.

Dr. Mahmoud specifically discusses Jinn or Iblis communication, which we may not hear but which penetrates our minds and influences us. The medicine is twofold:

1. The gift of Remembrance of God to His creation and the benefit it provides us in our stay on earth.
2. [Allah] said, "O Yahya [John the Baptist], take the Scripture with determination." And We gave him judgment [while yet] a boy (Quran 19:12).

In chapter three, Badri references a few Muslim and non-Muslim scholars who promote meditation's healing effects. He cites Herbert Benson, who also recommends switching affirmations with words of one's faith. For Muslims, Benson recommends:

1. The word for God, Allah.
2. Prophet's words: "The Lord is wondrous kind...."
3. Bilal's words when he was tortured: *Ahadun, ahadun...* [One God, one God]

However, while Benson recognizes the healing impact of meditation and the use of such words to help Muslims, he and others view healing as purely an emotional experience. In fact, Westerners who want to have a mystical experience are advised to avoid reasoned-based forms of worship. Benson comments on Karen Armstrong's book, A History of God, that the mystical experience is not rational but emotional and intuitive. Armstrong calls it "silent contemplation." Armstrong writes: *The mystical experience...is a subjective experience that involves an interior journey, not a perception of an objective fact outside the self; it is undertaken through the image making part of the mind-often* called imagination – rather than through the more cerebral, logical faculty. Finally, it is something that the mystic creates in himself or herself deliberately.

To help us understand the difference between non-Islamic meditation and the importance of Islamic meditation, let us reflect on the remembrance of God or dhikr.

In *"10 strategies of manipulation"* by the media, Noam Chomsky said:

6. Use the emotional side more than the reflection

Making use of the emotional aspect is a classic technique for causing a short circuit on rational analysis, and finally to the critical sense of the individual. Furthermore, the use of emotional register to open the door to the unconscious for implantation or grafting ideas, desires, fears and anxieties, compulsions, or induce behaviors ...

When we turn contemplation or meditation to strictly an emotional or mystical feeling, purely imagination, to reach inner peace and calm, we nurture ourselves and others to be targeted for implantation or *grafting ideas, desires, fears, anxieties, compulsions, or induce behaviors.*

If we weave the video on sounds, there are voices or sounds we do not hear, yet according to Islamic teachings, we are told they exist and aim to implant ideas against our teachings in our minds. Hence, remembrance of God is holistic, as it is not purely emotional, mystical, or imagination, but rational, intellectual, and encompassing cognition and reason, where the words do not just heal and calm but protect us from such implantation from sounds and voices that we do not hear. It also helps us to be aware when such ideas are promoted to manipulate us. Badri cites a few scholars on remembrance of God and the verse:

> *Exalted is He and high above what they say by great sublimity. The seven heavens and the earth and whatever is in them exalt Him. And there is not a thing except that it exalts [Allah] by His praise, but you do not understand their [way of] exalting. Indeed, He is ever Forbearing and Forgiving. And when you recite the Qur'an, We put between you and those who do not believe in the Hereafter a concealed partition.*

—Quran 17:43-45

Qur'an and the Contemplation of God's Creation

The fourth chapter of the book, Contemplation, discusses the various methods the Qur'an uses to nurture the human mind to contemplate and see signs of God in His Universe. I will emphasize some.

Attributes of God

The Qur'an has many verses that call the reader to reflect, bringing to the heart the Oneness of God, the Greatness of God, the Creator, the Originator of the Heavens and earth, the Strong, the Mighty, the Evolver and Bestower of forms, et cetera.

> *That is Allah, your Lord; there is no deity except Him, the Creator of all things, so worship Him. And He is Disposer of all things. Vision perceives Him not, but He perceives [all] vision; and He is the Subtle, the Acquainted. There has come to you enlightenment from your Lord. So whoever will see does so for [the benefit of] his soul, and whoever is blind [does harm] against it. And [say], "I am not a guardian over you."*

—Quran 6:102-104

Favors of God

Cattle, bees, and various creatures that we derive benefits from. Also, the multiple products include corn, olives, figs, date palms, grapes, and every kind of fruit and herb. Imagine if the sun decides to rise from the West one day. The heavenly orbits are in subjection by His command.

> *It is He who sends down rain from the sky; from it is drink and from it is foliage in which you pasture [animals]. He causes to grow for you thereby the crops, olives, palm trees, grapevines, and from all the fruits. Indeed in that is a sign for a people who give thought. And He has subjected for you the night and day and the sun and moon, and the stars are subjected by His command. Indeed in that are signs for a people who reason. And [He has subjected] whatever He multiplied for you on the earth of varying colors. Indeed in that is a sign for a people who remember. And it is He who subjected the sea for you to eat from it tender meat and to extract from it ornaments which you wear. And you see the ships plowing through it, and [He subjected it] that you may seek of His bounty; and perhaps you will be grateful. And landmarks. And by the stars they are [also] guided. Then is He who*

> *creates like one who does not create? So will you not be reminded? And if you should count the favors of Allah, you could not enumerate them. Indeed, Allah is Forgiving and Merciful. And Allah knows what you conceal and what you declare. And those they invoke other than Allah create nothing, and they [themselves] are created.*

—Quran, 16:10-20

Reprimands for unrelenting hearts

Tyrants, when they rule a land, if they cannot subjugate people to their will, will use the most vicious and malicious means of control and torture. We read of such stories in the past, such as the Pharaoh, Nimrod, et cetera. These are not just stories in books or scripture; we see them in the current day – when wars – have destroyed millions and people openly brag about flattening Gaza, the second Nakba is coming, et cetera.

This reminder was to wake them up so they might see their vulnerability and the vulnerability of others, not to oppress them. Tyrants have a hatred of weakness, be it in themselves or others.

> *They said, "O Shu'ayb, we do not understand much of what you say, and indeed, we consider you among us as weak. And if not for your family, we would have stoned you [to death]; and you are not to us one respected." He said, "O my people, is my family more respected for power by you than Allah? But you put Him behind your backs [in neglect]. Indeed, my Lord is encompassing of what you do. And O my people, work according to your position; indeed, I am working. You are going to know to whom will come a punishment that will disgrace him and who is a liar. So watch; indeed, I am with you a watcher, [awaiting the outcome]."*

—Quran 91-93

These questions and reprimands engage the reader through soul-provoking questions, instigating contemplation on the evidence that is in plain sight for all to witness:

Examples of such verses are:

> *Then, do they not look at what is before them and what is behind them of the heaven and earth? If We should will, We could cause the earth to swallow them or [could] let fall upon them fragments from the sky. Indeed in that is a sign for every servant turning back [to Allah].*

—Quran, 34:9

Then do they not look at the camels - how they are created? And at the sky - how it is raised? And at the mountains - how they are erected? And at the earth - how it is spread out? So remind, [O Muhammad]; you are only a reminder. You are not over them a controller. However, he who turns away and disbelieves - Then Allah will punish him with the greatest punishment. Indeed, to Us is their return. Then indeed, upon Us is their account.

—Quran, 88:17-26

[Pharaoh] said, "So who is the Lord of you two, O Moses?" He said, "Our Lord is He who gave each thing its form and then guided [it]." [Pharaoh] said, "Then what is the case of the former generations?" [Moses] said, "The knowledge thereof is with my Lord in a record. My Lord neither errs nor forgets." [It is He] who has made for you the earth as a bed [spread out] and inserted therein for you roadways and sent down from the sky, rain and produced thereby categories of various plants. Eat [therefrom] and pasture your livestock. Indeed, in that are signs for those of intelligence. From the earth We created you, and into it We will return you, and from it We will extract you another time. And We certainly showed Pharaoh Our signs - all of them - but he denied and refused. He said, "Have you come to us to drive us out of our land with your magic, O Moses?

—Quran, 20:49-57

The Pious

How do the pious see these same realities? Sometimes, we think we can argue or engage His creation better than Him. Instead of using His arguments that He teaches us in the Quran, we come up with egotistical views that cause more problems than solve them. The Quran is full of verses instigating the creation to reflect on their world, the beauties, benefits, and in-depth intelligence behind such realities and objects.

In the earlier-mentioned Reuben video, the seeker attempts to converse with God alone. Recall how the individual interacts with God and the signs God gives him in return. If one listens intently to the Quran and takes these divine dialogues to heart, their long-term response to the world around us is:

> *To Allah belongeth the dominion of the heavens and the earth; and Allah hath power over all things. Behold! in the creation of the heavens and the earth, and the alternation of night and day,- there are indeed Signs for men of understanding,- Men who celebrate the praises of Allah, standing, sitting, and lying down on their sides, and contemplate the (wonders of) creation in the heavens and the earth, (With the thought): "Our Lord! not for naught Hast Thou created (all) this! Glory to Thee! Give us salvation from the penalty of the Fire.*
>
> —Quran, 3:189-191

> *Behold! in the creation of the heavens and the earth; in the alternation of the night and the day; in the sailing of the ships through the ocean for the profit of mankind; in the rain which Allah Sends down from the skies, and the life which He gives therewith to an earth that is dead; in the beasts of all kinds that He scatters through the earth; in the change of the winds, and the clouds which they Trail like their slaves between the sky and the earth;- (Here) indeed are Signs for a people that are wise.*
>
> —Quran, 2:164

More Signs or Hearts that See?

Your conscience is a secret witness to prior knowledge. It knows of the meeting with God in the pre-eternal realm, and it recognizes the signs of God when presented by a Messenger, Prophet, or a pious person. When we do not accept the signs of God that are as clear as day, we will readily accept conjecture, disinformation, misinformation, and magic as truth.

Those who reject the signs will argue in this world; it is the lack of evidence or no evidence why they do not believe in God. Yet, if one studies their lives, they readily accept everything that inclines or resonates with their ego based on conjecture, disinformation, misinformation, and magic. In the case of Pharaoh, he was willing to accept magic. However, he was not open to the signs by Moses, upon him peace.

A case in point: walking across hot coals is a ritual for the thousands of followers of famed motivational guru Tony Robbins. Something went wrong at a fire walk in Dallas Thursday night as thirty people were treated for burns, and five had to be hospitalized. Inside Edition spoke to Melissa Seureau, who posted a photo of her burned and blistered foot on Twitter. Melissa also took a photo of the makeshift emergency room set up to treat the firewalk victims. She calls herself out for drinking the kool-aid. (Tony Robbins' Hot Coal Ritual Goes Horribly Wrong)

We sometimes look for magic, supernatural solutions, kool-aid, or inspiration that enable our desire to escape reality. We might call it meditation, inspiration, and motivation, but as the Inside Edition video shows, it is based on mind games, not nurturing the body, mind, and soul in harmony to see reality as it is. We call it overcoming our fear. However, God gives us many opportunities to face reality and overcome our fears by turning to Him, but we prefer the escape route, the magic.

If we want to overcome our fear, we can speak up against Apartheid in Israel or human rights abuses where we have power and influence, but when we reject to do so, we become inclined to such games and delusions. The image of ourselves overcoming our fears than the reality of facing and overcoming our fears. They took selfies as well.

During the first coming of Jesus, upon him peace, his people struggled to believe sign upon sign, miracle upon miracle, which they witnessed, despite the numerous sent. When God tested their hearts, they readily believed conjecture about Jesus, upon him peace, which they did not witness.

The children of Israel saw sign upon sign, yet questioned Moses, upon him peace. However, they readily believed as-Samiri in worshiping the golden calf.

Some might argue that we are not convinced these stories exist or are true. Well, look at the present day. Two cases to reflect on. Case one: Richard Dawkins and 'clock boy. I will address this later in this section. Case two: Christopher Hitchens did not believe in God, but he believed the Iraq War propaganda and ferociously defended it. This is why the Quran describes people with lip-service faith as "avid listeners to falsehood...They distort words beyond their [proper] usages."

If people say there is no evidence that God exists, look at how they live their lives, and listen to how much disinformation, conjecture, misinformation, and magic they readily believe about whatever they wish to acknowledge is true. When we look at the whole picture, is their statement accurate? Throughout my life, I reflected much on such voices and listened to them, not just on matters of religion but the discussions outside of religion. I realized we do not need more signs or signs but rather hearts that can witness the signs all around us. Prophet Muhammad, upon him peace and blessings, taught us to supplicate God: "Oh Allah (God), show us the truth as truth and enable us to observe it and show us falsehood as falsehood and enable us to avoid it."

In one of his lessons on science and religion, Dr. Mahmoud shared:

1. We do not use our minds to measure God; instead, God sends us signs that our minds can measure.
2. We know God with our conscience, the secret witness to the embedded knowledge in our hearts.

God knows how we will respond if we receive signs that are supernatural or signs that overpower our minds such that we cannot encompass or comprehend them. We would say we were bewitched to choose God.

> *Even if We opened out to them a gate from heaven, and they were to continue (all day) ascending therein, They would only say: "Our eyes have been intoxicated: Nay, we have been bewitched by sorcery."*
>
> —Quran 15:14-15

> *(Pharaoh) said: "If indeed thou hast come with a Sign, show it forth,- if thou tellest the truth." Then (Moses) threw his rod, and behold! it was a serpent, plain (for all to see)! And he drew out his hand, and behold! it was white to all beholders! Said the Chiefs of the people of Pharaoh: "This is indeed a sorcerer well-versed.*
>
> —Quran, 7-106-109

When the Pharaoh was shown the sign of a rod turning into a snake, he responded, "this is magic." This comes from someone using magic to prey on the ignorance of his people and overpower them. How many scientists and fields of science did humans need to take images with the James Webb Telescope? Hence, Richard Dawkins came to an 'Aha' moment. (Harris)

Dawkins just did not recognize it. He was furious at a child for saying he built a clock when he only disassembled and reassembled the clock. That is Dawkins' soul or the secret witness speaking, telling him you only disassembled and reassembled things or took an image; however, you are not the Designer (*Al Musawwir*) or the Creator (*Al Khaliq*).

We should ask God for hearts that see the signs around us and use our minds to witness His Greatness, the Creator Supreme, to develop a deeper understanding and appreciation for His infinite wisdom and power. This requires us to be mindful of our actions and intentions and constantly seek God's guidance and forgiveness. Only then can we truly experience the peace and contentment that comes with a heart at ease with its Creator.

> *"Is not He Who created the heavens and the earth able to create the like thereof?" - Yea, indeed! for He is the Creator Supreme, of skill and knowledge (infinite)!*

—Quran, 36:81

The Human Being

The brain looks like a small blob, about three pounds, and yet scientists admit how complex it is to study the human brain. Dr. Rachel Tompa stated that many fields of science are complicated, and anything under active scientific investigation needs to be fully understood. But the brain seems different. Extra complex. Extra mysterious. (Tompa)

Dr. Herbert Benson said: [the brain] is so complex, so constantly in motion, so mega-faceted and super-connected that all our attempts to describe its actions are, by Nature, simplistic. Every remarkable discovery we make only further elucidates how astonishingly elaborate is the brain and its circuitry that which affords us life and health, movement and memory, intuition, and wisdom. That which appears to be crude clump of jelly assemblies and then retains notes on every movement, every breath, every incident that has ever occurred to you or ever will, as well as every thought or dream you have ever or ever will have.

The brain is a gift from God. I shared many verses from the Quran that explore some of our creation's miracles. He says the divine call, which questions how people can be blind to the miraculous creation of their own selves.

> *On the earth are signs for those of assured Faith, as also in your own selves: Will ye not then, see?*

—Quran, 51: 20-21

Two theories: Backwards or Hoax

Faith is not a straight horizontal line or a straight upward line. The Quran is clear that there are days that will be for us and others where we will be in trial, including the Prophets' lives and stories. Hence why trade is allowed and usury or interest is not. This is by Divine Will to test everyone's faith:

> *If a wound has touched you, be sure a similar wound has touched others. Such days (of varying fortunes) We give to men and men by turns: that Allah may know those that believe, and that He may take to Himself from your ranks Martyr-witnesses (to Truth). And Allah loveth not those that do wrong.*
>
> —Quran, 3:140

A world where the oppressors or those with power are always in control, and those who are weak are always weak and oppressed. This brought about two theories:

1. The oppressed are backward. Blame the oppressed.
2. If the oppressed build or innovate anything, it is a hoax.

I reflected on these theories, and here is how I understand them. I agree with evangelicals that God allowed former President Trump into power, but He also allowed others, even Salman Rushdie. This power or opportunity does not mean theists or Islam is backward; instead, that—those who make such claims are insecure and lack conviction in their beliefs, such that were theists to build such great things or present their ideas, they would say, this is magic, or as Dawkins said, this is a hoax.

God gives turns to each people. Hence, God allows them to discover the truth through their power and hands and asks others to contribute to the conversation and help them reflect on what they built. Where some theists go wrong is they have hidden envy or awe of those in power instead of awe of God in their hearts, as they claim. Like Dawkins and Rushdie, they believe they are failures if they are not on top, winning, or the superpowers of the day. In fact, when winning, they make the same comments that Dawkins and Rushdie, which might also be a test for some theists to reflect on their inner reality.

> *For, Believers are those who, when Allah is mentioned, feel a tremor in their hearts, and when they hear His signs*

> *rehearsed, find their faith strengthened, and put (all) their trust in their Lord;*

> —Quran, 8:2

We can look to Dr. Malik Badri and Dr. Mostafa Mahmoud, both scientists in their own right, for guidance on how to approach other people's scientific discoveries with respect and humility in light of Islamic teachings.

> *But Allah has created you and your handwork!*

> —Quran, 37:96

> *...Nor shall they attain any of His knowledge except that which He wills...*

> —Quran, 2:255

> *It was We Who taught him the making of coats of mail for your benefit, to guard you from each other's violence: will ye then be grateful? (It was Our power that made) the violent (unruly) wind flow (tamely) for Solomon, to his order, to the land which We had blessed: for We do know all things.*

> —Quran, 21:80-81

> *It is We Who have created you: why will ye not witness the Truth? Do ye then see? - The (human Seed) that ye throw out, -Is it ye who create it, or are We the Creators?*

> —Quran, 56:57-59

At the end of chapter five, Badri mentions even during the time of Makkah, God drew the attention of the people of Makkah, Madinah, and the neighboring areas to the ships sailing smoothly across the oceans like moving mountains; it was a time when most of these ships were in the hands of people who had not yet embraced Islam. Nevertheless, it did not prevent the believers from contemplating a sign of God, the benefit and use He had chosen to put into the hands of unbelievers. Faith does not fear contemplating what God gives others power to build. We don't yell hoax when others build it or backward when we build them. We can appreciate and contemplate them in light of faith, witnessing God created us and all our handiwork. God calls us to see the signs all around us.

> *See ye the seed that ye sow in the ground? Is it ye that cause it to grow, or are We the Cause? Were it Our Will, We could crumble it to dry powder, and ye would be left in wonderment, (Saying), "We are indeed left with debts (for nothing): "Indeed are we shut out (of the fruits of our labour)"*
>
> *See ye the water which ye drink? Do ye bring it down (in rain) from the cloud or do We? Were it Our Will, We could make it salt (and unpalatable): then why do ye not give thanks?*
>
> *See ye the Fire which ye kindle? Is it ye who grow the tree which feeds the fire, or do We grow it? We have made it a memorial (of Our handiwork), and an article of comfort and convenience for the denizens of deserts. Then celebrate with praises the name of thy Lord, the Supreme!*

—Quran, 56:63-74

Contemplation of the Invisible and its Limits

There is a limitation on contemplating the Divine Being Himself since none but God knows Himself. We do not speak for God but convey what He shared about Himself. We do not interpret His inner reality, as only He knows this knowledge, even prophets do not know, as Jesus, upon him peace said: *I do not know what is within Yourself.* Ibn' Abbas said: "Some people tried to contemplate the Almighty, but the Prophet said to them: *Contemplate the creation of God and not God Himself*, for you can never give Him His due."

We cannot even guess the inner reality of others, as the brain remains a mystery to scientists. When we tried, we created more harm than good: We do not read minds and know that none of us can predict the future. In an article on Psychology Today, Dr. Alice LoCicero, and Dr. J. Wesley Boyd, wrote: We will not spy on our patients. We do not read minds, and we know that none of us can predict the future. (J. Wesley Boyd M.D.)

We can also reflect on His Divine Attributes and Names. The Attributes of God are the same Nature as His Being. Ibn Abbas said: "The Divine Being is shaded by His glorious Attributes and His Attributes are shaded by His deeds. So how do you feel about a Divine beauty shaded by Attributes of perfection, and adorned with epithets of grandeur and splendor."

Five Stages: Pre-eternal, womb, birth, sleep, and death

While we are limited in reflecting on the Divine, we can reflect on death, the *barzakh*, and the pre-eternal realm. We go through stages that are stored in our memory. We may not be able to access our memories in the pre-eternal realm where we bore witness that God is our Lord, then we entered the world of the womb similar to the world after death, the *barzakh* (the stage between death and resurrection). This time period represents the darkness before our birth or, in the case of the *barzakh*, our resurrection. Our sleep is a small reminder of our death. The Quran gives us sufficient information to help guide these reflections. Recent scientific discoveries by non-Muslims (so one can't accuse Muslims of confirmation bias) confirm the truth of the Quran on these matters.

Individual levels of contemplation

Contemplation should not replace obligatory prayer or any of the commands of God. It should not replace the pillars such as fasting, zakat (purification of wealth), planning the pilgrimage, and what God requires of one. Rather, contemplation supplements one's faith and increases it. It nurtures certainty and depth of faith. Contemplation is about worship, not egoism. It is not escapism. For example, taking care of your children or your parents are a form of *jihad* (struggling in the way of God) and supersedes contemplation. Jihad, or "striving against one's inclinations," also supersede contemplation. This inclination includes running away from the battlefield without just cause. This is important, so one does not pervert contemplation into what one feels, wants, or desires. The author mentions depth of faith, length of concentration, psychological state, environmental factors, the influence of culture, knowledge of the objects of contemplation, companionship, Nature of the objects of contemplation, and familiarity.

> *The day We shall gather the righteous to (Allah) Most Gracious, like a band presented before a King for honours, And We shall drive the sinners to Hell, like thirsty cattle driven down to water,*
>
> —Quran, 19:85-86

Depths of faith

Depths of faith come about by acting on the guidelines of one's faith. Sometimes people will assume someone who is an introvert has more depth of faith than someone who is an extrovert, or vice versa, depending on how both personalities are perceived in society. I am an introvert, and my daughter an extrovert. These are personality identifiers, not faith identifiers. Depth of faith is identified by how much one turns to God seeking guidance and follows the Sacred Laws sent to Prophet Muhammad, upon him peace and blessings.

Length of concentration

It is easy for an introvert to concentrate and listen to an eighteen-hour lecture on the scholarly commentary of the Quran. It is difficult for an extrovert to sit for more than ten to thirty minutes. They need stimulation and to be engaged. However, they can still concentrate on movies such as the Stellar Tours, Zoo animals, or nature sites. There are many opportunities and various means based on each person's personality to sit and watch the sunset or sunrise and praise God.

Psychological state

This one is quite complex. However, some people are persecuted and cave in themselves. Most do not recognize them; some might further attack or accuse them of a lack of faith, hatred, or falsehoods. While we cannot diagnose others, we can protect ourselves from harm based on what we see and hear, not speculation. Given their psychological state might not be healthy, reading daily morning and evening supplications might be beneficial. Given their state, they are heavily impacted by Jinns and less by their ego. I will not go further in-depth on this one, just to remind myself and others that God knows a person's internal reality. My knowledge is limited in this area.

The Covenant

And [mention] when your Lord took from the children of Adam—from their loins—their descendants and made them testify of themselves, [saying to them], "Am I not your Lord?" They said, "Yes, we have testified." [This]—lest you should say on the day of Resurrection, "Indeed, we were of this unaware." (Quran 7:172)

Islam is a way of life, and while you have heard me say not to focus on the dos and don'ts, this does not imply that we ignore the Sacred Law. There is a balance that we must embrace. The Sacred Law teaches us discipline and helps keep us on the Straight Path, but the law's spirit nurtures love, hope, and commitment.

The foundations or pillars of Islam should be done soundly. Therefore, reach out to teachers to understand the rules and guidelines of acts of worship that you are obligated to perform. If necessary, renew your understanding every few years to ensure proper performance. If you have children, they might have questions that need to be answered. You can schedule lessons with a teacher and answer their questions. Be sure to pay for the teacher's time. Do you know the rules and integrals of fasting, praying, and paying *zakat*? We mustn't treat the Sacred Law with irreverence.

In one of the lessons by Dr. Ramadan al-Bouti, he mentions that, as Muslims, all our actions are based on a covenant we made with God. He further explains that if we abide by this covenant or agreement, then we are rewarded in this worldly life and the next. However, if we disobey, we will be punished in this worldly life or the next. This agreement is for individuals who made the declaration of faith and took God as *Lord*, an authority, Majestic, one who is All-Knowing, and Judge, accepting His commands, et cetera.

However, if someone is not a Muslim and did not make such an agreement, it is important to note that God will not reward or punish them for obeying or not obeying these commands. They will be held accountable for the truth that reached them, that their soul recognized as true, in the hereafter. This is a matter between God and His creation, not for anyone of us to judge. There is a secret witness in each of us, our conscience, that will bear witness before God regarding such matters. As for us Muslims, we must be aware and show resolve to the agreement made.

In November 2019, I had a relative pass away, and as you go through the motions and review your notes, you understand the questions the angels raise when you are in your grave. These are questions that first determine if you took God as a Lord. You can now fully understand why Satan was accursed. Out of arrogance, not ignorance, he refused to take God as Lord. The angels took Him as Lord, and so did Adam, upon him peace. The questions we will be asked in our grave:

1. "Who is your Lord?"
2. "What is your religion?"
3. "Who is this man who was sent among you?"

Taqwa, or Obedience

Obedience, like physical exercise, requires effort and discipline to strengthen one's faith. We develop a deeper understanding and connection with our beliefs by overcoming challenges and difficulties. However, trust is demonstrated when one faces temptation or something that draws one away from God while remaining determined and firm on the straight path. According to the Quran, those who struggle in God's way will be rewarded with guidance and blessings. This means that obedience is both a test and a means of strengthening faith.

Therefore, Muslims believe that obeying God's commands and staying away from sinful acts is essential to lead a righteous life and attaining salvation in the hereafter. It is believed that the struggle to maintain obedience is a constant battle between good and evil within oneself. If God wants us to come to Him without any obstacle or antagonist in our faces, then the road is easy, and we will all go in that direction.

However, God wants to manifest that among His creation, there are people who come to Him by loving choice, and they have the free will and power to disobey. Why? Because this manifests the true love of God. This also shows that those who choose to follow God are doing so out of genuine love and devotion rather than simply because it is the easy or convenient path. True faith and character are developed through this choice and struggle.

Faith Is a Gift—Receive with Gratitude

Faith is like climbing a steep mountain, and we keep climbing. If faith were easy, there would be no value to it. The difficulties we face in Ramadan to fast and increase acts of worship make us value Ramadan, but more so our faith.

Just as a woman has a hard time giving up her child after struggling and carrying them for nine months, a strong bond is built. Likewise, a person strengthens their bond of faith with God within the hardships of Ramadan. Therefore, you will find people who fast but don't pray outside Ramadan. A bond is built such that Ramadan calls many of such people back every year. Hopefully, this bond will be strengthened outside Ramadan. There is value in striving and struggling.

Whenever you perform an act of worship, take time to thank God for enabling you to do so. You should feel happy and proud that you performed this action and ask God to enable you to do more out of His Grace.

> *O, my Lord! So enable me that I may be grateful for Thy favours, which thou hast bestowed on me and on my parents, and that I may work the righteousness that will please Thee: And admit me, by Thy Grace, to the ranks of Thy righteous Servants.*
>
> —Quran 27:18–19

Hope Is a Reality, Not Thoughts

True hope requires effort. Unless you have reached the state of Prophet Jacob, upon him peace, or Prophet Job, upon him peace. Both reached a state of physical illness outside their control. Yet neither allowed his soul to follow its caprice. They accepted this as a call to be alone with God. In such a state, you can just make prayers. It is your limbs that will do the talking.

> *That Day shall We set a seal on their mouths. But their hands will speak to us, and their feet bear witness, to all that they did.*
>
> —Quran 36:65

So hope requires effort. Prophet Muhammad, upon him peace and blessings, said, "The intelligent is he who takes his soul to task and works for that which is after death; and the incapable is he who makes his soul follow his caprice and merely hopes on Allah."

Commitment

Every vision one has and mission one undertakes faces obstacles. Commitment to a mission builds resolve and helps one become vigilant. To maintain resolve and focus, you put a security system to keep distractors or invaders out. Adam, upon him peace, was warned but forgot. God had warned him not to listen to Satan. You see references to avid listeners to lies in the Quran—people who pay lip service to faith. Adam, upon him peace, was a prophet, and he forgot the covenant he made. It was not intentional or deliberate; however, this story teaches us to be vigilant and on guard to demonstrate our commitment to the covenant.

> *We had already, beforehand, taken the covenant of Adam, but he forgot: and We found on his part no firm resolve.*
>
> —Quran 20:115

Our commitment to agreements builds firm resolve in our character and keeps us building and planting seeds, even when the Day of Judgment comes. The resolute prophets are Noah, Abraham, Moses, Jesus, and Prophet Muhammad, upon them peace and blessings. They did not waver once in their mission. Reflect on their stories if you wish to understand commitment to faith and build resolve in your character.

Anas ibn Malik reported that the Messenger of Allah, upon him peace and blessings, said, "If the Resurrection were established upon one of you while he has in his hand a sapling, then let him plant it."

The Sacred Law builds a security system to protect you and your faith while the Law's spirit drives you forward and keeps you moving. It does not matter if one person is flying, another driving a race car, and another limping. Just keep moving forward. Don't give up.

> *Journey to Allah limping and broken and don't wait for wellness, because waiting for wellness is inability.*
>
> —Imam al-Shafi'i

Choice and Consequences

> *Let there be no compulsion in religion: Truth stands out clear from Error: whoever rejects evil and believes in Allah hath grasped the most trustworthy hand-hold, that never breaks. And Allah heareth and knoweth all things.*
>
> —Quran 2:256

Our faith is based on principles and ethics. It is not based on desire and whim. The first pillar of faith is the *Shahada* or Declaration of faith. We begin by rejecting what is false and accepting what is true. Principles require us to know our beliefs—to what to say no and to what to say yes. For this reason, Adam, upon him peace, was tested. As humans, we go on autopilot sometimes and forget, but God, Most Loving, reminds us to be aware: we are not paying attention; there is a security risk here.

In addition, some have said to me during public speeches that God sent us to earth and just left us to fend for ourselves, like a parent abandons their child. I explained that our five daily prayers are like five appointments a day with God. And in the night, God asks: "Is there any who has a need?" We also have times of the year when God reminds us of our covenant and gives us opportunities to increase in wisdom and receive mentorship and nurturing to our higher selves. I explained that Ramadan is like a boot camp where Muslims review, remember, and reflect. This is a moment when we must say no to ourselves and yes to God. Even in arguing, we must say, "No [I am fasting]" to our ego and remind the other in kind: "I am fasting."

> *Allah the Almighty said: I am as My servant thinks I am. I am with him when he makes mention of Me. If he makes mention of Me to himself, I make mention of him to Myself; and if he makes mention of Me in an assembly, I make mention of him in an assembly better than it. And if he draws near to Me an arm's length, I draw near to him a cubit, and if he draws near to Me a cubit, I draw near to him a fathom. And if he comes to Me walking, I go to him at speed.*
>
> —at-Tirmidhi and Ibn-Majah

The angels who are pure and sinless could not see Satan's true self or Adam's secret, so how can mere human beings claim such purity and powers that are solely those of God alone?

We witness how human beings discriminate in matters of wealth, power, housing, et cetera—for that reason, God does not allow something that our salvation depends on to be in any hands but His own. If we look to the prophets, we see that they did not try to put a mirror in anyone's face, but rather, they turned the individual to God as God knows best their reality. Furthermore, Moses, upon him peace, did not know the magicians were compelled by fear; however, God knew, and it was God who put Moses before them, to teach them courage and purify them.

What Is a Mirror?

The mirror helps you see the darkness within. Imagine if God put someone who was cowardly before the magicians: would they have seen their cowardice? No. You need light to recognize the darkness. It is one whose being enacts the cure that can be a flashlight to help you walk out of that darkness. Hence, the prophets, who carried the message, lived that message, and were divinely protected from error, help us see our own imperfections, flaws, and shortcomings. So to put a mirror in someone's face is to put the cure before them. That is how purification works.

Likewise, God sent Moses, upon him peace, who asked the Pharaoh if he wished to be guided to Allah. When his Lord called to him in the sacred valley of Tuwa:

> Go to Pharaoh. Indeed, he has transgressed. And say to him, "Would you [be willing to] purify yourself And let me guide you to your Lord so you would fear [Him]?"
>
> —Quran 79:16–19

If you turn to God, and you are struggling with stinginess, God will place before you a generous person. If you are mean, God will place before you a loving person. If you are egotistical, God will place before you a humble person. If you refuse to repent and you are proud, defiant, and unremorseful, God will place before you a humble, repentant soul who is remorseful. Adam, upon him peace, was the mirror for Satan to see himself. If you want to be purified, turn to God, and He will place a mirror before you or use you as a mirror for others. Be yourself and let God.

Such words can only be uttered by one who accepts their human condition and has love in their heart for God. God knows we are weak. It was a Divine Plan that we would be on earth before Adam, upon him peace, was created. It is important to repeat that Adam, upon him peace, did not say Satan was a loser, but we.

We learn from this that our effort should not be to lash out at others if they do not believe and call them losers or mock them, but rather to acknowledge to ourselves and internalize deeply this reality such that if we stumble, we can privately and immediately turn to God and confess our need for His Forgiveness and Mercy, and without Him, we are losers. Notice Adam and Eve, upon them peace, and who and what they were focused on.

The first word Adam, upon him peace, spoke was "Alhamdulillah." *Hamd* is the highest station. This is a state we share with the angels, who are constantly praising God. Within that *Hamd*, his second reality is revealed, which is a confession to our need for His Forgiveness and Mercy. Here, we separate from the angels, who are sinless and cannot have this need in the way humans do. One can look at this as internalizing shame or as an invitation to know God in deeper and more intimate realities.

If we are made to believe that if we treat others well, then we will be accepted, we will only behave better for the same reasons that we behave badly: for attention and belonging. This leads to a lack of self-knowledge, which leads to people being afraid of themselves because they learn to doubt that they will be accepted as the real person that they are. This does not lead to faith but to multiple personalities, shallowness, and superficiality.

How? Dr. al-Bouti asked whether those listening had complained about their weaknesses and imperfections to God. We often complain about others to God. But do we sit with God and talk to Him about our own transgressions, dark thoughts, or feelings? Do we ask Him to help us or put us in the path of someone who can help us remove those imperfections?

If you have this conversation with God, then God is not going to shame you. If you look at Adam and Satan, yes, Adam made a mistake out of neglect. This mistake didn't bring him down in the eyes of God, although Adam did have to deal with the consequences of his actions. If you believe in *specific* imperfections, then you must deal with consequences. It doesn't mean you're a bad person.

The truth is that only God can accept you as you are as He created you and knows you better than you know yourself. First, He teaches you to accept yourself, then nurtures you so you can accept

Him as The Most Merciful, the Most Compassionate Lord of the worlds and *al-Mutakabbir*. So if you are searching for the one who will accept you as you are, you will find Him, or He will find you lost in the midst of the chaos and confusion and guide you.

al-Mutakabbir

One of God's names is *al-Mutakabbir*. It is important to pause and reflect on the meaning of His Beautiful Name as we proceed to understand the clarification.

Self-Acceptance versus Self-Oppression

What does it mean to accept oneself? And what does it mean to oppress oneself? Often, when we speak of self-acceptance, we are really using the logic and definition of self-oppression.

If I was to ask you, "Who are you?" how would you define yourself? Some will focus on their humanness, which is part of who we are, but there is more. We are also spiritual beings, and self-acceptance requires that we accept all parts of who we are. Read the following verse and reflect:

> When we have died and become dust and bones, are we indeed to be resurrected? And our forefathers [as well]?" Say, "Yes, and you will be [rendered] contemptible." It will be only one shout, and at once they will be observing. They will say, "O woe to us! This is the Day of Recompense." [They will be told], "This is the Day of Judgement which you used to deny."
>
> —Quran 37:16–21

I learned from Dr. Ramadan al-Bouti in one of his lessons that it is a sin to ask God to remove all animalistic-type desires from one, as there is a purpose for them within us. It is a form of arrogance, a being who is inherently weak in origin yet acts as *al-Mustakbir*, not according to their reality but as though they were a deity. I always use the term *playing God*. These desires, including our ego and conditions that make us prone to mistakes, are our reality, to push us to our need for His Mercy and His Forgiveness, as well as His Generosity. We were created from earth and will return to it; however, our purpose is to build this earth for our lives here and in preparation for our hereafter.

We oppress ourselves when we are in denial of our human condition or ask God to turn us into angels instead, as beautifully discussed by Dr. al-Bouti. Yet we also oppress ourselves if we are denial that we are spiritual beings who will be resurrected and face a day of account for our actions on earth. Most humans oppress themselves, denying one or the other. Hence, to accept oneself is to accept that we are spiritual beings living on earth for a temporary time until we return and give an account for this human experience. So, to further expand on the clarification point above, whose eyes are you using to nurture you? Are you defining yourself based on your ego, the opinions of others, or the guidance sent by your Creator?

Therefore, we must ask God to help us utilize these conditions and internal desires in accordance with the sacred law and, if we are not able to, to protect us from engaging in them in an impermissible manner. This is why I add the word *protection* to the prayers for forgiveness by Hasan al-Basri. As humans, we are always between fear and hope, between need of His Protection and Generosity and of His Forgiveness and Mercy. Everyone needs Him, but He needs no one.

For example, there is no sincerity or truthfulness if Joseph, upon him peace, was asexual. It is in the choice and the struggle to adhere to the call of God that the manifestation of his truthfulness and sincerity was witnessed by God. The other part missing in the story is that Joseph was tested with a very powerful, beautiful, and attractive woman, someone who was very desirable. Likewise, Joseph, upon him peace, was extremely beautiful and attractive to many women. They were a test for each other, and he acted according to his faith.

al-Mustakbir

Who is *al-Mustakbir*? Someone who desires to wear the robe of greatness although they are inherently weak. This is different from God honoring people with positions of high status or greatness. It is the internal state that we focus on here, not the external. He refuses to see the signs of Allah, regardless of how well you present them to him.

Explanations or any evidence you give has no benefit; the *mustakbir* responds by arguing and debating, scheming, twisting, and distorting to tire you out and drain you.

Shaykh al-Mustakbireen is Satan. The internal state of such a person is a very diseased heart. It is important to differentiate between *gafla* and *'i'raad*.

Gafla or heedlessness—this person had no intention or deliberation to disobey but was negligent. The person lacked resolve. God's Forgiveness and Mercy envelop such a person.

'I'raad or stubborn denial—this person is intentional and deliberate and has stubborn resolve to defy without listening or considering evidence or explanations. Given the diseased heart, God's Mercy and Forgiveness will not reach this person. They will not seek it and feel it is beneath them to ask for it. Instead, such a person will be obsessed with power, as Satan was. Instead of asking for Forgiveness and Mercy, Satan said, "Then, by Thy power, I will put them all in the wrong."

He asked for God's Power instead of His Forgiveness. To do what? To call Adam, upon him peace, and his progeny to disobedience. Hence, when he was doing good before and ridding the earth of evil, he was doing it for his ego, not God. The creation of Adam, upon him peace, manifested the reality of his diseased heart to him. If you are doing something for God, you should want the person to be guided, not misguided and disobedient.

God did not falsely accuse Satan. If you genuinely love someone or worship and internally acknowledge that He is Lord, why would you turn His creation against Him?

Then the *al-Mustakbir*'s life is internally in a state of anguish; he has a hard time being alone and in peace. He struggles to sleep and has nightmares. The heart has a key, and that key is with God, not with you or others. The house or the spouse is not the key to the heart. The heart's key is with God, and it is surrender to His commands and decree that brings about peace. God might test this person in various ways, including physical sickness, yet his heart is clean and at peace with God. When a person is in a state of *dunka*, or internal darkness, it means they are not at peace within themselves. *Dunka* is not depression or trauma. Focus on the words of Satan so you do not accuse everyone struggling with sadness, depression, or trauma of having an internal state of *dunka*:

Satan said, "Then, by Thy power, I will put them all in the wrong." Satan was not depressed or traumatized. He was scheming to misguide others.

Mustakbir versus Jahlil

A *jahil*, or ignorant person, has an excuse, and God will not hold such people to account for their ignorance. God forgives them and envelops them with His Mercy. The learned are held to account for not teaching them.

However, there is an arrogant type of person who knows and denies. For example, they send someone to you to make false claims. You know the rumors they are passing about XYZ are false as well as the scheme they plotted and planned, and they are throwing shade at you, so you throw the game out in the open. Instead of admitting fault and apologizing for their scheme, lies, and actions of a charlatan, they accuse you of slander and gossip.

Effort and Results

God rewards people according to what they seek internally. For example, whoever wants results in the *Dunya*, or this worldly life, and insists on it and strives for it, God gives it to them, like Qarun and Satan. He also gives it to believers if their faith is not strong enough to handle patience. God rewards them for their efforts in the *Dunya* in what they seek, ask for, and strive for. You work hard and strive; God rewards you.

God rewards people for their efforts, regardless of whether they are Muslim or non-Muslim, believer or *mustakbir*. He rewards their hard work and efforts and allows them to see the fruits of their labor. Those who strove, did not see the results in the *Dunya*, but acted on their faith and values will see the results in the hereafter. Prophet Ibrahim and his wife Hajar are two examples. Their souls and faith are in a much higher state than those who cannot wait and might lose faith if they do not see the results. God knows His creation and knows how to test them and what is best for them. If the person is true and sincere and is striving hard, God will pour trials upon them as He did for those He brought to His nearness.

The clarification point is simply to act according to what you believe; it will manifest in time, either in this world or the next. If you acted for desire of greatness, belonging, and attention, God will try to get you to graduate to the next level. We all are toddlers seeking attention and belonging at one point in our life. We are all born ignorant and engage in acts of *gafla*, or negligence. It is a need, and as humans, we are prone to err. Some had parents who fulfilled that need, and some did not. It is not a sin to have these desires, but when you are ready to graduate, and God knows you are ready, He will try you. Seek His Strength, Protection, Forgiveness, and Mercy and keep moving forward. A trial can just be a time to graduate to the next level of faith with God's Help and Strength.

What If There Are No Results?

Call with your actions. Abraham called people to God in the desert thousands of years ago, seeing little result. He prayed that he would be a guiding example for later generations, calling to God. His hope in God was overflowing. Millions answer his call every year. If you want to read a motivational or inspirational story that will make your eyes water, this is one to read as you witness the miracle before your eyes.

Manifestation of His Mercy

> *Do ye not see that Allah has subjected to your (use) all things in the heavens and on earth, and has made his bounties flow to you in exceeding measure, (both) seen and unseen? Yet there are among men those who dispute about Allah, without knowledge and without guidance, and without a Book to enlighten them!*
>
> —Quran 31:20

Taskheer—Subject to You

He made these creations as servants to us and our living. Not everything, just what we need. Some are subject without any effort from us. Some require effort, like fruits, plants, animals, electricity, et cetera. Even the moon and sun follow their own orbit, by design to nurture life.

Allah shows mercy to those who are merciful. Mercy is not just for Muslims, but this should extend to people of other faiths. In addition to this, we should have mercy in our hearts for all His creation and have a sincere desire for the guidance of all morally responsible beings on the surface of the earth.

This is also a time for expressing our true state, which is brokenness and neediness for God. This is the real meaning of prostration in Islam. These spiritual teachings are important as

Prophet Muhammad, upon him peace and blessings, taught Muslims that fasting is not just about hunger and thirst. It's about rededicating ourselves to God and becoming conscious of and grateful for God's enabling grace upon us. This is the month of self-evaluation and rebuilding community and family ties. It is an opportunity from the Divine to aid us in our struggles to perfect our character in every way.

1. How did we do since last Ramadan?
2. What milestones and goals will we work toward next year?
3. What have we done for the less fortunate?
4. What are we going to do? Did we remember them in our prayer at least?
5. Will we not even make a prayer for them this Ramadan?

Some traditions mention stories of Prophet Noah, upon him peace, that Muslims reject. These stories are similar to the stories of the savage Native Americans, violent thugs, or various oppressed people whose lives were written in a way to justify their oppression.

Likewise, people smear the lives of sacred figures to rationalize disobedience or defiance of the sacred law. Islamic teachings clear Prophet Noah, upon him peace, of such violations of the Sacred Law. The Quran mentions that his wife was not pious and betrayed him and undermined his mission.

Prophet Noah, upon him peace, did not kill her or harm her, even though she harmed him. At times, the betrayal of our mission comes from those closest to us. While we might be angry or hurt by such abuse, we can face it by turning to God, knowing that God will always make the truth come out at an appointed time.

> *Abu Mas'ud reported: The Messenger of Allah, peace and blessings be upon him, said, "Verily, among the words, people obtained from the Prophets are this: If you feel no haya, do as you wish."*

—Sahih al-Bukhari, 3483

Ibn Rajab said: The scholars interpret this saying in two ways. First, it is a command of caution and warning, meaning if there is no haya, do as you wish, for Allah will repay you accordingly... Second, it is a command of description, meaning that whoever does not have haya will do as he wishes, for it is haya that prevents evil deeds.

What is *haya*? Often, *haya* is translated as *shame*. Khizi is the translation of *shame*. In my writings, I translate it into *faith, life, self-respect, values, conscience, ethics,* and *dignity*. If one is shallow and hollow internally, then there is nothing of substance to prevent them from transgressing the boundaries of others. Hence, the saying of the prophets: you can do as you wish.

These people resemble a parched man searching for a mirage in the middle of the desert. To endure trials and tribulations, we must have a strong faith and trust in God's plan, as well as a willingness to learn from and grow from the challenges presented to us. As a result of these trying times, our faith increases, and we acquire wisdom.

Most of us now judge in this manner: You are innocent because I love you and what you stand for, and I can come up with a million and one reasons to explain your actions. I despise you and everything you represent. This kind of judgment is highly subjective and often biased, as it is based on personal feelings rather than objective evidence or facts. It can lead to unfair treatment and discrimination against individuals or groups not favored by the person making the judgment. To maintain a just and equitable society, promoting peaceful and nonviolent conflict resolution methods is critical.

Soon after Prophet Muhammad, upon him peace and blessings, passed away, a social decline started, and fighting resulted. We see people struggle to get justice in many parts of the world, not just in the United States. The difficulty in obtaining justice is not a reason to stop seeking justice or nurturing a better society but a reason to connect with people struggling for justice to help one another find support and comfort when the results in the court system are not favorable.

Justice is hard. We all benefit by finding ways to contribute to the security of others. When people feel safe, we can converse on many common goods that might help the truth emerge. However, oppressors love oppressing as they benefit from their system of oppression.

I believe that we should perfect our argument, its soundness, its truthfulness, the supporting evidence—devoid of manipulation and coercion—and make sure it is in harmony with our faith and ethics, then present it.

> *O, my people! I have indeed conveyed to you the Message of my Lord, and have given you good advice but you like not good advisers.*
>
> —Quran 7:79

Speaking for justice will open doors for more oppression and possibly plots of injustice. Hence, lower your expectations.

> *And there were in the city nine men (from the sons of their chiefs), who made mischief in the land, and would not reform. They said: "Swear to another by God that we shall make a secret night attack on him and his household, and afterwards we will surely say to his near relatives, 'We witnessed not the destruction of his household, and verily! We are telling the truth.'"*
>
> —Quran 27: 48–49

If the argument is sound and truthful, supported, and presented with faith, and the oppressor rejects it, God will call them to account. After three days, the warning of Prophet Saleh, upon him peace, manifested before them. The city of Thamud was destroyed.

God is the Most Merciful and a perpetual Forgiver: He loves to forgive. However, ignoring the warning to stop the oppression will be dealt with severely. Prophet Muhammad, upon him peace and blessings, used to pray: "I seek refuge lest I should oppress or be oppressed."

About a year ago, I discussed human progress with a group of women. They believed that once we overcome the social ills of the past, we advance and keep evolving into a more humane society.

> *Do people think that they will be let go merely by saying: "We believe," and that they will not be tested?*
>
> —Quran 29:2

I asked them why it is that we repeat historical atrocities. Genocide happened in Rwanda and Bosnia. "Never again" did not stop such atrocities.

If we go to school and pass elementary, high school, and college, is this knowledge inherited by our descendants? No. They must also go to school and learn some of the lessons, likewise other social lessons that the previous generations faced and were tested on. We do not inherit faith, bravery, resolve, or justice lessons.

As Moses, upon him peace, told the Pharaoh: "The knowledge of that is with my Lord, duly recorded: my Lord never errs, nor forgets." We will face similar trials and tribulations in our own lives and refer to those lessons of the past to help us pass the tests.

A couple of decades ago, Iraq was a very technologically advanced country, with women leading in various parts of civil society. Now they are fighting for rights that they established years ago. Likewise, within some Muslim communities, you see difficulties for women trying to learn or gain knowledge, even to drive as in Saudi Arabia, whereas women were scholars during the very early years. I disagree that we advance to a state at which the problems that those before us faced will not be faced by us. I think the same problems reappear in different forms, testing us, as those before were tested.

One lesson from the story of Prophet Noah, upon him peace, is that if we left it to people's conscience to stop oppression, a relative handful would listen to reason, even if you spoke and pleaded with the oppressors for 950 years.

People do not stop oppressing you just because you present a compelling argument and images and videos of abuse. Oppressors seldom have a conscience when such images move them. It is critical to recognize that change frequently necessitates collective action and sustained effort. We can create a safer and more just society if we band together and advocate for change. And we accept responsibility for resisting. And we collectively request that people assist in pushing the oppressor, their supporters, and enablers within their boundaries and forcing them to stop.

We are being tested in the same way that those who came before were tested. We know how the past's stories ended and how every level of oppression will end. It is up to us to learn from history and avoid making the same mistakes. We can create a better future for ourselves and future generations by standing up to oppression and fighting for justice, beginning with ourselves.

> *Truly dost thou marvel, while they ridicule, and, when they are admonished, pay no heed. And, when they see a Sign, turn it to mockery.*
>
> —Quran 37:12–14

Cowardliness is not a fear of something, like fear of Muslims or a jihad squad. No, it is a fear of seeing their false selves, a form of escapism.

The magicians were afraid of the Pharaoh and overpowered by that fear. The cure for that was Moses, upon him peace, as a sign from God. They accepted the sign, gift of courage and overcame their fear.

Cowardliness—or *jubn* as we say in Arabic—is more related to love of self-interest than fear of a tyrannical oppressor. Often, our vulnerability is masked with mockery. Mockery is often countered by the Divine threat I spoke of earlier. It does seem as though mockery and ridicule (*istihzah* in Arabic) are common traits of those engaged in active rejection of the Truth. The mockery is a mask, somewhat like a small animal's defense mechanism to make itself look bigger than it is. I suspect that some of those who have nothing to say about life's purpose and meaning engage in mockery of things that are sacred to assure themselves (at a level that rational arguments cannot) that there is no Divine; otherwise, they would have been struck down long ago.

In some way, they are testing their conjecture about the existence of God. But Allah, Most High, is not taunted into revealing Himself to the arrogant. He does respond to all concerned parties in revelation. God speaks to the reality of their (our) human condition, with which He, Most High, is better acquainted than we ourselves.

In "*Surah al-Waqiah*" (Chapter 56), it is as though the disbelievers are being asked, "How can you make light of something so tremendous when your reality is so fragile, so vulnerable, and you know that?"

> *We only send the messengers to give Glad Tidings and to give warnings: But the unbelievers dispute with vain argument, in order therewith to weaken the truth, and they treat My Signs as a jest, as also the fact that they are warned!*
>
> *And who doth more wrong than one who is reminded of the Signs of his Lord, but turns away from them, forgetting the (deeds) which his hands have sent forth? Verily we have set veils over their hearts lest they should understand this, and over their ears, deafness, if thou callest them to guidance, even then will they never accept guidance.*
>
> *But your Lord is Most forgiving, full of Mercy. If He were to call them (at once) to account for what they have earned, then surely He would have hastened their punishment: but they have their appointed time, beyond which they will find no refuge.*
>
> —Quran 18:56-58

We do not have power over people's hearts to make them believe. Moreover, if God's knows people are arguing in vanity and mockery to weaken and malign the truth, instead of elevating it, He will put a seal on one's heart so they do not understand the message and will not believe. This is critical to understanding that God is Majestic and does not beg anyone to believe in Him.

He has no need for us. We need Him. Our intention in arguing is of critical importance. Because God is All-Seeing and All-Hearing. God will *not* shatter our hearts to force us to believe. There is no compulsion to believe. Instead, He will put a seal on our hearts.

He will give us space and time to reflect on our actions and intentions, regardless of our taunting, to seek forgiveness and turn to Him for His Forgiveness and His Mercy.

In other words, you can fool people, but you cannot fool God. Allah puts a covering over the heart of a person who has a spirit of contention, dispute, taunting, mockery, and distorting words to defeat the truth with falsehood and sinful cunning weapons.

Allah gives people reprieve because He is Oft-Forgiving and Most Forbearing, and He does not punish people on the spot for their evil actions. He is Most Merciful and gives people time to change their ways. God chooses sincere advisers who exhibit humility, forgiveness, forbearance, and mercy, rather than mockery and sinful deception.

Knowing this, the sincere adviser is most concerned with the Majestic Message's delivery. Because their intentions are pure and clean, they are not held accountable before God for polluting the message and contributing to its being misunderstood, misapplied, or distorted. We have seen cases where a person was fired for misrepresenting a company's mission and values. They are penalized in cases where the misrepresentation has caused damage and harm. As a result, anyone who calls to God's Majestic Message should pray consciously and privately for a pure and sound heart.

Muhammad: The Gates of Heaven Are Open

What win I, if I gain the thing I seek?
A dream, a breath, a froth of fleeting joy.
Who buys a minute's mirth to wail a week
Or sells eternity to get a toy?
For one sweet grape who will the vine destroy?
Or what fond beggar, but to touch the crown,
Would with the sceptre straight be strucken down?

—Shakespeare, *The Rape of Lucrece*

Some scholars claim that the Prophet Muhammad, upon him peace and blessings, was born on the twelfth of Rabi al-Awwal. Typically, this month is used to educate and remind people about Prophet Muhammad, may Allah grant him peace and blessings.

When Prophet Muhammad, peace and blessings be upon him, was born, it marked the end of a period of darkness in the world and the beginning of a period of joy, happiness, grace, and hope. We look forward to spring and celebrate it as the end of winter (a symbol of sadness or difficult times) and, consequently, the start of happiness or joy. Similarly, the birth of Prophet Muhammad, upon him peace and blessings, brought hope and light to a world that was previously filled with ignorance, injustice, and oppression. His teachings and actions continue to guide over a billion people worldwide to strive for a better future filled with peace, compassion, and justice.

If we are reminded, we remember our history, heritage, and those who sacrificed the most for us with their lives in this world and the next. So we must take time to remember, to learn, to reflect, and to give thanks to him, his family, and his companions out of love, appreciation, and gratitude.

As we reflect on this month and its position in the Hijri calendar, as well as reflecting on Prophet Muhammad, upon him peace and blessings, and his beautiful names, we can see during difficult times or sadness that one can connect to Prophet

Muhammad, upon him peace and blessings, and learn from him how to connect to God.

The aim is not to worship him, but being the purified guide, we follow him on the straight path.

We might ask God for love, belonging, A, B, C, and He responds with people who are abusive, trials, and tribulations to teach us what these realties are, for how can we receive what we cannot recognize and know? Hence, the delay in the answer or saving it for the next life. You might have heard the saying "I asked God for wisdom, and He gave me problems to solve."

Or we might pray and claim to love the poor, yet deep within, we really want to get out of poverty, and although God gives us a suitable place to live with the poor, eat, and drink, we are hoping for a way out. So we will say, "I do not want any worldly stuff," but we do.

Or, we might pray for X, Y, and Z and find we are not really happy because, like a child who gets bored with a new toy and wants another one, we, too, find ourselves bored.

Or we might ask God for things that are considered a sin in every faith, including our own, and God answers our prayers, and we are misled to believe that God is with us. You have probably heard many people saying, "God is good" or "God is great" while they are disobeying Him within their own faith tradition and asking for success in doing so. They might even argue, "Why would God answer my prayers if He does not approve?"

Prophet Muhammad, upon him peace and blessings, modeled to us how to manifest our love to the Divine. In this book, I want to focus on the supplications he made.

Obligatory to Love Prophet Muhammad

> *The Prophet is closer to the Believers than their own selves. (Quran 33:6)*

In addition, Prophet Muhammad, upon him peace and blessings, said, "None of you will be a true believer until I am more beloved to you than yourself" (Bukhari).

We all look for celebrities to love or ways to love ourselves. Neither is healthy love. Loving the Prophet helps ground us in faith. People follow whom they love; hence, loving the Prophet helps us follow the purified guide and learn *how* to love God.

Umar al Khattab, may Allah be pleased with him, is a companion of the Prophet, upon him peace and blessings. Umar is known as *al Faruq* or distinguisher between truth and falsehood. It is important to study Umar and know his character to appreciate the beauty of Prophet Muhammad, upon him peace and blessings. Umar, may Allah be pleased with him, was not someone who could be easily manipulated or a blind follower.

He was walking with the Prophet, upon him peace and blessings, and expressed his love to him.

The Prophet asked, "More than your children, O Umar?"
Umar replied, "Yes, O Prophet of Allah."
The Prophet asked, "More than your money, O Umar?"
And Umar replied, "Yes, O Prophet of Allah."
The Prophet then asked him, "More than yourself, O Umar?"
Umar honestly replied, "No, O Prophet of Allah."
The Prophet then told him, "O Umar, your faith will never be complete until you love me more than yourself."
Umar briefly isolated himself and reflected on this.

Analysis

Umar was a direct speaker, and although Prophet Muhammad, upon him peace and blessings, was a gentle speaker, he spoke to Umar in a direct tone as that is how direct speakers like to be engaged.

I wanted to share this story of the companion's love for Prophet Muhammad, upon him peace and blessings, to illustrate that the love Umar had for him was not based on feelings and just fitting in. Umar was known for his honesty and directness and openly responded that he loved himself more. He was not someone who suffered from social problems, self-hatred, or a lack of self-esteem, nor was he a vulnerable person who was manipulated. Umar's love for the Prophet was based on knowledge, dialogue, openness, reflection, and intelligence.

Early on in Umar's story, before he became Muslim, he had set out to kill Prophet Muhammad, upon him peace and blessings. The beauty of Umar was that while he was passionate, fearless, and intelligent, he was open to being wrong and corrected. Intelligence without openness and the courage to being wrong is fruitless.

After some reflection, Umar returned, stood in the center of the Masjid, and then said: "O Prophet of Allah, now I love you more than myself."

Prophet Muhammad, upon him peace and blessings, replied, "Now, O Umar, now, O Umar." Umar's faith had become complete.

People asked Umar, "What did you do to increase your love for the Prophet and love him more than yourself so quickly?"

Umar replied by sharing his self-dialogue:

> *I asked myself who did I need more, myself or the Prophet of Allah? I found that I needed the Prophet more. I will not intercede for myself on the Day of Judgment, but the Prophet of Allah will. My deeds will not place me at the highest of levels, but my love for the Prophet will. I did not take myself from the darkness to the light, but the Prophet of Allah did. Accordingly, the love of the Prophet deepened in my heart as compared to my love for myself.*

Likewise in our love of God, when we take time out, have a self-dialogue, and reflect on who we need more, ourselves or God?

To love God Most High and Prophet Muhammad, upon him peace and blessings, requires that we turn to God and ask Him to guide us to sound knowledge to know Him and His Beloved and to engage in works that increase our love and complete the faith in our hearts.

For Muslims, it is important to also have love of the companions, given the sacrifices they made to stand by the Prophet and aid him as he built the faith community.

What Did He Ask of God?

> *Their salutation on the Day they meet Him will be "Peace!"; and He has prepared for them a generous Reward. O Prophet! Truly We have sent thee as a Witness, a Bearer of Glad Tidings, and Warner, And as one who invites to Allah's (grace) by His leave, and as a lamp spreading light. Then give the Glad Tidings to the Believers, that they shall have from Allah a very great Bounty. (Quran 33:44-47)*

Hopefully, by reflecting on what he prayed for, we can learn to be mindful of our prayers and pray for things that we are obligated to ask of God and to be reasonable and honest in other requests we are making as well. This might also help us pause and reflect on the prayers of other prophets in the Quran. What did they ask of God?

Ibn 'Abbas narrated on Prophet Muhammad, upon him peace and blessings, "O Allah give me faith and certainty after which there is no disbelief, and mercy, by which I may attain the high level of Your generosity in the world and the Hereafter" (at-Tirmidhi).

Al-'Afiyah or Well-Being

We should never pray for trials or tribulations. We should pray for al-'afiyah, or well-being, and follow the commands of God.

Abul-Fadl al-'Abbas bin 'Abdul Muttalib, may God be pleased with him, reported:

> *I asked the Messenger of Allah, upon him peace and blessings, to teach me a supplication. He, upon him peace and blessings, said, "Beg Allah for safety (from all evils in this world and in the Hereafter)."*
>
> *I waited for some days and then I went to him again and asked him: "O Messenger of Allah, teach me to supplicate something from Allah." He said to me, "O Al-'Abbas, the uncle of Messenger of Allah! Beseech Allah to give you safety (Al-'afiyah) in this life and in the Hereafter."*
>
> —At-Tirmidhi

Do not place yourself in a position in which you bring trials and tribulations upon you. If you do, ask God to help you remove them and repent.

Noted in Sahih Muslim, 'Abdullah bin 'Umar (may Allah be pleased with them) reported that the Messenger of Allah, upon him peace and blessings, used to supplicate thus:

> *O Allah! I seek refuge in You against the declining of Your Favours, passing of safety, the suddenness of Your punishment and all that which displeases You.*

In another *hadith*, noted in Sunan Ibn Majah, Ibn 'Umar said:

> *The Messenger of Allah, upon him peace and blessings, never abandoned these supplications, every morning and evening: "O Allah, I ask You for forgiveness and well-being in this world and in the Hereafter. O Allah, I ask You for forgiveness and well-being in my religious and my worldly affairs. O Allah, conceal my faults, calm my*

fears, and protect me from before me and behind me, from my right and my left, and from above me, and I seek refuge in You from being taken unaware from beneath me."

What Is *Al-'Afiyah?*

Afiyah is an all-encompassing word referring to overall well-being and safety, including mental health, faith, physical health, wealth, and safety from all harm to one and loved ones so as not to worry about them.

1. To be alive.
2. To guard your prayers, fulfill your fasts, health permitting, and zakat.
3. To have good health, mind, body, and soul.
4. To have enough money and be debt-free and financially independent.
5. To have children and family who are alive, protected from afflictions, in good health, and debt-free.
6. To be protected from trials and tribulations.
7. To be protected from actions that lead to declining of God's favors, passing of safety, the suddenness of His punishment, and all that which displeases Him.
8. To repent sincerely, repair the harm, and be forgiven.

What is the Source of Love?

When Muslims discuss loving God, we frequently advise people to offer God love as God needs it. On the other hand, our faith teaches us to receive God's love and the reality of love comes from the source of all love, God.

> *The Messenger of Allah, upon him peace and blessings, said: One of Prophet David's (upon him peace) supplications was: "O Allah! I ask You for Your Love, the love of those who love You, and deeds which will cause me to attain Your Love. O Allah! Make Your Love dearer to me than myself, my family, and the cold water."*
>
> —Mishkat al-Masabih 2496

Often, I wondered, *why water?* Later, I realized we are so privileged as many in various parts of the world need water, and it is very scarce, causing people to be displaced. Sometimes, we are protected from trials and tribulations that others face, and we should take a moment to thank God for that protection while praying for the afflicted.

Christopher Hitchens has done a video series confidently bashing God. Without understanding His speech, Hitchens misrepresented God as vindictive. His analysis of God is not "confident" as he claims but pure arrogance and rationalizations, a projection of his own character, given his actions and political activities during the Iraq War. He advocated for the Iraq war and fought ferociously for his position, regardless of the cost to civilian lives, and that the Iraq war was based on lies.

People reject faith and God for one of two reasons: they do not want to surrender, or they do not want to repent. Even though he was a prophet of God, the seal of the prophets, and a messenger, Prophet Muhammad, upon him peace and blessings, used to make this prayer to God:

> *O Allah, I seek refuge in You, lest I misguide others, or I am misguided by others, lest I cause others to err or I am caused to err, lest I abuse others or be abused, and lest I behave foolishly or meet with the foolishness of others.*
>
> —Abu Dawud, Ibn Majah, An-Nasa'i, At-Tirmidhi

A closer look at the prayer shows his concern for others being harmed by him preceded his concern for being harmed by others. We can witness the genuine love of God, which is a concern for others. As the Quran describes them:

> *For, [true] servants of the Most Gracious are [only] they who walk gently on earth, and who, whenever the foolish address them, reply with [words of] peace.*
>
> —Quran 25:63

We hear many questions on why bad things happen or why there are suffering and evil in the world. Some will respond with mystery; others will mock and reject and demand a thorough, in-depth explanation of why God allowed such things to happen.

Worst, yet, some want to judge Him and put Him on the witness stand for questioning. As Moses, upon him peace, told the Pharaoh, "The knowledge of this is with my Lord." God does not owe us an explanation for why some things are allowed to happen, and we are asked to surrender.

As humans, unless we are taught and nurtured, we can all fall into this path of arrogance, which leads to more suffering for us and those around us. One thing that, as Muslims, we should be grateful for is how Prophet Muhammad, upon him peace and blessings, modeled to us how to relate to God and to the suffering we face in the world.

Instead of putting God on the witness stand and questioning, blaming, and debating Him, the ending of his supplication at Ta'if drives an arrow into our hearts or souls to shake us up and reflect on "To You is Right to reprimand until you are satisfied."

As Muslims, we are grateful for how Prophet Muhammad, upon him peace and blessings, taught us to connect to God truthfully with pure intellect and clean hearts.

> *O Allah! I complain to You of my weakness, my scarcity of resources and the humiliation I have been subjected to by the people. O Most Merciful of those who are merciful. O Lord of the weak and my Lord too. To whom have you entrusted me? To a distant person who receives me with hostility? Or to an enemy to whom you have granted authority over my affair? So long as You are not angry with me, I do not care. Your favor is of a more expansive relief to me. I seek refuge in the light of Your Face by which all darkness is dispelled and every affair of this world and the next is set right, lest Your anger or Your displeasure descends upon me. To You is right to reprimand (call me to account) until You are pleased. There is no power and no might except by You.*
>
> —Safiur Rahman Mubarakpuri, Sealed Nectar

Faith or religion need not be hard; if we find practicing difficult, we can turn to God and ask for ease in practicing our religion and handling world affairs. However, in doing so, we must not forget the hereafter. We do not look at the world as bad, but as a farm where we want to maximize doing good. And when we exit this world, we want to be comforted from the trials and tribulations we experience in life.

> *O Allah, make my religion easy for me by virtue of which my affairs are protected, set right for me my world where my life exists, make good for me my Hereafter which is my resort to which I have to return, and make my life prone to perform all types of good, and make death a comfort for me from every evil.*
>
> —Riyad as-Salihin 1472

In addition, before we ask God to ease our trials and tribulations, it is essential to acknowledge that God, has a right to reprimand us, the way Prophet Muhammad, upon him peace and blessings, modeled to us.

Trials can be a reprimand or an elevation. In the case of Prophet Muhammad, upon him peace and blessings, trials are an elevation, given his station and his being pure and sinless.

In the case of children who die of cholera, they are an elevation in the next life. The children might be the means that will prevent or pull their parents from hellfire. They will plead to God for their salvation since they were denied their company in the world. If their parents are righteous, they will raise their parents' rank in heaven.

However, none of us are at that station, so we should be open to the possibility of transgressions with God, not people. People have egos and will harm us. When this happens, read the Quran, and God will either comfort you with verses to help you be patient or bring to your attention boundaries transgressed.

Always make your reading of the Quran engaging God with what is happening or going on in your life. The prayers of Prophet Muhammad, upon him peace and blessings, teach us how to communicate with God emotionally, mentally, spiritually, and verbally. Shaddad ibn Aws (may Allah be pleased with him) narrated, The Messenger of [Allah], upon him peace and blessings, taught us to say:

> "O [Allah], I ask you for steadfastness in this matter, and I ask You for the resolve to adhere to the path of guidance, and I ask You for gratitude for Your blessings and to worship You well, and I ask You for a truthful tongue and a sound heart, and I seek refuge with You from the evil of what You know, and I ask You for the good of what You know, and I ask You for forgiveness for what You know; You are the knower of the Unseen."

—Mishkat al-Masabih 955

If we generally desire what is mentioned in this supplication, then God will facilitate for us the path and the necessary reminders to stay steadfast on the straight path and to have resolve while doing so. What is important to note from this supplication is that the companion is narrating what they were taught and directed for these things to their Source or God. We cannot purify ourselves; only God can do that. We should seek purification of our hearts from God.

> *Hast thou not regarded those who purify themselves? Nay; only God purifies whom He will; and they shall not be wronged a single date-thread.*
>
> —Quran 4:49

Keep Turning and Returning

Shahr bin Hawshab said:

> *I said to Umm Salamah: "O Mother of the Believers! What was the supplication that the Messenger of Allah, upon him peace and blessings, said most frequently when he was with you?"*
>
> *She said: "The supplication he said most frequently was: 'O Turner of the hearts, make my heart firm upon Your religion.'" She said: "So I said: "O Messenger of Allah, why do you supplicate so frequently: 'O Turner of the hearts, make my heart firm upon Your religion.'"*
>
> *He said: "O Umm Salamah! Verily, there is no human being except that his heart is between Two Fingers of the Fingers of Allah, so whomsoever He wills He makes steadfast, and whomever He wills He causes to deviate."*
>
> —At-Tirmidhi

I understand from the emphasis on the frequency that we need to keep returning with our supplications. We do not make a supplication once, and that is it. Rather, this supplication is repeated. We have supplications for morning and supplications for evening. If we reflect on them, they help nurture, purify, and correct us and remind us of God.

We are between fear and hope

Anas ibn Malik reported: The Messenger of Allah, peace and blessings be upon him, said, "Even if the Resurrection were established upon one of you while he has in his hand a sapling, let him plant it" (Musnad Ahmad, 12902).

One of the worst trials and tribulations that we can face is for God to allow us to deviate from the path. It teaches us that although we are practicing now, if we misuse our faith to harm others or defiantly misapply its teachings, God will allow us to deviate out of the faith. That is what happened to Satan.

We learn from the story of Adam, upon him peace, the importance of steadfastness and resolve. So, we take that lesson and pray for steadfastness and resolve continuously as Prophet Muhammad, upon him peace and blessings, practiced.

We turn to God with our hearts and with our limbs or deeds and actions. We want to make sure our actions are in harmony with the state of our hearts.

> 'Abdullah bin 'Amr bin Al'As (May Allah be pleased with them) reported: "The Messenger of Allah, upon him peace and blessings, supplicated: 'O Allah! Director of the hearts, direct our hearts to Your obedience.'"

—Riyad as-Salihin 1470

Oftentimes, we say it mindlessly, but it is packed with meaning and correction of our worldview. Try reading it and think of corrections and reminders of your worldview. In particular, review the question "Why do children die of cholera?" Why does God allow it to happen and not prevent it? He is God, and if He is omnipotent, He should stop it. 'Abdullah bin Mas'ud, may Allah be pleased with him, reported:

> When it was morning, the Prophet, upon him peace and blessings, used to supplicate:
>
> "We have entered upon morning and the whole kingdom of Allah entered upon morning. Praise is due to Allah. There is none who has the right to be worshiped but Allah, the One who has no partner with Him."
>
> He (the narrator) said: "I think that he, upon him peace and blessings, used to follow the recitation with these words:
>
> 'To Allah belongs all sovereignty, and all praise is for Allah, and He is Omnipotent. My Lord, I beg of you good that lies in this morning and good that follows it, and I seek refuge in You from the evil that lies in this morning and from the evil of that which follows it.
>
> 'My Lord! I seek refuge in You from lethargy and the misery of old age. O Allah! I seek Your Protection from the torment of Hell-fire and the punishment of the grave.'"

—Muslim

Why Adam?

Usually, when we challenge God, God allows us to discover our answer in our own journey. Satan discovered this when God showed him how Adam, upon him peace, sought forgiveness and repentance, and he would not.

At times, the answer is in the mirror: discovering that the one who is sadistic and inconsistent, justifying and rationalizing human suffering is ourselves. Christopher Hitchens discovered that with his support of an illegal war against Iraq which killed many civilians.

Other times, we might be on the left, debating that women have a right to their bodies and do not owe anyone an explanation for having an abortion. Our bodies, our business. Likewise, God's universe is God's business, and He does not owe you or anyone an explanation.

Yet others see that children dying from cholera is a call for us to investigate the international laws that elevate the strong over the weak and create such conditions and horrors. A wake-up call to change our laws that affect the lives of others.

Still others see this as a call to help children dying from cholera and see what can be done to raise awareness. Such people turn to God for help, creating a campaign to provide necessary aid. They reason that God will question them on why children are dying from cholera and what they did, not the other way around.

Those who debate God and challenge Him are never pleased. If God warns us with natural disasters, we judge or complain. If God allows them to see the consequences of their selfish dealings and actions, they blame God. Whatever God does, they are never pleased. In the next life, it will be God questioning us on why children died unjustly:

> *When the souls are sorted out, (being joined, like with like); when the female (infant), buried alive, is questioned for what crime she was killed; When the scrolls are laid open; When the world on High is unveiled; When the Blazing Fire is kindled to fierce heat; And when the Garden is brought near; (Then) shall each soul know what it has put forward.*
>
> —Quran 81:7-14

If we reflect on human experience and relationships, there are many songs about such individuals who are never pleased, regardless how hard you try to please them.

We do not want to have such a relationship with God. Hence, another supplication from our recommended daily and evening supplications is:

> *"Whoever says when he enters the morning or evening, 'I am pleased with Allah as a Lord, with Islam as a religion, and with Muhammad as a prophet,' it will be a duty upon Allah to please him."*
>
> —al-Tirmidhi 3389

Instead of daily self-love affirmations, we can make such affirmations or supplications that strengthen and nurture our relationship with God and our faith.

Dr. Martin Luther King Jr. said: "Normal fear motivates us to improve our individual and collective welfare; abnormal fear constantly poisons and distorts our inner lives. Our problem is not to be rid of fear but rather to harness and master it."

The way we master it is by turning to God the way Prophet Muhammad, upon him peace and blessings, showed us in his life and via the supplications he made.

When you learn about oppression, you learn that the oppressor has an agenda to promote themselves as a Lord in people's hearts and eyes. In the story of Moses, upon him peace, the Pharaoh said very directly, openly, and boldly, "I am your Lord."

Today, the pharaohs do not say the words directly but indirectly. Over time, the oppressed seek their approval and their pleasure instead of the pleasure of God. Some manifestations are "white gaze," "male gaze," or the gaze of whatever group has been tested with privilege in society.

Once an oppressor builds a nest in your heart and you develop an awe of them, they become the director of your life and, unconsciously, your lord. Without your awareness, you might start to go through this conversion therapy such that whatever they love, you love, and whatever they hate, you hate.

We can see the benefit of nurturing our hearts to only praise God every morning and evening. Prophet Muhammad, upon him peace and blessings, taught Muslims to recite three times each morning and evening:

> *Glory is to Allah and praise is to Him, by the multitude of His creation, by His Pleasure, by the weight of His Throne, and by the extent of His Words.*
>
> —Muslim

> *Thou canst [truly] warn only him who is willing to take the reminder to heart, and who stands in AWE of the Most Gracious although He is beyond the reach of human perception: unto such, then, give the glad tiding of [God's] forgiveness and of a most excellent reward!*
>
> —Quran 36:11

And since Adam, upon him peace, received the Divine Breath with "*Alhamdulillah*" or "Praise be to God," he was able to be corrected. So, the only gaze we concern ourselves with or seek to please is the Gaze of God.

> *And be thou patient under the judgment of thy Lord; surely thou art before Our eyes. And proclaim the praise of thy Lord when thou arises.*
>
> —Quran 52:48

Of course, we all fall short in putting these teachings fully into practice. However, God gives us many opportunities to reflect on how Prophet Muhammad, upon him peace and blessings, modeled this reality and teachings for us to follow.

Your ego is not your amigo

Dr. Umar Faruq Abd-Allah said: "The ego is more powerful than 70 satans!" The angels do not have an ego; hence, they are sinless. However, we have an ego, and if that ego is not disciplined or purified, it can throw the soul off, like a horse throws off its rider.

The following supplication was given to us by Prophet Muhammad, upon him peace and blessings, to turn to God, seeking His help in purifying our egos.

> *O Allah! I seek refuge in You from the inability (to do good), indolence, cowardice, miserliness, decrepitude and torment of the grave.*

> *O Allah! Grant me the sense of piety and purify my soul as You are the Best to purify it. You are its Guardian and its Protecting Friend.*

> *O Allah! I seek refuge in You from the knowledge which is not beneficial, and from a heart which does not fear (You), and from desire which is not satisfied, and from supplication which is not answered.*
>
> —Riyad as-Salihin

> *What can Allah gain by your punishment, if ye are grateful and ye believe? Nay, it is Allah that recogniseth (all good), and knoweth all things.*
>
> —Quran 4:147

We are always seeking to be delivered from the evil of others, and we should as there is some truth to that. However, since we are not angels and have egos, and ego can betray us, it is also wise to ask God to deliver us form the evil within us. Prophet Muhammad, upon him peace and blessings, taught us: "O Allah! Inspire in me guidance and deliver me from the evils within myself" (Abu Dawud and at-Tirmidhi).

The *nafs*, or ego, has a shadow. Turning to yourself with love does not mean you will always love yourself. As Carl Jung said, the more loudly you proclaim something, the inverse is true. Your shadow.

To clarify, we do not hate the self as well. That is not the aim. C.S. Lewis, who said, "Humility is not thinking less of yourself, it's thinking of yourself less."

In self-help books, they teach you that if you tell someone not to think about X, they will think about X. Rather, occupy your mind with what you should be thinking about. Praising God nurtures humility within us as we think about ourselves less.

I recall a scholar who taught a group of mental health counselors to teach patients to focus on the gaze of God instead of themselves. We see this response in the Quran when Moses, upon him peace, meets the Pharaoh. Whether the illness is self-hate or self-love, the cure is the same: Praise God.

Prophet Muhammad, upon him peace and blessings, did not have a shadow because his heart was constantly preoccupied with the remembrance of God.

With every need, Prophet Muhammad, upon him peace and blessings, taught us how to turn to God and seek help for that need. Of course, this does not mean we act irresponsibly and refuse good work to answer the supplication. It means we strive as much as reasonable while making the supplication, asking God to help us with the debt. 'Ali, may Allah be pleased with him, reported:

> *A slave who had made a contract with his master to pay for his freedom, came to me and said: "I am unable to fulfill my obligation, so help me."*
>
> *He said to him: "Shall I not teach you a supplication which the Messenger of Allah, upon him peace and blessings, taught me? It will surely prove so effective that if you have a debt as large as a huge mountain, Allah will surely pay it for you.*
>
> *Say: "O Allah! Grant me enough of what You make lawful so that I may dispense with what You make unlawful, and enable me by Your Grace to dispense with all but You."*

—At-Tirmidhi

Lying by omission

Lying by omission and vagueness is a trademark of an abuser, a manipulative liar, not a healer or a believer. Lying is a powerful tool used by manipulative people to gain control and power, and can be done by omission, vagueness, and withholding crucial information. Be mindful to not use God or hide behind "a litany of true facts" to manipulate, abuse, or mislead people to falsehood or a story that is layers of lies upon lies.

If you do not want someone to expose parts of the truth, do not harass them with those lies from every direction, bombarding them like the US carpet-bombs countries into submission.

We have two figures in the Quran in the story of Moses, upon him peace, to reflect on: al-Khidr and as-Samiri. Hopefully, this will help us differentiate between a trustworthy spiritual teacher supported by God and a charlatan using God for egotistical purposes.

The following supplication is unique in that it is also a verse in the Quran. This supplication manifests how God nurtured Prophet Muhammad, upon him peace and blessings.

> *And pray in the small watches of the morning: (it would be) an additional prayer (or spiritual profit) for thee: soon will thy Lord raise thee to a Station of Praise and Glory!*

> *Say: "O my Lord! Let my entry be by the Gate of Truth and Honour, and likewise my exit by the Gate of Truth and Honour; and grant me from Thy Presence an authority to aid (me)."*
>
> —Quran 17:79-80

There is a saying from Prophet Muhammad, upon him peace and blessings, that there will come a time when people will believe a liar, and the truthful one will be called a liar. Both sides in a dispute can claim to be the truthful person treated as a liar and find friends to accuse the other as the liar believed to be truthful.

However, this is not how I understand the *hadith*. I understand it as saying there will come a time when human beings will not be able to tell the liar from the truthful person because they will make their decisions based on nepotism, tribalism, and all manifestations of egoism. And we are witness to this reality throughout the world. Look at the Iraq War, for example.

The prophets were also accused of being liars. So, if you are accused of lying—and you can stand in prayer, enter your grave, and stand before God with your truth—then comfort yourself with the stories of the prophets. I mentioned this before. It actually was shared by a counselor I respect.

> *The truthful prayer is never a prayer of supplication (plea or request), but a prayer of gratitude. The reason is that when you pray with a plea, your request is a statement of lack and encourages a constant focus on a feeling of being short of Allah's mercy. This conveys a sense of lack of gratitude to Allah Almighty and therefore recreates the perception of being lacking in life.*

Most of us cannot claim this reality. If we were honest, we would say there are days we need to repent for failing that test. However, if we study the life of Prophet Muhammad, upon him peace and blessings—his whole life—we find this does fit him well.

When he told God, "You have right to reprimand me until you are pleased," this showed a manifestation of the depth of his tremendous gratitude to Allah. You can say this to one who has been very good to you, and you do not deny that goodness. You do not say it to a tyrant or an abuser.

You can ask, "Well, what about the trials and tribulations he faced? How can one be grateful for that?"

Ibn 'Ata'Allah, a world-renowned scholar, said in one of his aphorisms, "Whenever you are elated when given to, but unhappy when withheld from, you may infer from it you are still in your dependency, and your lack of sincerity in your servanthood."

Prophet Muhammad, upon him peace and blessings, would supplicate to God, saying:

> *O Allah, by Your knowledge of the unseen and Your power over creation, keep me alive so long as You know that living is good for me and cause me to die when You know that death is better for me.*
>
> *O Allah, cause me to fear You in secret and in public. I ask You to make me true in speech in times of pleasure and of anger. I ask You to make me moderate in times of wealth and poverty. And I ask You for everlasting delight and joy that will never cease. I ask You to make me pleased with that which You have decreed and for an easy life after death. I ask You for the sweetness of looking upon Your face and a longing to meet You in a manner that does not entail a calamity that will bring about harm or a trial that will cause deviation.*
>
> *O Allah, beautify us with the adornment of faith and make us among those who guide and are rightly guided.*
>
> —Sunan an-Nasa'i 1306

In life, we want the best. That is natural as humans being born in a state of honor. We can seek the best according to our human perception or turn the matter over to God. Prophet Muhammad, upon him peace and blessings, taught us to supplicate:

> *O Allah, I ask of You the best request, the best supplication, the best success, the best work, the best reward, the best life and the best death. And make me firm, let my balance [of good] be heavy, fulfill my belief, elevate my position [in your eyes], accept my prayer and forgive my sin. And I ask of You the highest degrees in Paradise. Ameen.*
>
> *O Allah, I ask of Your the beginnings of good and its endings, all its aspects, its first and its last, its apparent [side] and it unapparent [side], and the highest degrees in Paradise. Ameen.*
>
> *O Allah, I ask of You the good that comes to me and the good of what I do and the good of my work and the good of what I conceal and the good of what I reveal and the*

highest degrees in Paradise. Ameen.

O Allah, I ask You to raise high my reputation [in your eyes], relieve me of my burden, set right my affairs, purify my heart, guard my chastity, illuminate my heart, and forgive my sin. And I ask of You the highest degrees in Paradise. Ameen.

O Allah, I ask You to bless me in my hearing, in my sight, in my soul, in my body, in my manners, in my family, in my life, in my death and in my work and to accept my good deeds. And I ask of You the highest degrees in Paradise. Ameen.

—Al-Hakim and at-Tabarani

Debt and poverty can overwhelm a person mentally, emotionally, and socially. Being poor is not fun, and it can lead to temptation to fall in grave sins, just to get out of debt or avoid poverty. This is a reasonable concern that can preoccupy one's mind. We are given the below to call on God, for help and aid.

O Allah! Lord of the seven heavens and Lord of the Magnificent Throne. Our Lord and the Lord of everything. Splitter of the grain and the date-stone. Revealer of the Torah and the Injeel (Bible) and the Furqan (the Quran), I seek refuge in You from the evil of everything that You shall seize by the forelock. O Allah You are the First and nothing has come before you, and You are the Last, and nothing may come after You. You are the Most High, nothing is above You and You are the Most Near, and nothing is nearer than You. Remove our debts from us and enrich us against poverty.

—at-Tirmidhi 3481

[A]nd shown him the two highways [of good and evil]?

—Quran 90:10

We do not appreciate the following supplication until we understand how it protects us from a state of *kufr*, or ingratitude. This ingratitude does not just harm one; it is also a state embedded with arrogance—not ignorance where one learns from their oppressors how to justify and rationalize such oppression onto others.

Instead of learning what not to do, we absorb the spirit of our oppressors and learn what to do. Refuse the first call to lie via omission. Prophet Muhammad, upon him peace and blessings, taught us the following:

> *When something happened that pleases us, say: "Praise is to Allah Who by His blessings all good things are perfected. And if something happened that displeased us, say, "Praise is to Allah in all circumstances."*

—Hisn al-Muslim, 218

An example is Pharaoh wanted to question God and Moses, upon him peace, regarding the accidental death of the Egyptian soldier while overlooking his oppression of the children of Israel.

Another example, is the life of Elie Wiesel and how he wanted to question God on the Holocaust while overlooking his own lack of compassion toward Palestinians as well as his hatred and justification for the ongoing ethnic cleansing of Palestinians.

We seek refuge from God in following in such footsteps or for any trial to turn us to such a state of arrogance. We then find a choice to make when we are shown the two highways.

When you accept the first call to lie via omission with respect to God, you continue to accept the subsequent calls to lie via omission with respect to His creation.

May Allah enable us to choose the path that pleases Him. The steep path is described in the verses following Verse 10 of Chapter 90 in the Holy Quran.

Alhamdulillah, or Praise be to God, were the first words of Prophet Adam, upon him peace, when he received the Divine Breath. While we cannot change the past—meaning we did not say this during the first strike of a calamity—we can repent for those moments and say it going forward.

If you see one in calamity, take a moment, and ask God to open the doors of all good for them, relieve them of their trial, and bring happiness to their lives. If you are able to be the means of that prayer, do so. If not, keep praying for them:

> *Nor does he say (aught) of (his own) Desire.*

—Quran 53:3

We appreciate this verse and how God describes Prophet Muhammad, upon him peace and blessings, when we clash with people who love *laghw*, or vain talk and rumors. Whatever you entertain in your ears will come out of your mouth. Hence, if you are an avid listener to lies, you are someone addicted to *laghw* or vain talk that has no value and possibly can fall into slander and telling lies. Maybe you are empty inside and need lots of attention, and this is the means to get it. Maybe you are afraid to know your true self and talking aimlessly is your means of escape.

Whether it is in religion or any field of science, such people spend so much time talking, speculating, assuming, and rationalizing out of their own desire. There is no methodology to measure and evaluate their speech.

Prophet Muhammad, upon him peace and blessings, taught his followers to beware of the evil of the tongue and hearing: Shakal bin Humaid, May Allah be pleased with him, reported:

> *I asked: "O Messenger of Allah, teach me a prayer." He, upon him peace and blessings, said, "Say: O Allah! I seek refuge in You from the evils of my hearing, the evils of my seeing, the evils of my tongue; the evils of my heart and the evils of passions."*

—Abu Dawud and At-Tirmidhi

Prophet Muhammad, upon him peace and blessings, taught Muslims to say: "O Allah, I ask of You beneficial knowledge and I seek refuge in You from knowledge that does not benefit."

Some knowledge is a healing, and some is harmful. A case in point is the Chernobyl incident, which has much to teach us if we pause and reflect. I mentioned in *God Intervenes Between A Person And Their Heart*, a documentary about the nuclear containment zone called "Radioactive Wolves" shows the containment zone, where people have been barred since the 1986 nuclear accident. Although it was turned into a "dead zone" for humans, the documentary shows the different species that thrive there. Ultimately, we see how toxic humans can be and how, if we are not in touch with the Divine, we can be more harmful than nuclear waste.

> *Behold, We have willed that all beauty on earth be a means by which We put people to a test, [showing] which of them are best in conduct; and, verily, [in time] We shall reduce all that is on it to barren dust!*

—Quran 18:7-8

It is narrated on the authority of Abu Sa'id that the Messenger of Allah, upon him peace and blessings, said:

> On the Day of Judgment there will be a flag for every person guilty of the breach of faith. It will be raised in proportion to the extent of his guilt; and there is no guilt of treachery more serious than the one committed by the ruler.

—Sahih Muslim 1738b

It was narrated by Abu Sa'eed al-Khudri that the Messenger of Allah, upon him peace and blessings, said: "For every traitor a banner will be set up on the Day of Resurrection, commensurate with his treachery. "In another saying narrated by Abu Hurairah:

> The Messenger of Allah, upon him peace and blessings, said: "O Allah, I seek refuge in You from hunger, for it is a bad companion, and I seek refuge with You from treachery, for it is a bad inner trait in one's heart."

In yet another saying, Sufyan ibn Usayd al-Hadrami reported that he heard the Prophet, may Allah bless him and grant him peace, say, "It is great treachery to tell something to your brother so that he believes you when you are lying to him."

> Call unto your Sustainer humbly, and in the secrecy of your hearts. Verily, He loves not those who transgress the bounds of what is right.

—Quran 7:55

Praising God Protects You in Times of Trial

> And had he not been of those who exalt Allah, He would have remained inside its belly until the Day they are resurrected.

—Quran 37:143–144

Imam Ahmad ibn Hanbal narrated that the Prophet, upon him peace and blessings, said: "Whatever you say in celebration of Allah's Glory, Majesty, and Oneness, and all your words of Praise for Him gather around the Throne of Allah. These words resound like the buzzing of bees, and call attention to the person who uttered them to Allah. Don't you wish to have someone there in the presence of Allah who would call attention to you?"

It is not enough that we speak to God but we must do so at His Station, not ours. We must use His Most Beautiful Names. At a human level, we acknowledge and talk to people with the respect of their station: president, doctor, queen, et cetera.

Likewise, when we supplicate to God, we must do so with the respect due to His Majesty.

Abu Hurairah reported that whenever the Prophet, upon him peace and blessings, was faced with a serious difficulty, he would raise his head to the sky and supplicate, "Subhan-Allah al-'Azhim (Glory be to Allah, the Mighty)."

And when he implored seriously and strongly, he would say "Ya Hayyu, Ya Qayyum (O Ever-Living One, O Self-Existing One upon Whom we all depend)" (*hadith* of Tirmidhi).

One should begin by praising God and follow with sending peace and blessings upon Prophet Muhammad.

Supplication should be done in humility as I mentioned, for oneself or on behalf of others. Use God's Most Beautiful Names. Face Mecca while doing so if you can conclude by sending peace and blessings upon Prophet Muhammad, upon him peace and blessings.

Make it private and lower your voice. This is meant between you and God. Be persistent as a child is persistent when they want something from their parents. Do not use blame or accusatory statements. Ask God for His Pleasure. The supplication should be in a state of gratitude seeking God's pleasure, not blaming Him for the blows of life.

> *This is a recital of the Mercy of thy Lord to His servant Zakariya. Behold! he cried to his Lord in secret, Praying:*
>
> *O my Lord! infirm indeed are my bones, and the hair of my head doth glisten with grey: but never am I unblest, O my Lord, in my prayer to Thee!*
>
> *Now I fear (what) my relatives (and colleagues) (will do) after me: but my wife is barren: so give me an heir as from Thyself.*
>
> *(One that) will (truly) represent me, and represent the posterity of Jacob; and make him, O my Lord! one with whom Thou art well-pleased!*
>
> —Quran 19:2–6

Those who are afflicted with a trial should say for themselves or others:

> *Umm Salamah narrated: "I heard the Messenger of Allah, upon him peace and blessings, saying, 'When a person suffers from a calamity and utters: "We belong to Allah and to Him we shall return. O Allah! Compensate me in my affliction, recompense my loss and give me something better in exchange for it), then Allah surely compensates him with reward and better substitute." '"*

—Muslim

It is a reminder in our trial that this is His universe, His dominion, and we are His property. It also reminds us of the destination. We can ask God to help us weather the trials and tribulations of life.

> *[H]e cried through the depths of darkness (saying): "There is no God but You, Glorified be You! Truly, I have been of the wrongdoers."*

—Quran 21:87

> *Then the fish swallowed him, while he was blameworthy. And had he not been of those who exalt Allah, He would have remained inside its belly until the Day they are resurrected. But We threw him onto the open shore while he was ill. And We caused to grow over him a gourd vine. And We sent him to [his people of] a hundred thousand or more. And they believed, so We gave them enjoyment [of life] for a time.*

—Quran 37:142–148

And regarding holding people accountable to their own law:

> *(The Egyptians) said: "What then shall be the penalty of this, if ye are (proved) to have lied?" They said: "The penalty should be that he in whose saddle-bag it is found, should be held (as bondman) to atone for the (crime). Thus it is we punish the wrong-doers!"*

—Quran 74–75

You might want to read a few scholarly commentaries on these verses. In doing so, you will connect to the Quran holistically.

If one is feeling distressed or anxious, they can turn to God and ask Him by His Mercy to protect their soul. Again, here the reference to the two names of God: *Al-Hayy* and *Al-Qayyum*.

> *O Ever-Living One, O Eternal One, by Your mercy I call on You to set right all my affairs. Do not place me in charge of my soul even for the blinking of an eye (i.e., a moment). There is none worthy of worship but You.*
>
> —Abu Dawud 4/324; Ahmad 5/42

Some suggested to say these one hundred times before dawn break. We see the two names mentioned together in the magnificent verse of the throne.

Direct, clear, and straightforward

God was direct, clear, and straightforward in the Quran that this is an abode of trials and tribulations. Hence, sometimes the shock is our false expectations of the nature of this world or life's journey, not the trial itself. We had a false view of reality, and the pain we feel is due to that false understanding and those false expectations.

At times, this is why we hurl accusations at God. Sometimes, the trials come to awaken us to the reality of this life. If you are falling asleep during the test, the trial might be the means to wake you up, to educate you on God's Message, and bring you to a higher knowledge of God.

> *Be sure we shall test you with something of fear and hunger, some loss in goods or lives or the fruits (of your toil), but give glad tidings to those who patiently persevere, Who say, when afflicted with calamity: "To Allah We belong, and to Him is our return," They are those on whom (Descend) blessings from Allah, and Mercy, and they are the ones that receive guidance.*
>
> —Quran 2:155-157

The verses reinforce each other time and time again in the Quran, clarifying to us, that trials are faced with God, by God, and for God. They are not for the ego or to be a spiritual guru.

As the verses above mention: "(Descend) blessings from Allah, and Mercy, and they are the ones that receive guidance."

The cure or blessings to weather the trial does not come from the self, but from God. Hence, there is no benefit to self-love or forgiving ourselves. Rather, we are asked to turn to God, and He will guide us. The Forgiveness that comes from God can give us the strength to face the Pharaoh in his own kingdom.

> *[But when Moses had delivered his message, Pharaoh] said: "Did we not bring thee up among us when thou wert a child? And didst thou not spend among us years of thy [later] life? And yet thou didst commit that [heinous] deed of thine, and [hast thus shown that] thou art one of the ingrate!"*
>
> *Moses said, "I did it then, when I was an ignorant (as regards my Lord and His Message). So I fled from you when I feared you. But my Lord has granted me religious knowledge, and Prophethood, and appointed me as one of the Messengers. And this is the past favour with which you reproach me, and that you have enslaved the children of Israel."*

—Quran 26:18–21

At times, the guidance is to repent; at other times, it is to be patient, seek knowledge, or stand up to an oppressor, and still other times, it is to accept God's decree as everything belongs to Him, including ourselves. Mu'adh bin Jabal, May Allah be pleased with him, reported:

> *Messenger of Allah, upon him peace and blessings, held my hand and said, "O Mu'adh, By Allah, I love you and advise you not to miss supplicating after every Salat (prayer) saying: O Allah, help me remember You, expressing gratitude to You and worship You in the best manner."*

—Riyad as-Salihin 384

This includes remembrance, gratitude, and worshipping God as He wishes to be worshipped, also come from God and not the self. So, we should persistently seek them, as what we sincerely and truthfully seek from God will find us, in this world or the next.

The Possessor of the Strong Rope

What does the strong rope refer to? Research scholarly commentary on the following verse:

> *It is He who supported you with His help and with the believers. And brought together their hearts. If you had spent all that is in the earth, you could not have brought their hearts together; but Allah brought them together.*
>
> —Quran 8:62-63

Years, ago, I recall trying to make peace between people, and I could not. When I read the Quran to calm myself down after things got worse, and I ran across the verses above. When I read the verses again in the context of the life journey of Prophet Muhammad, upon him peace and blessings, and the Ansaar, they took a whole new meaning and dimension.

Before Islam, the Ansaar's disbelief had them standing at the edge of a pit of the fire, but Allah Most High saved them from it and delivered them to faith. The Messenger of Allah, upon him peace and blessings, reminded the Ansaar (from both Aws and Khazraj) of this bounty when he was dividing the war booty of Hunayn.

During that time, some Ansaar did not like the way the booty was divided since they did not get what the others did, although that was what Allah Most High directed His Prophet to do. The Messenger of Allah, upon him peace and blessings, gave them a speech, in which he said,

> *O Ansaar! Did I not find you misguided, and Allah directed you to guidance because of me? Were you not divided beforehand, and Allah united you around me? Were you not poor and Allah enriched you because of me?*
>
> —Scholarly commentary of Ibn Al Kathir

To each question, they would answer, "Indeed, Allah and His Messenger have granted us the bounty." Reflect on the following supplication as well. Note the names of God used, the reference to self and God, the glorification to God, et cetera.

What does it mean to you in your life journey? In the journey of the Ansaar? A companion of the Prophet, Ibn Abbas, may God be pleased with him, narrated:

> *I heard the Messenger of Allah, upon him peace and blessings, saying:*
>
> *"O Allah, I ask You of Your mercy, that You guide by it my heart, and gather by it my affair, and bring together*

that which has been scattered of my affairs, and correct with it that which is hidden from me, and raise by it that which is apparent from me, and purify by it my actions, and inspire me by it with that which contains my guidance, and protect me by it from that which I seek protection, and protect me by it from every evil.

O Allah give me faith and certainty after which there is no disbelief, and mercy, by which I may attain the high level of Your generosity in the world and the Hereafter.

O Allah, I ask You for success [in that which You grant, and relief] in the Judgment, and the positions of the martyrs, and the provision of the successful, and aid against the enemies.

O Allah, I leave to You my need, and my actions are weak, I am in need of Your mercy, so I ask You, O Decider of the affairs, and O Healer of the chests, as You separate me from the punishment of the blazing flame, and from seeking destruction, and from the trial of the graves.

O Allah, whatever my opinion has fallen short of, and my intention has not reached it, and my request has not encompassed it, of good that You have promised to anyone from Your creation, or any good You are going to give to any of Your servants, then indeed, I seek it from You and I ask You for it, by Your mercy, O Lord of the Worlds.

O Allah, Possessor of the strong rope, and the guided affair, I ask You for security on the Appointed Day, and Paradise on the Day of Immortality along with the witnesses, brought-close, who bow and prostrate, who fulfill the covenants, You are Merciful, Loving, and indeed, You do what You wish.

O Allah, make us guided guiders and not misguided misguiders, an ally to Your friends, an enemy to Your enemies. We love due to Your love, those who love You, and hate, due to Your enmity those who oppose You.

O Allah, this is the supplication (that we are capable of), and it is upon You to respond, and this is the effort (that we are capable of), and upon You is the reliance.

O Allah, appoint a light in my heart for me, and a light in my grave, and light in front of me, and light behind me, and light on my right, and light on my left, and light above me, and light below me, and light in my hearing,

> and light in my vision, and light in my hair, and light in my skin, and light in my flesh, and light in my blood, and light in my bones.
>
> O Allah, magnify for me light, and appoint for me a light. Glory is to the One who wears Glory and grants by it. Glory is to the One for Whom glorification is not fitting except for Him, the Possessor of Honor and Bounties. Glory is to the Possessor of Glory and Generosity. Glory is to the Possessor of Majesty and Honor."

—at-Tirmidhi 3419

Supplication and Response

I listened to a few reminders of making prayers during blessed nights. Most, if not all, stressed the importance of having certainty that God will address your prayer.

I address the issue of psychotherapy and prayers repeatedly. However, I stress less on getting a material issue and more on the blessings within, mainly to ensure our prayer is not a complaint or an accusation.

We all have moments in our lives when we struggle with what we can say is temporary mental illness as a result of various life events and factors. This is aimed at such conversations.

Part of worship is to make prayers or supplications to God. Growing up, I used to read books on thought stopping. I also looked into monitoring one's breath, as well as receiving biofeedback. I learned from that experience the importance of monitoring our thoughts. Hence, I look at the feelings and thoughts embedded in supplications. Here is an example from Prophet Zakariya.

In Chapter 19 of the Quran, Maryam, at the end of Verse 4: "[A]nd never have I been in my supplication to You, my Lord, complaining in an accusatory manner."

This leads to a question: What if we do not get what we want or what we supplicated for? Do we stop supplicating?

Some scholars teach that supplication repels the Lord's Decree, which leads to supplicating and supplicating and do not get what they we supplicated for and stopping supplicating altogether. How does one reconcile this and help people?

Shaykh Ramadan al-Bouti's addressed this in one of his lessons on "Learn, Then Speak."

A questioner asks me, and he says, "You once said that supplication (du'a) does not repel the Lord's Decree (qadaa')."

Shaykh al-Bouti: Yes, and I say, once again, that supplication is part of the decree. The decree repels the decree.

Supplication is not something outside the decree.

Our master, Umar, when he was approaching Amwas and heard about the plague of Amwas, that it had spread inside Amwas, he didn't enter it.

One of the Companions then came to him and said, "Are you fleeing from the decree of Allah?" In other words, enter it. What are you worried about?

He replied, "I am fleeing from the decree of Allah to the decree of Allah."

In other words, this fleeing of mine, and returning to the al-Madinah; is this outside the decree of Allah?

Let's say someone has fallen ill and I ask Allah to cure him, and he is thus cured; is my supplication not part of Allah's decree? Was it not recorded in Allah's knowledge that I would supplicate to Him?

Was it not in Allah's knowledge that He would answer me? And what is the decree? It is Allah's knowledge of what will happen.

Yes, and the hadith that only supplication repels decree does not mean that supplication is outside the decree. No.

Rather, the meaning of this hadith is that man must supplicate, and not say, "By Allah, why should I supplicate?"

"If Allah has decreed that such and such will happen, it will happen, whether I supplicate or not. If Allah has decreed that such and such will not happen, I could supplicate for twenty years and it still won't happen."

Just as the illness is part of the decree, the supplication is part of the decree. Any prayer that I do, by my choice, is part of the decree.

My fasting is part of the decree. My reading of the Quran is part of the decree. My seeking refuge in Allah is part of the decree. Thus, the decree repels the decree.

And Allah's decree, Glorified and Exalted is He, can be

> repelled. And this the meaning of His statement, Glorified and Exalted is He: "Allah erases whatever He wills or endorses it. The Master Copy of the Book is in His Hands. (Quran 13:39)"

Thus, He erases something decreed and replaces it with something decreed. Maintaining the ties of kinship, what do you do? This increases your lifespan, and you prolong the time. You extend the time. The same goes for charity. These are facts.

What if God does not give you what you asked for? Shaykh Ramadan al-Bouti and Imam al-Sha'rawi shared the following:

1. First, repent privately, not for show and tell.
2. Repair the harm, give people their rights, or return to people their property.
3. Find more powerless and helpless people than you and help them, seeking nothing in return.
4. Fix your income and purify it from impermissible wealth.
5. Do not ask why or question God's wisdom. Trust and have a good opinion of God.
6. The oppressed will be aided according to God's timing. Keep supplicating and follow steps 1–5.
7. God will respond to your prayers according to His wisdom and timing. Be patient; we do not know the timing.
8. We pray out of need, but we do not obligate Him. If you stop, who are you going to run to?
9. Some righteous people do not pray to God for dunya (materialism); they only pray for akhirah (beneficial deeds for the next life), like a good ending, honorable resurrection, et cetera.
10. It is not obligatory to pray for dunya. Still, it is obligatory to pray for akhirah (prayer, hajj, faith, guidance, salvation, acceptance of deeds, making good deeds, love of God, love of the prophets, etc.).

How Do We Know We Are Sincere or the Saliheen (Righteous)?

You cannot investigate yourself; doing so would be equivalent to Israel investigating its soldiers. Anyone who investigates themselves is delusory. Self-investigation can lead to biased conclusions and hinder one's ability to see their transgressions objectively. Instead, following the example of the Prophets by having faith in God, following His commands, and striving for righteousness through prayer may lead to more genuine self-improvement. The Prophets simply had an awe of God, obeying His commands, trusted His judgment and decree, and prayed to be of the *saliheen* (righteous).

> *And admit me, by Thy Grace, to the ranks of Thy righteous Servants.*
>
> —Prophet Suleiman (Solomon), upon him peace

> *Take Thou my soul (at death) as one submitting to Thy will (as a Muslim), and unite me with the righteous.*
>
> —Prophet Yusuf (Joseph), upon him peace

> *O, My Lord! Let my entry be by the Gate of Truth and Honour. and likewise my exit by the Gate of Truth and Honour; and grant me from Thy Presence an authority to aid(me).*
>
> —Prophet Muhammad, upon him peace and blessings

They tasted His Love. We learn from these verses, and there are others; just keep supplicating and doing good work that pleases God, Most High. Your grade will be given to you after you transition to the next world, not before.

Always, always be in a state of *dua* (supplication) and keep the end in mind.

> *We will remove whatever amount of malice they had in their hearts. Rivers will flow beneath them, and they will say, "All praise is to Allah who has guided us to this. We would not have been able to find the way, had Allah not guided us. Surely, the messengers of our Lord came with the truth." Then they will receive a call, "Here is the Paradise which you have been made to inherit because of the deeds you have been doing."*
>
> —Quran 7:43

Ego (*Nafs*) versus Faith

O Humanity! What has seduced thee from thy Lord, the Most Generous? Who created you, proportioned you, and balanced you? Fashioned thee in due proportion, and gave thee a just bias; In whatever Form He wills, does He put thee together. Nay! But ye do reject Right and Judgment! (Quran 82:2-9)

What prevents us from receiving love from God? Our ego. How do we know if it's the ego taking the lead or the soul? The ego is constantly searching for validation, for reassurance, win an argument, and for material support. The soul, on the other hand, is always seeking its Creator.

The soul knows that happiness doesn't come from the sort of "success" in which we aim to be better than others. Happiness comes from a state of contentment, or spiritual peace, that only God can grant us. If we're not happy, then we need to seek happiness from God and to open our hearts to receive it through remembrance of Him and constant repentance.

When we remember God often, we put our souls back in charge, and slowly, God aids us in controlling our egos and polishing our hearts. When our hearts are polished, we begin to see egoism and materialism as unhealthy. Our love for guidance grows greater than our desire for external validation. We begin to love seclusion and moments of silence. We become conscious of the tremendous beauty of the universe.

Cleansing Our Idols

When we think of cleansing a place of "idols," or of "idol worship," we think of things outside ourselves. But just as Mecca was cleansed of idols, so, too, we must cleanse the idols that lurk inside our hearts, leaving only God to dwell within. In this way, our ego cannot "hijack" our faith.

These idols are not always material. Sometimes they are our fears, desires, dreams, insecurities, plans, and/or loves. This does not mean we should not have dreams and desires. But if they compete with God, we will be tested with them until we rely on Him alone, instead of our insecurities or failed plans.

The same can be said of how some people use religion. Satan used religion as an idol or a stepping stone to reach his ambitions, instead of as a guiding light and a path to God. Satan talked the religious talk, but he did not know the first thing about real love of God. Satan feared love and could receive love neither from God nor from Adam, upon him peace.

The road to a love of God and to self-love is the road of self-purification. As we grow in religion, we must face our fear of rejection, abandonment, and loneliness with faith and closeness to God. We do not need to fear these psychological struggles. But it is important not to paper over them with feel-good strategies of validation and motivation.

How Do We Open Ourselves to Receive Love?

Often, we hear the word *love* and immediately think of romantic love. All humans need some kind of connection with others and some sort of love. But if you have in your mind a fixed image of what that love is, then you might be blind to the gift of love that God is sending you.

If we find ourselves resentful over what we have lost, we can pray to God to gift us peace and surrender. Sometimes it helps to think about our last day. This is not just true for religious people but for everyone. Steve Jobs said, "Remembering that I'll be dead soon is the most important tool I've ever encountered to help me make the big choices in life."

Almost all external expectations—pride, fear of embarrassment or failure—fall away in the face of death, leaving only what is truly important. Remembering death is the best way to avoid the trap of fear. You are already naked. There is no reason not to follow your heart to God.

No one wants to die. And yet death is the destination we all share. No one has ever escaped it, and that is how it should be as death is life's great agent of change.

By remembering our death and imagining that today is our last day, we can focus on what is right. We can focus prayers, our children, our responsibilities, and our purpose.

Purifying one's heart is hard work, especially after a marriage has ended. Peace is not fluff. We have to learn and implement healthy boundaries.

Learning boundaries is hard. You have to know what each person's rights are and commit to fulfilling them, no matter how you feel about that person. In doing so, you learn to live Islam by learning and seeking guidance and then by modeling, guiding, teaching, and counseling with loving care and concern.

> *All humans are dead except those who have knowledge. And all those who have knowledge are asleep, except those who do good deeds. And those who do good deeds are deceived, except those who are sincere. And those who are sincere are always in a state of worry.*
>
> —Imam al-Shafi'i

A life of struggle and noble effort builds trust with God. If we do not call ourselves or answer the call to that road, then we end up abusing Islam when we embrace a holier-than-thou judgmentalism that is used to oppress and control others. We want others to be more "Islamic" or "obedient" to us, instead of to God.

We have to let go and not wait for anyone else to change for us. We have to allow others to live their own lives. Sometimes that can be difficult as we are emotional beings. But if we can commit to praying for them, without placing conditions on that prayer, then we can move forward. Then if an ex-spouse changes and has a successful marriage with someone else, you will hold no resentment. If you find yourself resisting, remember that Prophet Muhammad, upon him peace and blessings, was willing to let his spouses go with a handsome gift.

Our mind is a tool, and we must reclaim it from the society that wants us to define success or love by material means. By taking that path, we grow to hate each other in the competition for status and power. When we are instead remembering God, our consciousness will start to unfold and remove the chains imposed by society. Then we can begin to relate to this world as a bridge to the next world.

When we make other people our competitors and judges, then either they or we become vindictive and rejoice in the misfortunes of others. We can overcome this by increasing our self-knowledge and becoming determined to live according to our values, free from dependence on others or the ego, seeking reliance on God.

Aisha, may God be pleased with her, was nurtured toward this road after facing the pain of a scandal. Society turned against her, so she had to fully rely on God and seek His protection.

If we do not measure up to our values, then we can always repent and continue forward. Islam is not a religion of despair and self-hatred. We can engage ourselves and try to accept the gifts God sent to aid us on our journey. In this way, the feelings of discomfort will be purged so we can start to feel at peace with who we are.

A Different Question

Instead of constantly asking ourselves, "Am I happy?" or "Do I love this person?" or "Does this person love me?" we should ask ourselves, "Is God pleased with my actions and my thoughts?"

One man asked 'Ali ibn Abu Talib about his *nafs* or ego. 'Ali ibn Abu Talib replied, "Of which *nafs* are you eager to become aware?"

"Is there more than one *nafs*?" the man asked.

"Yes," said 'Ali ibn Abu Talib. "There are four: *nafs* of growth, *nafs* of sensibility (animal spirit), *nafs* of pure intellect, and *nafs* of wholeness and divinity.

"Each one of the *nufus* (plural of *nafs*) has powers and qualities of its own." We learn about the different aspects that come into play with our true intentions toward any act, person, or thing. The level of self-interest affects the outcome.

We might also learn that specific environments are debilitating, and others lead to equilibrium. We might also understand that peace comes from God and not from our ego or others.

After each prayer, Prophet Muhammad, upon him peace and blessings, taught us to say:

> O Allah You are the Peace and from You comes the Peace. Give us the Peace. Blessed art Thou the most High. O Lord of Majesty and Bounty.
>
> —Sahih Muslim 592

In this process, we become more aware because we have become more familiar with who we are and who others are. When this happens, confusion dissipates because the clarity of what influences and egos are at play and our relationship to them becomes more transparent. Thus, we become less confused, God willing.

I was listening to Shaykh al-Sha'rawi on *Al-Fatiha*. One of the things that the scholar said was that the Quran is a miracle, and God took it upon himself to guard the Quran. It has its own station of respect as it is the word of God. No one can fully interpret the Quran; however, we turn to the Quran seeking knowledge and understanding based on our life experiences. Each person has their limitations. A scholar can do commentary, a jurist can pass religious edicts, while a common person can extract reflections to strengthen their faith and connection to God.

Prophet Muhammad, upon him peace and blessings, was very honest and trustworthy in receiving the Quran, implementing the rulings or Sacred Law that are agreed upon by jurists in each generation. However, the secrets of the Quran will be revealed when their realities are given birth upon mankind. For example, fornication, murder, and stealing are sins. They are agreed upon in each generation and place.

When God told us to seek refuge from Satan when reading the Quran, He wanted us to approach the Quran by first purifying our hearts and minds from any falsehood. What does Satan do? He puts whispers and thoughts into our hearts and pollutes our minds, so our reading becomes polluted with his thoughts and whispers. Faith does not absorb what is outside. Faith absorbs the light and knowledge from the Quran. To absorb people around you, you are going to be following the crowd. You are not going to be following what the Quran is inspiring, teaching, making permissible or prohibited.

Can Men and Women Play Games?

> *(Allah) knows of (the tricks) that deceive with the eyes, and all that the hearts (of men) conceal. And Allah will judge with (justice and) Truth: but those whom (men) invoke besides Him, will not (be in a position) to judge at all. Verily it is Allah (alone) Who hears and sees (all things).*
>
> —Quran 40:19–20

Hawa is wind. There is a value in wind, such as sailing boats, pumping water, and generating electricity. Winds can also remove rooftops, destroy homes, blow down power lines, and cause damage.

Mind games do not just exist between men and women where the context is sex and love. Satan did not play games with Adam, upon him peace, and ask him to engage in fornication or passion. Games are calls to disobedience to God. This behavior needs to be called out, and for too long, we would just say that men play mind games. Instead, men fear God and do not play games. If we always assume they have to do with sex or love and just obsess with "do not approach *zina* or fornication," we do not resolve using games to call to disobedience.

God cursed Satan for plotting and planning for another to slip or calling for disobedience and using religion's cloth to do so. I have never heard of lectures online or offline in Muslim settings in which playing games was addressed, and people were told to repent for doing so. As we are human beings, every sin is not far from us, so I always add the word *protection* as an acknowledgment of God's grace upon me for not engaging in it as well as an acknowledgment of our need for His protection from engaging in it.

By the grace of God, I lived a very chaste and noble life. The teachings in this theme are not aimed at making permissible what Islam made impermissible. My mother taught us to pray and fast at a very young age. I also wore hijab out of my own volition at a very young age. However, while we judge matters on the outside, God judges matters of the heart. Our faith requires us to learn matters of the heart and check ourselves, not others. Arrogant people obsess with checking others, instead of checking themselves.

Likewise, we should encourage people not to play games and teach ourselves not to play games with others. We study ostentation, pride, arrogance, et cetera. We also need to discuss playing games or sinful, cunning behavior that aims to cheat, manipulate, insult, deceive, or call others away from God.

Often, our evil is hidden. We mask it while playing Mr. and Ms. Piety. We gaslight the victim that the games we played are all in their mind. It could be an insult, a false accusation, slander, shade, or emotional and mental abuse, using means that hide us from facing judgment or rebuke. These are the actions of cowards who cannot face their opponent or fear being exposed as liars or penalized for harassment. While we cannot see this treacherous inner world outside, God reminds us that He sees it and will call us to account for it.

Shaykh al-Sha'rawi relates a story where Prophet Muhammad, upon him peace and blessings, had to judge between two people. And one person was better at arguing his case. In other words, he was a good lawyer. Prophet Muhammad, upon him peace and blessings, judged on his behalf. Yet he said, "If I decide in favor of one who is guilty, the person goes to hell as he knew he was lying." If you are so skilled at playing games and lying that even the Prophet judges in your favor, yet God can see your inner treacherous world—what does that say about you? There is a *hadith* that the Messenger of Allah, upon him peace and blessings, said:

> *The first of people against whom judgment will be pronounced on the Day of Resurrection will be a man who died a martyr. He will be brought, and Allah will make known to him His favors and he will recognize them. [The Almighty] will say: And what did you do about them? He will say: I fought for you until I died a martyr. He will say: You have lied—you did but fight that it might be said [of you]: He is courageous. And so, it was said. Then he will be ordered to be dragged along on his face until he is cast into Hellfire.*

> *[Another] will be a man who has studied [religious] knowledge and has taught it and who used to recite the Quran. He will be brought, and Allah will make known to him His favors and he will recognize them. [The Almighty] will say: And what did you do about them? He will say: I studied [religious] knowledge and I taught it and I recited the Quran for Your sake. He will say: You have lied—you did but study [religious] knowledge that it might be said [of you]: He is learned. And you recited the Quran that it might be said [of you]: He is a reciter. And so, it was said. Then he will be ordered to be dragged along on his face until he is cast into Hellfire.*

> *[Another] will be a man whom Allah had made rich and to whom He had given all kinds of wealth. He will be brought, and Allah will make known to him His favors and he will recognize them. [The Almighty] will say: And what did you do about them? He will say: I left no path [untrodden] in which You like money to be spent without spending in it for Your sake. He will say: You have lied—you did but do so that it might be said [of you]: He is*

> *open-handed. And so, it was said. Then he will be ordered to be dragged along on his face until he is cast into Hellfire.*
>
> —Muslim, Tirmidhi, and an-Nasa'i

This should not discourage the actions but encourage us to engage in these actions for the sake of God. We can turn to God and ask for a sincere intention.

In one of his lessons, Dr. Ramadan al-Bouti explained how we should look at blessings, whether they are in grace or material possessions. We should be between two extremes: reward for good deeds and delusion for insincerity within. This reflection or view of the good we do for God purifies our inner world from using religion to harm ourselves and others.

Trust and security are essential for a relationship that provides the necessary foundation for building a community. Playing games is a form of betrayal, which undermines trust and faith. It nurtures feelings of insecurity in the one who is the target of the games of manipulation. Every relationship that lacks security robs those involved of giving and receiving, as well as compassion and mercy for one another.

A lack of trust and security breeds a lack of growth and resilience in the face of hardships and challenges. Betrayal can shake our faith and undermine inner resilience. Our reactions rob our community of creativity, security, and learning from situations that unfold.

Forgiveness becomes a struggle, not because of expectations of perfection but because of a lack of security and trust in the relationship. In the struggle between the ego and soul, the fight for the reins emerges. The games we rationalize teach some manipulation, control, exploitation—all of which limit our potential as human beings and members of our community. These games never teach us to want the best for one another. This creates an environment where we "mask" our true feelings for one another. We smile but not from the heart. We preach, but we do not transform. We communicate, but we do not listen to what is said. We read without reflection or understanding.

However, some take advantage of others' weaknesses, nurturing further insecurity and lack of trust. The games breed a cycle in which maturity is not nurtured. If we look at our communities, we witness double standards in social values, allowing men to violate their values yet demand angelic perfection from women. This creates a cycle of hurting each other and is evident in our relationships within the community.

We must challenge the game playing and ask, "Is there a particular situation that enables the games?"

Most men's and women's egos desire a partner or friendship that will be submissive, unquestioning, and selfless, and yet their souls will crave a partner or friend with character traits that help free them, not entrap them in their egoism and bad habits. The former partner burdens the community by making us weaker, vulnerable, and unable to grow.

Examples:

A woman was married to a man who was a nurturer, but she dumped him for a submissive, unquestioning, and selfless husband. She ran from her first husband and clashed with another person who was like her ex-husband. She was constantly fighting with this person because deep down within her soul, she was crying to be freed from the manipulation games that entrapped and shackled her. Subconsciously, a target of manipulation is chosen for the character traits the offender needs to free themselves from the games and manipulation that entraps them. They are in a spiritual and psychological prison. This is also true for men.

Some like to remain in the "boys will be boys" and "girls will be girls" club because they have become addicted to the attention and fame this brings. They have a nice wife yet claim to need another. They have another sweet and kind soul, yet their soul is never satisfied because it was never a partner they were seeking, but attention and escape from their true selves.

Some have a self-perception that cannot handle being confronted for fear of discovering their true self or not wanting to be responsible for fulfilling a role faithfully. They see themselves as leaders of the community and confuse respect with worship.

Peter Pan and Neverland. Why grow up when you can live in Neverland? Games allow us to avoid adulthood's realities and what requires us to nurture our community's sense of security and trust.

When we refuse to rationalize games or manipulation, we open doors for our community to grow and heal. We must turn to God and seek His forgiveness for avoiding the challenge of confronting this situation. As we confront these games, we can appreciate the many spiritual lessons that can help rewire our brains and thoughts toward each other. "People disappoint" becomes an enabling voice that undermines our need to confront the critical situations before us.

Imagine if we taught that we human beings are the property of God, and God has obligated us to responsibilities that we will be required to fulfill. I, as a community member, will nurture our community's sense of trust and security by not undermining that role that another person needs to fulfill, as well as the obligations that are required of them. Suppose we challenge ourselves to pray, *"I seek refuge that I should come between You and your creation, the target person and their responsibility, as well as this person and their heart."*

Moreover, if you are blind to a matter, God will make you aware of it and answer your prayer by removing the person from your life.

God made Joseph, upon him peace, aware of Zulaikha's inner world to grant Joseph, upon him peace, the choice to stay or remove himself. Likewise, although we can only judge the outside, God will make us aware if someone is not clean inside and is attempting to play games of manipulation directly or via third parties. Remove yourself and close the door.

Joseph tried to teach the women in the Kingdom the skills they needed to grow, opening new communication lines to learn about and understand one another faithfully. If they are sincere and faithful to God, they will repent instead of doubling down, and God will transform them. If not, and they continue with tricks and games and practice them on other people, God will discipline them at an appointed time.

> *But for such as fear the time when they will stand before (the Judgment Seat of) their Lord, there will be two Gardens. Then which of the favours of your Lord will ye deny?*
>
> —Quran 55:46–47

The word *maqam* is translated here as *judgment seat*. It can also be translated as *station*. As I pointed out before, we are called to worship God at His Station, not ours. Hence, we must think "Lord of the Worlds" and "Master of Day of Judgment."

I discussed Joseph, upon him peace, but some ask if there is an example of a woman like Joseph, upon him peace. Yes, there are many. An angel appeared in the form of a man before Mary, the mother of Jesus, upon them peace. She said, "I seek refuge from thee to (Allah) Most Gracious: (come not near) if thou dost fear Allah" (Quran 19:18).

We do not always control the environment. At times, our lives are such that we do not always find the boundaries that Islam puts in place between the opposite genders can be implemented by choice or faith.

Some examples:

1. A young woman in a coma for ten years in Arizona is found in labor pain, giving birth.
2. Refugees and orphans.
3. Your car stopped on the road.
4. Target of a scheme by a psychopath, charlatan, and their cult crew.
5. Case of when Aisha was left alone, caravan left.

As much as we want to assume that we can always control the environment, the truth is we cannot. This is not a signal to violate Islamic teachings in gender interaction, but to do the work within. We fast because God sent down commands for fasting, be you poor or rich. Likewise, we practice boundaries between gender interaction because God sent down commands to do so. However, in the fasting is a call to work on jIhad (*an-nafs*). Likewise, in the boundaries, you must work on yourself and how you view the opposite gender: as a sex object or a human being who is the property of God with responsibilities.

God might remove these boundaries and test you by force, choice, scheme, or otherwise. A well-known Muslim scholar of the past, Imam al-Ghazali, said:

> *If the first inward thought is not warded off, it will generate a desire, then the desire will generate a wish, and the wish will generate an intention, and the intention will generate the action, and the action will result in ruin and divine wrath. Just so, evil must be cut off at its root, which is when it is simply a thought that crosses the mind, from which all the other things follow on.*

We saw these examples in Mary and Joseph, upon them peace. What will God witness of you if He was to test you?

Saving Women

Research the sex cult NXIVM (pronounced "nexium") that sold itself as a self-help group to empower women. They see themselves as "badass." In this case, it was a man using a cocktail of knowledge in many areas and preying on people's desire for empowerment.

Keith Raniere could heal them of emotional traumas, set them free from their fears and attachments, clear patterns of destructive thinking. Some believed he could heal them sexually too. "This is the white-collar spiritual path," an ex-member says. "You're on the monk's path, but you're not wearing a red robe with a shaved head."

We will be tested in life with good and bad people. If you resist both and cannot differentiate between a good person and a bad person, then you are oppositional and have a hatred of authority. The reference to the Israelite who resisted the soldier must be compared with Moses, upon him peace, who also resisted the soldier, accidentally killing him to save a fellow Jew.

The Israelite resisted the soldier and threw Moses, upon him peace, who just saved his life, under the bus. He accused him of wanting to be a tyrant in the land, which was a projection of his own reality. Not everyone supported Martin Luther King Jr. or Malcolm X. There were Blacks who were against them.

However, although Moses, upon him peace, was living under the Pharaoh, he could recognize and live under Prophet Shuy'ab, Asiya, and his brother Aaron (Haroon), upon them peace. Some of the children of Israel did not welcome Moses or Aaron as leaders. Reflect on your "Why?" when you resist. Sometimes we claim a faith, ethics, or principles that are pure lip service when put to a test.

Hijab and Modesty

If men and women cannot play games, shouldn't that be sufficient as a reminder and admonition? As human beings, we forget or become distracted—we need more visual reminders.

I recall during the COVID-19 pandemic reading a few articles from various colleges explaining that masks not only protect you from spreading or catching the virus, but they also serve as a visual reminder to be cautious and take all necessary precautions when engaging each other. We tend to forget when we talk that we are living during a pandemic; hence, the mask is a visual reminder to all of us to be cautious.

Similarly, the hijab, worn by both men and women, serves as a visual boundary. For Muslim women, it is a symbol of modesty and religious piety and symbolizes their devotion to Allah and desires to please Him above all else. While for Muslim men, it is a sign of respect for women and a reminder to lower their gaze.

Finally, as we wear hijab, we must understand that our focus is on God, not on how others wear or do not wear it. There is a saying by Prophet Muhammad, upon him peace and blessings, that if you can safeguard your tongue and your private parts from engaging in unislamic behavior, he will guarantee for you heaven or *Jannah*. The reality is that if you are not mindful of one, you are not mindful of the other.

> *And [they are] those who do not testify to falsehood, and when they pass near ill speech, they pass by with dignity. And those who, when reminded of the verses of their Lord, do not fall upon them deaf and blind. And those who say, "Our Lord, grant us from among our spouses and offspring comfort to our eyes and make us an example for the righteous."*
>
> —Quran 72–74

We should learn from those who got COVID 19 after calling it a hoax and died. When truth hits, it does not care if you believe in it or not. Investigate issues genuinely, respect experts in the field, or say, "I do not know." So, how do we respond?

Acknowledge the struggle in faith and allow people to struggle; however, the representatives of God to humanity are the prophets. The leader of the prophets is Prophet Muhammad, upon him peace and blessings. Encourage the youth to have a connection to the prophets. Discourage youth from taking any celebrity as a role model for their faith, whether or not they wear hijab.

Humble their expectations of people of faith. Prophet Joseph's brothers threw him in a well, and they were children of a prophet. Later, they repented and reunited with Joseph, upon him peace. The stories of the prophets should be amplified for youth and teenagers, nurturing their hearts and souls on the reality of life as a place of trials, tribulations, and tests.

Teach them *al-Fatiha* and its commentary as it is a torch that lights the way in good and bad times. Review its full meaning and read it while fully present with God in times of confusion, with a heart seeking guidance and the straight path. We have before us a situation in which we can see our contribution if we recall how often we pressured women to promote Islam in such a way that comes off as marketing for desperate attention and approval, instead of inviting people to reflect on the core message or on the Beautiful Names of God.

I know a lot of women who took off their hijab and are not social media influencers but, in the past, were giving presentations on stage for MSA or during Islam Awareness Week.

Mary, upon Her Peace

There are two extremes in expectations. One is that the person who wears hijab sees herself as the venerated and honorable Mary, the mother of Jesus, upon them peace. The other extreme is that people expect those who wear hijab to be at the station of *Sayyidah* Maryam or the venerated and honorable Mary, the mother of Jesus, upon them peace.

> *Behold! the angels said: "O Mary, indeed Allah has chosen you and purified you and chosen you above the women of the worlds."*
>
> —Quran 3:42

Maryam is a role model, a religious leader, and a person chosen by God to give birth to and nurture one of the five resolute prophets: namely, Prophet Jesus, upon him peace. Her story, wisdom, piety, and character should be studied and reviewed. While we cannot reach her station or have false expectations that others may be at her station, we can study her life year after year and review the lessons. And, there are other women, such as Hajar, Khadijah, Asiyah, Fatima, et cetera.

When you engage, you do not know, clarify, verify, and communicate with faith and ethics. If you do not trust the other person or think they are a liar, avoid them. If you cannot avoid them and keep running after them to compel them to your perception and narrative, this reflects that you are projecting realities and flaws that you see in yourself but are unwilling to accept onto them. Truth does not force another person to their narrative; falsehood does.

People violate their values for many reasons. I am focusing on modesty here, so I will not touch on abuse or sexual harassment matters. I am speaking about an intention to lure, seduce, flirt with, or meddle with another party without right or permission. Marriage gives one permission.

Remind and Educate

Prophet Muhammad, upon him peace and blessings, talked to a man who openly said he loved *zina*, or fornication. The Prophet questioned him, if he likes others to treat his female relatives in kind, and the man said no. Briefly, he educated him to treat other females how he loves his female relatives to be treated.

He did not say; men play games or men's nature is to seduce women. Rather, he taught him to stop this behavior through education. The Prophet did warn men that women are a temptation, meaning that is an area of weakness; hence they need to be on guard, not put their guard down and act irresponsibly.

We see this in both Joseph and Mary, who placed God before the other. Although the Angel did not call Mary like Joseph was called, his entrance in her private quarters is a reason for her to place God before him.

Use Your Power and Remove Yourself

If reminders and education are not working, and you realized you do not trust the person, then use your power and walk away. Joseph, upon him peace, *ran* away. So, if you accuse someone of being a violator, you have the responsibility of removing yourself from their presence. You might want to send them a "cease and desist" letter if they continue.

At times, you will need to report the person. Once verbal communication is violated, keep all communication written, as such individuals will backpedal, change their story, and claim you violated them. In short, violations will take place, intentionally, unintentionally, knowingly, and unknowingly, out of ignorance, arrogance, and all the permutations in between.

We need to be responsible and follow guidelines of the Sacred Law and not compromise our values for acceptance and belonging. Any deviations from these boundaries could cause individuals to experience significant distress.

Friendship

CONSIDER the flight of time! Verily, man is bound to lose himself. Unless he be of those who attain to faith, and do good works, and enjoin upon one another the keeping to truth, and enjoin upon one another patience in adversity.

—Quran 103:1–3

As we begin with the end in mind, taking *al-Fatiha* with us as a torch, we experience the passage of time and face adversities along the way. According to Islamic teachings, what does friendship mean, or how do we understand the meaning of friendship? Let us review some questions:

Can the Pharaoh and Asiya be friends? They are married. No, the Pharaoh killed his wife.

Can Prophet Noah and his wife be friends? He is a prophet, and they are married. No, she betrayed him, and so did his son.

Can Satan and Adam be friends? Satan said he was a sincere adviser, and Adam, upon him peace, was a prophet. No, Satan deceived Adam by twisting and distorting the truth, then projecting his reality unto him.

Can Abraham and his family be friends? They are family. No, his father had him exiled after throwing him in a fire.

Can Joseph and his brothers be friends? They are children of righteous people. No, they threw him in a well and sold him into slavery. Why? If we reflect on the chapters: *Al-Fatiha*, the opening, and *al-Asr*, the passage of time, emphasize:

1. Believe in God and the Day of Judgment.
2. Need for guidance.
3. Journey or straight path to a destination when many are calling you away from that path, such that it will lead you to loss.
4. To avoid the loss, you need someone with the same worldview who will give and receive advice and provide and receive reminders to be patient, as this is the abode of trials and tribulations.
5. Call each other to do good deeds that are acceptable to God.

Aisha, may God be pleased with her, was slandered. Prophet Muhammad, upon him peace and blessings, did not run after the hypocrites as with hypocrites, you leave them to God. God, Most High, does not purify some people because there is no goodness in them to purify. Purification is for people who have goodness in them and need to be polished as the view is not that they are bad, but more like gold or diamonds in the dirt. With friends, you invest and nurture. There is a commitment, responsibility, and accountability to a worldview and faith in this companionship. The Quran describes this relationship as *awliya*, or protecting friends. Other translations for this word are *helpers, supporters, friends*, and *protectors*.

> *And the believers, men and women, are protecting friends one of another; they enjoin the right and forbid the wrong, and they establish worship and they pay the poor-due, and they obey Allah and His messenger. As for these, Allah will have mercy on them. Lo! Allah is Mighty, Wise.*
>
> —Quran 9:71

The Quran that describes Muslim men and women are protecting friends. Let us unpack the implications in the question:

1. It is immodest.
2. If men and women are friends, that means they can be alone with each other.
3. If men and women are friends, that means they have premarital sex.
4. If men and women are friends, that means they will flirt.
5. If men and women are friends, that means impermissible actions will take place.

However, that is not the definition of friendship in Islam. A friend is someone who helps you on the straight path, be they a man or woman. When you commit to being a friend to someone, you commit to giving and receiving advice and reminders of patience. It is a two-way street. Friendship in Islam is not about luring and games. It is a special relationship embedded in faith and commitment to sincere and truthful traveling on the straight path, reminding each other of the commands of God and abiding by the boundaries of interaction set by God. This includes the saying of Mary, the mother of Jesus, upon them peace, who said to the Angel who appeared to her as a man, "Indeed, I seek refuge in the Most Merciful from you, [so leave me], if you should be fearing of Allah" (Quran 19:18).

Ego Games Disguised as Help

Many years ago, a Turkish series titled *Mohannad*, which was dubbed in Arabic, made waves in the Arab countries. The series was about a Turkish couple who were worlds apart and got married via an arranged marriage. I did not watch the series, but it was very hot among Arabs when it came out, and everywhere you visited, people were discussing the latest episode or watching it.

One scene showed Noor, the wife, arguing with Mohannad as he was always dropping everything to help other women. Although this was a show, it contained some lessons that are worthy of reflection. I know a man who destroyed his marriage because he was always running after the damsel in distress while ignoring his wife.

Likewise, Noor wanted his attention and love, and he was always obsessed with helping other women. In this case, Mohannad is a beautiful and attractive man, and the women called for his help and welcomed it. His wife was so angry that he would drop her needs and her desire for attention from him to run after these helpless damsels in distress.

Mohannad was married and had a mother and father, and his focus should have been on his wife and family, resolving problems and giving them attention and love. However, men who lie to themselves or whose egos lie to them or both spend, considerable time helping women out there.

What about people who need our help? Get your priorities right. There is nothing wrong with helping people; however, it should be welcomed and not sacrifice the rights of those who God obligated you to look after. If your marriage is shaky or your help is going to create marital problems, find someone else to help the individual and protect your marriage and family from falling apart. Adhere to Islamic guidelines while doing so, as Moses, upon him peace when he helped the two women near the well.

Between Egoism and Conformity

People are blind to the boundaries that protect others from their harm and the boundaries they can set to protect themselves from others' harm, whether the boundaries are physical, emotional, or psychological. The interpretation a person places on others' actions and words is based on the light that dominates their heart. If you listen and observe, people tell on themselves. What might they be disclosing and unconsciously confessing? Throughout history, shaming has been the tool of oppressors, imperialists, and supremacists. To feel good about myself, I need you to feel small.

A case in point: Toni Morrison broke down racism in a sweeping 1993 interview with Charlie Rose. Her famous quote: "If you can only be tall, when someone is on their knees, then you have a very serious problem." I call it egoism. This quote raises the bar to more critical and reflective questions we should be exploring.

Am I Oppressing Myself or Others?

In order to center ourselves in that question mode, we can use the following supplication by Prophet Muhammad, upon him peace and blessings:

> *O Living! O Sustainer! I call upon Your Mercy for assistance, and from Your punishment I seek refuge! Make good all my affairs and do not entrust me to myself or any of Your creation even for the blink of an eye.*

The creation we witness is not artwork. Rather, it is a sign from God. You are not in a museum asked to fall in love with a work of art, then meet and greet the artist. Rather, there are meanings and purpose in the creation.

Whether you reflect on Pacific sunsets, a full moon rising on the ocean, the clouds from an airplane, the autumn forests in Raleigh, or the first fallen snows, the Quran teaches Muslims how to reflect on these signs, what to say to ourselves, and how to engage God, our Lord.

Guilt, Remorse, and Getting beyond the Self-Help Placebo

> *O Allah, I seek Your forgiveness for every sin that overtook me because I disrespectfully complained and objected to You for withholding Your subsistence from me, and because I turned away from You and inclined instead toward Your [powerless] servants in submissiveness and earnest petition; whereas You had let me hear Your clear statement in Your Book, "But they humbled not themselves to their Lord, nor did they submissively entreat [Him]" (al-Qur'an 23:76)*

> —*Hasan al-Basri, Prayers for Forgiveness*

It is important to distinguish between two very different emotional processes: *guilt* and *remorse.*

We sometimes think of the two as interchangeable, but in truth, they are very different. Guilt is connected to control, obligation, and fear. When we are feeling guilty, we are being shamed and disempowered. At times, this shame can be personal, part of a private controlling force. But often, guilt is part of a broad societal shaming.

For instance, Muslims have been pressured for the past twenty-one years, to feel guilty for the horrific events of September 11, 2001, as well as other violent attacks. We have been put on the guilt track, where we need to constantly excuse, explain, and apologize for a crime that took us by surprise as it did everybody else.

Indeed, this guilt denied American Muslims the space to grieve. We, too, needed to share with the rest of the community the process of loss. We, too, needed to work through our sorrow and fear.

Instead, we were roped by a feeling of guilt and shame and a burden to prove that we were *not* guilty. But in this case, there is nothing we can do to prove we are not guilty.

Still, the president's executive order evokes September 11, when permanent residents' access to their homes, jobs, and lives was revoked.

Remorse, meanwhile, is something entirely different. Remorse is personal, and remorse is empowering. We have all done something wrong, and we all know the feeling of having done wrong. This remorse—like the feeling of pain when we have cut ourselves, which directs us to wash out our cut and bandage it—is important. Without remorse, we would end up thinking we had never done anything wrong. We would never worry about violating our values or the rights of others.

What Is Remorse?

Remorse is not feelings of being bad. Remorse is an acknowledgement of our lack of God consciousness, our resolve to stay on the straight path, and the awe of God in our hearts coupled with love for God. How so?

> *Thou canst but admonish such a one as follows the Message and fears the (Lord) Most Gracious, unseen:*

> *give such a one, therefore, good tidings, of Forgiveness and a Reward most generous.*
>
> —Quran 36:11

Let us review the prayer or *dua* of Prophet Adam, upon him peace: "Our Lord! We have wronged ourselves. If You forgive us not, and bestow not upon us Your Mercy, we shall certainly be of the losers" (Quran 7:23).

First, an acknowledgement of God as Lord, not your buddy or peer. Second, an acknowledgement of wronging—not by God, but by oneself. Third, an acknowledgement of our need for God's Mercy and Forgiveness. Fourth, an acknowledgement that without God, we are losers. In a nutshell, that is remorse, hope for God's pleasure and acceptance.

Guilt allows us to be controlled from the outside. Remorse helps us take control of our own actions, accept them, cleanse our soul of actions that violate our values, repent, and become better people. Repentance is about nurturing our best and strongest selves.

Beyond the Hope Placebo

When I was early in my healing process, I turned to self-help motivations, positive thinking, and hope. It does make you feel good in the short term, or at least, it seems to. Much like the politics of hope, hope healing is ultimately a placebo that can distract us from the real issues in front of us.

As Professor Benjamin Bratton discussed in his talk, "What's Wrong with TED Talks," "placebo politics" can be much like "placebo medicine." Inspiration, hope, and positive thinking can make us feel good. But true transformation is about facing the hard stuff: injustice, political economy, policy.

A placebo can seem to have positive effects. But ultimately, on both a political and a personal level, the placebo is harmful because you cannot just say nice things and expect that everything will be OK. You have to deal with the heavy stuff—the social-justice issues and the racism—and, on a personal level, with trauma, remorse, and rebuilding. If you invest in things that make you feel good but do not solve problems, then you have only moved further away from healing.

What Does Repentance Have to Do with It?

Remorse is not something that makes us feel good. It is different from staring into a mirror and saying, "I'm a good person, and everything's going to be all right." Remorse can fill us with an unpleasant dread as we know we have to reach out and apologize or work to make ourselves better. We have to accept that we have done something that violates our values. It is hard. But it is also the path to real healing.

The process begins through connection and through emptying and cleansing our internal spiritual selves. We can use prayers of forgiveness for every time we violated our values and for every time, we failed to put our gifts to their best use. In an ideal world, we would take some sort of daily account of our actions and seek forgiveness for every time we violate our values.

This is not about self-flagellating or self-policing. Indeed, it is the motivational self-positive talk that's self-policing. By attempting to force your thoughts to change—to force away the negative—you are just shoving down the pain and not healing it. I have been down that route, where I tried to "fix" my thoughts and check my feelings, where I was very diligent in monitoring all these things.

But policing ourselves ultimately does not help. It is by really dealing with what we have done, calling ourselves to account, and repairing harm that we are being honest with ourselves and building from the ground up.

Repentance through Helping Others

Part of cleansing our soul of ego and finding our way to repentance is through using our gifts to help others. We must look for people we can help with our gifts without robbing them of their dignity or self-worth. It is very important we do not note or remind them that we are offering support—or even remind ourselves. But if we do, that is all right. It just becomes a moment to ask for forgiveness.

When we are helping somebody, we must try to do it in a state of servitude, not reminding them and not expecting any reward from them. This connectivity creates links between ourselves, others, and God.

We might say, if we are feeling low, that we have nothing to give. But if we search within ourselves, we can find a way to comfort someone hurting, to read to the blind or elderly, or to mentor a child.

There are many ways and many people to help, people with whom we can connect without asking for anything in return.

Through this process, we can cleanse ourselves of our ego and receive spiritual light. This does not mean we are reaching God through a bridge of our own making or that we are connecting because of our good deeds. As Ibn Ata Allah says:

> *If you were only to reach Him after all your misdeeds had been eliminated and your pretensions all obliterated you would never reach Him. But rather, when He wants to make you reach Him, He conceals your nature with His nature and your attribute with His attribute and makes you reach Him with what is from Him to you, not from what is from you to Him.*

It is important to remind ourselves through this process of repentance and vulnerability that we are not doing something *for* God, but rather, we are receiving *from* God.

We all act in ways that violate our values. We may not have killed someone, but there are many small acts we can find: looking at someone in disdain or speaking in a hurtful way. These are all things we can work on weeding out of our hearts.

In this way, we are not policing our thoughts or feelings or telling ourselves, "You must think positive thoughts!" We are recognizing that we are flawed and weak and that we can build ourselves into stronger people by recognizing that we are human beings who are bound by human limitations.

Toxic Guilt and False Responsibility

People with dark personalities who lack a conscience often blame innocent individuals, causing some to feel guilty even when they are innocent. Toxic guilt occurs when someone takes responsibility for something they didn't do.

We often become consumed with false guilt regarding our human relationships, preventing us from seeing the importance of our relationship with God. This false guilt causes us to unfairly judge ourselves and can lead to self-abuse rather than genuine repentance. It is essential to recognize and overcome this toxic guilt.

False responsibility has nothing to do with what's true and accurate, nor is it related to true repentance. Instead, it is usually the fear of rejection, and this disguise is seen by people who have a conscience and repent to God often. This repentance is to seek His pleasure and not people.

People driven by toxic guilt must shift their gaze from pleasing people to pleasing God. A quick look at the lives of the Prophets shows: they are divinely protected from sin, yet people, including family, still plotted to murder them.

Remorse and repentance, after all, are not acts of self-punishment. They are acts of great love for ourselves and the world around us. They show our willingness to work hard for ourselves and improve our lives and the world around us based on the laws sent down by God.

Muslims: Finding a Place of Contentment

> *He who wishes that people always remember him with goodness is neither God-fearing nor sincere.*
>
> —Shaykh Ibrahim ibn Adham

We start to feel inferior when we judge ourselves through the eyes of others. This is a trap, as material success, status, money, power, and privilege can never be enough. The more we have, the more we want. More of them leads not to more happiness but to a more impressive façade of happiness.

The ego-driven desires are often superficial and temporary, while soul-driven needs are more meaningful and long-lasting. By prioritizing the latter, we can achieve a sense of contentment and fulfillment that cannot be found through material possessions alone. Our ego is much like a horse, that the soul disciplines and rides.

Learning from Charlatans

> *Have you not seen those who claim themselves to be pure? Rather, Allah purifies whom He wills, and injustice is not done to them, [even] as much as a thread [inside a date seed]. (Quran 4:49)*

Sometimes you meet people with knowledge. These people both expand your horizons and strengthen your faith in God. Sometimes you meet charlatans. At first, they seem to offer you sincere advice and assistance, and yet it turns out to be toxic. A charlatan is someone who pretends to possess knowledge that they, in fact, lack. The word comes from the sixteenth-century Italian *ciarlatano*, or *quack*, and charlatans are often marked by the elaborate schemes they cook up to fool and control others.

How can we tell the difference, and what can we learn from charlatans?

Sometimes God puts you in the path of charlatans. This is not so they can teach you wisdom but so you can learn gratitude and humility from those who—like Satan and Pharaoh—try to pressure you into pledging your allegiance to them instead of God.

Knowledge and wisdom are a form of power. However, when they are misapplied, as by charlatans, they can do serious damage. It is important to learn from charlatans what *not* to do.

Charlatans often try to pressure us into being increasingly grateful. It is important for us to remember that *none* of us are sufficiently grateful. We can never enumerate the blessings of God as they are infinite. We all have room to increase our gratitude, but this should be directed primarily at God, not someone who tries to force us to be their followers.

Charlatans Who Act Like Satan: Lying by Omission and Vagueness

One of the characteristics of a certain type of charlatan is lies that operate on omission and vagueness. Obfuscating the truth is one of the most effective ways to manipulate others. But lies do not always directly mislead another person or tell a direct untruth.

Satan, for example, used lies of omission when he deceived Adam. Satan did not come right out and say: "Adam, you should disobey God." Instead, Satan approached Adam in a sneaky way, telling him, "Eating from this tree will help you." Satan reminded Adam about God, but then distracted him when it came to the facts. He kept things hidden and surrounded Adam with a haze of misinformation.

Often, when people manipulate us through lies of omission, they are not operating on a level playing field: emotionally, socially, or spiritually. They know more than we do, and they hold back key details while pretending—like Satan—to be a sincere adviser.

This form of lying is sometimes called gaslighting, and it involves making the other person uncertain of the world around them. If someone treats you in this way, the first thing you can do is to level out the playing field. Ask the person in question to see a counselor or mediator with you so that an independent person can listen to both sides and help the truth come out.

In our own lives, Satan keeps coming at us from every direction, trying to cause us to slip and fall by using deception. He is not going to come right out and say: "Don't pray." Instead, Satan might say: "Pray now or later." And then, he might say: "Wait another ten minutes." But his ultimate aim is to get you to obey him instead of God.

Pharaoh's Emotional Power: A Different Kind of Charlatanism

Pharaoh did not withhold information and create a haze of misinformation as Satan did. Instead, Pharaoh counted on the fear he instilled in others and a web of emotional power. Sometimes, abusers huff and puff and make themselves super powerful to their victims, so their victims live in perpetual fear.

Pharaoh counted on this sort of power and that no one would ever stand against him. When the magicians stood by Moses, that was the first sign Pharaoh's empire was crumbling. Pharaoh's raw emotional power is also a form of charlatanism. Instead of using lies of omission, gaslighting, and obfuscation, Pharaoh used outright physical power.

What links the two forms of charlatans is that Satan and Pharaoh, both placed themselves in the position of God's authority. They placed themselves between humans and God.

Why? Charlatans, like Satan, often act out of envy. Deep down, Satan could not accept the honor that Adam had been given. We all suffer from various degrees ingratitude, jealousy, and envy. The difference with Satan was that he felt he should be at the same station as God. Pharaoh, on the other hand, felt he *was* God. According to Islamic Law, Satan felt himself superior to man when, in fact, man was, by Allah's decree, superior. Although he does say Allah Most High is "Lord," he debates God's decree regarding Adam, upon him peace. When you debate someone, you place yourself at their station of knowledge.

As Susanna Barlow notes in "Understanding the Healer Archetype," sometimes a would-be healer can turn into a charlatan as they attempt to maintain control of a patient. The charlatan depends on "helping" others for validation and reinforcement. But ultimately, they put themselves in the place of God.

A charlatan is desperate for approval, and this need for approval keeps them worried and stressed. They cannot walk away from those they believe they are helping. Yet as Imam Ibn Hazm has noted, those who cross the line when offering advice and become a "seeker of submission and possession" are wrongdoers and not advisers.

One of the other commonalities is that both Pharaoh and Satan refused to lose. Instead of living and fighting for their beliefs, they fought with a result in mind, bending their values to suit the result. Both Pharaoh and Satan plotted in secret to bring down others who they perceived threatened them.

Handling loss is a sign of one's faith. Those who insist only on outcome are in danger of losing their moral compass entirely and ending up like Hitler or ISIS.

It is important to remember that God does not need us to reach out and help somebody. If God wants to use you, he will use you. If God wants to use someone else, he will. It is not for any individual to force their will and to compel others to submit to their advice and counsel. That kind of force is a sign not of an adviser, but of a charlatan. How do you know if you are acting as a charlatan?

Try to Walk Away

Sometimes, we *should* ask ourselves, "Am I acting more like an adviser or a charlatan?" If someone rejects your advice or assistance, are you able to let it go? Or do you try to force people to accept your love and support?

If someone says no, then it is time to walk away. You should not run after that person or compel them to accept your help.

It is impossible for us to say why our help was not wanted or needed in that moment. Maybe God did not will for that person to be healed. In the end, you cannot enter the domain between God and his servant, nor can you interfere with someone else's boundaries and force your will upon them. That is the act of a charlatan.

Finding the Right Guide

> *Without an escort you are bewildered on a familiar road;*
> *do not travel alone on a way you have not seen at all; do*
> *not turn your head away from the Guide.*
>
> —Rumi, Mathnawi

For one reason or another, you've decided that it's important to study Islam. How do you go on? How do you know if you've found the "right" teacher or guide in this quest?

One important thing to remember is that, in learning about Islam, you are not looking for someone who resonates with you. After all, part of learning about Islam is becoming aware of all that you *do not* know. You also have to recognize the relatively small role that conscious thought plays in decision-making. Subconscious thought plays a much greater role, and there is much about your own choices that you can never know.

Whether we are newly literate or a PhD, an elder or a teen, we must approach faith with an open mindedness and open heartedness. As the Egyptian Nobel laureate Naguib Mahfouz wrote early in his career, "What we have learned is still but a wave of light on an infinite ocean of darkness." In such a wide-open space, we must seek guidance and connect to others who can help us make the right decisions in learning and in life.

But how do we know if we are being guided to the right people?

We can know we are being guided by the right person by gauging how it feels to be guided. The wrong sort of guide is controlling. They lead, and you follow. When you have found the right sort of guide, you are not being led but nurtured, and you are being made aware of who you are.

When someone is guiding you well, they help you better understand yourself. After all, you cannot know God without knowing yourself. The right guide gives you a sense of power in the discovery of who you are, how you relate to others, and even what your weaknesses are. However, the right guide does not take advantage of your weaknesses, and their goal is not to connect you to themselves. They are connecting you to knowledge, self-knowledge, and God, *Al Hadi* (The Guide), who guides every creature to what it needs for its existence.

A good teacher wants to help you understand the material, not for you to be overly attached to them. At any moment, the right kind of teacher might leave, and you are on your own.

But when you are being poorly guided, you are guided to bond with the leader themselves. In an extreme version, young people are disconnected from their families and communities and are guided toward a militant or fascist philosophy like that of the so-called extremists of any faith. They are made to feel dependent on this bad-faith guide.

A nurturing guide will help you fully understand not only Islam but also the sciences because how can you decide in ignorance? As Shaykh Qays Arthur has said, "In reality true faith cannot obtain without knowledge."

Knowing God is not just a feeling. We have to dig into the sciences. In the Quran, faith in God is based on knowledge and conviction, not birth or affiliation.

But how can we know?

> *Show us the straight way, The way of those on whom Thou hast bestowed Thy Grace, those whose (portion) is not wrath, and who go not astray.*

—Quran 1:6-7

At times when we are ignorant, we cannot tell the difference between someone guiding us in the right direction and someone who is taking us down the wrong path.

Even though it might seem counterintuitive, it is important to find guides who say things that *do not* always resonate with us. First, turn to God, and seek His guidance, not once but repeatedly and sincerely. Be open to God, not others. I recently saw an interview with a woman who said she would follow Donald Trump wherever he went. Whatever he said, it resonated with her. This woman was not acknowledging ignorance or looking for knowledge. She was looking for someone to put the "God" stamp on the things she already believed.

If someone is a blind believer, then they're looking to be misled. They're looking for someone who'll echo their conscious and subconscious prejudices, and they don't want to wake up from their trance. In this woman's case, it was Trump, but it could've been any bad-faith guide who tells people what they already believe.

A blind believer is somebody who is not looking to be changed. On the outside, it might look like they're worshiping a leader, but in fact, they're just worshiping their own ego and beliefs. They're not looking to grow. They just want to hear what they already believe.

In any community, you will find these bad guides who make you feel as though you already know what needs to be known. They don't bring you to a place of self-knowledge or help you understand your limitations or weaknesses. For that, you need the right sort of guide.

Psychology and Spirituality

In finding the right sort of guide and learning more about ourselves and the people around us, it might help to study some psychology, but it's also good to understand a spirituality that helps us detect the diseases of the heart, such as arrogance and envy. Some of these diseases can blind a person from being guided.

Psychology at times acknowledges these spiritual illnesses: envy, jealousy, and arrogance. When someone is a habitual liar or they suffer from envy, for instance, there can be psychological effect. But often psychology doesn't acknowledge the envy, just the result, just as contemporary medicine often deals only with disease, not the causes of disease.

Yet these spiritual diseases have to be dealt with. The medicine psychology sometimes gives is a promotion of the ego. Spirituality, on the other hand, tends not to strengthen the ego but to subdue it. Spirituality is recognizing that I didn't pull myself up by my bootstraps or do everything by myself. That's ego. Spirituality helps us understand the concept of privilege. It helps us understand that, where we've benefited a lot, we need to give back.

With spirituality, we realize that if something good has reached us, there are a lot of people who helped out. Or perhaps it wasn't people but the gifts we were given or the landscape or the physical environment. When we see someone who's lost out to us, spirituality tells us not to see ourselves as better but to recognize that we have been privileged over that person and to take it with humility. After all, we were not created for ourselves alone. The strengths that God gave us are to be shared with others.

Spirituality teaches sharing, connectivity, selflessness, and generosity. These are some of the cures for spiritual illnesses and the medicine that a spiritual teacher might give.

Humility is very important here. If you ever reach a point where you think you know it all, then you are not leading but blindly following. Seeking knowledge is an imperative of life and an imperative of religion. We should seek knowledge from the cradle to the grave as we will never reach a point at which we know everything that we need to know. "And mankind have not been given of knowledge except a little"(Quran 17:85).

That which we are in ignorance of is greater than that which we know.

The Use and Misuse of Logic

Logic is an important tool for humans. However, as we are all probably aware, people often use facts to lie or to confirm and validate their prejudices.

"The point behind acknowledging our ignorance is keeping our feet firmly on the ground and rooted in reality." If one fears Allah, He will teach them. [Angels]They said: "Glory to Thee, of knowledge We have none, save what Thou Hast taught us: In truth it is Thou Who art perfect in knowledge and wisdom" (Quran 2:32)

In comparison, Satan answered his own question, which led to his loss. As we seek knowledge, we should ask God for humility so we not lose sight of the truth which is that it is all from God."

Envy: Curable and Incurable

> *Then know that the sickness of ignorance is of four sorts, one curable and the others incurable. Of these which cannot be cured, [the first] is one whose question or objection arises from envy and hate, [and envy cannot be cured for it is a chronic weakness] and every time you answer him with the best or clearest or plainest answer, that only increases his rage and envy. And the way is not to attempt an answer. One hopes for the removal of every enmity Except enmity arising from envy.*
>
> —Imam Ghazali, O Beloved Son

Why do people envy?

To envy is to feel discontent or to rebel against God in His distribution of His Gifts: a pious child, talent, strength, wisdom, wealth, et cetera. God's Gifts are gained without oppressing others; hence, you cannot steal and say, "God gave me this."

The truth is that all of us envy. However, some people envy more than others. Some turn to God and asked Him to cure them of envy while others hide their envy behind a veneer of superficiality and civility. A person who claims never to struggle with jealousy declares a purity that is not real.

In addition, some do not act on their envy or the evil traits or thoughts within themselves. If one does not act on their envy, hopefully, their envy does not harm them. Still, it is a disease. It is best, first and foremost, to examine our egos! We can tell others not to envy, but if we are honest about ourselves, we are hiding our envy.

Don't be content with your self-investigation. Ask Allah, knower of the unseen, to cleanse and protect your heart from envy. He is the best of judges. Ask Him to grant you a clean heart (*qalb saleem*), a sanctuary for you and others.

Many confuse response to oppression with envy. If you transgressed someone's boundaries then played the envy card, that is oppression as well. If someone wants to take back what is not yours, that is justice and not envy.

If you worked hard on something without oppressing others and someone wanted the fruits of your labor or wanted you to lose God's gifts upon you that you gained without oppression, that is envy. The story of Satan and Adam, upon him peace, can help you understand envy.

When you accuse someone of being envious of you, ask yourself the following: Did you engage in actions that harmed the accused? We know that Adam, upon him peace, did not. Likewise in the story of Cain and Abel. Did you respond to the accused as Adam, upon him peace, or Abel did?

As you reflect on these questions, you might discover that the envious person is you, and you are projecting it onto others, claiming they are envious of you. Reflect on the questions privately. Many people who harm others are telling stories that people are envious of them.

Trauma, Abuse, Pain, and Suffering

And never think that Allah is unaware of what the wrongdoers do. He only delays them for a Day when eyes will stare [in horror]. (Quran 14:42)

When we witness or experience oppression, we wonder why God is not responding. He is witnessing everything and responds at an appointed time. Oppression or abuse is a transgression of boundaries, including physical, psychological, mental, verbal, emotional, and spiritual. In addition, it is a misapplication of knowledge or violation of an agreement or covenant. I address the covenant between God and His creation in an earlier section.

Trauma consists of three main types. If it's a single incident, it is acute. Repeated and prolonged abuse such as domestic violence, colonization, and social ills is chronic. Exposure to varied and multiple traumatic events, often of an invasive, interpersonal nature such as rape, followed by domestic violence, discrimination, or abuse is complex. Trauma is the impact of the abuse on the victim.

Some therapists differentiate between retraumatization and successful reprocessing of trauma. With God's guidance, protection, and strength and immersive treatment, a person can be nurtured in hope for overcoming triggers during and after treatment without being overpowered. Without God's guidance, protection, and strength, a person will fall into a loop of retraumatization and not come out.

There is a difference between how Moses, upon him peace, faced oppression under the Pharaoh and how his followers faced their oppression. The key lesson is with God, by God, and for God.

Pain is inevitable. We will all face trials that will bring us emotional, mental, social, spiritual, and physical pain. I cannot comprehend some trials such as rape, the murder of loved ones, and arson. Suffering is based on how we interpret the trial and tribulation we are going through. Suffering comes when we reject the trial and go into denial. We might go from denial to questioning God.

Healing comes through surrendering to His Love, Mercy, and Wisdom. In doing so, we accept the pain and seek knowledge and insight to understand and heal. We are not asked to like it or be happy, but to seek His help to prevent suffering that might overpower us.

The stronger our relationship, not lip service, to God, the more we are able to heal the pain and protect ourselves internally from suffering and trauma.

> *In God, there is no sorrow or suffering or affliction. If you want to be free of all affliction and suffering, hold fast to God, and turn wholly to Him, and to no one else. Indeed, all your suffering comes from this: that you do not turn toward God and no one else.*
>
> —Imam al-Ghazali

When trials and tribulations hit, many people struggle in search for meaning while others fall into despair or seek means of escape.

Many faiths offer counseling on how to deal with trials and tribulations. In Islam, trials and tribulations are expected to hit as a test of faith and growth, and in the face of them, Muslims are to remind themselves and each other that "Allah suffices us and is the best to rely on" (Quran 3:173).

The 2010 earthquake in Haiti is one such example. The earthquake destroyed homes and damaged infrastructure, and the Haitian government confirmed a death toll of 170,000 and estimated over 300,000 injured. To add to the disaster, the rescue and relief efforts were severely limited by a shortage of resources.

Considering such large-scale destruction, many are left asking how this could happen and are now searching for answers. Where is the Divine Mercy in all this? Where is justice? Where is the Divine Wisdom? Many atheists are now using this as another sign that God does not exist.

In 2010, in the aftermath of the earthquake in Haiti, it was said that some questioned God while others came out of the rubble thanking God and singing His Praises.

I am not sure how I would respond to such a disaster, but trials and tribulations squeeze you and shake you. Hence, the question is "Where are you and I?" "Where is God?" indicates that the questioner is lost or disconnected from God.

> 'Ali ibn 'Abu Talib said, "Do not ask these three kinds of people to satisfy your needs: the liar, for surely they will make things seem near when they are in distant; the fool, for surely he will want to help you, but will only harm you; and the man whose own need is linked to your needs, for surely he will use your need as a means to secure his own need."

Every day we wake up in the morning to the call of our soul to free it or enslave it. The only way for our soul to be free is by turning and keeping it connected to our Creator, who honored it.

The best book that can help you face any trial and tribulation is the Quran. By reflecting on the stories of the Quran, you will create an emotional distance between you and your trauma, abuse, or pain. Hence, you can just listen and continue reading as it unfolds and repeats certain important junctions. It will help you understand what you are going through without focusing on your trauma.

Since we can only see the outside, our ability to understand what anyone else is going through is very limited. At best, we conjecture.

By reading the Quran as a book of reflection on yourself, comparing your actions and words to those God identifies as true and sincere, you will be able to distinguish those who are true from those who are false around you. You will also recognize the work you need to improve yourself to get closer to God Most High.

Turn to God, *Al Ghani*, the one free of need and want, in your needs, in prayer, and in supplication. He is always there when no one else is. The supplication cleanses the heart and strengthens your vision to see things differently. As you turn to God, He will direct your path toward Him.

Two Faces of the Trial

Trials and tribulations face us from two directions. In one direction, we are the underdog: oppressed and unprotected.

From another direction, if we are observant, the trial comes wrapped in another face, and we are the one with power, the enabler, the offender, et cetera.

If we are accurate in our claims for justice, the logic and spirit of oppression from both sides will be repulsive to our souls and spirit, and our hearts can find ease in seeking help with patience and prayer when we are the underdog.

If our claims for justice are motivated purely by egoism, tribalism, or any self-interest group, we will find it hard to seek help through patience and prayer.

We will be condemning injustice and oppression against us and our kind and passionately defending it when it is against others, and we stand to gain. Do you see the two faces or directions of the trial that God is testing you?

Case Studies of Guidance from the Quran

> *Just as he [Abraham] and his son reclaimed the foundation left by Adam and rebuilt upon it, sometimes our lives are left destroyed, and we too must rebuild upon the foundation which God gave us and ask Him to accept from us.*
>
> —Dar al-Ifta

If you want love, compassion, and kindness, seek it from God, and He will give it to you via the many means He has created. Sometimes, people we seek love from are incapable of giving or receiving love, or God sealed their hearts. We can obsess about why they are not perfect or leave the matter to God, as He is their creator.

In a world full of narcissists and trauma, how does one survive and continue their journey to Allah in a dignified manner?

As I mentioned in the last chapter, *God Intervenes Between A Person And Their Heart*: "Praising God inoculates you from becoming a narcissist or being drawn to narcissists. The best protection against narcissism is praising God...not taken in by strength, charm, or voice hogs."

What are the signs and symptoms of narcissism? Through the trial of Islamophobia, God taught us many lessons by our being profiled through the eyes of others. Concern yourselves with rights and responsibilities, not profiling. Did you fulfill the requests God will require of you? Did you transgress?

What are the roots of narcissism? Being great in the eyes of others or one's own eyes. Narcissists cannot accept being wrong or being defeated. They respond to being wrong with sinful cunning or *kade*, overpowering their opponent, manufacturing evidence, rumors or lies, creating chaos or sedition, or cheering crowds.

How to tell the difference between healthy self-esteem and arrogance? Healthy self-esteem is the courage to bring your evidence for investigation. Moses said, "Your appointment is on the day of the festival when the people assemble at mid-morning."

Oppressors hate transparency and accountability. When people fail to respond like Moses, upon him peace, and resort to sinful cunning games, behind the charm is denial, anger, fear, shame, anxiety, guilt, numbness, and projection. One can say that a narcissist will avoid clarity at all costs. However, they employ projection with skill.

The story of Joseph, upon him peace, teaches us that you can love someone and oppress him. You can hate someone and oppress him. Focus on rights and responsibilities, yours and others', not psychoanalyzing.

There is a belief that most people seek love in all the wrong places. I disagree. Most people seek security, not just now but historically. Our faith emphasizes that one of the names of Prophet Muhammad, upon him peace and blessings, is *Al Amin*.

Al Amin is translated as the trustworthy one and also as the sanctuary, the safe person. Currently, our discourse is saturated with love. This misleads people into looking for love or accepting claims of love in all the wrong places. In restorative justice, the emphasis is on safety.

The Messenger of Allah, upon him peace and blessings, said: "The Muslim is the one from whose tongue and hand the people are safe, and the believer is the one from whom the people's lives and wealth are safe." Again, the emphasis in Islamic teachings is on safety, not love.

In Joseph's story, "Emphasis on the Name of God, *Al-Waali*": "Thou art my Protector." Indirectly, *Ash Shaheed* or The Witness: "Verily my Lord understandeth best the mysteries of all that He planneth to do, for verily He is full of knowledge and wisdom."

Throughout the Quran, God reprimands those who seek protection other than God. "The parable of those who take protectors other than Allah is that of the spider, who builds (to itself) a house; but truly the flimsiest of houses is the spider's house—if they but knew" (Quran 29:41).

Easier said than put into practice, I agree. Usually, the failure might carry a message or training that the individual chose the means for protection rather than a means God uses to protect you. In Joseph's story, he was nurtured, repeatedly, to rely "completely on God." A case in point:

> *And of the two, to that one whom he consider about to be saved, he said: "Mention me to thy lord." But Satan made him forget to mention him to his lord: and (Joseph) lingered in prison for a few (more) years.*
>
> —Quran 12:42

What Is Emotional Abuse?

Emotional abuse is a non-physical form that manifests in various ways, including constant criticism, intimidation, manipulation, and unwillingness to be pleased.

Emotional abuse can brainwash the victim, slowly eroding their self-worth, self-trust, and overall sense of self. This abuse can take many forms, including constant criticism, intimidation, and humiliation disguised as help, support, or advice. Regardless the means used, the end result is always the same: the victim feels helpless, worthless, and powerless. Emotional abuse can have lasting effects, often leaving deeper scars than physical abuse.

The University of Tennessee Knoxville website's Counseling Center page outlines basic rights and an explanation of the types of emotional abuse, which include aggressing, denying, and minimizing. Some we've heard about from many speakers. However, one that might surprise you is the indirect aggressive type of emotional abuse: "helping."

> *[D]isguised as "helping." Criticizing, advising, offering solutions, analyzing, probing, and questioning another person may be a sincere attempt to help. In some instances, however, these behaviors may be an attempt to belittle, control, or demean rather than help. The underlying judgmental 'I know best' tone the abuser takes in these situations is inappropriate and creates unequal footing in peer relationships.*

Such individuals act in this emotionally abusive way in the community or among friends to compensate for their "victim" status in their home relationships. When a person spends a considerable amount of time giving unsolicited advice, they show signs of being overpowered by a person or possibly bad upbringing.

> *In friendships, however, you may play the role of abuser by withholding, manipulating, trying to "help" others, etc. Knowing yourself and understanding your past can prevent abuse from being recreated in your life.*

If we listen to their advice, they will indirectly and secretly offer it. They share with us that people tend to judge them and their family problems but forget that even the prophets were tested with domestic issues. The prophets did not have perfect families. However, while asking people not to judge them and their families, they exhibit a spirit that is very judgmental of others. Instead of learning what not to do, they absorb the spirit of their abusers and act accordingly with others.

We need to know and understand the basic rights of a healthy relationship to understand types of emotional abuse and assess where the violations have taken place. Therefore, learning about emotional abuse can help us heal and take precautions not to abuse others.

What's the Difference between Being Gaslighted and Being Triggered?

When I was young, our home burned down. Afterward, every time I saw a fire truck or heard of a fire; it would trigger memories of that difficult event. Over time, I was no longer triggered, although I still remembered it clearly. A trigger is anything stored in a person's memory that brings back a whole traumatic event. For a long time, if I saw or heard a fire truck, I would smell smoke, feel myself choking on it, and feel the panic I felt during the fire.

What of the person who triggered you or is being triggered?

Sometimes, the person who has triggered you has done something wrong. Perhaps you are triggered when you feel demeaned, and it brings up experiences of being humiliated. Those experiences can be from society, such as racism, sexism, or xenophobia, or childhood experiences from school or family members.

First, you should manage your trigger by calming yourself down. Later, you can address the demeaning comment as itself and not for all the feelings it's brought up inside you. I try to do this with Islamophobes.

To be gaslighted is much different. Gaslighting is a tactic whereby a person or people attempt to gain power by making someone question their reality, past or present. Triggering is generally incidental and accidental—the firefighters who turned on the siren didn't mean to harm anyone. But gaslighting is purposeful and intentional: the abuser tells someone, over and over, that an event *did not* happen, in order to gain or secure power. It is a way of undermining a person's confidence in themselves and their perceptions of the world.

Anyone can be susceptible to gaslighting. The term first became popular after it appeared in a 1938 play, *Gaslight*, by Patrick Hamilton, in which a husband dimmed the lights and told his wife she was imagining it. But it's a common technique of abusers at all levels of society, from family members to dictators. It's also used as a tool by particular groups. Islamophobes, for instance, use it against Muslims. Some use it against those with whom they disagree.

For example, sending people to harass you in various ways, then denying it or, if you react, accusing you of being triggered or being crazy. With gaslighting, the victim does not recall a past event but, rather, is having trouble processing the present event, given the actions and the denial of those actions by the abuser. Another example is creating a fake Facebook profile or using shade to attack someone. When questioned, the abuser denies it.

Triggers are about trauma or unprocessed events in one's life. Gaslighting is about power and control like Hegelian dialectic. Brad Thor explained this tool in the following way:

> *Hegelian dialectic—a psychological tool used to manipulate the masses. In this case, you create a problem, wait for the reaction, and then offer the solution. What people historically fail to realize, though, is that those offering the solution are the same people who caused the problem in the first place. They also fail to realize that no matter what the solution is, it always ends up providing its creators with more power.*

The gaslighter likewise engages in mental abuse, wearing an individual down until they completely depend on the reality and perception of the gaslighter.

Sometimes, those who gaslight others can seem well mannered and virtuous. The abuser might turn down the lights on their victim and tell them that they're mistaken about the dimness in a very civil way. As Syed Muhammad Naquib al-Attas has warned, we shouldn't view the concept of good manners in a simplistic way, by confusing virtue with social etiquette. A person can certainly be civil sounding and gentle sounding and also be an abuser. Many use social etiquette as a false cloak of softness.

However, an abuser cannot be virtuous. Professor al-Attas explains that values and social etiquette are human created. Yet virtue—like hope—is from God.

But just as being virtuous shouldn't be confused with civility, it shouldn't be confused with perfection either. The famous jurist and scholar Ibn 'Ata Allah al-Iskandari said, "If you were to be united with Him only after the extinction of your vices and the effacement of your pretensions, you would never be united with Him."

Instead, when God wants to unite you to Himself, He covers your attributes with his own, uniting you to Himself "by virtue of what comes from Him to you, not by virtue of what goes from you to Him."

Just as Mary inspired Zakariya to turn to God with true hope, the prophets and those near to God encourage us to seek virtues and hope from Him.

If you lost hope or feel angry is just the right moment to turn to God and seek hope from Him. When we do, we might use these prayers found in many books on supplications by Prophet Muhammad, upon him peace and blessings:

> O, God! I beseech You for guidance, piety, chastity, and contentment.
>
> O, God! Forgive me, have mercy on me, guide me, guard me against harm and provide me with sustenance and salvation.
>
> O God, make my religion easy for me by virtue of which my affairs are protected, set right for me my world where my life exists, make good for me my Hereafter which is my resort to which I have to return, and make my life prone

to perform all types of good, and make death a comfort for me from every evil.

O, God! I have considerably wronged myself. There is none to forgive the sins but You. So grant me pardon and have mercy on me. You are the Most Forgiving, the Most Compassionate.

O, God! I seek refuge in You from hunger; surely, it is the worst companion. And I seek refuge in You from treachery; surely, it is a bad inner trait.

O God I ask You for good surprises, and I seek refuge in You from bad surprises.

Gaslighting and Spiritual Abuse

How do we protect ourselves from spiritual abuse? First and foremost, we shouldn't rationalize and justify our own abuses of others. We should turn to God, seek protection, and remember Him often.

During Muhammad's time, Umar ibn al Khattab, may God be pleased with him, treated accusations of abuse seriously. If a person was suspected of abuse, al Khattab removed the suspect from their position before investigating. He made it clear who had brought the complaint and who was being investigated. These investigations were not done in the dark, amid clouds of confusion. No one has a right to a certain position, and stopping potential future abuse outweighs other considerations.

This is true even of those who had "good intentions." It is actions themselves that matter, and only God knows a person's real intentions. Even the Nazis and the architects of other large-scale atrocities claimed good intentions. We have to judge people by their actions as the Prophet, upon him peace and blessings, taught us to do: openly and transparently, not through secret clubs, stalking, spreading rumors, conjecture, and gaslighting.

Transparency versus secrecy

Transparency means being honest and straightforward in one's dealings with others. An authentic leader does not have a hidden agenda and does not gaslight. With an authentic leader, people know where they stand because this leader openly expresses their thoughts and feelings. There is no projection. We hear loudly the voices seeking clarification, verification, and confirmation.

God does not tell us what Satan thinks or feels. Instead, He asks Satan, "Why did you not prostrate as I commanded you to?" This is the opposite of Satan.

"(God) said: 'What prevented you (O Iblees) that you did not prostrate, when I commanded you?'" (Quran 7:12).

Satan gives us his reason and projects his thoughts and feelings onto God, then tries to guilt God.

> *[Satan] said, "I am better than him. You created me from fire and created him from clay."*
>
> *[God] said, "Descend from Paradise, for it is not for you to be arrogant therein. So get out; indeed, you are of the debased."*
>
> *[Satan] said, "Reprieve me until the Day they are resurrected."*
>
> *[God] said, "Indeed, you are of those reprieved."*
>
> *[Satan] said, "Because You have put me in error, I will surely sit in wait for them on Your straight path. Then I will come to them from before them and from behind them and on their right and on their left, and You will not find most of them grateful [to You]."*
>
> *[God] said, "Get out of Paradise, reproached and expelled. Whoever follows you among them—I will surely fill Hell with you, all together."*
>
> —Quran 7:12–18

An authentic leader has a self-regulated ethical core. They know the right thing to do and are driven by a concern for ethics and fairness executed through ethical decision-making, judgment, and behavior.

Betrayal, cheating, and deception are heinous sins. They will be a source of shame to those guilty of committing them. The Prophet, upon him peace and blessings, said that, on the Day of Judgment, every traitor will be raised, carrying the flag of his betrayal: "Every traitor will have a banner on the Day of Resurrection, and it will be said: This is the betrayer of so-and-so" (Sahih al-Bukhari).

Sometimes, the more a person grows in their religious practice, the more they—like Satan—are able to manipulate others. This is a sign of disease lurking in the heart. Growing in religion should make us grow in truthfulness, not in manipulation or scheming. A mind that is busy scheming is born of a heart empty of God. If the heart is full with God, that enables ethical and truthful communication, not just an outward use of social etiquette.

Not all can be fixed with words

Jesus, upon him peace, realized that not all people could be reached with words. Jesus said: "God has given me the power to give life to the dead, sight to the blind, sound to the deaf; but He did not give me the power to heal the fool of his foolishness." When dealing with abuse and gaslighting, remember these ten things:

1. Do not accept stories at face value or just because the person is a public figure. Sometimes it's important to recognize you don't know the truth of the matter.
2. Don't create, spread, or accept rumors. Learn to seek clarification, verification, and confirmation.
3. Don't attempt to take the place of God.
4. Don't give unsolicited advice or life coaching. Focus on your spiritual state and on that of those you will be asked about.
5. Don't spy, eavesdrop, stalk, or make assumptions.
6. Say what you mean. Don't give hints or communicate vaguely in order to avoid judgment.
7. Don't psychoanalyze others who haven't requested your analysis.
8. Do not chase after those who do not want to engage you.
9. Don't act like Satan and plot and plan to fool people.
10. Live your life. Enjoy it.

Brainwashing Versus Surrender to God

> *(It is) a Quran which We have divided (into parts from time to time), in order that thou mightest recite it to men at intervals: We have revealed it by stages.*

> *Say: "Whether ye believe in it or not, it is true that those who were given knowledge beforehand, when it is recited*

> *to them, fall down on their faces in humble prostration, 'And they say: 'Glory to our Lord! Truly has the promise of our Lord been fulfilled!'" They fall down on their faces in tears, and it increases their (earnest) humility. Say: "Call upon Allah, or call upon Rahman: by whatever name ye call upon Him, (it is well): for to Him belong the Most Beautiful Names. Neither speak thy Prayer aloud, nor speak it in a low tone, but seek a middle course between." Say: "Praise be to Allah, who begets no son, and has no partner in (His) dominion: Nor (needs) He any to protect Him from humiliation: yea, magnify Him for His greatness and glory!"*
>
> —Quran 17:106–111

There is an article titled "How Brainwashing Works," by Julia Layton and Alia Hoyt. It is good to reflect on how it is done to review the Quran study and how the Prophets nurtured people to God and faced social injustices.

The study of brainwashing, also known as thought reform, falls under the umbrella of "social influence" in psychology.

Every minute of every day, social influence occurs. It is the collection of methods by which people can influence the attitudes, beliefs, and behaviors of others.

Brainwashing is a severe form of social influence that combines many approaches to change someone's thinking without consent and frequently against their will. It is an invasive form of power; it necessitates the subject's complete isolation and dependency, which is why brainwashing is most commonly associated with prison camps or totalitarian cults.

For example, the compliance method is concerned with changing a person's behavior rather than attitudes or beliefs. Persuasion, on the other hand, seeks an attitude shift, or "Do it because it will make you feel good, happy, healthy, or successful."

When you don't have a core set of values or a guiding book, or you don't believe in what's being taught, the education method (the "propaganda method") tries to change the person's beliefs. When a trial's wind blows, it controls your will. This emphasizes the significance of establishing a solid foundation of values and beliefs that can withstand external influences. Without it, societal winds can easily sway one's beliefs and actions. For example, during the Cultural Revolution in China, Mao Zedong implemented a propaganda campaign to indoctrinate young people with his ideology. Through slogans, songs, and mass rallies, he aimed to create a generation of loyal followers who were willing to do whatever he asked. This destroyed many traditional cultural practices and the brutal persecution of those who resisted the regime. Those without a book of guidance or strong beliefs were easily swayed by Mao's propaganda and became complicit.

The agent (the brainwasher) must have complete control over the target (the brainwashee), so sleeping, eating, using the bathroom, and meeting other basic human needs depend on the agent's will.

During brainwashing, the agent gradually erodes the target's identity until it crumbles. After that, the agent replaces it.

In the late 1950s, psychologist Robert Jay Lifton defined a series of steps involved in the brainwashing cases he investigated: Assault on one's identity, guilt, self-betrayal, the tipping point, leniency, obligation to confess, guilt channeling, getting rid of guilt, harmony and progress, reincarnation, and final confession.

Each stage occurs in an environment of isolation, meaning that all "normal" social reference points are unavailable, and mind-clouding techniques such as sleep deprivation and malnutrition are standard.

There is frequently the presence or constant threat of physical harm, which makes it difficult for the target to think critically and independently. Lifton identified three stages in the process: breaking down the self, introducing the possibility of salvation, and rebuilding the self.

Identity assassination: You are not who you think you are. This is a methodical assault on a target's sense of self (also known as identity) and core belief system.

The agent denies everything that defines the target, and the target is constantly attacked for days, weeks, or months, leaving them exhausted, confused, and disoriented. When our beliefs are not solid, we will be heavily affected. While the target is experiencing an identity crisis, the agent instills an overwhelming sense of guilt. He relentlessly and mercilessly attacks the subject for any "sin" committed by the target. This "sin" could be framed in a non-religious context.

If the target does not have a station of repentance with God, the use of guilt and humiliation will force them to change. When one faces humiliation, they must turn to the Source, who needs no protection from any humiliation. Turning to God is done through prayer and remembrance of God, magnifying God's Glory and Greatness. In doing so, the person can break the brainwashing process by focusing on God.

The Quran nurtures a person's conscience in stages. The nurturing process increases one in faith, a sense of tranquility, and self-knowledge and removes confusion and disorientation. Unlike the brainwashing process, the nurturing process strengthens a person's resolve and direction, as the Quran states: "Then, where are you going?"

The writers quote a study that shows that faith in a higher power can assist a target in mentally detaching from the process. How people are nurtured does affect their chances of being brainwashed.

Prisoners of war are taught survival techniques as part of their training. Through visualization, constant repetition of a mantra, and various other meditative techniques, soldiers are trained to psychologically detach from their actual surroundings. Likewise, Muslims are trained to reflect on the Quran, which contains certain visualizations, and we are taught to make *dhikr* daily. The *adhkar*, or daily supplications, make it difficult for Muslims to be brainwashed.

Furthermore, if we established a connection with God, and guarded it, we can never be alone and isolated, or targets of such an attack. Don't wait for a trial to happen to prepare yourself.

> *It was We Who created man, and We know what dark suggestions his soul makes to him: for We are nearer to him than (his) jugular vein.*
>
> —Quran 50:16

Projection

Projection is denying one's unpleasant traits, behaviors, or feelings by attributing them (often in an accusing way) to someone else. It is essential to recognize when we are projecting and take responsibility for our thoughts and feelings.

Projection is a defense mechanism and escapism that allows individuals to avoid confronting their flaws, sins, and shortcomings by attributing them to others. It can harm relationships, personal growth, and more critically, our souls if not recognized and addressed. It is the workings of the mind without any purification of the heart.

Sometimes, the projection exaggerates something that has a basis. For example, the person may accuse you of "hating" them when you feel irritated. Sometimes the projection may come entirely from their imagination: for instance, they accuse you of flirting with a sales clerk when you were just asking for directions or clarifying a matter.

People who do not engage in purification of the heart and repent to God regularly, are more than likely to project their unpleasant traits and behaviors onto others.

Handling Uncertainty: Harness the Wind

Now, as for man, when his Lord trieth him, giving him honour and gifts, then saith he, (puffed up), "My Lord hath honoured me." But when He trieth him, restricting his subsistence for him, then saith he (in despair), "My Lord hath humiliated me!" (Quran 89:15-16)

We just experienced a pandemic during which our lives were turned upside down, plans failed, and we felt a loss of control. If we look to the Prophet's life, a major battle happened after he returned to our Lord. Such trials can shake one's faith. Muslims fought each other. As a youth, when I first read about the companions, I remember feeling very bothered for days. I had expected utopia would emerge, but I was reading of battles taking place between Muslims, among those who were closest to the Prophet, upon him peace and blessings.

It took me awhile to reconcile that utopia does not exist. There was much discussion of the "fall" regarding Prophet Adam, upon him peace. Then I read about Prophet Noah, upon him peace, one of the most resolute prophets. He showed tremendous resolve, yet, again, no utopia.

We Are Not Prophets

We all need a role model who will practice what they preach (word, action, and spirit), and in order for us to follow the commands of God, we need to love them. We see how people imitate celebrities or any action that comes out of people they love. Imitating the actions of people we love is human nature. We take the lessons from the prophets, and move forward into uncertainty. During these difficult times, the trials manifest the benefit and beauty in the lessons as one watches the stars and moon in the dark nights.

Given how religion is often twisted and distorted, a true and genuine love of the Prophet more than ourselves can protect us from the misapplication and distortions of religion to the whims of our desires and egos.

This love can drive us to follow him such that "He does not speak out of his own desires."

Prophet Muhammad, upon him peace and blessings, manifested his love for God and how he sacrificed and endured oppression, sanctions, rejection, and mockery, at times standing alone, refusing the power that was offered to him to punish his tormentors severely. It is in our interest to imitate him.

Always listen to extremists and listen to those who disagree with them in their own faith community. This will help you understand how those who love God understand His message and how those who love their egos more than God understand His message. I share a poem to help us reflect on despair.

> [Acceptance]
> Turn away from your worries,
> and entrust your affairs to the Decree.
> [Hope]
> Rejoice at the good which will soon be,
> you will then forget what has gone by.
> [Alhamdulillah]
> Perhaps an issue which upsets you,
> holds at its end what will gladden you.
> [Trust]
> Perhaps the tight road will constrict moreso,
> and perhaps the universe will expand even more.
> [Surrender]
> Indeed Allah does what He wishes,
> So never be one who opposes (Him).
> [La ilaha illalLah]
> Allah is your beautiful source of strength,
> so determine things by what has elapsed...."

—Safi al-Din al-Hali (an Arab poet)

They say that despair is an unforgivable sin because the despairing judge God in a way that denies His Attributes of being Most Merciful, Most Compassionate, Most Generous, Most Loving and that He is the Creator and Sustainer of the world.

Then, how do we embrace our worries without despair? I share a lovely poem for reflection. The comments in brackets are mine. In short, despair comes about by how we *judge* the Creator and interpret the event. We can be open and turn to God with *Alhamdulillah' ala kulli hal* (All Praise and thanks are only for Allah in all circumstances) and not place conditions and limits on God.

I came across the book *The Antidote* and read articles about the it. One can read this book if they are against faith completely or they can explore the ideas the book raises within the faith context. The Quran explores these ideas. From Amazon's description of the book:

> *The Antidote is a series of journeys among people who share a single, surprising way of thinking about life. On the surface, they might not seem to share much else: they are philosophers and experimental psychologists, Buddhists and terrorism experts, New Age dreamers and hard-headed business consultants. But what they have in common is a hunch about human psychology: that in our personal lives and the world at large, it's our constant efforts to eliminate the negative that cause us to feel so anxious, insecure, and unhappy. And that there is an alternative negative path to happiness and success that involves embracing the things we spend our lives trying to avoid. Oliver Burkeman's new book is a witty, fascinating and counter-intuitive read that turns decades of self-help advice on its head and forces us to rethink completely our attitudes towards failure, uncertainty and death.*

Around that time, I started to explore facing death from a faith context and dealing with trials and tribulations. In doing so, I feel I learned more about my faith and it helped me understand and appreciate the lives of the Prophets more.

I will not focus on the book here, but on how faith helps us to face uncertainty, failure, and death. This is not just Islamic understanding, but one can find such verses in the Bible:

> *"Trust in the LORD with all your heart and lean not on your own understanding; in all your ways submit to him, and he will make your paths straight."*
>
> —Proverbs 3:5-6 NIV.

I understand this verse as "Don't conjecture or assume. Turn to God and He will help you weather the trial and tribulation according to His knowledge of what is before you, around you, and ahead of you."

Often, we discuss human beings as "fallen creatures" given the cut-and-paste understanding of the story of Adam, upon him peace. We assume, had Adam, upon him peace, not done this deed, we would not be here. And we go further by opening other "if" doors, until we arrive at this: it is all Adam and Eve's fault that we are fallen creatures. This is the door of Satan and his soldiers. When we read the Quran, we are faced with a verse that corrects our worldview:

> *Say: "I have no power over any good or harm to myself except as Allah willeth. If I had knowledge of the unseen, I should have multiplied all good, and no evil should have touched me: I am but a warner, and a bringer of glad tidings to those who have faith."*
>
> —Quran 7:188

How do we reconcile the story of Adam, upon him peace, and the story of Noah, upon him peace, in the context of this verse?

As you read the Quran, think of your mind like going treasure hunting. Suppose you are studying power, make this reading focused on what the Quran says about power. Maybe you want to know about praising God—go through the Quran and find when, how often, and in response to what, believers are told to praise God. Try reading the Quran and just focus on "handling uncertainty." One of the descriptions of Al Quran is Al Furqan, as it helps correct your vision and understanding on matters.

A case in point is Noah and "the most abject amongst us." The conversation between Prophet Noah, upon him peace, and the chiefs is throughout the Quran from various angles and perspectives. Each perspective sheds light on one aspect of the conversation. Reflect on how faith communicates and how abusive power communicates.

> *We sent Noah to his people (with a mission): "I have come to you with a Clear Warning: "That ye serve none but Allah: Verily I do fear for you the penalty of a grievous day."*
>
> *But the chiefs of the Unbelievers among his people said: "We do not see in thee anything but a mortal man like ourselves; and we do not see that any follow thee save those who are quite obviously the most abject among us; and we do not see that you could be in any way superior to us: on the contrary, we think that you are liars!"*
>
> *He said: "O my people! See ye if (it be that) I have a Clear Sign from my Lord, and that He hath sent Mercy*

> unto me from His own presence, but that the Mercy hath been obscured from your sight? shall we compel you to accept it when ye are averse to it?
>
> "O my people, I do not ask you for any money for this; my reward comes only from God. I will not drive away those who believe; they shall surely meet their Lord. Yet I see that you are a people who act out of ignorance.
>
> "My people, who would support me against God if I were to drive them off? Will you not take heed?
>
> "I do not say to you that I possess God's treasures, or that I have knowledge of the unseen, or that I am an angel. Nor do I say concerning those upon whom you look with contempt, that God will not bestow any good upon them—God knows best what is in their hearts. If I did, I would certainly be one of the wrongdoers."
>
> "Noah," they replied, "you have argued with us, and argued to excess. Now bring down upon us what you threaten us with, if you speak the truth!?"
>
> He said, "It is God who will bring it down upon you, if He wishes, and you will not be able to escape.
>
> "My advice will not benefit you, no matter how sincerely I want to advise you, if God lets you go astray. He is your Lord and you will all return to Him."
>
> If they say, "He has invented it himself," say to them, "If I have indeed invented this myself, then may I be punished for my sin; I am innocent of the crimes that you commit."
>
> God's will was revealed to Noah, "No more of your people will believe in you than those who already believe; do not grieve, therefore, over what they have been doing.
>
> "Build the Ark under Our Eyes and in accordance with Our revelation. Do not plead with Me concerning the evil-doers. They shall certainly be drowned."
>
> —Quran 11:25–38

We need to reflect on the reality that we are all the children of the eighty who followed him and boarded the ark. The rest were all drowned. This means all of us, the good, bad, and ugly (character-wise) are descendants of the eighty followers.

Likewise, when the angels came to destroy the whole town after they harmed Prophet Muhammad, upon him peace and blessings, he said no, that maybe their children or descendants might follow Islam. So many of the ancestors of people who are now followers of Prophet Muhammad, upon him peace and blessings, were about to be wiped off the face of the earth.

Sometimes the trial is within your home. God gives us examples in which one spouse is pious, and the other is treacherous.

The betrayal of Noah's wife is akin to today's government surveillance, informants, and entrapment techniques. There is a saying that if you have nothing to hide, you have nothing to fear from people spying on you in the privacy of your home. Often, what is left unsaid is that those who spy on others in the privacy of their own home have something to hide. As we have seen, the stories they tell are not accurate but a package of lies, conjecture, projection, and slander. There is always some hidden agenda behind the spying.

Such treachery does make a person psychologically unsafe due to psychological torture by outside forces within the home, mosque, workplace—either via family members or informants. We must note that the judge, jury, and executioner cannot also be your abuser.

Deception Has a Short Lifespan

Over a billion and a half Muslims teach their followers that Prophet Noah, upon him peace, was one of the five most resolute messengers of God, who was divinely protected from sin or violations of the sacred law.

> *We have made some of you as a trial for others: will ye have patience? for Allah is One Who sees (all things).*
>
> —Quran 25:20

Sometimes God wants to elevate someone in rank and pour a trial upon them or test another who is deluded and arrogant. If the believer weathers these trials by turning to God, seeking help via patience and prayer, then God will elevate their rank, or they will climb the spiritual mountain of faith closer to Him.

There is a verse in Chapter 18 that I like to repeat. The emphasis is on 'asa, or "I hope/wish/pray/aspire to." Hope for what? Listen: "I hope that my Lord will guide me ever closer (even) than this to the right road" (Quran 18:24).

Because the trials are a means to receive or nurture forbearance, forgiveness, and learn to pardon people, how can you rule over people who have faults, might be wrong as day? How can you avoid using guns in matters that can be handled via nonviolent means?

They might be a clear enemy yet still do not require a shot to the head, destruction of an entire village, torture, et cetera, rationalizing our enemy's hatred and justifying the unjustifiable. Remember Christopher Hitchens?

Turn to God, ask Him for wisdom to respond, and trust He will direct your actions on what is best in this situation. He knows "all that is beyond the reach of a created being's perception as well as all that can be witnessed by a creature's senses or mind—the Almighty, the Wise" (Quran 64:18).

We are not prophets or angels, so we are not divinely protected from transgressing and oppressing others. Laws are intended to ensure that everyone is treated fairly and justly, regardless of social status or position. They help people understand what is and is not acceptable behavior, resulting in a more harmonious and equitable community.

Examples:

Susan Bro, the mother of Heather Heyer, who was killed when a car plowed into a crowd of counter protesters at a rally in Charlottesville, says she's "glad [the jury was] able to recognize the preponderance of evidence definitely showed the clients to be guilty."

In Portland, Oregon, fifty-three-year-old Ricky John Best, and twenty-three-year-old Taliesin Myrddin Namkai-Meche died while trying to intervene when a man shouted racial slurs at two women, one of whom was wearing a hijab. Micah David-Cole Fletcher, twenty-one, of Portland was also stabbed in the attack and faced serious injuries.

In the case of the trial of Ahmaud Arbery's killers, one attorney representing Arbery during the trial said very beautifully, "It began with assumptions." It helps to listen to those in the heat of the trial and reflect on their journey and lessons we can learn for our own journey.

> *O you who have believed, avoid much [negative] assumption. Indeed, some assumption is sin. And do not spy.*
>
> —Quran 49:12

We see people struggle to get justice in many parts of the world, not just the United States. The difficulty in getting justice is not a reason to stop seeking justice or nurturing a better society but to connect to people struggling for justice to help them find support and comfort when the results in the court system are not favorable.

We all benefit by finding ways to contribute to the security of others. When people feel safe, we can converse on many common goods that might help the truth emerge. However, oppressors love oppressing, as they benefit from the system of oppression.

> *O my people! I have indeed conveyed to you the Message of my Lord, and have given you good advice but you like not good advisers.*
>
> —Quran 7:79

Speaking for justice will open doors for more oppression and possibly plots of injustice.

Be Proactive

What I share next is what I found beneficial for me to process some events in life:

> *[A]nd of Abraham, who to his trust was true: that no bearer of burdens shall be made to bear another's burden; and that naught shall be accounted unto man but what he is striving for; and that in time [the nature of] all his striving will be shown [to him in its true light], whereupon he shall be requited for it with the fullest requital; and that with thy Sustainer is the beginning and the end [of all that exists]; and that it is He alone who causes [you] to laugh and to weep; and that it is He alone who deals death and grants life.*
>
> —Quran 53:37-44

Initially, the revelation of God was sent down in books: that is, they were written as the revelation came down—for example, the Ten Commandments. However, the original books have become extinct. The following principles were true then and are true now:

1. That every person is responsible for what they do.
2. That the responsibility of one person's actions cannot be transferred to another unless they have a share in the commission of the act.

3. That even if a person wishes, they cannot take on themselves the responsibility of another person's act, nor can the actual offender be let off on the ground that another person is willing to suffer the punishment on their behalf.

What you strive for, you find: three principles are derived from this teaching:

1. That every person will get only the fruit of their deeds.
2. That the fruit of one person's deeds cannot be given to another unless they have a share in that deed.
3. That none can attain anything without striving for it.

Some people wrongly apply these three principles to the world's economic problems and conclude that no person can become the lawful owner of anything except their own earned income. However, this conclusion clashes with several laws and injunctions in the Quran. Some examples:

Laws of inheritance: many individuals inherit from a person and are regarded as their lawful heirs, although the heritage is not earned income.

Laws of *zakat* or purification of wealth and voluntary charities, according to which one person's wealth is transferred to others based only on their legal and moral entitlement, and they become its lawful owners, although, in the production of this wealth, they did not make any contribution at all.

Therefore, it is against the spirit of the Quran to take a verse and derive conclusions that clash with the bedrock teachings of the Quran. There is a breadth and depth of scholarly discussion on these principles concerning the hereafter.

Supplications and prayers of one person are beneficial for the other because the Quran confirms it; however, they differ only in details and not in principles as to whether the sending of spiritual rewards for another and doing good work on behalf of another are beneficial or not.

If one wants to understand the complete discussion, they must not enter the discussion late, leave early, and share their notes. The discussion began; sound arguments came from all sides; the change of positions continued with the sound arguments presented back and forth.

The rich scholarly discussion shows that in the beginning, it was permissible to perform acts of bodily worship such as prayer and fasting on behalf of others. However, the practice that became established in the end was that it was not permissible. Still, one needs an academic degree to enter the discussion and use it for issuing religious edicts. Hence, if you want a religious edict regarding yourself or a loved one, seek a scholar you trust who has the qualifications to issue a religious edict and follow them.

What is essential for us to understand at the individual level is that the fulfillment of an obligation on behalf of another can be beneficial only to those who have, themselves, been keen and desirous of fulfilling their obligations and might have been unable to do so, rendered helpless by circumstances. This should motivate us to strive to fulfill them, and if the door is closed, we have a valid excuse and our striving to support our claim.

However, a person who deliberately shirked going for hajj, although he had the necessary means for it and had no feeling whatever of this obligation in his heart cannot be benefited, even if several hajj be performed on his behalf afterward. Although scholars might disagree, do not use the disagreement as an excuse not to strive to fulfill the duties of hajj. In the hereafter, the striving will be seen and judged.

> *That (the fruit of) his striving will soon come in sight: Then will he be rewarded with a reward complete; That to thy Lord is the final Goal;*
>
> *That it is He Who granteth Laughter and Tears; That it is He Who granteth Death and Life.*
>
> —Quran 53:40-44

Allah provides the means both for joy and for grief. He controls all those means. This does not mean we hurl blame at God, but instead, we turn to God and keep returning for relief, aid, support, mercy, and whatever means are needed to turn tears into laughter or to help us surrender to our own or a loved one's passing away.

I recall watching a movie in which a woman had a daughter who had diabetes. When her daughter died as she was not taking her insulin as prescribed, the mother raged at God with blame. I know many cases of people who acted similarly. Hence, the comforting reminder to us all: "To God we belong and To God is our final return." Patience in the face of trials is only by God, with God, and for God.

Disagreement versus *Kade* (Sinful Cunning)

In the book *God Intervenes Between A Person And Their Heart*, I explored some lessons on Aisha, may Allah be pleased with her. She is one of the spouses of Prophet Muhammad, upon him peace and blessings. I titled one chapter "Let Aisha Speak for Aisha."

So many people were exploring her thoughts and feelings without researching what she said or expressed during the trials that faced the community after the passing of Prophet Muhammad, upon him peace and blessings.

Likewise, everybody spoke for Ali, may God be pleased with him, instead of amplifying what Ali said or did. Their narratives of the companions used fallacies. I will note a few for reflection.

A *red herring* is a fallacy in which an argument uses unrelated topics to draw the attention of listeners or readers away from the main point. This fallacy is frequently used in mystery or suspense novels to mislead readers or characters or to lead them to incorrect conclusions. We see this fallacy used by those who oppose the prophets throughout the Quran.

The *psychologist's fallacy* is when an external observer assumes that their subjective interpretation of something represents the objective nature of that thing. Most notably, this is associated with the mistaken assumption that your (third-person) interpretation of someone else's mental state (e.g., how they feel or what they think) is necessarily correct and identical to their (first-person) experience of it.

Another typical fallacy is the *straw man fallacy* which misleads people by disagreeing with and defeating an opponent's argument through misrepresentation (i.e., "stand up a straw man") and their refutation ("knock down a straw man") instead of the opponent's argument. This fallacy is often used in political debates and media, where opponents are misrepresented and attacked for positions they do not hold.

Given the many fallacies, to know people, one should let them speak for themselves and listen to how they tell their stories over time. This allows for a better understanding of their thought processes and beliefs and can help to identify if they are honest and seeking understanding or argue to win using fallacious reasoning.

When we disagree, we must avoid using fallacies to promote our understanding or interpretation of historical events. Unless Ali or Aisha expressed specific thoughts and feelings, over time, we should reject anyone telling us how they felt or thought.

I am sharing excerpts from the book *The Jurisprudence of the Prophetic Biography* by Dr. Ramadan al-Bouti. I found it a very excellent read as it clarifies the disagreements between the companions without using *kade* or fallacies. I recall reading about the political rivalry between Umar al-Khattab and Khalid ibn al-Waleed, and Umar and Ali ibn Abu Talib.

The companions worked together to aid Prophet Muhammad, upon him peace and blessings. And they continued within that same spirit after he returned to our Lord. They are the gold star families of the Muslim community and should be treated as such. A careful study of the lives of the prophets can help us appreciate their support of Prophet Muhammad, upon him peace and blessings. No other prophet of God had such a gift of companions who disagreed with each other in the healthy spirit of faith and goodwill.

Clarification, Verification, and Confirmation

One beauty of the Quran is that humans are taught to think critically and use intelligence. Throughout the Quran, righteous people or the prophets engage in questions that seek to clarify or verify. Chapter 55, Verse 4 reads, "He has taught him speech (and intelligence)."

Bayyan is the art or skill of making things clear, which requires intelligence and critical thinking. It is also a mark of faith as we study how disinformation and misinformation spread, leading to sedition or war.

Each of the rightly guided Caliphs was able to shut down malicious disinformation campaigns, preventing the Divine message from being maligned or undermined. We appreciate this when we read about the past Divine messages and how certain events were made to appear.

For example, the Quran says, the crucifixion was made to appear like that. What does that mean? It means a rumor or disinformation campaign regarding an event took place, and the community's faith was too weak to clarify, verify, and confirm the event's truth; hence, the message was maligned. The Quran gives the example of the slander of Aisha. The hypocrites planned this event to discredit the Prophet, yet God used it to purify and nurture the community to use their intelligence in the face of disinformation campaigns.

One of the descriptions of people with lip-service faith is that they are avid listeners to lies. There is much to say about Ali, may God be pleased with him, and his relationship with the other companions. I was very impressed with his handling of the event regarding Uthman, may God be pleased with him.

A wrongdoer spread malicious lies in the name and using the seal of Uthman, which appeared to be an act of treachery against other companions. Ali, whose nobility, and faith shined in this event, responded by presenting the accusation and evidence to Uthman. Upon clarification, verification, and confirmation, it was clear that the letter used the seal of Uthman but it was not in his handwriting. I have experienced something in my life in which a wrongdoer used notary public signatures and sheriffs to falsify documents. Many were misled, and few verified the information.

Uthman is known for compiling the Quran, preventing the message and its language from being distorted. Imagine if Uthman had been discredited by this disinformation campaign, and Muslims were led to believe falsehood about Uthman until the Day of Judgment as some believe of other prophets? Imagine what would have happened to the Quran as a result. One wave of *fitna* or sedition after another faced each companion, who immediately shut down attempts to undermine the Divine message. It is easy to read, and it is another reality to live through and face.

Although Ali could not prevent Uthman's death, he tried his best. However, Ali did prevent Uthman from being discredited as a righteous Caliph and an honest leader. This act helped prevent the Divine message from being distorted. We cannot prevent trials and tribulations. However, the strength of the companions' faith and character is something to take time and reflect on for our growth.

What Can We Learn from This Event?

As you read about Uthman's assassination, followed by Ali becoming a Caliph, you see the primary failure in the disinformation campaigns was they're not seeking clarification, verification, and confirmation in the face of fallacies and the inability to get their facts straight, which led to the many insurrections that followed.

False Accusations

I have mentioned that God is All-Knowing and knows how people will process events and accusations that will arise in the future. If Ali, the fourth rightly guided Caliph, believed power belonged to him after Prophet Muhammad, upon him peace and blessings, returned to God, he would have gone to battle against Abu Bakr, Umar, or Uthman. However, he was the leading adviser, not to one but to all three. Ali also passionately disagreed with Uthman. Yet his interactions with Uthman were not kade or sinful cunning. In the aftermath of the murder of Uthman, Ali was chosen by the companions as the next Caliph. He did not need a unanimous vote to become a Caliph. What was essential was receiving enough votes from the companions. Those who disagreed were entitled to their political positions.

Having such honorable and righteous companions was a gift from God to Prophet Muhammad, upon him peace and blessings. The gift of righteous companions was not given to any prophet before him or even to his companions, as the murder of Ali shows. He died as he lived, supporting the Messenger of God, and protecting the Divine message from distortion, allowing it to reach us for centuries to come. His final words were, "There is no deity worthy of worship, except Allah," the Muslim declaration of faith.

1. Ali defended Uthman to the extent of asking his sons to be on guard at his palace.
2. Ali could have used the letter by Marwan, an act of treachery, and just refused to make things clear for the community. However, his response, as mentioned here, cleared Uthman's name.
3. Mu'awiya refused to give his pledge to Ali, claiming Uthman's murder.
4. As Uthman's kin, Mu'awiya had a right to demand justice for Uthman's murder; however, he did not have the right to be a Caliph.
5. Ali opened himself up to arbitration to defuse the brewing tension among Muslims regarding Uthman's murder. He was seeking clarity and reconciliation.

6. Mu'awiya did not trust the process but agreed to it. *Kade* was used in the arbitration process to promote Mu'awiya as Caliph. In other words, it was a farce.
7. *Kade* was used to stir the passions of the community against Ali.
8. The story of the Caliphate of Ali plays out in similar realities to the stories of the prophets. As he was going to fight Mu'awiya and demand he surrender to Ali's Caliphate, he instead went and fought the Kharijites as they were causing major problems to the teachings of Islam.
9. Even though people stood against Ali, while he was facing battles from many corners to undermine his Caliphate, he continued to defend the faith from the Kharijites, who had very poor critical thinking skills, were causing mayhem in the name of God, extracted such nonsense as declaring Ali himself a non-Muslim, and later murdered him.
10. After Ali's assassination, Hasan, Ali's son, was appointed Caliph in Kufa. Hasan's appointment was challenged by Mu'awiya, who requested Hasan surrender the Caliphate to him.
11. As a result of the political unrest among Muslims, Hasan engaged in a peace agreement whereby he would accept Mu'awiya if he would comply with the Quran and *Sunna*; a council (*shura*) would appoint his successor, grant safety to the people, and grant Hasan's supporters amnesty.
12. Hasan returned to Kufa and surrendered his control of Iraq after a seven-month reign.
13. Although Mu'awiya accepted the peace treaty terms, he selected his son Yazid as ruler upon his death, instead of allowing a council (*shura*) to appoint the successor.

The final chapter of his life refutes the false accusations made in various corners that he believed he should be the rightful Caliph instead of the appointed companions (Abu Bakr, Umar, and Uthman) whom Ali supported.

What Is Our View of Mu'awiya?

The mainstream Islamic teachings differentiate between disinformation campaigns that promote seditions and insurrections and a rebellion based on reasonable claims for justice. They do not shut down dissent based on reasonable demands. Dr. Ramadan al Bouti explains the view of Mu'awiya's rebellion. The murder of Uthman was not a simple matter; it was a declaration of war against the state, as we would now view the murder of a head of state.

We cannot overlook the psychological, social, and emotional impact such a murder had on Muslims. This act shook the Muslim community. We are emotionally removed from the impact of that time, so it is important to separate Mu'awiya from the Kharijites and from rebels without a just cause. Dylann Roof is a case in point. Roof, is an American white supremacist, convicted of perpetrating the Charleston church shooting on June 17, 2015, killing nine people, all African Americans, including senior pastor and state senator Clementa C. Pinckney, and injured one other person.

Ashura and the Martyrdom of Husayn

Ashura means *tenth*—in this case, the tenth of Muharram. It is a day that Muslims fast in gratitude to God for saving Moses, upon him peace, and his followers. God split the Red Sea and allowed Moses and his followers to flee.

Yazid was not a righteous ruler and was not chosen by a council (*shura*). Before Gandhi or Martin Luther King, al-Husayn led a nonviolent revolution against political and religious tyranny. Imam al-Husayn did not sacrifice innocent civilians for a political cause or power sharing. He refused to compromise his values and faith and refused to accept the new ruler. He fought with courage and sacrificed his life and those of his own family for the elevation of truth.

Yazid's soldiers refused his conditions and demanded he either fall on his knees and pledge to Yazid or face death. He declined to give his pledge to the new ruler and was martyred with his family and a few followers. Thousands had professed that they would stand by Husayn if he stood up to Yazid. Yet when the time came, they betrayed him and did not come to show him support. As magicians who followed the Pharaoh out of compulsion, many pledged their support to Yazid out of fear, not conviction.

Unlike the magicians who found the courage to break through the fear and became honorable witnesses by embracing the courage of Moses, upon him peace, Husayn's supporters disappeared.

These trials and tribulations were their life test. Those who followed God passed, and those who did not are getting their due.

The lesson of the martyrdom of Imam Ali and his two sons, Hasan and Husayn, is this: "And say not of those who are slain in the way of Allah: 'They are dead.' Nay, they are living, though ye perceive (it) not" (Quran 2:154).

However, their murderers are dead and being punished. A lesson we can take from those who did not show up to defend Husayn or those who mocked and insulted Moses, upon him peace, after God liberated them from the Pharaoh is the value and station of the companions of Prophet Muhammad, upon him peace and blessings.

We understand the critical role the companions played and what would happen to the Prophet, upon him peace and blessings, and the message he carried had they deserted, betrayed, harmed, or insulted him. God chose them to accompany and support the final Messenger and guard the Majestic Message.

> *And remember, Moses said to his people: "O my people, why do you harm me while you certainly know that I am the Messenger of Allah to you?" And when they deviated, Allah caused their hearts to deviate. And Allah does not guide the defiantly disobedient people.*
>
> —Quran 61:5

At an appointed time, our tests will end. And we will be discussed by people after us as we discuss these current-day events.

> *We granted not to any man before thee permanent life (here): if then thou shouldst die, would they live permanently? Every soul shall have a taste of death: and We test you by evil and by good by way of trial. to Us must ye return.*
>
> —Quran 21:34–35

Professing love to Moses, upon him peace, or Husayn, may God be pleased with him, now is akin to professing love to Moses and Husayn then. When the test time comes, will we support the current-day Yazids or Pharaohs, or will we do what we can with the power, voice, and influence we have to support and elevate the truth?

Truth is from your lord

If you make demands on Him, you doubt Him. If you seek Him, you are absent from Him. If you seek other-than-Him, you are shameless before Him. If you make demands on other-than-Him, you are distant from Him.

—Ibn Ata'illah Iskandari

At times, we face trials that make us wonder—why? When we tell stories that if you do everything right, God will open a way for you, we lose people who are oppressed and are left wondering what they did wrong.

We might say, "Pray." Moses and Aaron (Haroon) prayed, and victory was open for them. However, John the Baptist and his father, Zakariya, upon them all peace, prayed, and they were martyred.

We might say, "Give charity"; "Did you pray *istikhara* (prayer of seeking guidance)"; et cetera and give a list of all the things we should do. Then people wonder, *well, these people who have doors open for them—they did not do all these things, and doors are opening for them.*

The stories of Umar, Uthman, Ali, Hasan, Husayn, and countless others, may God be pleased with them all, help fix our vision of life and reality. Why didn't God grant them victory as He granted Moses, upon him peace?

When answering people, we must be mindful of all these stories and reconcile them, then answer people with wisdom, instead of pop-pill spirituality.

I learned that Imam Husayn prayed and made *istikhara*—the prayer of seeking guidance on permissible matters—before he set out to Kufa. He sought advice from knowledgeable people around him regarding the matter. Some advised him to not go. However, he did his research and prayed hard on what was needed at that moment. Husayn was hoping for something similar to what Prophet Muhammad, upon him peace and blessings, found in Medina.

Yet things fall apart, and the situation looks very grim. *Karbala.* Some say it comes from the root word *bala',* which means *tribulation.* You know you are facing your death. We don't have God wrapped around our fingers. Yet there is inspiration in this story for many who are oppressed worldwide.

In the case of Palestine, arbitration and negotiation was tried (Ali); so was peacemaking (Hasan). People are realizing they have two roads before them: ethnic cleansing or showing resolve and pushing invaders back to their boundaries.

We listen to stories of mothers having amazing hope, finally conceiving a child after years of trying. Then they spend their lives raising their only child and dreaming of holding *their* children. Then, suddenly, that child is killed. Another story of a family of four beautiful children, all killed in a bombing, et cetera.

Those are not our stories to tell and share with others. Rather, we must amplify those stories of faith so others facing similar situations can reconcile their faith.

How many prayed *istikhara*, did their research, sought advice, and followed it, only to see a trial and tribulation unfold?

You prayed for good things; however, you assumed you knew what was good for you. God answered your prayer by giving you what was good for you according to His knowledge, not yours. Hence, the question "Why does God not answer my prayers?" needs to be clarified. You asked God to give you what was good for you, and God answered your prayers.

You should pray, give charity, et cetera so you can receive the answer to your prayers. This is where resolve and faith come into the picture. Resolve and faith are good for you.

Lesson two: The first debate of Christianity

The first great debate of Christianity was about the crucifixion, like the debate among Muslims about Ali and Husayn, may God be pleased with them. The lessons for Muslims and Christians are the same. Don't conjecture and interject your own understanding on the unknown. We love to point out to Christians the message regarding the crucifixion but fail to take heed with regards to Ali and Husayn, may God be pleased with them.

The messengers were carrying a message, and the message to humanity must be protected and delivered.

Abraham: Unless My Lord Guides Me

"O my Lord! bestow wisdom on me, and join me with the righteous; Grant me honourable mention on the tongue of truth among the latest (generations); Make me one of the inheritors of the Garden of Bliss;" (Quran 26:83-85)

We came into this world knowing nothing. We were given faculties of hearing, seeing, and reasoning. We are learning creatures capable of so much. In the book *God Intervenes Between A Person And Their Heart*, when I discussed the life journey of Prophet Abraham, upon him peace, I focused on surrender or submission. I reflected on the experience of hajj, or pilgrimage. In this book, I focus on wisdom.

> *So also, did We show Abraham the power and the laws of the heavens and the earth, that he might (with understanding) have certitude. When the night covered him over, He saw a star: He said: "This is my Lord." But when it set, He said: "I love not those that set." When he saw the moon rising in splendour, he said: "This is my Lord." But when the moon set, He said: "Unless my Lord guides me, I shall surely be among those who go astray." When he saw the sun rising in splendour, he said: "This is my Lord; this is the greatest (of all)." But when the sun set, he said: "O my people! I am indeed free from your (guilt) of giving partners to Allah. For me, I have set my face, firmly and truly, towards Him Who created the heavens and the earth, and never shall I give partners to Allah."*
>
> —Quran 6:75–79

The emphasis is on his prayer or supplication as he was using his faculties of hearing, sight, and reason. He said, "Unless my Lord guides me, I shall surely be among those who go astray."

God is not asking us to figure it out and debate the reality of His Existence with each other. He is asking us to turn to Him and seek guidance from Him. He is not going to trick us and misguide us when we do.

How? Chapter 14 of the Holy Quran is titled *"Ibrahim."* Ibrahim is the Arabic name for Prophet Abraham, upon him peace. It begins with the verse:

> *Alif Lam Ra. A Book We have sent down to thee that thou mayest bring forth mankind from the shadows to the light by the leave of their Lord, to the path of the All-mighty, the All-laudable.*
>
> —Quran 14:1

There seems to be a critical misunderstanding of who God is. I see many cases in which God is presented as needy of our love, praise, and acceptance. In the same chapter, a few verses down, we read:

> *And Moses added: "If you should [ever] deny the truth— you and whoever else lives on earth, all of you—[know that] verily Allah is Free of Need, Owner of Praise.*
>
> —Quran: 14:8

When we speak about God, there seems to be this mentality: we are begging people to accept God. Trials and tribulations help us discover our need of God and turn to God, begging for acceptance from Him.

I mention this again: Adam, upon him peace, said: "Our Lord! We have wronged ourselves, and if You do not forgive us and have mercy upon us, we will surely be among the losers."

And Prophet Noah, upon him peace: "O, my Lord! I seek refuge with You from asking You that of which I have no knowledge. And unless You forgive me and have Mercy on me, I would indeed be one of the losers."

I shared the supplications of Prophet Muhammad, upon him peace and blessings. Let me use literature to clarify my point. Umar al Khattab, companion of Prophet Muhammad, upon him peace and blessings, said, "Our conscience is the most secret witness of an evil deed."

The tragedy *Othello*, written by William Shakespeare, is a story that revolves around two characters, Othello and Iago. Othello, a Moor, is a military commander who recently married Desdemona, a beautiful and wealthy Venetian lady much younger than himself, against her father's wishes. Iago is Othello's malevolent trusted adviser, who maliciously plants seeds of jealousy in Othello until the usually stoic Othello kills his beloved wife in a fit of blind rage.

Iago is a fictional character, but he helps us understand that people have intentions, aims, and motives hidden in their hearts and camouflaged with words of freedom, democracy, justice, love, loyalty, and possibly faith. On the Day of Judgment, the inner realities of the hearts will be exposed and examined to distinguish good from evil.

Secular laws, in principle, agree that a person should not be punished merely based on their apparent act but their motive. However, secular laws are limited in what they can see and measure. We cannot see the intentions, malice, and sinful cunning and declare someone like Iago guilty before a court of law.

Many seemingly good acts escape punishment because we do not see the person indiscreetly planting seeds of evil or doing good deeds for ulterior motives. If we only consider this, we cannot help admitting that absolute and complete justice can only be done in the court of God.

This X-ray vision into our hearts and the secrets they hold is within the knowledge of God alone. God will examine these locked secrets and the underlying motives behind every apparent act of man and decide what reward or punishment they deserve.

On Resurrection Day, these secrets will be brought out openly before the people. After thorough scrutiny in the court, it will be shown what was good and what was evil.

Tahsil or *hussila ma fissudur* means to bring out something in the open and sort out different things from one another. Thus, the use of *tahsil* concerning hidden secrets of the hearts contains both the meanings: to expose them and to sort out the good from the evil.

This same theme has been expressed in Surah At-Tariq thus: The Day the hidden secrets are held to scrutiny (Verse 9), God will allow the heart to unfold and reveal the secrets within for all to see.

There are chapters (112, 113, and 114) in the Holy Quran that specifically teach us to acknowledge such people as Iago in society. It is recommended to read them after every prayer for protection.

When Messengers come to call to God, in a way, they are taking people from the shadows, where evil is done in secrecy, and they are unconscious recipients of evil seeds being planted in them. They encourage their audience to turn to God, who can see the wrong intentions, secret plans, and rotten seeds unconsciously planted by those with evil intent.

While Iago is a fictional character, Satan is not. There are people who act like Satan in society. I gave an example of a psychologist who went to therapy. His therapist continuously planted evil seeds in his mind that he was sexually attracted to him, even though the patient did not recall such feelings or have them. The patient's psychologist had a dream that warned him of danger, and he never visited that therapist again. Our conscience will communicate to us if someone is trying to plant evil seeds within us.

God might also separate you from them. We saw this in the Messengers' lives. Noah built the ark and invited his wife and eldest son to embark, and they refused. In the story of Abraham, he is exiled with his wife, Sarah. We are told that God bestowed children upon Abraham *after* he separated from his family to protect his offspring from such evil seeds being planted. If Othello, a military commander, can be affected, children can be affected as well.

You might have nothing to hide, but someone like Iago or that therapist might have some evil seeds to plant. Hence, the first wisdom that all messengers convey is to ask people to turn to God alone.

As human beings, we have the power to choose whether or not to surrender to God. In Islam, the most significant way to do so is by submitting our will or ego to God by following His commands. This surrender brings ultimate peace.

Messengers are entrusted with removing all distortions and conveying the message with crystal-clear clarity and openness to ensure surrendering to God is a conscious choice.

> *CONVEY [unto others] whatever of this divine writ has been revealed unto thee, and be constant in prayer: for, behold, prayer restrains [man] from loathsome deeds and from all that runs counter to reason; and remembrance of God is indeed the greatest [good]. And God knows all that you do.*
>
> —Quran 29:45

Prayer serves as a form of remembrance and a means of protection against outside influences if we are present during worship.

Hence, humans are endowed with an intelligence capable of conceiving the Absolute and with a will capable of choosing what leads to the Absolute.

Prayer invites us as humans to remember the Divine Absolute and our human weakness and need for guidance and protection before the manifestation of His Greatness.

Trust

We will be tested with those nearest to us—in particular, those in whom we place our trust. The key lesson here is that our trust should, primarily, be in Allah. We should never trust anyone to a higher degree than God.

We always think we are immune from being like Iago or having trusted relatives or friends like Iago, but we are not. When we place our trust first in God, we protect ourselves from the worst form of mental and emotional abuse: gaslighting. Many talk about gaslighting but fail to realize that gaslighting requires trust. Lying and denying without trust are lies. The person does not trust you, so there is no invasion of their conscience, making them question reality or brainwashing them.

In the example of Othello, had he turned to God and asked Him to guide his heart, God would have inspired him to stay away from suspicion and not spy. God would have inspired him to cut off ties with Iago.

At times, some might be very tenderhearted like Prophet Abraham, upon him peace, and find it hard to leave an abusive situation. If we turn to God, God might direct our hearts to stay and be patient, to leave, or to separate and grow before reconciling like Prophet Joseph, upon him peace, for He knows best the reality of situations. Hence, instead of telling women to leave or stay or asking why they do not leave or stay, tell them to turn to God, and ask Him to plan on their behalf what is best for them. Share with them the prayer of seeking guidance or *istikhara*.

How does this happen when we have a trusted person who is abusive?

(They prayed): "Our Lord! in Thee do we trust, and to

> *Thee do we turn in repentance: to Thee is (our) Final Goal. "Our Lord! Make us not a (test and) trial for the Unbelievers, but forgive us, our Lord! For Thou art the Exalted in Might, the Wise." There was indeed in them an excellent example for you to follow for those whose hope is in Allah and in the Last Day. But if any turn away, truly Allah is Free of all Wants (Al Ghani), Worthy of all Praise (Al Hameed).*
>
> —Quran 60:4–6

Chapter 60 of the Quran is titled "*Mumtahana*" or "*Mumtahina*" ("She Who Is to Be Examined").

It is important to identify the social reality of the time to help us extract the true meaning of the words. The social context was war and violations of a peace treaty between Muslims in Madinah and Quraish in Mecca.

A case example was referenced when the verses were revealed. The scholarly commentators and Ibn Abbas, Mujahid, Qatadah, Urwah bin Zubair, and others also had unanimously reported that revelation was sent to Prophet Muhammad, upon him peace and blessings, regarding a letter by Hatib bin Abi Baltaa to the pagans of Mecca.

The Meccans violated the *Hudaibiyah* peace treaty. Prophet Muhammad, upon him peace and blessings, was preparing a military response. Only a few knew the plans. During this time, Hatib conversed with a woman and gave her the secrets to give to the Meccans. Allah sent revelation regarding this case of espionage. Prophet Muhammad, upon him peace and blessings, immediately sent Ali, Zubair, and Miqdad bin Aswad to find her before she revealed the plans. In brief, they found her, got the letter, and gave it to Prophet Muhammad, upon him peace and blessings.

Prophet Muhammad, upon him peace and blessings, publicly questioned Hatib on his actions and presented the letter as evidence. Hatib responded that he had family in Mecca who did not have protection from any clan and was worried this military response would lead to their persecution.

He was requesting that the Quraish in Mecca not harm his children. Hearing what Hatib had to say, the Prophet, upon him peace and blessings, spoke to the people: Hatib has told you the truth. He added that this man had participated in the Battle of Badr. The Muslims were taught to accept Hatib's excuse and pardon him.

God reveals to Muslims that they cannot trust treacherous people. If they violated the Hudaibiyah peace treaty, then you can expect the following:

> *If they could overcome you, they would act as your foes and would hurt you by their hands and tongues, and would love to see you become unbelievers.*
>
> —Quran 60:2

While Muslims accepted and pardoned Hatib, God educated all Muslims regarding this event.

God adds that, on the Day of Judgment, family relations will be void. Only those based on faith will remain; others will be separated. Family members will not be able to defend each other; each will worry about themself and saving themself. No one will come forth and take the burden of another's sins on them.

God will render worldly relations and bonds of love and friendship void in the hereafter. The people will not be judged as groups, tribes, classes, and families, but every person will have to present himself as an individual and only render their account.

The key lesson is not to commit a wrong for the sake of a relationship, friendship, or tribe because you will face all its consequences, and no one else will become a partner in the matter of his responsibility.

Key lessons: Hatib's actions were a dangerous kind of espionage on a critical occasion. Motives and intentions were not essential or justifiable. These were not peace but wartime conditions, yet the Prophet, upon him peace and blessings, did not place Hatib in confinement without giving him a chance to defend himself.

Hatib was not prosecuted in secrecy or killed without a fair trial, even though the Prophet had revelation and Hatib's letter as evidence. Even under grave situations, Islam does not allow a ruler to imprison a person or prosecute them only based on their knowledge or suspicion.

Islam also does not recognize the method of prosecuting a person in secret. While Hatib's motives were unjustifiable as his actions put the community in grave danger, he was not only one of the emigrants but also a participant in the Battle of Badr. He was one of the distinguished companions, and God teaches us how to view the errors of the companions of the Prophets, upon them peace and blessings.

The companions can commit errors because of human weaknesses. Muslims should take them to task, which should be a teachable moment for the community.

Umar believed his actions were treachery to Allah and His Messenger, upon him peace and blessings, and the Muslims. However, the Prophet, upon him peace and blessings, disagreed and explained his decision. While Hatib's motives were not justifiable, one needs to consider his past life, the general character of the person who happened to commit the act, and the circumstances under which he committed it.

One can also see how God teaches and pardons humans through events, even when their motives or intentions are not justifiable. Still, they are ignorant of other realities in this world and the hereafter.

This case helped me a lot in reconciling mistakes by the companions and how to view the lack of utopia or trials and tribulations after Prophet Muhammad, upon him peace and blessings, returned to God. I mentioned some insights by looking at a few verses before, on Abraham, upon him peace. Let me look at a few verses after:

> *Allah forbids you not, with regard to those who fight you not for (your) Faith nor drive you out of your homes, from dealing kindly and justly with them: for Allah loveth those who are just. Allah only forbids you, with regard to those who fight you for (your) Faith, and drive you out of your homes, and support (others) in driving you out, from turning to them (for friendship and protection). It is such as turn to them (in these circumstances), that do wrong.*
>
> —Quran 60:8–9

The Quran was revealed in a span of twenty-three years, and changes were taking place to prepare Muslims to receive its revelation. As the Quran was revealed, Muslims were not sitting down in a classroom learning and being divorced from life and its challenges; instead, they were prepared internally either through trials, hardships, or challenges with others to receive its wisdom and understanding fully.

The Quran has a holistic and balanced approach to war and peace, teaching us how to understand, discern, and practice war when necessary and peace in all other circumstances. If we enter the Quran seeking guidance, we can see the two realities—war and peace—and reconcile them. If we enter the Quran looking for verses to attack others or distort its message, we cut and paste what feeds our ego and desires. In doing so, we either ignore the lessons and guidance on war or distort the lessons and guidance on peace.

The Sincere Adviser

Satan claims to Adam, upon him peace, to be a sincere adviser. However, he confesses that he will disassociate from those he advised or listened to.

Imam al-Sha'rawi gives great wisdom about this reality. He says that if the person advising you is not going to shoulder the consequences of their advice or the impact of that advice on you, you should not listen to that person or their advice.

Abraham, upon him peace, was truthful and told his father, "I have no power over Allah to obtain anything on your behalf" (Quran 60:4).

Abraham, upon him peace, was placed in the fire, and God saved and protected him. He put his trust in God and turned to God for guidance. Likewise, those who turn to God in this world will be saved from the fire of the hereafter. However, we cannot save others or make such claims that we have power over God to obtain anything on anyone's behalf. We must be firm and truthful in sharing this wisdom.

However, Satan does not say that. Instead, he makes false promises and claims: "Satan makes them promises, and creates in them false desires; but Satan's promises are nothing but deception" (Quran 4:120).

We learn from this that everyone must turn to God alone, seek their guidance, and not accept false promises of hope from others, including Satan.

Don't Follow People Blindly

> *They will all be marshalled before Allah together: then will the weak say to those who were arrogant, "For us, we but followed you; can ye then avail us to all against the wrath of Allah?" They will reply, "If we had received the Guidance of Allah, we should have given it to you: to us it makes no difference (now) whether we rage, or bear*

> *(these torments) with patience: for ourselves there is no way of escape."*
>
> —Quran 14:21

It is essential that we learn to turn to God and not expect others to protect us from judgment should God judge against us. We do not follow a mob mentality or find comfort in the mob having our back or people who are tested with power and privilege.

Likewise, we should be honest and truthful with others that if God judges in their favor, we have no right to protest the decision. However, if God judges against them, we have no power to protect them or protect ourselves.

In short, if we reflect on the Iago character in the story of Othello, we realize that all will be exposed on the Day of Judgment.

The Arabic word *baruz* means *to emerge*. As the chapter begins, guide humanity from the shadows to the light. It also implies becoming known. Hence, some translators translate it to *shall appear before Allah*, for it implies both these meanings.

In fact, we are all fully exposed all the time before Allah, but we are negligent or do not realize it. We will, however, realize it on the Day of Judgment when we will face judgment before the best of judges. As noted, before, everything will be on the table so that every deed we did and each and everything we thought and desired is known to Him.

The verse above warns all who follow others blindly or obey and submit to tyrants because they say, "We are weak." One should consider it well today where the people we follow or obey are heading. Our true intentions on why we followed such people will be made manifest on the Day of Judgment.

Such individuals lie to themselves and others, claiming: "If we had received the Guidance of Allah, we should have given it to you." Guidance means to point someone in the correct direction. Those in power and those who are weak were told to turn to God alone and seek His guidance, like Abraham, upon him peace, sought guidance from God.

Their record will show if they accepted this advice and turned to God seeking His guidance or not.

As Muslims, we read *al-Fatiha* seventeen times a day, at least daily, seeking guidance from God. One can argue that God does not exist, and we just came out of a random accident or chance, so how can we turn to God? We can put that theory on the table and use science to respond. Let me put my science hat on for a moment.

Scientists aim for their studies to be replicable—meaning that another researcher could perform a similar investigation and obtain the same basic results. When a study cannot be replicated, it suggests that our current understanding of the study system or our methods of testing are insufficient.

So if you can produce life and intelligence from random accident or chance and replicate your understanding or theory, you have an argument. You do not have a sound argument if you cannot produce evidence to replicate this understanding.

To my knowledge, every time there was a big bang or bombs were dropped on life-forms in various countries, people died. No new life-form or intelligent life-form was discovered. This study was replicated repeatedly throughout history via earthquakes, tornadoes, volcanoes, tsunamis, et cetera. No one has ever claimed an intelligent life-form emerged as a result of natural disasters. In all cases, people, animals, and life-forms died. COVID-19, a virus that came out of an accident, hit the global community, killed people globally, and overwhelmed the health-care systems worldwide. No new life-forms were discovered by anyone. Too many examples of this as a false and delusional theory to count.

Logic on a false worldview is simply logical falsehood. Since this theory has been postulated, I have not seen any replication studies producing intelligent life-forms from random accidents, natural disasters, or chance. You put a seed in the ground, water it, give it sun, and expect a plant. That has been replicated repeatedly. Where are the replication studies that random accidents, natural disasters, or chance produce intelligent life-forms? None exist.

In addition, if a random accident or chance brought us to life, then we can bring people back to life by planning and science. After all, look at all the amazing things we build from what God created, including robots. Hence:

> *Then why do ye not (intervene) when (the soul of the dying man) reaches the throat, And ye the while (sit) looking on, But We are nearer to him than ye, and yet see not, Then why do ye not, If you are exempt from (future) account, Call back the soul, if ye are true (in the claim of independence)?*

—Quran 56:83–87

We had plenty of time to figure out how to bring people back to life by now. So why haven't we brought one back? Regardless of how much we lie to ourselves and others, the truth is that we know.

> *It is We Who have created you: why will ye not witness the Truth?*
>
> —Quran 56:57

On the Day of Judgment, it will be manifested that it was arrogance and not ignorance that prevented us from turning to God and seeking His guidance. If we wait for that moment to see our shadow self-manifested to us, it will be too late, and "there is no way of escape."

Acceptance

> *And remember Abraham and Isma'il raised the foundations of the House (With this prayer): "Our Lord! Accept (this service) from us: For Thou art the All-Hearing, the All-knowing.*
>
> *"Our Lord! Make of us Muslims, bowing to Thy (Will), and of our progeny a people Muslim, bowing to Thy (will); and show us our place for the celebration of (due) rites; and turn unto us (in Mercy); for Thou art the Oft-Returning, Most Merciful.*
>
> *"Our Lord! send amongst them a Messenger of their own, who shall rehearse Thy Signs to them and instruct them in scripture and wisdom, and sanctify them: For Thou art the Exalted in Might, the Wise."*
>
> —Quran 2:127–129

As I mentioned earlier, we often treat God like He is chasing us, begging us for any crumbs of love or attention. Yet, when we value something, we strive hard to gain it, cry if we don't, and beg God for it. If it is acceptance of our deeds or ourselves, likewise, our internal state should reflect that. At the very least, we should be as worried as we are about getting into Ivy League and medical schools, passing bar exams, et cetera, for which we exhaust ourselves to the end and, afterward, worry frantically if we got accepted or passed.

When we value our relationship with God and do our deeds for God, our state should indicate that instead of being pompous and boasting.

Why would Prophet Abraham pray to God: "Our Lord! make of us Muslims, bowing to Thy (Will)"?

Because God is *Al-Ghani*— Free of Need or Want—our faith is a gift from Him. As we beg for acceptance in many areas of our lives, we should likewise beg of Him. In this spirit, we understand the words of Imam al-Shafi'i:

> *All humans are dead except those who have knowledge. And all those who have knowledge are asleep, except those who do good deeds. And those who do good deeds are deceived, except those who are sincere. And those who are sincere are always in a state of worry.*

Why worry? Worry is an expression of our value for something or someone. We have all experienced an emotional roller-coaster moment when we felt tremendous agony and worry, waiting for good news or acceptance from someone or something we held in high esteem.

The Promise

It is not a one-time event or test. Instead, if we pass, we are tested to a higher level of trust. Reflect on the supplication: "I leave your religion in the care of Allah, as well as your safety, and the last of your deeds."

Allah manages everything in the heavens and on earth—the sun, the moon, the stars—with perfection, and yet we don't trust Him to manage others' lives! Sometimes, we can do amazing acts of sacrifice for God regarding ourselves. Prophet Abraham, upon him peace, faced the blazing fire placing his trust in God.

He had to learn to accept that some family members were now his enemies, not just the enemies of God, and face exile with his wife Sarah, upon them peace.

The difficult test came to him when he learned to trust God when He placed his only companion in faith, Sarah, in a tyrant's hands. This is a difficult test. The mother of Moses, upon them peace, struggled to place her son in the basket. Many of us faced separation anxiety when we had to separate from our children for the first time. However, it is hard to trust God—when we are asked to trust Him—when He places our most dear and cherished in the hands of a tyrant.

Prophet Jacob, upon him peace, also struggled with this test. In a way, the death of a loved one invites us to embrace that test. We do not struggle to place them in the hands of God but in the cold and dark grave. All alone. And we struggle and hold on because we find it a difficult test to bear.

And after having firm faith in God and hope with regards to Joseph, upon him peace, Jacob was tested again at a higher level with the loss of Benjamin and his oldest son.

And Prophet Abraham, upon him peace, was tested again, with his son, Ishmael, and Hajar, placing them in Mecca. And then again, when asked to sacrifice his only son, Ishmael.

Hence, trust is not a one-time event. It has many levels. If you fail, the same test repeats itself. If you pass, a new test emerges with a higher and steeper level of trust. Most of us will not be tested to such a degree. However, we can learn and reflect on the lessons we face in much smaller manifestations of such tests.

I found this *dua* or supplication helpful in preparing myself to separate from my mother as she faced her final days. I would tell God, "I am placing her in the hands of the Most Merciful of those who show Mercy or *fiaman Arhum Ar Rahimeen*."

Generosity

> *Has there reached you the story of the honoured guests of Ibrahim? When they entered upon him and said, "[We greet you with] peace." He answered, "[And upon you] peace, [you are] a people unknown. Then he went to his family and came with a fat [roasted] calf. And placed it near them; he said, "Will you not eat?"*

—Quran 51:24–27

My mother was from a Palestinian town called Khalil. The town was named after Prophet Ibrahim, upon him peace. *Khalil* means *Friend*, as he was given the title "The Friend of God" or "*Khalil ul Allah*."

One thing that people in that town insist on following is the generous spirit of Prophet Ibrahim, upon him peace. The townsfolk are known for this character that they uphold and pass on.

Honoring guests and feeding strangers are among his character strengths. In this passage, the angels, appearing in human form, come to visit Prophet Ibrahim, upon him peace. He did not recognize them but treated them with hospitality and generosity.

Prophet Abraham, upon him peace is known as an *ummah* or nation all by himself.

In an interview with Charlie Rose, Toni Morrison raised some interesting questions. She asked the following questions of racists: "Who are you without your race [crowd]? Are you any good? Are you still strong? Are you smart?"

Very good critical thinking questions. Let us use these questions to reflect on Prophet Abraham, upon him peace, his wife Sarah, and his other wife, Hajar.

1. When Abraham was taken away from his family, was he still faithful, strong, and committed to God?
2. When Sarah was taken away from Abraham and faced the tyrant alone, was she still a strong woman of pure faith?
3. When Hajar was taken away from her community and husband and placed in the desert, was she still a strong woman of pure faith?

What about us? Who are we without our crowd? If you contemplate this further and ask, "Who was Satan without his crowd of angels? Was he any good? Was he strong? Was he smart?" No. He was accursed. He was unrepentant and delusional. God tells us his argument was weak—the permutations of sinful cunning.

In general, oppression of oneself or others does not have a sound argument. And that is how some people are. Avid listeners to the lies of Satan and others. Whom do they harm? Themselves. Over time, their actions cause their hearts to be sealed: "Those are they whose hearts God desired not to purify."

I end with Morrison's famous quote: "If you can only be tall when someone is on their knees, then you have a very serious problem." I call it egoism.

I discussed that God is *Al-Hameed* and *Al-Ghani*. God did not command us to build a house or community of faith on the oppression of others. When He chose Abraham and his spouses and children to build the faith community, God did not do so on the oppression of others. God manifested their purity of faith, strength, intelligence, and commitment to Him. They obeyed and then faced tribulation; they were tested and passed.

Like the tests of *Ta'if* or the birth of Jesus, upon him peace, these trials are the means that God uses to manifest to us, those pure in faith. Who are they without their crowd? Only the sincere and pure of faith can survive such trials and remain committed to God.

When the house of worship was built, others were not killed, massacred, or ethnically cleansed to make this happen. A place without a people for a new faith community without a place. Likewise, when Prophet Muhammad, upon him peace and blessings, went to Medina to build the budding Muslim community, it was at the invitation of the *Ansar* or helpers, who were the people of Medina. He was welcomed with nobility. No one was massacred or killed.

Abu Dharr al-Ghifari, may Allah be pleased with him, reported that the Prophet, upon him peace and blessings, narrated that His Lord said: "Oh my servants, I have forbidden oppression even for myself, and I have made it forbidden among you as well, so do not oppress one another."

> *And remember Abraham and Isma'il raised the foundations of the House (With this prayer): "Our Lord! Accept (this service) from us: For Thou art the All-Hearing, the All-knowing. "Our Lord! Make of us Muslims, bowing to Thy (Will), and of our progeny a people Muslim, bowing to Thy (will); and show us our place for the celebration of (due) rites; and turn unto us (in Mercy); for Thou art the Oft-Returning, Most Merciful.*
>
> *Our Lord! send amongst them a Messenger of their own, who shall rehearse Thy Signs to them and instruct them in scripture and wisdom, and sanctify them: For Thou art the Exalted in Might, the Wise.*
>
> *And who turns away from the religion of Abraham but such as debase their souls with folly? Him We chose and rendered pure in this world: And he will be in the Hereafter in the ranks of the Righteous. Behold! his Lord said to him: "Bow (thy will to Me):" He said: "I bow (my will) to the Lord and Cherisher of the Universe."*
>
> —Quran 2:127–131

If we read the Quran, there is a general theme that is repeated through the lives of all the prophets: God will test your sincerity and truthfulness to Him before fulfilling His promise.

There is a narrative that Sarah asked Abraham to send Hajar to the desert out of jealousy and a claim that Hajar was banished.

However, a close look at the facts and allowing Sarah to speak for Sarah, not interjecting or conjecturing our own conjured ideas, helps us gain a more honest view of the story.

It was Abraham and Sarah whom Abraham's family banished and who came to Palestine as refugees. A tyrant took possession of Sarah; because of her strength of faith, he was hit with a calamity. To free himself, he let her go with Hajar as a gift to serve her.

Sarah gave Abraham Hajar as a wife, hoping she would bear him a son who would inherit the covenant. Sarah was a strong and loyal believer. She reached very old age and wanted to aid his mission.

Imam Ghazali said, "The believer despairs of everyone but God, while the hypocrite has set his hopes in everyone except God."

The stories of Sarah and Hajar can help us ask questions about patience, generosity, and sacrifice.

Forbearance

> *[A]nd every People plotted against their prophet, to seize him, and disputed by means of vanities, therewith to condemn the Truth; but it was I that seized them! and how (terrible) was My Requital!*
>
> —Quran 40:5

Prophet Ibrahim, upon him peace, was known to be a very forbearing person. He was able to endure much pain and suffering from his people, as all prophets had to. While we can share his message, we must admit that we struggle to follow his example. Hence, it is essential that whenever we share a message from any prophet, we humble ourselves and share it first and foremost with ourselves.

The prophets were not ordinary people, getting applause on stage for preaching the word of God. Rather, they were encompassed with the plots and plans to kill and harm them.

Their forbearance is also proof against the people who rejected them solely to condemn the truth of the message they shared with them. As we prepare every year for lessons during Hajj, we should reflect on this reality and not claim a station of faith at their level.

Prophet Ibrahim, upon him peace, taught us the importance of showing gratitude when God fulfils our prayers. In addition, the importance of asking God to make us among those who establish prayer and to include our children. Also, pray for our forgiveness and include all the believers in these prayers.

Power and Proofs

> *"Uff to you and to what you worship instead of Allah. Then will you not use reason?" They said, "Burn him and support your gods if you are to act." Allah said, "O fire, be coolness and safety upon Abraham." And they intended for him harm, but We made them the greatest losers.*
>
> —Quran 21:67–70

In a scholarly commentary video on Chapter 18 of the Holy Quran, Shaykh al-Sha'rawi mentions the proof that Prophet Abraham, upon him peace, presented to his people and the importance of understanding this proof.

When a trial happens, know there is a pearl of great wisdom. Is it a punishment or a test? Look at your actions. If they align with the sacred law, there is higher wisdom that you must surrender to. If not, you might have violated the sacred law, and God is waking you up to repent, which is a blessing and a sign of His loving concern for you.

People always see accountability by God as a bad thing. Instead, it is a good thing. A case in point is Satan. If God lets you go after you did something wrong, it is because He saw nothing good in you and does not wish to purify you, so delusion is your punishment in this world and hellfire in the hereafter.

Faith has a strong argument. Many people think that the argument of faith is to believe in God, just in case there is a hell and a heaven—a safety net to protect one from the worst-case scenario. That is simply not true.

The prophets came with proof as clear as day to humanity. At first, people had to bear witness to their character and honesty. They would acknowledge they were a noble and trustworthy citizen. The prophets were not common folk who lived unethical lives and suddenly decided to preach God to people for attention.

The proofs were of the kind that showed the power of God over His creation and the universe. They cannot be replicated.

For example, if Abraham fell into the fire and wind or rain blew out the fire, that is not proof. Another example he gave is if Prophet Ibrahim, upon him peace, escaped them and the chiefs could not throw him in the fire, then this is not proof. Both can be replicated.

However, for Prophet Ibrahim, upon him peace, to be thrown into the fire, and the fire, which is known to burn people, is ordered by God to be cool to Ibrahim, that is a proof of God's power and that Prophet Ibrahim, upon him peace, is speaking the truth. It cannot be replicated.

We study the mechanics of creation and the biological matter we are made of, yet we cannot bring a soul back to life. We can freeze embryos or implant them in surrogate mothers, yet we cannot bring them back to life. Jesus, upon him peace, was given the power to bring the dead back to life to show God sent him. We cannot replicate this.

> *"O fire, be coolness and safety upon Abraham."*

The fire is under the command of God. The community bore witness with their own eyes that the fire only burned the ropes that bound Ibrahim, upon him peace. The fire was peaceful and cool as the smoke suffocated them. The fire kept burning, its smoke darkening their faces, reflecting their dark hearts, as they waited for it to burn out. When it did, to their amazement, Prophet Ibrahim, upon him peace, walked out of the fire, face bright with spiritual light, untouched by the fire as if he was walking out of a garden.

> *"And they intended for him harm, but We made them the greatest losers."*

Imagine working very hard to harm someone, and it backfires in your face in front of everyone. The same happened with the Pharaoh and Moses, upon him peace.

Despite the evidence right before them and their souls acknowledging that they were wrong, they could not surrender to the truth witnessed as clear as day. In this way, God guards the message He sends with His Prophets to humanity. If you look through the Quran, people plot and plan, and God allows their plans to unfold; however, they only unfold at the command and power of God. In this way, truth is separated from falsehood. I mentioned earlier that God allows falsehood to prevail before the truth comes and knocks out its brains.

An example would be if someone kills you or a loved one today. Well, one day, they, too, will die. We will all die.

> *And We did not grant to any man before you eternity [on earth], so if you die—would they be eternal? Every soul will taste death. And We test you with evil and with good as trial, and to Us, you will be returned.*
>
> —Quran 21:34–35

So getting rid of someone in this life simply pushes the person into the next world, as Joseph's brothers threw him into the well and slavery. Eventually, we will die, and just like Joseph's brothers were forced to seek help in Egypt and came face-to-face with Joseph, we will also die and come face-to-face with those who killed or harmed loved ones or us or vice versa. The oppressors will be under the mercy and power of those they oppressed.

The Shaykh goes into more detail on trials and tribulations in Chapter 18. However, I will not discuss the examples he gave. You are welcome to listen to them for greater understanding. The critical point or lesson to derive is that trials and tribulations manifest God's power over His creation and universe. They are reminders to turn to Him or surrender to His Divine Plan. When people's evil plans hit the prophets, God allowed them to do so, to verify, confirm, and strengthen the argument of truth and faith.

What does this have to do with love? God wants love, meaning He gives you the power and choice to disobey Him, and you lovingly choose to obey Him.

Shaykh al-Sha'rawi presented an example of two enslaved people who serve you: Saad and Saeed. One is compelled to serve you, and you have him metaphorically held by the neck and pull the rope whenever you want him to do something. Does he have the power to disobey? No. He serves you by compulsion.

The other has the power to disobey, with no rope attached to his neck. You call him, and he comes willingly to serve you. *Marhab* or welcome. Which one can manifest his love for you? The one who comes willingly to serve and obey you.

God made some matters that we must obey, and we are compelled to abide by them such that we are not permitted to kill, steal, et cetera. Some matters measure our love of Him and conviction in our faith.

Also, heaven and hell. God will grant heaven to those who serve Him with their hope of going to heaven. And those who serve Him to be protected from hell, God will protect from Hell. This is acceptable, and God rewards them such. In the last verse of Chapter 18, we are invited to a higher level of faith.

> *Hence, whoever looks forward [with hope and awe] to meeting his Sustainer [on Judgment Day], let him do righteous deeds, and let him not ascribe unto anyone or anything a share in the worship due to his Sustainer!*
>
> —Quran 18:110

Heaven is considered such a means of worship. Whoever works for heaven will be granted heaven. No doubt. We all start our faith with baby steps. Here we are invited to seek the Creator of heaven, a desire to meet Him and come close to Him. We are invited to grow in depth and breadth of faith.

There is a saying that translates to "If I did not create heaven and hell, do I not deserve to be worshiped?" The Shaykh quotes a saint, Rabi'a al-'Adawiyya, known for her devotion and piety, as saying,

> *Everyone worships You for Your heaven or fear of Your hell. God, if you know that I am worshiping you out of greed for your heaven, then forbid it to me. And if you know that I am worshiping you out of fear of your hell, throw me in it. I obey you because You are worthy of being obeyed.*

This is a high station to reach, and we should strive to worship God out of love, for He is most worthy of our love, more than anyone or anything.

We must understand our limitations and seek forgiveness to better understand God's Mercy and Compassion, leading to a deeper appreciation of His Beautiful Names and a stronger faith in His Divine Plan and Promise.

When Satan attempted to sow sedition between humanity and God, God responded by expelling him from heaven for the sake of humankind. And made heaven open for us. However, we failed to show gratitude to our Loving Creator. When Satan tried again, this time whispering to Adam to create a schism between humanity and God. We listened. Our weakness is that we do not turn to God for guidance and instead listen to doubt and lies about God. We must learn that when Satan throws into our psyche what troubles our soul to cultivate a false opinion of God within us or others, to turn to

Allah: "And if (at any time) an incitement to discord is made to thee by the Evil One, seek refuge in Allah. He is the One Who hears and knows all things" (Quran 41:36).

Which of the favors of your Lord would you deny?

> The Most Merciful or the Most Gracious! It is He who has taught the Quran. He has created man: He has taught him speech (and intelligence).
>
> The sun and the moon follow courses (exactly) computed; And the herbs and the trees—both (alike) prostrate in adoration. And the heaven
>
> He raised and He has set up the Balance (of Justice), In order that ye may not transgress (due) balance. So establish weight with justice and fall not short in the balance.
>
> And the earth He laid [out] for the creatures. Therein is fruit and palm trees having sheaths [of dates] And grain having husks and scented plants.
>
> So which of the favors of your Lord would you deny?
>
> —Quran 55:1–13

Making peace is a good thing to do between people, but it is not obligatory. However, justice is obligatory.

Instead of asking why bad things happen to good people, the Quran encourages us to ponder on "Which of the favors of your Lord would you deny?"

It is hard to find the best translation of the Quran. It is good to look at a few as the verses are full of meaning and difficult to translate.

> He created man from clay like [that of] pottery. And He created the jinn from a smokeless flame of fire. So which of the favors of your Lord would you deny?
>
> —Quran 14–16

Djinn references another set of beings, devils or satans, although according to Islamic tradition, some of them accepted Islam. They rejected the call of their forefather Iblis. However, in general, satans are enemies of human beings and God.

Why did God allow this powerful djinn to trick Adam? When people ask this question, they blame God for their slips, implying that a good or just God would not allow Satan to exist. But to answer the question of "Why Satan?" we must also ask," Why humanity?" Angels and djinn existed long before God created humans.

God created humans because angels couldn't know God the way humans do. God has said that He created humanity so that we might know Him differently. We can discover the attributes of God that can only be discovered by beings who have the freedom to choose well or poorly. As God said, "I was a hidden treasure, and I wanted to be known."

We can say it's our purpose in life to get to know God. But how do we get to know God's hidden treasures—His intimate and loving reality? It is through our flaws and failings and overcoming them with His Mercy, by His Mercy, and for the Most Merciful.

Humanity manifested to Satan his arrogance. And Satan manifested to humanity their weakness. And by knowing ourselves, we can know God sincerely. So, which of the favors of your Lord would you deny?

> [He is] Lord of the two sunrises and Lord of the two sunsets. So which of the favors of your Lord would you deny?
>
> —Quran 55:17–18

If you have ever watched a sunset or sunrise, you must have felt amazed at the moment's beauty. We can look at these verses physically as in reference to the sunrise and sunset. On Altafsir.com, one of the commentaries on this verse says:

> *(Lord of the two Easts) the East of winter and the East of summer, (and Lord of the two Wests) the West of winter and the West of summer! There are two Easts and two Wests.*
>
> *The East of winter and the East of summer have 180 phases, just as the two Wests and the moon have 180 phases. It is also said that the Easts of summer and winter have 177 phases and the Wests of summer and winter, as well as the moon, have 177 phases. The sun rises throughout the year two days in the same phase, and it also sets two days in the same phase.*

We can also look at this verse metaphorically; other commentaries on this verse say:

> *He is Lord of the two risings and Lord of the two settings.*
>
> *He said: Its inner meaning refers to the rising of the heart and its setting, the rising of the tongue and its setting, and the rising of the profession of His oneness, [whose] setting is the witnessing (mushahada) of Him.*
>
> *And He also says, [I swear] by the Lord of the risings and the settings [70:40], meaning the risings of the bodily members through sincerity (ikhlaṣ) and their settings through subservience to people (ta'a li'l-nas) inwardly and outwardly. His words, Exalted is He.*
>
> *He released the two seas, meeting [side by side]; Between them is a barrier [so] neither of them transgresses. So which of the favors of your Lord would you deny? From both of them emerge pearl and coral. So which of the favors of your Lord would you deny? And to Him belong the ships [with sails] elevated in the sea like mountains.*
>
> *So which of the favors of your Lord would you deny?*
>
> —Quran 55:19–25

The injustice that we as humans bring into the world, whether as victims of it or as offenders, keeps us focused on the fight, the argument, the pain, the oppression, et cetera.

God responds by opening our eyes to the natural world and how it is just and functions in order and harmony. When Moses, upon him peace, met with the Pharaoh, he was challenged by the Pharaoh on how God would treat people of the past, overlooking how he was dealing with people under his power. Likewise, Moses, upon him peace, turned his sight to look beyond himself, see the world, and look outside the circle of oppression. I wrote in my book *God Intervenes Between A Person And Their Heart*, in the chapter on lessons on power and oppression from Moses:

> *Tyrants project their fears not just on the people they oppress but also on God. They accuse God of what they are doing, and instead of allowing the pharaoh to do that, Moses closes that door. In this dialogue, the pharaoh questions God's power and justice, overlooking his own reality: That he's a vulnerable human being enslaving*

> others. Moses, upon him peace, directs the pharaoh to focus on the present moment, which he can see clearly before him, the diversity of God's creation and how each is nurtured. Open your eyes to the present moment, he says.
>
> Interestingly, this advice is that many healers likewise encourage their patients to go into nature and look at the diversity of plants and creation and observe them. There is a healing effect in just looking at stars and sky and the present moment.

Here is their conversation:

> When this message was delivered, Pharaoh said: "Who, then, O Moses, is the Lord of you two?"
>
> He said: "Our Lord is He Who gave to each (created) thing its form and nature, and further, gave (it) guidance."
>
> Pharaoh: "What then is the condition of previous generations?"
>
> He replied: "The knowledge of that is with my Lord, duly recorded: my Lord never errs, nor forgets,
>
> "He Who has made for you the earth like a carpet spread out; has enabled you to go about therein by roads (and channels); and has sent down water from the sky." With it, We produced diverse pairs of plants, each separate from the others.
>
> Eat (for yourselves) and pasture your cattle: verily, in this are Signs for men endued with understanding.

Look outside of yourself.

> Everyone upon the earth will perish, And there will remain the Face of your Lord, Owner of Majesty and Honor. So which of the favors of your Lord would you deny? Whoever is within the heavens and earth asks Him; every day, He is bringing about a matter. So which of the favors of your Lord would you deny? We will attend to you, O prominent beings. So which of the favors of your Lord would you deny?

—Quran 26–32

If you have ever had engaged in thought monitoring, you might have wondered how such horrific loss of life can happen in wars, genocide, mass shootings, et cetera.

It can take on a life of its own if not stopped and countered. It helps to ground our thoughts and delusions with reality or faith to help us face such trials and tribulations. If some tyrant feels they have the power to give hell to another country, you can rest assured that he will perish in time. Hence, killing someone doesn't bring a win as we are all going to pass and die. Eventually. And justice will be served.

You might have also heard news of individuals who, during their time, were celebrated as great people, but, either before their death or after, they were recognized as bad people who harmed others or enslaved them. Although they were seen as heroes during their time, now we remember them in history as fascists, psychopaths, or abusers. And the reverse is true: people were condemned, and before their death or after, history recognized them as people of valor.

This helps us make choices and not be deluded by applause and praise. When we are reminded that all that remains will be our Lord, Possessor of Majesty and Generous Giving, we know whom to take our prayers and complaints to first and foremost. People are means, and when we seek their help, we seek them as instruments of God.

This is the same as He says elsewhere: "What is with you runs out, but what is with God subsists" (Quran 16:96).

This also helps us not be yes men to abusers for fear of death or greed. "Prefer what subsists over what undergoes annihilation."

We can make better choices when we recognize that this world is the Abode of Delusion and the next life the Abode of Joy.

When we recognize that this world is the Abode of Annihilation and the next life the Abode of Subsistence, this helps us make decisions. Hence, intelligence prefers subsistence over what undergoes annihilation and the Abode of Joy over the Abode of delusion.

Even if all power and all the world were given to you, the outcome of all would be annihilation. So seeking that is a delusion.

Whatever is in the heavens and the earth asks of Him. Each day, He is upon some task. In the scholarly commentary of Chapter 55, on Altafsir.com, it is mentioned that:

> *The faithful are two groups: the worshipers and the recognizers. The asking of each group is in the measure of their aspirations, and the caressing of each is suited to their capacity. The worshipers want everything from Him, the recognizers want Him Himself.*

We all seek God with our needs. The commentary continues: "Each day He is upon some task." He lifts one group and puts down others. To one group, He says, "So rejoice!" (Quran 9:111); to another, He says, "Die in your rage!" (Quran 3:119).

Everything we do shall be recorded in the life of the world and will be addressed on the Day of Judgment, both for djinn and for human beings.

The Witnesses

The same facts can have different meanings and be told as countering: i.e., in varying contradictions to each other. How can we tell the two or the many apart, for we all tell stories claiming ourselves and our tribe as the protagonists, using assumptions and conjecture that often carry and implant seeds of prejudice and malice about people's intent or specific actions?

The prophets' stories, as related in the Quran by God, provides a light to answering these and many questions.

In addition, human power has a master narrative that carries assumptions, bias, pride (not dignity), and conjecture that people believe to be accurate and blindly use to engage each other, even God. These assumptions and conjectures are normative life experiences and shared meanings we construct or adopt to speak for others and God. They are framed within cultural, social, and political systems of power.

The unchallenged assumptions and conjectures made when people tell and listen to stories can malign, silence, or distort the truth, particularly the stories of the prophets and the words of God.

> *It is He Who has sent His Messenger with Guidance and the Religion of Truth, to proclaim it over all religion: and enough is Allah for a Witness.*
>
> —Quran 48:28

When the stories in the Quran are shared as counternarratives to the dominant voice, these stories enable a different "truth" to emerge and be heard, allowing an enlightened heart a lens of understanding through which to view the exact facts of an event. It will help us distinguish the reformer from the corrupter.

Sin Means Saying No to God

> *The foolish among the people will say, "What has turned them away from their qiblah, which they used to face?" Say, "To Allah belongs the east and the west. He guides whom He wills to a straight path."*
>
> *And thus, we have made you a just community that you will be witnesses over the people, and the Messenger will be a witness over you. And We did not make the qiblah which you used to face except that We might make evident who would follow the Messenger from who would turn back on his heels. And indeed, it is difficult except for those whom Allah has guided. And never would Allah have caused you to lose your faith. Indeed, Allah is, to the people, Kind and Merciful.*
>
> —Quran 2:142–143

Qiblah means the direction of prayer. Al Masjid Al Aqsa, or the farthest mosque, was the first *qiblah* for Muslims, and it has been a significant and important place of worship for the Prophets and Messengers of God. Currently, it is toward the Ka'abah, in Mecca. I will not give the wisdom that scholars mention behind changing the direction of the *qiblah*. What is important to note is how Prophet Muhammad, upon him peace and blessings, responded when God told him to face Al Masjid Al Aqsa. His unwavering, unhesitating response to the command of God.

When we consider sin, we often look for evidence that something is a sin or evidence that it is not. In doing so, we conjecture much. Sin is simply saying no to God's command. Hence, the question Hajar asked demonstrates how to interpret scripture: "Is this from God, or did God command this?"

Here, God mentions that Prophet Muhammad, upon him peace and blessings, will be a witness over us Muslims. Now, if we turn to God seeking guidance, and we are following Prophet Muhammad, upon him peace and blessings, out of genuine faith and not tribalism or other motives, God says, "[I]t is difficult except for those whom Allah has guided. And never would Allah have caused you to lose your faith. Indeed, Allah is, to the people, Kind and Merciful."

Sometimes God brings forth commands or trials to offer people who are following for ulterior motives a chance to turn to God for guidance. In fact, whenever we find something difficult, and we will all find something in our faith difficult to put into practice, we should turn to God and ask Him to make it easy for us.

I mentioned that Prophet Muhammad, upon him peace and blessings, will be a witness over us Muslims. We Muslims will be witnesses for previous prophets.

How So?

Imam Ahmad and Ibn Maajah narrated that Abu Sa'eed al-Khudri, may Allah be pleased with him, said:

> The Messenger of Allah, upon him peace and blessings, said: "A Prophet will come on the Day of Resurrection accompanied by one man, and a Prophet will come accompanied by two men, or more than that. Then his people will be called and it will be said to them: 'Did this one convey the message to you?' and they will say, 'No.' It will be said to him: 'Did you convey the message to your people?' and he will say: 'Yes.'
>
> "It will be said to him: 'Who will bear witness for you?'
>
> "He will say: 'Muhammad and his followers.' So Muhammad and his followers will be called.
>
> "It will be said to them: 'Did this one convey the message to his people?'
>
> "They will say: 'Yes.'
>
> "It will be said: 'How did you know that?'
>
> "They will say: 'Our Prophet came to us and told us that the Messengers had conveyed the message.'"
>
> Some will say, "How can you bear witness when you were not there?"
>
> Muslims say: "Enough is God as a Witness."

God did not make us witnesses to the creation of the heavens and the earth or to the creation of ourselves, and He would not have taken the misguiders as assistants. (See Quran 18:51)

We investigated the Message that reached us and the Messenger who brought it while those who rejected it ran after conjecture, guessing at the unknown, playing with doubt, and amusing themselves. Those who rejected it are quite comfortable bearing witness to the creation of the heavens and the earth and ourselves, when we were not there as witnesses to our creation.

We should be open to investigating the Message and the Messenger, upon him peace and blessings, and believing him and accepting that the Message he brought is from God.

As Muslims, we must realize the Prophet and God will be witness over us. This means we cannot use our faith as a weapon for power or other forms of egoism. We ask God for refuge and guidance. Below are verses for reflection regarding this theme:

> *And [warn of] the Day when We will remove the mountains and you will see the earth prominent, and We will gather them and not leave behind from them anyone.*
>
> *And they will be presented before your Lord in rows, [and He will say], "You have certainly come to Us just as We created you the first time. But you claimed that We would never make for you an appointment."*
>
> *And the record [of deeds] will be placed [open], and you will see the criminals fearful of that within it, and they will say, "Oh, woe to us! What is this book that leaves nothing small or great except that it has enumerated it?" And they will find what they did present [before them]. And your Lord does injustice to no one.*
>
> *And [mention] when We said to the angels, "Prostrate to Adam," and they prostrated, except for Iblees. He was of the jinn and departed from the command of his Lord. Then will you take him and his descendants as allies other than Me while they are enemies to you? Wretched it is for the wrongdoers as an exchange.*
>
> *I did not make them witness to the creation of the heavens and the earth or to the creation of themselves, and I would not have taken the misguiders as assistants.*
>
> —Quran 18:47–51

Examples of witnesses

- The Gathering (similar to the Day of Festival in the story of Moses)
- Appointed Day

- The record or book of deeds
- The angels or the recorders
- Human conjecture without any witnesses

Our Heart Is Also Witness

> *And that which is (locked up) in (human) breasts is made manifest—That their Lord had been Well-acquainted with them, (even to) that Day?*
>
> —Quran 100:10–11

We can see very clearly: God's justice is open and transparent. Beautiful verses if one reflects on them. May God grant us His grace to be true and sincere to Him.

You cannot see your reflection in dirty water. Similarly, you cannot see the truth if your heart is full of diseases. When hearts are purified, clarity comes. What does this mean?

It means use your mind, and don't let your mind use you. We know this realization is true. Scientifically, it is true. Prejudice, pride, love, hatred, and bias obscure the truth. And you and I know we are human. Hence, when we come to this realization, it should push us to turn to God and to earnestly seek that our hearts be purified so we can see the truth as truth.

Otherwise, our hearts will remain full of impurities, and we will lose awareness of the message embedded in our souls.

The Messenger of Allah, upon him peace and blessings, said: "O Allah grant my soul its piety, and purify it, for you are the best who can purify it. You are its protector and guardian. You are its Protector and its Guardian" (Sahih Muslim, 2722).

This is the same message of all the Prophets of God: use our reason and intelligence and seek a pure heart. Prophet Ibrahim, upon him peace, said:

> *And let me not be in disgrace on the Day when (men) will be raised up; The Day whereon neither wealth nor sons will avail, But only he (will prosper) that brings to Allah a sound (pure) heart.*
>
> —Quran 26:87–89

May Allah grant us pure hearts, sound minds, and certainty of faith as we age. May we be written of those who ever turn to Him.

Divine Connection?

> *And of the people is he whose speech pleases you in worldly life, and he calls Allah to witness as to what is in his heart, yet he is the fiercest of opponents. And when he goes away, he strives throughout the land to cause corruption therein and destroy crops and animals. And Allah does not like corruption. And when it is said to him, "Fear Allah," pride in the sin takes hold of him. Sufficient for him is Hellfire, and how wretched is the resting place. And of the people is he who sells himself, seeking means to the approval of Allah. And Allah is kind to [His] servants.*
>
> *O you who have believed, enter into Islam completely [and perfectly] and do not follow the footsteps of Satan. Indeed, he is to you a clear enemy. But if you deviate after clear proofs have come to you, then know that Allah is Exalted in Might and Wise. Do they await but that Allah should come to them in covers of clouds and the angels [as well] and the matter is [then] decided? And to Allah [all] matters are returned.*
>
> —Quran 2:204–210

When God takes us as a witness, we cannot claim God is on our side. Instead, we comfort our soul that God is Witness when we're falsely accused, and on the Day of Judgment, God will judge based on the truth.

As I mentioned, Islam calls for accountability and responsibility. A person must always have witnesses in case a need or a false accusation is made. Law-abiding documents must have witnesses. A marriage must have witnesses. We need witnesses in many areas of our lives. A court of law cannot be obligated to judge the unseen or claims based on town gossip.

God commanded that we take truthful witnesses and protect our rights. Hence, we cannot act irresponsibly, go to court, and say God is my Witness. Likewise, we cannot transgress, go to court, and say God is my Witness. Both actions are in violation of God's commands. If anyone act in such a manner, then God is a witness that this person violated His commands.

Example:

> *And if you are on a journey and cannot find a scribe, then a security deposit [should be] taken. And if one of you*

> entrusts another, then let him who is entrusted discharge his trust [faithfully] and let him fear Allah, his Lord. And do not conceal testimony, for whoever conceals it—his heart is indeed sinful, and Allah is Knowing of what you do."
>
> —Quran 2:283

When we take God as a witness to an event, we are not speaking for God, but to God, pleading that He bears witness to an event that requires a witness in typical life experiences, but there are no witnesses or the witnesses are giving false testimony due to circumstances beyond our control. An example is the story of Joseph, upon him peace.

Trusting in God's justice and relying on Him to reveal the truth at the appointed time can bring a sense of inner peace and calmness, even in the face of false accusations. This faith can also help individuals avoid getting caught up in the drama and negativity accompanying such situations.

Say, "Bring it to court." Usually, such individuals will go from place to place, smearing your name and engaging in sinful cunning games but refuse to come before a court of law. Why? They prefer to operate outside the legal system, where they can manipulate and deceive people without being held accountable for their actions. It's essential to stand firm and insist on resolving disputes through legal means to protect yourself from such individuals. A court of law is obligated to judge based on truthful witnesses. They cannot listen to testimony from the world of the unseen. Below is a case in point:

> And [beware the Day] when Allah will say, "O Jesus, Son of Mary, did you say to the people, 'Take me and my mother as deities besides Allah?'" He will say, "Exalted are You! It was not for me to say that to which I have no right. If I had said it, You would have known it. You know what is within myself, and I do not know what is within Yourself. Indeed, it is You who is Knower of the unseen.
>
> "I said not to them except what You commanded me—to worship Allah, my Lord and your Lord. And I was a witness over them as long as I was among them; but when You took me up, You were the Observer over them, and You are, over all things, Witness."
>
> —Quran 5:116–117

When we are falsely accused, taking God as a Witness is speaking to God. As Jesus, upon him peace, said, "If I had said it, You would have known it." In other words, we ask God to judge based on what He witnessed, and we are open to His judgment of the matter without any opposition.

Let God Speak for God

> He [Noah] said, "My Lord, I take refuge with Thee, lest I should ask of Thee that whereof I have no knowledge; for if Thou forgivest me not, and hast not mercy on me, I shall be among the losers."
>
> —Quran 11:47

We do not like people to speak for us, about us, or what is within us without our knowledge or consent. Likewise, we cannot speak for God or what is within Him. We can convey His Message, Commands, and Words in the Quran as Jesus, upon him peace, said, "It was not for me to say that to which I have no right."

God can speak for us, about us, and what is within us as He created us and knows us more than we know ourselves. Despite this tremendous knowledge of us, to the depth of our inner world and more hidden and secret to us, He Most High and Exalted uses witnesses to respond to those who deny and oppose His Judgment. God does not use human conjecture, corrupters, or mind games. He is God. *Al Khabir* could say you are lying on the Day of Judgment. However, He brings evidence and witnesses to make it clear as day to all that the individual opposing Him is lying.

The lesson is that if God says, "I witnessed from you X, Y, and Z," beg for Forgiveness and Mercy. Do not argue or oppose Him. If we do not oppose and deny what He Witnessed when He calls us to account, the witnesses will not be needed. Corrupters will argue, as they have a contentious, oppositional, and defiant spirit.

What If People Reject the Witnesses?

A person of faith finds God sufficient as a witness. For a corrupter, God, the angels, and the Prophets are not enough witnesses. They will argue and debate.

God will bring those affected by their oppression and transgressions as witnesses for questioning. Again, God brings people as witnesses who are trustworthy, not dishonest and corrupt.

The angels will bear witness. However, Satan will not. It will be clear that the witnesses brought forth to testify are innocent and credible. As the Prophets are questioned, the victims are questioned.

> *When the souls are sorted out, (being joined, like with like); When the female (infant), buried alive, is questioned—For what crime she was killed.*
>
> —Quran 81:7–9

To help you appreciate this passage, I want to share a story. Growing up in the States, we heard much about women's rights here compared to the Muslim communities globally. We believed or expected that going to court would be very easy to get our rights heard and addressed.

Briefly, it was just as difficult as that which women are facing in Iran. This is not to say that Muslim communities are beacons of women's rights. They struggle in different ways and, at times, to skirt our responsibilities or deflect the multiple ways we oppress, we focus on how women are oppressed over there. Muslim communities will focus on women's rights in non-Muslim communities and vice versa. You probably saw how Israel, which fought ferociously to avoid any investigation into the targeted assassinations of Shireen Abu Akhleh and Rouzan al-Najjar and the imprisonment of Ahed Tamimi, could not help but defend the women in Iran in the recent protests.

In this manner, we keep focusing on how others over there are oppressing and nurturing blindness to our areas of needed growth. We were summoned to court in Chicago to respond to the usual false accusations by my sister's ex-husband. As we prepared to leave for Chicago from Minnesota, her young daughter swallowed something harmful, forcing us to rush to the emergency room. We left the hospital very late and needed to inform the court that we could not make the court date. As we were calling to reschedule, given the crisis, we learned that the sheriff had a warrant for my sister for attempted murder. My sister's ex-husband even had witnesses to give testimony that they saw my sister approach in a car and shoot many times at her ex-husband, then flee. Not one witness, but many.

So we asked the sheriff and the police department if the hospital staff would be sufficient witnesses that we never set foot in Illinois, much less Chicago, on that date or time. After investigating with the hospital, they verified that my sister had been in Minnesota.

Likewise, transgressors will bring witnesses to give false testimony on the Day of Judgment. I have never argued with a transgressor who did not get or manufacture witnesses. People will blame each other. They will even throw blame at the prophets. Each will absolve themselves from the other.

> *And they will turn to one another, and question one another. They will say: "It was ye who used to come to us from the right hand (of power and authority)!" They will reply: "Nay, ye yourselves had no Faith! Nor had we any authority over you. Nay, it was ye who were a people in obstinate rebellion!" So now has been proved true, against us, the word of our Lord that we shall indeed (have to) taste (the punishment of our sins). "We led you astray: for truly we were ourselves astray."*
>
> —Quran 37:27-32

> *And they all shall appear before Allah (on the Day of Resurrection); then the weak will say to those who were arrogant, "Verily, we were following you; can you avail us anything against God's Torment?" They will say, "Had God guided us, we would have guided you. It makes no difference to us (now) whether we rage, or bear (these torments) with patience; there is no place of refuge for us."*
>
> —Quran 14:21

> *The Satan will say when the matter will have been decided, "Allah promised you a truthful promise while I gave you a promise and did not fulfill it. I had no authority over you, except that I invited you and you accepted my call. So,* do not blame me, but blame yourselves. Neither I can come to your help, nor can you come to my help. I disown your associating me with Allah in the past. Surely, there is a painful punishment for the unjust."
>
> —Quran 14:22

They admit they called people to disobedience, but they blame those who followed them. Therefore, I began on the theme of "Can men and women play games?" A pious person does not call to disobedience at all. In the case of the Prophets, they called people to obedience of God, not disobedience. The Prophets were practicing what they were preaching, and their people did not follow them. If you reflect on the argument of transgressors like Satan, they even blame God: "had God guided us."

Blame, Harass, or Hold on to the Strong Rope?

- After calling others to disobedience, do you argue like Satan, "Do not blame me; blame yourselves"?
- When someone calls you to disobedience, do you argue, "I cannot follow you, because on the Day of Resurrection, I cannot protect you, and you cannot protect me. In addition, I cannot blame you and you cannot blame me"?
- When God shows you that you are wrong, do you say to yourself, "I cannot blame anyone for the choices I made or who I followed. I can turn to God and seek His Mercy and Forgiveness. God is Oft-Forgiving"?
- In our troubled times, do you turn to God and read *Al-Fatiha* from your heart, seeking guidance, wisdom, knowledge, and aid to stay firm on the straight path?
- When called to guidance, do you argue, "If God wants to guide us, He will guide us"?
- Do you say to yourself in the Presence of God: "Our Lord! we have heard the call of one calling (Us) to Faith, 'Believe ye in the Lord,' and we have believed. Our Lord! Forgive us our sins, blot out from us our iniquities, and take to Thyself our souls in the company of the righteous" (Quran 3:193).
- Do you argue with others: "O ye that reject Faith! I worship not that which ye worship, Nor will ye worship that which I worship. And I will not worship that which ye have been wont to worship, Nor will ye worship that which I worship. To you be your Way, and to me mine." (Quran 109:1-6).

Spiritual Boundary

After ten years of fighting this case, it was evident that the justice system was in favor of those who had strong attorneys, a large network, and money to keep the fight going. This is no different than in other societies or faith communities. It is the human condition. Money talks. Keep in mind, this is someone who crossed from Canada into the US, and law enforcement found arms in his car. He was able to vacate this charge against the backdrop of Islamophobia. It does not take much to reflect on what connections he had. We did not have money to spare to fight further. The court system realized he was making stuff up; however, the judge told us, the prisons are full. This part of our lives opened our eyes to the justice system and to justice in general, here and elsewhere, including the UN. We saw how the Iraq War unfolded, given the testimonies of petty criminals.

The Quran describes the reality of injustice best, in the most truthful description: "*Weak* will say to those who were *arrogant*."

We prayed to God to protect us from his harm and later learned that he was arrested for attempting to buy a gun illegally to harm someone. He was convicted and went to jail for some years, giving us a break from his harm. As one recalls this and reads the Quran, it is striking how this passage reads when the transgressors are brought for questioning:

> *His Companion will say: "Our Lord! I did not make him transgress, but he was (himself) far astray." He will say: "Dispute not with each other in My Presence: I had already in advance sent you Warning. "The Word changes not before Me, and I do not the least injustice to My Servants. "One Day We will ask Hell, "Art thou filled to the full?" It will say, "Are there any more (to come)?"*

—Quran 50:26–30

In this passage, his companion admits that he had knowledge that he was far astray; however, instead of setting a boundary, he chose to enable his transgressions. The few verses before share how God uses angels, sinless, who prostrated to Adam out of respect, to record our deeds, while the arrogant use people who are far astray. This is what I meant: if you see someone who is far astray, do not play games. Our faith does not allow us to use people who are far astray to commit injustice or transgressions or rationalize oppression.

Shame, Humiliation, or Mercy?

If you do a search on the root letters of witness in the Quran, you will find 123 verses or *ayahs*. Before I continue, I want to remind that God is Oft-Forgiving and Most Merciful. This grilling process on the Day of Resurrection is only for people who deny, before God, their record of deeds and the accounting, and rejected the many opportunities to repent. How people live on earth is how they will be resurrected.

Let me give an example. Fourteen years ago, I was driving and saw a school bus stop and raise the stop sign arm. The street was four lanes, two in each direction, with an island in between. I assumed I could pass because I was on the far right, and the bus was on the far left. There was a police car, and I passed. The police car stopped me. I was penalized and given a ticket. I assumed I knew the rules regarding school buses, but it appeared I did not in such cases. Is this shame, humiliation, or mercy that I was immediately warned? I saw it as a mercy for myself, as I would hate to accidentally cause the death of a child and any school child.

Similarly, God sends us warnings to wake us up regarding our actions that could potentially lead to harm to ourselves or others. At times, we are confused and assume we are doing things right. A warning makes us cautious, and we take extra measures to protect ourselves and others.

On the Day of Resurrection, the grilling process that I mentioned earlier only unfolds when people deny, give false testimony, blame others, distort and malign, and ferociously argue. How one lives on earth is a telling sign of how one will be resurrected. If you accept God's warnings and ever turn and return to Him, that will be your state on the Day of Judgment.

If we tried our best but had shortcomings and faults that we did not address, God will call us to account for these issues between Him and us privately. If we do not deny but accept His accounting, it will go very smoothly, and we will be forgiven.

However, not everyone surrenders and confesses to the wrong they engaged in. Some lived on earth engaging in sinful cunning games to overpower the truth, distort, or kill the messenger. For example:

> *They said, "Take a mutual oath by Allah that we will kill him by night, he and his family. Then we will say to his executor, 'We did not witness the destruction of his family, and indeed, we are truthful.'"*

—Quran 27:49

They die in that state, never facing accountability or justice. As they lived and exited their life, they will be resurrected.

Produce Your Proof

And We will extract from every nation a witness and say,

> "*Produce your proof,*" *and they will know that the truth belongs to Allah, and lost from them is that which they used to invent.*
>
> —Quran 28:75

I found the whole process of the Day of Judgment amazing. At the finest degree of utmost justice, God engages with His creation when calling them to account.

This passage baffled me, in that God asks them to present their arguments and evidence, even though He knows every minute detail, including what is most hidden.

I found it interesting that while people blame God and project their issues onto Him, on the Day of Resurrection, they do not blame God but each other. They turn against each other and disassociate from each other. Satan confesses, "Allah promised you a truthful promise while I gave you a promise and did not fulfill it."

Just because people turn against each other and do not have an argument does not mean they will stop arguing. They denied God, the angels, the Messengers, and truthful and innocent people as witnesses. They will disassociate from each other and continue to argue.

Until . . .

> *That Day, We will seal over their mouths, and their hands will speak to Us, and their feet will testify about what they used to earn.*
>
> —Quran 36:65

> *And they will say to their skins, "Why have you testified against us?" They will say, "We were made to speak by Allah, who has made everything speak; and He created you the first time, and to Him you are returned. And you were not covering yourselves, lest your hearing testify against you or your sight or your skins, but you assumed that Allah does not know much of what you do. And that was your assumption which you assumed about your Lord. It has brought you to ruin, and you have become among the losers.*
>
> —Quran 41:21–23

As of 2023, it is still true that what we do not know about outer space is far greater than what we do know. Furthermore, it is still true that in history, what we do not know is far greater than what we do know. This should not deter us from continuing to learn and research. It should humble us from making conjectural claims denying God, the next world, the origin of creation, or the origin of the world.

Instead of conclusion shopping, *as we study outer space and history, we can explore the message brought forth by the Messengers and give it serious study for our souls*, knowing we will exit this world.

> *And if they deny you, [O Muhammad], then say, "For me are my deeds, and for you are your deeds. You are disassociated from what I do, and I am disassociated from what you do."*
>
> —Quran 10:41

This study should not harass, bully, or compel others to submit to our beliefs: physically through violence or mentally, emotionally, or spiritually. Likewise, we must protect ourselves from harassment, bullying, and brainwashing, making it difficult to accept our faith. We have a right to practice Islamic teachings. This means that we do not distort the message and commands of God in exchange for acceptance and belonging or turn them into a weapon for power and control.

> *If they turn away, say: "Bear witness that we are Muslims."*
>
> —Quran 3:64

> *"Our Lord! we believe in what Thou hast revealed, and we follow the Messenger; then write us down among those who bear witness."*
>
> —Quran 3:53

The meaning of spiritual, mental, and emotional boundaries is as follows. We do not feel the urge to hurt or make fun of others when we are working to be convinced of our faith; the message we assert is from the Divine and put into practice.

Boundaries and Transgressors

These are the limits ordained by Allah; so do not transgress them if any do transgress the limits ordained by Allah, such persons wrong (Themselves as well as others). (Quran 2:229)

Human life is marked by its many tribulations. Some of our tribulations come from outside oppressors, as Pharaoh's attacks on the Jewish people. Yet many come from within our very families and own communities, as did the attacks on Joseph. Even Prophet Muhammad, upon him peace and blessings, suffered attacks from abusive family and community members.

The Quran reminds us of the limits or boundaries set by God in resolving problems and protecting ourselves, whether domestic or foreign. We all have responsibilities to our families: siblings, spouses, and children. But we also have rights. Having family doesn't ever mean they belong to us, and the attachment we have shouldn't be a blind attachment, causing us deny wrongdoing or abuse. One of the worst things we can do in the face of abuse is to deny it.

Trials run in all directions: parents can be a trial, as can children; siblings can be a trial; either spouse can also be a trial. Sometimes one person is clearly at fault. Other times—many other times—the interaction is simply difficult.

The ways in which the prophets dealt with complex and abusive behavior from family members are a light for all of us. We have their examples to guide us. But cognitive therapy is also crucial as we need to have a witness outside ourselves, someone in a position of authority, to keep us centered and to help us establish positive boundaries.

Case Studies: Family, Community and Boundaries

O you who have attained to faith! Behold, some of your

> *spouses and your children are enemies unto you: so beware of them! But if you pardon [their faults] and forbear, and forgive—then, behold, God will be much-forgiving, a dispenser of grace. Your worldly goods and your children are but a trial and a temptation, whereas with God there is a tremendous reward.*
>
> —Quran 64:14–15

Case one: a parent who is abusive and controlling, trying to live vicariously through their child.

In all communities, there are abusive parents and spouses. Both therapy and getting closer to God can help us establish boundaries so that we can live positive lives: connected to our family members yet not allowing them to push us around.

This may take a lot of practice, particularly with very difficult family members. When we are parents, we need to constantly remind ourselves of what it was like to be a child. And as children, we need to remind ourselves of how difficult it is to be a parent. It's difficult for everyone—parent and child—to identify their thoughts and feelings and to see their own actions in a fair light.

At times, we have a hard time accepting imperfect family members. We need to reduce our expectations in order to learn to accept them. This doesn't ever mean we should accept abuse. In situations of physical abuse, physical distance is necessary.

But in many cases, we can mitigate the harm by responding with kindness, refusing to argue, and establishing clear boundaries. And we can always—every day—wake up and choose peace and forgiveness.

Case two: male and female siblings who have different cultural expectations and have become estranged from each other based on differing beliefs of the "right" way to act.

Even the Prophet had family members who were abusive. Yet despite their abuse—which stemmed from their inability to understand his life and choices—he would still visit his family. There were members of his family who tried to hurt him and who spoke about him in abusive terms. Yet he remained calm and loving toward them.

As for us, sometimes we need to check our feelings. It's possible we have a sibling who's being abusive. But we also might be feeling jealousy, anger, or rancor. It's important to look at the issue through multiple lenses and to continually reach out to family members who have drifted away.

Certainly, we don't want to approach every family member at once, particularly in a large family. But there will always be some family members who are open to dialogue and conversation. We can go slowly and start to feel connected, build boundaries, and understand each other.

Remember, as we constantly pray for our family members, that we cannot control or change anyone.

We also need to look both ways! Try not to speak to your family members in an accusatory way but in a way that helps them *consider*. As in, *consider that there's a possibility…*

And just as we try to better our relationships with our family, we also need to work on ourselves. In particular, we shouldn't work on our family as a way to deflect and avoid working on ourselves and our own issues.

And always, the hearts of people are in God's hands. We shouldn't violate that or assume that people's hearts are in our hands. Even the Prophet Muhammad, peace be upon him, didn't have the hearts of others in his hands but could only set boundaries and speak to them of God's light.

As adults, we can never really make someone else "do the right thing." We can insist that others treat us properly and that they fulfill their responsibilities and respect our rights. But we are not responsible for how our family members behave. And understanding boundaries helps us understand what God expects from us.

Case three: a family in which no one is at fault, but there is an aging parent or other issue for which family members must come together and act, but there are different ideas about responsibilities and boundaries that make this difficult.

Sometimes it's not an issue of anyone acting badly. Instead, entrenched habits or different ideas about responsibility can lead to difficult situations. After all, people are creatures of habit, and we do not like change. When family members are called on to take up new responsibilities, not everyone will be ready to do that. Setting boundaries can help people live up to their responsibilities.

We have to accept that, while there are things that are obligatory, and we can expect these things from family members, we can't expect others to take the high road or do good works: those have to happen by choice. And we certainly can't blame or guilt others into taking the high road.

We don't want to break our bonds of kinship or our obligations to family members. Yet we are also free to choose because God gives us the choice to say no. When setting limits and boundaries, it's important to know our rights and responsibilities, and a first step is to seek God's guidance to make sure our conscience is clear. This will help us be firm but polite.

In these situations, it's also good for us to pace ourselves, make lists, start small, and introduce changes gradually.

In a family situation, we can let others know that things will be changing. We love our siblings, but the situation has changed, so there are new boundaries that need to be set. It's important to remember that none of us are superheroes, and we all need to be aware when something is beyond our capacity. As it says in the Quran, "God does not impose upon any soul a duty but to the extent of its ability." Sometimes, we have to say, "I can't do this," or "I can't do this alone."

Once you've set boundaries, it's important to keep them clear. Sometimes, boundaries should be written in order for them to be clear to all parties. And we should always notice when people have changed as we asked! When we thank God's creation, we are also thanking God.

But being clear doesn't mean you take the responsibility for endless explanations. You can even set a "personal explanation limit," and you shouldn't feel the need to constantly justify your position or to take responsibility for the emotional responses of others.

Also: as much as we'd like to connect with everyone, it's not possible for everyone to be close all the time. At times, you must allow tense moments to enable people to reflect on their behavior.

How do you know if a boundary is the "right" boundary? In deciding if you're setting up the right boundaries in dealing with family members, it is sometimes helpful to set up a meeting with some sort of mediator. It's also helpful to talk with authorities: doctors, teachers, scholars, therapists.

Certainly, you don't want to impose on anyone else an authority they wouldn't trust. At times, you may have to agree on a mediator to assist in boundary creation, but this needs to be a mediator trusted by all parties: a neutral person who has good intentions.

Of course, at times, people understand a boundary is right, but they still want to resist it. Boundary creation can take time. It's often not an issue of "good" or "bad" but averting harm and helping everyone take responsibility for their own actions.

Khawlah bint Tha'labah

So what is the solution? In many cases, we can extract knowledge and insight from Prophet Muhammad, upon him peace and blessings, on how to nurture healthy boundaries within families and communities. I discussed his relationships with his wives in *God Intervenes Between A Person And Their Heart*. Let me discuss a companion where the family and community were nurtured and taught healthy boundaries. Compare this with the cases above.

Khawlah bint Tha'labah was a companion of the Prophet, upon him peace and blessings. There is a chapter titled after her: "*Al Mujadilah*," or "The Woman Who Complained."

She was married to Aws ibn al-Samit, another companion. During an argument, Aws used an utterance that meant at the time she was divorced from her husband. It was a cultural tradition that was very disrespectful to women.

For brevity, I will fast forward and bypass details as that is not the important part of the story. Khawlah went to complain to the Prophet, upon him peace and blessings.

Prophet Muhammad, upon him peace and blessings, could only give her what he knew and practiced, so he told her to be patient. He was very forbearing and patient himself with his spouses and people in general. However, Khawlah complained to God.

The important part to note here is how the Prophet, upon him peace and blessings, responded.

I wanted to give this example from our faith. Oftentimes, extroverts—and my daughter is an extrovert—love to talk and express our feelings. The problem with that is our feelings are understood as facts.

For example, when we express love, we refuse to acknowledge the suffering even when presented with facts, and when we hate, we refuse to acknowledge the good, even when presented with facts.

People experience that in various forms and to various degrees. However, the issue becomes a problem when we fail to comprehend the boundaries and the right of the oppressed to push the offender to their boundaries. Or a boundary needs to be created as another human is being abused.

God sent down revelation to the Prophet, upon him peace and blessings, in her defense. The language was bold, firm, and strong, and a big penalty was prescribed for such behaviors. How you feel about it and whether you cried or not are irrelevant. The world does not revolve around your tears and feelings.

Her rights were restored. The man was penalized. A social ill was called out boldly and strongly. A community was educated. The powerless and helpless felt relieved. Now, it opens another door for a conversation on healing, reconciliation, and trust.

Trust and Healing

Prophet Muhammad, upon him peace and blessings, told her, "Let him release a slave." She responded, "O Messenger of Allah, upon him peace and blessings, he does not have the means to do that."

He then said, "Then let him fast for two consecutive months." She said, "By Allah, he is an old man, he is not able to do that." He said, "Then let him feed sixty poor people." She said, "O Messenger of Allah, he does not have that much." He said, "Then we will help him." She said she would contribute to the penalty fee. He said, "You have done right and done well. Go and give it in charity on his behalf, then take care of your husband properly." And she did so.

Analysis

God is Most Wise, and He knows what is behind all the complaints. At times, we spend hours talking and projecting our conjured ideas and sharing our feelings, but we do not hear or listen to a word said.

Boundaries are set firmly to help us listen to and hear our inner souls. At times, behind anger are love and feelings of not being needed or of worthlessness.

While she came to complain about her husband, she also pleaded with the Prophet regarding the big penalty and went from complaining to contributing to the penalty fee.

The Prophet did not psychoanalyze her based on social ills, conjured ideas, or prejudices toward women at the time. He did not blame her or belittle her pain or suffering but called her to what he practiced himself.

The revelation that came down was healing and nurturing, not just for her and her husband but for the whole community.

Through the dialogue with the Prophet, she was made to discover, without the Prophet shoving it in her face, that her husband was old, poor, and sick and needed to be taken care of well. Her husband's actions were probably due to his feelings of not being able to provide for or take care of his wife, possibly feeling worthless and not needed.

He discovered her feelings of genuine love for him, which nurtured him to be a better man, and he became kinder to his wife afterward. The community learned the importance of respecting women in general.

Women and the helpless learned to take their complaints to God if they were not heard or understood. God opens doors for everyone to listen to what they need to hear. More importantly, Prophet Muhammad, upon him peace and blessings, did not respond like some psychologists or teachers of religion, using his position to dehumanize another human being.

Peacemaking versus Mischief-Making

Peacemaking between individuals, communities, or nations requires all parties' knowledge and consent. Engaging in secret plots that you use to gain access to someone's private life without their awareness or permission is a form of sedition.

A teacher who fears Allah does not infantilize community members and treat them as objects to manipulate and overpower emotionally, socially, psychologically, or spiritually.

If you lack the good upbringing to talk directly with both parties, seeking their permission to intervene, find the dignity and self-respect to mind your own business and not meddle. Under the façade of democracy or making peace, we have many examples of nations meddling in Muslim affairs without the consent of all parties, creating major sedition.

Likewise, when community members engage in practices that they would not condone against themselves or their loved ones by people they passionately do not like, it is an act of spiritual and psychological abuse.

If a community member suspects that they are the target of such a secret plot and pushes you within your boundaries using harshness and verbal whipping, this is their right. You are not a victim and have no grounds for retribution. You are a wrongdoer, a transgressor, and you need to be disciplined.

In summary, do not engage in secret plots between family or community members meddling in personal and private affairs without the consent of all parties. If you do and the target responds with retribution, that is not bad *adab* or bad character. That is justice served.

It is oppression to engage in secret plots that compel, overpower, and infantilize a community member and steer them against their will to engage people they decided to cut off.

Claiming your response to the discipline is self-defense or retribution is nonsense. Call it whatever you want. You are *not* engaged in self-defense when you are engaged in sedition. Know where your boundaries with others begin and end. Do not transgress the bounds.

If You or Someone You Know Feels Wronged

> *(All) faces shall be humbled before (Him)—the Living, the Self-Subsisting, Eternal: hopeless indeed will be the man that carries iniquity (on his back). (But he who works deeds of righteousness, and has faith, will have no fear of harm nor of any curtailment (of what is his due).*
>
> —Quran 20:111–112

First, ask yourself if you are able to forgive. Can you either move on without the person or else move on from the hurt feelings and continue to engage?

If you can, then do so. However, as you do, communicate your feelings about being wronged to someone you trust who has shared values. You might feel wronged, but another set of eyes and ears might look at the situation differently, and they might be able to help you see your contributions to the hurt. You might even be the one in the wrong. It's best that, if you decide to engage, you learn how to communicate your feelings.

But perhaps you are not able to forgive. Are you, then, able to call the person before an independent judge or conflict-resolution mediator?

If you can, do this, and work through the complicated process of seeking your rights or explaining your thoughts and feelings.

Yet perhaps you cannot forgive, and you also cannot call on the person to resolve the wrong they did. What next?

Can you take the matter to court? If you can, then do so. The courts have authority over the person, and in this way, you can get your rights or penalize the person. Make sure all communications are recorded, although you should be transparent about it, so that you act with fairness, integrity, and ethics. You don't want to manufacture evidence to win an argument or bend the situation in your favor.

But perhaps you are not able to forgive, resolve the situation, or settle it in court. Are you, then, able to wait until the Day of Judgment? We will all face people from whom we cannot get our rights in this world. In this case, we will need to ground ourselves in our faith and wait until the Day of Judgment for rights and justice. Imam al-Sha'rawi said, "The matter will be so grave and meticulous that a person who is headed to hell will not go to hell until they get their rights from one who is going to heaven."

But perhaps you cannot forgive, resolve the situation, settle it in court, or wait until the Day of Judgment.

In this case, seek therapy and work through your feelings. Create healthy boundaries between you and the person who wronged you. If you don't wish to engage the person, let them know your feelings in writing. Keep repeating the message. Block them on all social media and avoid them at events. This is called *hudna* in Arabic—*sulha*, or peacemaking—and it represents a cessation of hostilities.

And What if the Individual Is a Family Member?

Then learn how to maintain minimum contact and protect yourself from harm. If anyone tries to meddle in your life, ask them to stop. Meddlers can cause more damage than good. See this person who has wronged you as a lesson in what not to do or be. If they are an abuser, as you think, then they may have saturated the community with false news about you before you could even speak a word. As the saying goes, "He hit me and cried, then raced ahead of me and complained."

Remind yourself that you are responsible before God for the words that came out of your mouth, the actions carried out by your limbs, the plotting carried out by your forelock, and the intentions of your own heart, not someone else's. It is okay if someone believes lies. To keep the fight going, such people will try to bait you with false claims. Provide them with a just path to justice. If they refuse, don't waste any more time over-analyzing their false claims after you've stated your truth once.

Addressing individuals who break the rules is crucial. However, unclear or ambiguous rules may result in innocent people being unfairly accused. Additionally, people in positions of power may misuse their authority and unjustly criticize or punish others without proper justification.

What if Someone Says You Have Wronged Them?

If someone comes to tell you a story about how you have wronged or hurt them, then ask them to share their story in writing. People who are telling the truth will repeat the same basic story, while those who are caught in a lie will backpedal and change the story once you show evidence to refute parts of it. In this case, the story keeps changing.

If you agree with the person's claims, work through resolving the matter between the two of you. If you were joking, realize that if both parties aren't laughing, then your joke was probably an insult disguised as a joke. This is verbal abuse.

If you disagree with the person's claims and their description of events, then ask them to go before an independent mediator. Tell them you would like to resolve the matter according to your values.

What if someone tells you that they have been wronged?

Start with step one above. But don't interfere without the permission of both parties. Refuse to be a meddler. However, allow the wronged party to express their pain privately. Listen. Make *dua* (prayer) for them. If their life is in danger, help them contact law enforcement and seek shelter; otherwise, encourage them to seek counseling.

It's critical to remember that toxic and abusive behavior is never acceptable, especially if we've done nothing wrong but are still mistreated. The situation needs to be looked at objectively. We do not have to tolerate or accept harmful or immature behavior. We must resist attempts by others to degrade or devalue us. We may not have been able to set boundaries before due to spiritual, mental, and emotional blackmail, including guilt trips.

Still, as we grow and recover, we can stand up for ourselves, set healthy boundaries, or leave an unhealthy situation because we have a responsibility to protect ourselves from harm. It is critical to prioritize our mental and emotional health.

> *I have more respect for a man who lets me know where he stands, even if he's wrong, than the one who comes up like an angel and is nothing but a devil.*
>
> —Malcolm X

Finally, when it comes to justice, and when people's rights are at stake, do not use hints or be so discreet that someone might misinterpret your behavior or not catch the message. We are all different in many ways, and we transgress each other's boundaries both unintentionally and intentionally.

Badawi Explains Coexistence

Dr. Jamal Badawi, a prominent Muslim scholar on Christian-Muslim relations, discussed the challenges posed by some commentators and religious leaders against the Quran and Islam.

Badawi explained that Islam does not divide the world into believers and infidels. God addresses people "O mankind" more than two hundred times in the Quran and "O children of Adam" many times. The term for Jews and Christians is not *infidel* but *Ahlil Kitab*, or *people of the book*. Badawi elaborated on coexistence by explaining that the inclusive address "O mankind" is an address by the Divine that embraces all.

> *It reminds humanity that they belong to one family with the same set of parents, albeit a diverse family. This is a reminder that diversity in unity and unity within diversity are possible. Humanity is like a bouquet of flowers in which each flower is beautiful in its own right, yet, the combination of all flowers and the rich diversity of their colors is more beautiful. This sweeping statement in the Quran about broad human brotherhood is a profound basis for peace for and among all.*

Badawi added, "The basic principle in dealing with non-Muslims is 'birr.'" There is no good definition of the word *birr* in English; however, it can be most closely translated to mean honor, compassion, and kindness. God uses the same word *birr* when advising Muslims on how to deal with their parents. Furthermore, the Quran clearly states there is "no compulsion in religion."

Finally, Badawi touched upon the word *jihad*, which means *struggle* but is often mistranslated as *holy war*. *Jihad* has many forms, from the spiritual struggle against the self to the physical struggle against aggressors, whether Muslims or non-Muslims.

Badawi emphasized, "This [physical struggle against aggressors] is not a holy war. It is the lesser of two evils. There is nothing holy about destruction, killing or suffering."

As we dialogue and work on solutions to make our country secure, we must realize the importance of understanding Islam and Muslims to ensure that our policies and solutions for security are within the spirit of justice and peace, not revenge and hatred.

Lead by Example

If we expect Muslims to condemn terrorism, we must set a good example by denouncing all forms of terrorism, including state-sponsored terrorism, even if those states claim to be democratic. If we genuinely want to end terrorism, we must recognize that condemning violence by the weak while financing, supporting, and condoning it by those in power is futile. The weak always try to emulate the strong.

Hope versus Obligation

I listen to the prayer of every supplicant when he calleth on Me: Let them also, with a will, Listen to My call, and believe in Me: That they may walk in the right way. (Quran 2:186)

Often, when we think about hope, we think about an expectation or desire for a particular concrete result. We hope to have Friday off, or we hope for a war to end, or we hope to be reunited with a friend or beloved.

Understood in this way, hope is tied directly to an achievable result, and we can determine if the hope was worthwhile by looking at whether that result was achieved. In this way, hope is driven not by our values but by our expectations and desires. And often, with this sort of hope, we deceive ourselves and bend our values to make them line up with our expectations and desires.

I have heard many stories of people who brought their hopes to God, and, when these hopes did not achieve a result, the people changed their values and beliefs.

Recently, I was speaking with a coworker who was Hindu but became an atheist after he experienced a trauma during which he prayed to God, but God did not come through for him. Once this coworker realized God was not going to give him what he wanted, he gave up on God.

In a different job, I knew a Catholic who was also in a difficult situation and prayed to God. He had hope, but then he didn't receive what he'd hoped for, and he became disillusioned. This feeling made him think he'd been believing in illusions.

I also knew a Muslim woman who wanted very badly to be reunited with her husband. She prayed and prayed for their reunion, and she had hope that she would hear the right answer, the one she wanted. Yet what she got was something else, and they were not reunited. When she heard that, she told God, "I'm not going to pray to you any longer."

One thing to remember through all these stories is that prayer is a gift. When we pray, we're not doing God a favor. Instead, we're receiving a gift from God. If you pray, you should be grateful that you've prayed and thank God that you've received that gift of prayer.

Hope Is Not Obligation

Where hope is about a particular result, it's not really hope. Instead, it's creating an obligation. It's putting God to a test. At times we verbalize this test, and at times we don't. Yet in all cases, God can read our hearts, and he knows that behind our verbalized requests can be hidden ones, such as "If you don't fulfill my demands and needs, then I won't believe in you."

If God knows this, He might bring us to that state in order to purify that lack of faith and to give us the gift of choice in receiving faith.

Sometimes, when we say we're hoping for something, what we're really doing is trying to guilt God into action. We say, "If you don't do XYZ, you're not a loving God. If you're not going help me out, then you're not God." By speaking like this, we're asking God to prove Himself to humanity.

We know it's wrong to treat other people like this. So why direct these behaviors toward God?

We don't like to be controlled, but we want to control God. We don't like others to guilt us or speak for us, but we do that to God. We don't want to be put in a situation where we have to prove our humanity, and yet we put God in that self-same situation. We say, "You must prove to us that you're a loving God."

We understand that these things are wrong at a human level, but often, when it comes to God, we want Him to prove His Kindness, Compassion, and His Mercy. But God knows Himself better than we know Him. And just as we have the right to choose how to represent ourselves and to choose who can speak for us, so God has the right to choose who He wants to speak for Him.

The problem is not the lack of reciprocity; rather, it is a false belief in God that falls short of acknowledging His transcendence.

What Is Hope?

There is an older meaning to the English-language word *hope*, and that is a feeling of trust. Indeed, true hope is not result based. It's a condition of heart and mind. We saw real hope in the Quranic story and life of Hajar. When she was left in Mecca, she had hope in herself and her skills. Then, after running seven times between the hills in search of water, her hope in a positive result ended. Still, she didn't change her values or her faith in God. She trusted God, and she was able to bear witness to the power of God.

Hajar didn't know how the answer to her prayer was going to come. Likewise, her husband, the prophet Abraham, was asked to call people to the pilgrimage in an empty desert. From a results-based point of view, such a thing is ridiculous. There's nothing to suggest it makes logical sense. And indeed, Abraham didn't see the results and never knew that millions go on pilgrimages.

Hope is a light that comes into the heart. Hope is, in fact, desiring a specific outcome while taking its means, The outcome being the pleasure of Allah and the true goodness that goes with it. The means is obedience to Him. However, hope is not making demands. It moves us, but we may never see the result or the end of the story. Still, we continue acting in accordance with our values, not our desire for any particular result.

Nobody's Perfect

People often say, "Nobody's perfect." Many motivational speakers and life coaches are fond of the phrase. Even Adam, the first among us, wasn't perfect. It's undeniably true, and obsessing over perfection can be a harmful practice. But what sorts of things can we hide behind the phrase "nobody's perfect"?

Imagine a child who is raised in a family in which every time he does something wrong, his parents make excuses: "He didn't mean it"; "He's a good boy"; "Everyone makes mistakes." Instead of the child facing the consequences of his actions, accepting responsibility, and repairing the harm, he avoids them because "He's only human."

This can result in a case like Brock Turner's, in which, even when he was convicted of rape, his parents made excuses and helped him evade responsibility. Here, the mantra that "I'm not perfect" became a way of refusing to deal with his crimes.

Indeed, those who are in denial about their own specific imperfections are often obsessed with the imperfections of others.

We need to ask ourselves, *what have I done to nurture my soul and purify my heart? How many times have I genuinely apologized for wrongdoing?* There is an exercise any of us can do: write down on a sheet of paper how many times you have deeply apologized to another. How did it make you feel?

Those of us who are honest with ourselves likely felt dread and fear before a genuine apology. Those who aren't likely bypass responsibility and perhaps even attack others. They say, "I'm imperfect; we're all imperfect; let's move on." These people apologize without apologizing.

So What Is the Solution?

The first is acceptance. We need to accept not that humans in general are imperfect, but our specific imperfections. We need to recognize the environment and causes of these imperfections.

The second is admitting when we have done wrong, repairing the harm, and working to overcome our imperfections. Just saying "Nobody's perfect; I accept myself" isn't enough. When we transgress against others, we need to acknowledge this and work to repair the harm we've created.

Everyone needs to continue working on themselves. The great scholar and teacher Shaykh Ramadan al-Bouti has decades of knowledge, and yet he carries it with humility and attended a talk by one of his students—he said—to purify his heart.

In that lesson, al-Bouti asked whether those listening had complained about their weaknesses and imperfections to God. We often complain about *others* to God. But do we sit with God and talk to Him about our own transgressions, dark thoughts, or feelings? Do we ask Him to help us or put us in the path of someone who can help us remove those imperfections?

Yet what's most important is to acknowledge our flaws not to the world, but to ourselves. Only we can answer these questions. There's no need to answer them to the crowd because speaking to an audience can distort how we talk about ourselves.

For myself, I remember a time in school when I was a classroom monitor, and I was making tea for a Korean teacher in her classroom. I accidentally broke the pot, but instead of telling her, I snuck out of the classroom and didn't come back. I spent weeks dealing with dread and guilt before I was able to pray to God, asking

Him to help me. Finally, I went and explained that I had broken the pot. It was a very difficult conversation to have, but crucially, I had turned to God.

If you have this conversation with God, then God is not going to shame you. If we look at Adam and Satan, yes, Adam made a mistake out of neglect. This mistake didn't bring him down in the eyes of God, although Adam did have to deal with the consequences of his actions. If you believe in *specific* imperfections, then you have to deal with consequences. It doesn't mean you're a bad person.

But if you walk around telling others, "I'm not perfect," then that might be a way of seeking not understanding but attention. God doesn't want us to say, "I'm bad; I'm bad" but, instead, "Forgive me"; "Strengthen me"; and "Help me repair the harm."

We each need to recognize our areas of weakness and ask God to strengthen us in these areas.

We're always—all of us—discovering things we have to work on. We need to help ourselves and others connect with God in a humble way.

Umar, for instance, one of the companions of the Prophet, peace upon him, would take an hour each day to call himself to account. Umar would go through everything he'd done that day, good and bad, and he would deal with each specific flaw in turn. This isn't a game of blame or guilt, but an honest assessment of our behaviors. This is something for which we can all strive.

Wanting What You Can't Have

It is good to want things! We humans aren't meant to sit around all our lives without desiring anything. It's in our nature to want. Some of us may want a better job while others may want power to help the weak. Or we might want to understand complex scientific phenomena or to create beautiful art.

The desire for things we don't have is part of human nature. Whether we crave the material or nonmaterial, there is nothing wrong with wanting. A good person can want a PhD, an end to war, or a new car. There isn't anything wrong with praying to God for any of these things or in asking God's help to achieve our material and nonmaterial goals.

But we should remember that each time we pray for something, we are opening our heart. When we look toward some particular goal, it affects our soul. So, as the saying goes, we need to be careful what we wish for. If we're looking for something illusory or impossible—such as a fairy-tale romance—these illusions can blind us and make us vulnerable to harm. An example of this is Harvey Weinstein and the celebrity culture, in which abusive men and women use their celebrity to groom people and sexually abuse them.

When we ask God for things, we need to ask for things that are real. These should be things we are really working toward and things that—if we got them—would be a positive force in our lives.

What if God Doesn't Answer Our Prayers?

But what if we're asking for something reasonable, and we don't get it? What if this seems like it should be within our reach—a relationship, a promotion, a baby—but we don't get it?

Sometimes we can become intensely focused on one particular goal. Society might be telling us we really must have a baby or an important career. Sometimes it's a thing we deeply desire. At times, we might grow obsessed with this one thing, thinking our entire life's meaning rests in this achievement.

Yet sometimes, no matter how much we pray, we don't get what we want.

When this happens, we should remember Moses's travels with al-Khidr, upon them peace. We must remember how even Moses couldn't understand al-Khidr's actions because Moses was human. Only al-Khidr could see the unseen and know the past, present, and future. It's important for us as individuals to realize that, as with Moses, our ignorance is far, far greater than our understanding.

We might even lose what we desire: the job, the house, the spouse. Even though we've prayed and prayed, we might not get it back. There might seem no possible positive outcome, no possible reason for our suffering. But always, we must practice patience and trust in God.

After all, we see things only from our limited human view, which means we don't have the whole picture. God's name *Al-Aleem* means that He is the one who knows all. By comparison, what we humans don't know is infinite.

Always Being Tested

What does it mean to be tested by God? A life test is anything that causes us either loss or gain, to which we are expected to respond with gratitude or patience or both. As Dr. 'Abd Lateef Krauss Abdullah has said, "Our lives are a personal education program designed and created by God."

In the examples given us from the lives of the prophets, we can see many different ways in which humans can be tested. We might be tested with power, as Solomon was. During this test, Solomon turned to God in gratitude. When we think about his story, we are reminded that very few humans can wield power and not lose their humility and gratitude.

We can be tested as Jacob and Joseph were, and, like them, we can turn to God in patience. Both of them were later elevated. We can be tested with illness, as Job was. Or we can be tested with a slip, as Adam was. Like Adam, when we slip, we must turn to God in remorse and repentance.

Every part of our lives is a test, both the big and the small. Sometimes we're tested by getting what we want. Sometimes we're tested when we don't.

Through all this, it's important that we don't focus too much on wanting one thing because if our desire goes too far, it can lead to feelings of anger at God. It can also lead to an internal anger that becomes depression and hopelessness. Satan encourages this hopelessness—a loss of faith is exactly what he wants for us.

Sometimes, when we want something very badly, the world doesn't seem fair. Let's say you worked very hard for a promotion, but someone else, a lazy and undeserving person, got it instead. This isn't just a test for you. It's a test for both parties: you and the person who got the promotion. Sometimes a person is tested through deprivation, and sometimes they are tested through gifts. We never know what's going on between God and another person.

Certainly, tests can be very difficult. Yet through them, we can be protected, purified, or elevated. If we don't get what we want right away, it can be a sign that God is pushing us to a different path. But it's also possible that what we desire will come much later. Prophet Joseph's dream only became real twenty-two years after he first had it.

Your trial may be just as difficult as Joseph's. But through it all, it's critically important not to make the thing you aren't getting the center of your universe.

All Tests Are Unbearable if We Don't Turn to God

Some people seem to have everything. They have the job you want; they have beautiful children; they have an apparently perfect spouse. But their tests are different from yours. It's even possible that their trials—to them—feel unbearable.

Both good and bad trials should cause us to constantly turn to God. We should never underestimate prayer, in good times or in bad.

Constantly turning to God can help us stick to our values. If we stop turning to God and make a fetish of the thing we want—a job, for instance—then Satan might offer us another fancy job that goes against our values.

A trial may, of course, feel overwhelming. There are times we can feel crushed by the world around us. A trial can leave us shocked and bewildered. But when a trial hits, it cannot be larger than the soul. The body can be overwhelmed, and the mind might face a nervous breakdown, but that only means we need to turn to God for help, mercy, and relief. By turning to God, our hearts are expanded.

Indeed, every trial—even a positive trial—is difficult to bear without turning to God.

Neither are we meant to bear our trials without help from the people around us. Just so, we are also expected to share in the trials of those who are being tested with pain and suffering. If others are suffering around us, we must reach out and help them, although without robbing them of their dignity or their sense of self-reliance.

In this, too, we are constantly being tested. God may have given you wealth, power, knowledge, or a kind heart. Yet it is not an end simply to have these things. What's important is what you do with them.

Allah Testing You versus You Testing Allah

> *Once Jesus met Iblis [Satan], and Iblis said, "Is it not true that only what has been decreed will happen?"*
>
> *Jesus replied, "That is true." Then Iblis said, "So throw yourself down from the top of this mountain, and let us*

> *see if you live or not!"* Jesus answered, *"The servant does not test his master; rather, it is the master who tests his servant."*
>
> —Imam Abu Nu'aym Ahmad ibn 'Abdullah al-Aswbahani

My mom was in the emergency room. The doctors told us no visitors as my mother's blood pressure might rise, and this could cause a deadly stroke. However, some visitors hated rules or reason. They confused *tawakkal*, or trust in God, with bungee jumping.

They would say, "Nothing can happen to you except what God wills." They assumed they could break the laws of the natural world set by God, as Moses, upon him peace, did when he bulldozed into the Red Sea without thinking. Moses was a messenger of God with a Divine Message. All Divine Messages to humanity must be delivered. Moses, upon him peace, sought guidance before entering.

Tawakkal is using your faculty of reason to understand what God requires of you in such a situation, seeking counsel if you do not know, praying for guidance, and proceeding without placing God under obligation to a set of results.

What Is Security, and How Do We Find It?

Allah is He, than Whom there is no other god; the Sovereign, the Holy One, the Source of Peace (and Perfection), the Guardian of Faith, the Preserver of Safety, the Exalted in Might, the Irresistible, the Supreme: Glory to Allah! (High is He) above the partners they attribute to Him. (Quran 59:23)

A sense of security—in our families, our homes, and our communities—is a basic need and a human right. None of us is ever completely safe from the unpredictable dangers of our world. At any moment, a storm might blow up, or another driver might lose control of their car. But we do need to feel reasonably protected in our relationships with others, both near and far. We need to feel that the other drivers of this world are staying in their lanes.

What is reasonable protection? Does our security mean driving an enormous Humvee or blocking other drivers from using the road? The concept of "security" can easily become distorted, driving us to aggressive measures that make us progressively less secure.

How do we tell the difference between real security, with everyone staying in their lane, and a false one, in which we prevent other drivers from using a public road? The first thing to consider is whether our security is looking out for "me" or whether it's interested in the protection of the collective "we." Only the second one pushes us toward coexistence.

With false security, an individual or community insists on their own security but doesn't have any concern for the security of others—or for how their sense of security was gained. False security is, for instance, when a middle-class White community is concerned about their own safety but not that of neighboring African Americans. Or when Israelis allow only Jewish settlers onto certain roads.

Real security happens when everyone in an interconnected set of relationships—local or international—is concerned about healthy boundaries for coexistence. Real security is the protection of "we," as when one person is insecure, ultimately, we're all insecure. Eventually, those who are insecure are going to rise up.

No, I Don't Sleep at Night

Concerning ourselves with security for all is not about charity—it's about common sense. Menachem Begin, who was prime minister of Israel during the Sabra and Shatila massacres, was once asked how he slept at night, seeing as he was contributing to a system that was making the Palestinians very insecure. He responded that he didn't sleep at night and that he was always worried.

Security is a two-way street. None of us can be secure at the expense of another's insecurity. We need to see that everybody in a network of relationships is treated fairly and equally before there can be real security.

In many blogs, I wrote about a woman who was being abused by her husband and in-laws. She was feeling insecure and transgressed upon mentally, emotionally, and spiritually. For that reason, she was struggling with anger and hatred.

There were many possible outcomes here. Certainly, no one was safe: there are cases of women so abused that their hatred was turned on their abusers.

Even in this situation, inequality doesn't justify a violent response. But if one party in a relationship is insecure, then it's likely there will be conflict. In any situation where one party is secure and privileged and the others aren't, the others are going to want to rebel.

Rationalizing Inequality Away

It's often hard to see ourselves as the oppressor. It's very easy to rationalize away our actions in the name of security for ourselves and our children. Even Pharaoh said that he was trying to secure and defend his country.

But there is a way to think through the situation without just relying on our feelings about security. First, we have to ask about a given relationship, "What are each person's rights?" Then "What are each person's responsibilities?" For instance, Israelis and Palestinians both want to feel secure. But what are each party's rights under international law? Which rights are being transgressed?

A person might *feel* insecure even while driving down a private road in a Humvee, defended by armed guards. But security cannot be boiled down to emotion. It's about rights and laws.

Indeed, one of the biggest obstacles to having a dialogue about security is that many of us in these discussions are driven by our emotions.

Security Means Accepting Difference

The solution is not to say that we're all alike—that we can allow African Americans or Muslim Americans into "our" bubble of security because "They're just like us." Security also means accepting differences. The solution to a fear of immigrants or African Americans or the impoverished is not to force the outsiders to show how they are just like "us." It's to say that we're all different, and that's OK.

We will find our security when we can nurture good leaders.

The Quran tells the story of Bilqis, Queen of Sheba, who faced a society that had made the worst people its nobles. Yet Bilqis was very intelligent. She gained her position through respect, and eventually, all the men turned to her to make decisions. She nurtured society to better know themselves. She worked on society as a whole.

In the same way, we must deal with our insecurities by nurturing society. Although "security" fears in the US are currently being targeted at the Muslim community, we shouldn't just be concerned about fellow Muslims. I could try to prove that even though I wear a hijab, I'm just like a "normal American." But then the fear is transferred from me to Mexican immigrants or to a Syrian family that's just arriving in the US. Instead of protecting any particular group, we need to challenge America to accept difference.

The land of the Midian was not a paradise—they also had problems. But when Moses arrived, they were receptive to him and his differences. Moses married a Midianite woman and lived there for many years before returning to Egypt to lead the Israelites out of slavery. The acceptance and hospitality he received in Midian played a significant role in shaping his character and leadership style. After all, disenfranchised groups are transformed into groups that can enrich and contribute to society when given voice and space.

Countering Violence Extremism

> *The camel sees all of the other camel's humps but never his own.*
>
> —Bedouin Proverb

In the immediate aftermath of the 9/11 attacks, the Bush administration framed the entire country as the innocent victim of an out-of-the-blue declaration of war. This framing was deceptive: in painting the whole country as the wounded target of unprovoked aggressors, the administration avoided drawing attention to its foreign policies—and redeployed the memory of the 9/11 victims in service of an interventionist war on terror.

Prophet Muhammad, upon him peace and blessings, taught Muslims that a society should not "inflict the legal punishments on the poor and forgive the rich." This is not just an Islamic teaching—it has also been a teaching of those noble Americans who have nurtured our country to a higher understanding of human dignity and value.

Yet with ISIS, we seem again to be forgiving the rich and focusing the brunt of our punishments on the poor.

A newly aired PBS *Frontline* documentary titled *The Secret History of ISIS*, produced by Michael Kirk, Mike Wiser, and Jim Gilmore, examines how ISIS or Daesh came to be. The documentary discusses how the US contributed to the rise of ISIS through many mistakes, as well as lies told to create a link between 9/11 and Saddam Hussein so that we could make a case for invading Iraq.

Experts, including CIA officials, discussed how mistakes were made and lies and exaggerations told along the path to a US war against Iraq, which, in turn, gave rise to ISIS, also known as ISIL or Daesh.

One of the mistakes outlined in the documentary was made by Secretary of State Colin Powell, who made a seven-minute speech at the UN that turned the founder of Daesh, Abu Musab al-Zarqawi, from a nobody into a powerful terrorist and the founder of ISIS. In the speech, he connected the dots between Saddam Hussein, Osama bin Laden, Zarqawi, and weapons of mass destruction. Upon closer analysis, those dots were not connectable, and Iraq did not possess weapons of mass destruction. Yet Zarqawi was turned into a powerful warrior in the eyes of the region and the world.

Powell appeared in the documentary and argued that Zarqawi did not play a major role in the presentation he gave to the UN. However, the documentary shows that, in his speech, Powell mentioned Zarqawi by name twenty-one times. Reporter Eric Black writes on MinnPost:

> *I read the full text of Powell's presentation to see how heavily he relied on the bin Laden-Zarqawi-Saddam nexus. The answer is that he relied on it heavily, but always by implication, still clearly intended to convince the world that Zarqawi was the middleman through whom WMD could flow from Iraq's (non-existent) stockpiles to bin Laden.*

As Black notes, at the time, Abu Musab al-Zarqawi was a Jordanian-born Palestinian petty criminal. A falsified version of his story helped justify the Iraq War, which, in turn, helped create ISIS—turning Zarqawi into the powerful terrorist Powell said he was.

If the secretary of state and others in the government can make major blunders that helped give rise to Daesh and Zarqawi, and they are forgiven, then we must ask why we are holding a bunch of youth suffering from social problems to a higher standard before the law.

Wanting to protect ourselves, our families, our communities, and our countries is an essential human desire. Lately, many in Minnesota have been talking about countering violent extremism or CVE.

This program that stigmatizes the local Muslim community, particularly the Somali community, as it reaches into communities and entraps young Muslim men.

Yes, those who are plotting violence must absolutely be stopped. But what if, to protect ourselves and our country, we challenge each other to think differently than Satan, who plots and plans to entrap others? Satan sees our weakness and, in the shadows, conspires to make us slip and stumble. As the documentary shows, working with criminals as informants eventually backfires.

How about, in this time of chaos, if we are just as forgiving of the powerless as the powerful, and we take a different approach to community engagement?

What if we challenge ourselves to think like the angels and anchor each other? If we think that someone—out of weakness, ignorance, or lack of coping skills—might engage in actions that harm us, we might seek that person out, entice them with ideas of glory. Or we might instead anchor that person and nurture them, and our society, to a higher level of understanding.

Can We Say No to Entrapment and Yes to Anchoring?

Imagine that there are young men who came to this country as immigrants. They are dealing with language and adjustment issues in schools, and their parents are likely overwhelmed as they try to settle in a new culture. These kids are struggling, and they don't have the necessary social and emotional support in the family.

We have used acts of violence by these young men to justify more screening and more surveillance on an entire community.

There is another model: rehab. Instead of entrapping and criminalizing, we can put these young men to work in the community, and we can find ways to fold them back into the fabric of our society.

God sent down messengers to humanity to remind us, to guide us, and to anchor us. We need to listen to them and be the angels our vulnerable youth and our communities need.

What Makes a Good Judge?

There is a story attributed to Abu Hurairah, a seventh-century narrator of *hadith*. He told of a cleaner who lived during the time of the Prophet, upon him peace and blessings.

It happened that the Prophet noticed this cleaner was suddenly missing from the mosque. When he was told the cleaner had died, the Prophet asked, "Why didn't you inform me?" It seemed that the Prophet's companions had found the matter trivial, but the Prophet went to the cleaner's grave to offer prayers.

In this story, we learn about the attentions of the truly just—the sort of person who would be a good judge. The Prophet didn't ask, "Was this person a high achiever? Did they go to Yale?" This person's worth, for the Prophet, didn't rest on having reached a particular station in life or put together a stunning CV.

Although ways of measuring human worth have changed, much has stayed the same. It is important for us to remember that innocence and guilt are not built on a person's place in the social hierarchy.

When US Supreme Court nominee Brett Kavanaugh testified before the Senate about the charges laid against him by Dr. Christine Blasey Ford, many people had already made up their minds about him. People were either in camp "I believe him" or camp "I believe her." But we learn a lot more by listening to his testimony and trying to judge him on the evidence before us.

Repeatedly, Kavanaugh stated in his defense that he was a hard worker, he went to Yale, he studied a lot. For instance, during the September 27, 2018, hearing, in response to a question about overconsumption of alcohol, Kavanaugh said, "Senator, I was at the top of my class academically, busted my butt in school. Captain of the varsity basketball team. Got in Yale College. When I got into Yale College, got into Yale Law School. Worked my tail off."

Success Doesn't Prove Innocence

Kavanaugh did, indeed, attend Yale College. And while it seems he lied when suggesting he had no connections there—his grandfather was a Yalie—going to Yale is hardly a mark of shame. Yet the problem is not that Kavanaugh went to Yale. The problem is that he's suggesting his time at Yale demonstrates *innocence*.

There have been many people who justified their abuse of others by saying, "But I'm a high achiever!" We often accept this logic in daily discourse. For instance, scientist Richard Dawkins said there was a lack of Nobel Prizes among Muslim scientists to support his opposition to contemporary Muslims. Dr. Dawkins also tweeted about fourteen-year-old Ahmed Mohamed, a boy who was detained and questioned because he had brought a clock he'd built to school. Mohamed was called "Clock Boy" in the popular media.

Dawkins's argument against the boy wasn't that children shouldn't be allowed to build clocks. It was that Ahmed Mohamed's clock wasn't particularly sophisticated. Dawkins dubbed the boy "Hoax Boy."

Dr. Ford certainly showed evidence of being credible and should have been given the opportunity of a fair investigation. But based on what was presented at the hearings, we cannot prove whether Kavanaugh is guilty or innocent of sexually assaulting Dr. Ford. We simply don't have sufficient evidence. But Kavanaugh's statements about himself are in themselves concerning. If being a high achiever proves innocence, then what does being a low achiever prove?

How will Kavanaugh look at cases of immigrant workers and other vulnerable people? Those from marginalized groups are often perceived as more likely to commit violence. Kavanaugh showed no sign of sympathizing with them or with anyone outside the elite.

What the Senate hearings revealed about Kavanaugh was not the complete truth of whether or not he assaulted Dr. Ford. What it revealed was what he believes about justice.

Unlikability Doesn't Prove Guilt Either

Sometimes we come across people in this world who we passionately dislike. We may find them loud, obnoxious, and irritating. Indeed, they may be loud, obnoxious, and irritating! But we can't use our feelings about them to rationalize accusations. We must step back from their unlikability and look at the facts as dispassionately as possible. It is possible for someone to be a jerk and be innocent. It's equally possible for someone to be charming, kind, and loveable yet be guilty.

People who have later been shown to be murderers—even serial killers—were thought of as charming and lovable. Many abusers are initially very kind and validating to those they later abuse. Being charming doesn't mean a person is not violating others.

This is something the Prophet Muhammad, upon him peace and blessings, taught his followers. Once, a man came to claim his rights. As he did, he spoke in an abusive manner and was so belligerent with the Prophet that his companion, Umar ibn al-Khattab, wanted to strike the man. Yet the Prophet admonished Umar. He addressed the man's rights first, before he addressed his aggressive behavior and tone.

Anger Is OK, But . . .

Some people mocked Kavanaugh for his expressions of anger during his September 27 hearing. But anger in and of itself shouldn't be a disqualifier, and shaming people for their anger isn't healthy. People who have been the victims of a crime, for instance, have a right to feel angry. It's easy for us to forget that Martin Luther King Jr. was animated by anger at the treatment of African Americans. But he recognized this anger, and he used it to organize and transform.

Marginalized people are often shamed for expressing anger in public. We don't want to do the same to Kavanaugh. But we can ask questions about his anger.

1. Is this anger related to a particularly unjust event?
2. Does this anger prompt him to take action to correct a wrong?
3. Is the angry person concerned primarily for their own status or for others?

So what sort of anger was Kavanaugh's? Of course, we can't get inside his head. But it seems that this anger was primarily about himself, on his own behalf. He did not express anger about sexual assault or about the abuse of women or about other injustices. Instead, it seemed that his anger was about how he, personally, might be denied a job.

What Could a Good Judge Have Said?

Most—if not all—of us have made mistakes. Most—if not all—of us have done things we now regret. If Kavanaugh did attack Dr. Ford, he could have admitted this and asked, "How can I repair the harm?"

If he knew for certain that he didn't attack Dr. Ford, then he could have talked about how he, as a judge, has dealt with the crime of sexual assault. He could also have talked about how he would deal with it as a Supreme Court judge. He should have shown that he empathized and identified with the victims of sexual assault. All that was missing from his statements.

It's exceptionally important that a judge be able to identify with all sorts of different people: those in power and those who are not. If a judge has no way to identify with people who are different, then how will they be able to properly express and uphold the law?

Anger is an important and healthy emotion. However, a judge also has to be able to take a step back from their personal emotions. A judge must be able to give everyone their rights, including the marginalized.

"I Made It"

Throughout the hearings, Kavanaugh talked about himself and what he had achieved in life but also how hard he had worked to achieve it. He said:

> *I busted my butt in academics. I always tried to do the best I could.*
>
> *I worked very hard in college, in my studies, and I also played basketball, I did sports and I also did socialize.*
>
> *I got into Yale Law School. That's the number one law school in the country. I had no connections there. I got there by busting my tail in college.*

Yet what does "busting your butt" have to do with being a Supreme Court judge? Kavanaugh is speaking here as though he's applying for a position as a CEO, not a position that requires him to relate to the people of the country. At the hearing, Kavanaugh had an opportunity to talk about how he wanted to serve the American people. But saying "I got it" and "I worked very hard" and "I busted my butt" doesn't suggest he's seeking to help the American people or that he intends to use his skills in the service of others.

In the end, Kavanaugh might or might not be guilty of the particular assault accusations leveled against him. Based on the evidence presented at the hearing, we can say she was a credible witness and that we believe her. We can't say he is, in a legal sense, guilty of sexual assault. When we judge an issue—for we all act as judges sometimes—we must examine it from as many sides as possible, accept that we might be in error ourselves, and try to get at the truth rather than to please or find fault with others.

We can learn from these hearings: about critical thinking, about treating others with respect, and about talking to teens about sexual assault. As Anita Hill said, we cannot offer results, but we can offer a fair and thorough process. Even if, in the end, we don't have enough evidence to say whether Kavanaugh is guilty of this particular act, it doesn't mean Dr. Ford is lying or should be silent. It only means we can't definitively judge guilt about the event in question.

What we can say is that Kavanaugh is unqualified to be a Supreme Court judge, or any judge at all.

Give Muslims a Platform

A Somali MPR reporter is stopped at the courthouse where he's been going every day.

A sixth-grade Muslim schoolgirl in New York is called "ISIS," put in headlock, and punched as middle school boys try to pull off her headscarf.

A fourteen-year-old boy who wants to show his clock to a teacher is treated as a terrorist.

My daughter is called a terrorist in school.

These are not isolated incidents but part of an increasingly powerful narrative about Muslims. I get up early to read the news. When I do, I find Muslims all over the world, mainly in a negative light, often framed as a stereotype of violence and hatred.

Year after year, the voices of ISIS and their supporters have been saturating the internet—both because of their shocking acts and because of how well they fit with stereotypes of the "eternally violent" Muslim. One would think they were the majority of Muslims rather than a fringe minority.

All around the world, Muslims are working as journalists, attending school, inventing things—but extremists get the coverage and the mic. They overwhelm the picture, and they seem like the majority.

Here in Minnesota, we're watching a trial of Somali youth unfold. Many of us feel a sadness about how these youth were misled and who failed them. But meanwhile, Mukhtar Ibrahim, a Somali MPR reporter, is stopped at the courthouse.

"They know who I am; they see me every day," Ibrahim said of the security guards. "I'm not a stranger coming to cover this case from the East Coast. I've been covering this case since day one. They know I'm a reporter."

What happened to make security see Ibrahim not as a reporter but as a threat? The problem is the imbalance of the platform. Even though there are a few "positive" stories about Muslims here and there, there isn't a platform where people are able to respond to false accusations, clarify misunderstandings of Islamic teachings, and reach the masses.

When someone is allowed to speak on behalf of Muslims, it's often not the people who are targeted but someone whose story fits with the violent narrative.

Back in 2005, Thomas Friedman wrote an essay titled "Brave, Young and Muslim," in which he praised Irshad Manji's book *The Trouble With Islam Today*. Manji is a self-proclaimed Muslim refusenik who, in her book, magnifies every social ill present in Muslim societies, portraying Muslims as morally bankrupt people for mainly non-Muslim audiences.

Certainly, Muslims should not be above criticism! But through Manji's book, Muslims are shamed into seeing themselves as flawed and defective just by being Muslim, which creates feelings of worthlessness, pushing them into emotional rage or isolation instead of dialogue and peacemaking. But there is another way.

My daughter attends public school. In sixth grade, I took her out of Al Amal, a Muslim school in Fridley, feeling that she should be OK now in the broader community. Sometimes, I've been alarmed by her coming home asking me about ISIS or feeling angry that she was called a terrorist or having all eyes look at her when the teacher discusses 9/11.

When I was her age, I used to get into physical fights with people who would try to bully me or my siblings because we were foreigners, Muslims, or Palestinians. I lacked the tools to do anything else, but I don't want my daughter to use that approach. I want my daughter to be able to speak up for herself. To do that, she needs a platform.

Last month, my daughter was called a terrorist in school. Right away, she reported the person to the dean. The boy was found and brought to the office, and my daughter got a platform to tell him how his words made her feel.

Face-to-face.

The boy was compelled to listen. After that, he apologized and told her he didn't mean it. She felt better—she was able to face the boy openly and transparently and to express how his words had affected her. This was because she knew how to respond to discrimination but also because the school principal gave her a small platform, a place to speak.

On the national level, this has been much harder. Clock Boy became instantly famous when he brought an invention to school and was treated as a terrorist. The fourteen-year-old was detained, questioned, and hauled off in handcuffs.

It wasn't resolved at the local level, so the story made headline news, and people gave the boy moral support. Yet sadly, the platform quickly became skewed toward people like Richard Dawkins, who could not help attacking the boy on social media. "Don't call him 'clock boy' since he never made a clock. Hoax Boy, having hoaxed his way into the White House, now wants $15M in addition!" Dawkins tweeted.

We need to have more empathy and compassion for young children being abused and bullied in school. We need to give those children a platform to speak, just as Muslims across the United States need to have a place to speak, to respond, to share their stories.

Loyalty and Cooperation Are Two-Way Streets

There are frequent calls—from law-enforcement officials, from radio personalities, and from ordinary people—for Muslims in the United States to be "loyal." It's not new. The loyalty of many other groups has been questioned: Japanese, Catholics. But what does it mean to be a loyal citizen of the United States, and how can loyalty be fostered?

Loyalty doesn't mean that you agree with every action taken by your country's government. As a US citizen, I have some criticism of US foreign policy. But loyalty does mean that I will address this in the public square. I will raise my questions not to attack America but in a way that will benefit the country. When you're speaking up as a loyal citizen, you're speaking openly—you're not plotting and planning in the shadows.

Loyalty also doesn't mean staying quiet or even following every law. It means that you're speaking and acting with the intent to benefit the greater community. Martin Luther King Jr. showed great loyalty to the United States, as did the boxer Muhammad Ali.

When Moses wanted to call out oppression and discrimination, he went and spoke to the Pharaoh. He didn't hype up people in Midian because Moses spoke as loyalty speaks. Even in a situation of extreme oppression, he didn't try to catch the rulers of his society off guard or create an unequal power play. He spoke directly and openly to power.

Disloyalty is its opposite: where a citizen in *not* seeking the benefit of everybody but is instead seeking power and self-aggrandizement. For instance, in Yemen, there is broad anti-American sentiment. I don't agree with the drone policy in Yemen. But when I traveled there, it would've been wrong for me to play on that by bad-mouthing America.

Terrorist groups hide in the shadows, hyping people up against their own. If you disagree, that's not disloyalty. But you have to fight the good fight and speak up conscientiously in the public square.

Is the Government Loyal to Us?

When the story broke that US officials had detained dual Canadian-Syrian citizen Maher Arar during a layover at JFK Airport and sent him not to Canada but to Syria, where he was detained and tortured, Muslim American citizens had good reason to wonder about their government's loyalty. It took a year before Arar's case was properly examined, and he was declared innocent by both the Syrian and Canadian governments.

This news came in an environment where federal and local law-enforcement officials were asking the Muslim community to spy on each other and report on themselves. Certainly, I want to protect my community from anyone who is planning violence. But I *also* want to make sure individuals who might be innocent—and even those who might be guilty—have their rights protected too. If I'm being asked to report somebody, and then I hear the person is being tortured, that makes it difficult for me to report anyone else in the future.

In an attempt to be loyal to America, I harmed another human being. Even if he was planning something, everyone deserves a trial and due process.

On the other hand, in July 2009, Minnesota Muslim leaders met with Congressman Keith Ellison to discuss challenges that were facing Muslims in Minnesota. The discussion focused on everything from positive contributions to the growth of the community, including the free Muslim-run health clinics in the Twin Cities, to the missing Somali men and Muslims' cooperation with law enforcement.

Congressman Ellison encouraged everyone to contribute to America and answer President Obama's call to service. This was the sort of two-way loyalty that everyone present could get behind and stood in stark contrast to Senator Joe Lieberman's refusal to accept an invitation to meet with Minnesota Muslims, even though he was leading a terrorism investigation into Minnesota Somali Muslims.

False Accusations Are Also a Reality

I am not a fan of "I believe her." I am not a fan of "I believe him" either.

I am a fan of "I don't know," and if my knowledge about this situation is of importance to the victim, whether it is a man or woman, then show me the evidence and give me space to verify and investigate.

Let me begin by saying that I do not believe whatever a woman is wearing or doing justifies any sexual harassment or abuse. Without her explicit consent while she is of a healthy mind and conscious of what she is saying and agreeing to, nothing justifies any abuse. If a woman were twerking in the public square while naked, that would not justify any groping or harassment.

That justifies a charge of indecent exposure but not harassment, rape, or groping. From an Islamic perspective, it is a sin to look at the woman and to move into her personal space.

In my experience, I have seen women being abused and sexually harassed without their consent, but I have also seen people falsely accuse others, both men and women.

I have also seen women sexually harass men and destroy marriages once they set their eyes on someone who is married. I used to find women in my brother's bedroom who got in by climbing and entering through an open window while he was not there. My brother never ran after them, but they ran after him all the time.

A teenager who is a senior is a mentor at her high school who helps first-year students get settled. She tells me stories of high school girls having a crush on this new freshman boy and running after him.

I was in a mosque once, and the teacher was giving the lecture. The mosque was situated such that the women were sitting in the back, and the men were in front. I was in the middle, and women were chatting very loudly behind me. I got annoyed and turned around to see what they were talking about. They were passing around a banana and making sexual comments regarding men's genitals and laughing.

There is no doubt that women's experiences of sexual harassment by men are greater than men's experiences of sexual harassment by women.

However, blind and uncritical support without evidence is not healthy and can harm the vulnerable and weak more than those in power. Let me give some examples.

A woman was falsely accused of attempted murder by her ex-husband, who created a scene and paid witnesses to claim she was shooting at him. The sheriff was out looking to arrest her while she was in the hospital with her sick child at the time of the alleged shooting.

I know another woman who was accused of throwing a stone at a grocery store, yet this relative cannot drive to reach the store, which is far from her home, nor does she know how to get there or have the ability to throw a stone such that it would break a window. She suffers many health issues. During a fight, the other party paid witnesses to claim the accused threw a stone and destroyed her store window. She found people to falsely bear witness, including relatives of the accused. A few women created the whole scene and brought forth false witnesses. Their evidence did not hold water in court, and they withdrew the case.

The third case is one we are all familiar with and are still paying the price for. The Iraq War. That war was based on lies and paid informants who were petty criminals and testified to falsehoods. How many people died because we were hyped up and refused to ask for evidence or investigate the evidence?

How many were whipped up and imprisoned as an aftermath to the chaos that emerged? How many were tortured? How many are still paying the price for this war?

The numerous campaigns to malign Muslims or minorities are based on lies or distortions while ISIS and other extremist groups who hype people are also based on distortions and feelings of pain and hurt. You get the point.

Beware of Hype

Victims have every right to call out their abusers. In fact, I believe they should. Loudly, whether people believe them or not, it is their responsibility to call out abusers. Historically, truth seekers have stood up to abusers regardless of the threat to their lives or whether people believed them. Some have even been killed.

Those who justify the abuse by talking about what a woman was wearing or saying she was a porn star need to be sternly silenced. A man always has the power to walk away. However, false accusations are also a reality.

Our starting point is to say we do not know, and encourage a woman to speak up if she is indeed a victim and to bring evidence that we can investigate and verify if she wants our support against the accused party.

If we always believe an accuser, this campaign can be used to harm minority groups or social justice movements. After all, it is easy to recruit individuals with pay to falsely bear witness against another.

Guilty Until Proven Innocent

The American legal system is meant to be built around the excellent premise that everyone accused of a crime is innocent until proven guilty.

Yet according to Somali Voices, a coalition of nearly a dozen local Somali organizations, the entire Somali community has been under suspicion and scrutiny for the harmful actions of a handful of men for almost a decade. In a 2009 press release, Somali Voices stated:

> [M]embers of the Somali community have reported being stopped on the streets and in the malls, Somali businesses have been raided, students have been approached by federal agents in campus libraries, community leaders have been denied boarding passes without due process, agents have talked their way into homes without warrants, non-English-speaking Somalis have been interviewed without translators, agents in unmarked cars have staked out in front of Somali mosques, informants have allegedly been sent inside the mosques.

If anything, things have intensified with Minnesota's Countering Violent Extremism (CVE) program, which launched in three pilot cities in 2014, including Minneapolis. The CVE is administered by the US Department of Justice, and a number of groups have spoken out against it for the way it discriminatorily targets the Muslim and Somali communities, increasing policing and intelligence gathering under the guise of providing social services.

After this many years of intense observation, the community is feeling harassed, transgressed upon, and that they have no rights.

Instead of loyalty, this is a breeding ground for mistrust, resentment, and anger.

Somali Muslims in Minnesota are being psychoanalyzed and watched, and there are informants in their mosques. These practices inhibit the kinds of social and emotional growth that connect the Somali community with the greater community. They don't have space to hear themselves, to define themselves, or for beneficial criticism.

Instead of fostering loyalty, an atmosphere of neighbor spying on neighbor fosters the sort of mistrust that drives young people to look for alternative authority figures, gangs and extremist groups among them. We absolutely shouldn't be in denial that there *are* cases of missing Somali youth who have gone to fight with violent, fringe extremist groups. But a fear-based, oversimplistic approach will do nothing but make the problem more expensive and more difficult to solve.

When you want loyalty, you have to promote trust. What can individuals do to show loyalty to marginalized communities?

In October 2015, Asma Jama was attacked in a Coon Rapids, Minnesota, Applebee's for speaking Swahili—a forty-three-year-old woman walked up to Jama and allegedly smashed her face with a beer mug.

The attack left Jama with a deep gash in her lower lip and cuts across her face. Afterward, Jama said that, after calling the state home for fifteen years, she felt unwanted and unsafe in Minnesota. But after a solidarity gathering to support her, Jama said she changed her mind.

Scores of Minnesotans, including Coon Rapids city officials and social-justice leaders from across the area, met to support Jama, sending a message not just to her but to the whole community.

By listening with compassion and pushing back on anger and hatred, we as individuals can help steer the larger society in the right direction and nurture those with unhealthy sentiments without condemning them.

Justice versus Revenge

Justice is at the core of Islam. Yet the practice of being just in our lives, and particularly being a just leader, is not easy.

On the one hand, justice is something that comes naturally to us. We're all, in our lives, *seekers* of justice. But it's also human nature not to want to *give* justice when we, or our friends, may have transgressed against others. Giving justice to others means we have to recognize when we're wrong. And that's a difficult thing for humans to do.

Being a judge, a mediator, or another leader in the community who has to examine a case both deeply and impartially requires rigorous training. The top judges in Islamic history had knowledge not just of the law but also of the communities and contexts in which they worked. When the judge Imam al-Shafi'i moved to Egypt in 814 CE, he changed his practice and judgments in order to reflect the particular ills that plagued that country and culture.

For instance, although many associate FGM with Islam, it's instead part of the local cultural context in countries where Islam has been widely accepted. Islam doesn't come to kick out a local culture but rather to nurture people to justice.

Thus, justice is about understanding context, and anyone who works in a position in which they judge others must not just be a critical thinker but also have an openness to accountability and self-criticism. The more influential the judge's position, the higher the standards to which they must be held, just as the Prophet, peace and blessings on him, held himself and his family to the highest standard of all.

Holding ourselves and others to account—such as through peer reviews and other checks and balances—helps us all stay accountable. A judge who preaches accountability to others must absolutely *be* accountable to a review of their work.

Umar al-Khattab and Openness to Criticism

Umar al-Khattab first encountered Islam when his sister accepted its teachings into her life and her heart. He started out by criticizing his sister. But she corrected him and told him he was transgressing her rights. He accepted this criticism and went to meet the Prophet for himself. He grew into a senior companion of the Prophet's, but he never grew above criticism and correcting.

Another case in point, a Muslim scholar at ISNA convention, related a historical story of when two men who fought, and during the course of this heated, passionate fight, one ended up accidentally killing the other. The killer was remorseful, and he neither ran away nor tried to rationalize what had happened. He went to Calipha at the time and asked if he could go wrap up a few things before he came back to accept his punishment.

The Calipha asked, "Who will be this man's sponsor and accept responsibility for him?" A man who didn't know the killer stepped forward. He said he had no connection with this man but that he didn't want anyone to say that mercy had left the hearts of the Muslims. And so the man left, and later, as promised, he came back.

The Calipha asked him, "Why did you come back?" The man said to him, "I didn't want it to be said that trust had left the hearts of the Muslims." Then the guardian of the man who had been killed stepped forward and said that he forgave this man, who had killed his relative in a fight. "I didn't want people to say that forgiveness had left the hearts of the Muslims," he said.

In this case, we have a justice system that is not abusive nor based on revenge but is instead a careful process of dispassionate and restorative justice. Yes, the man did wrong, but he was trying to repent and accept punishment. This doesn't ever make the murder OK, but we must be able to allow people to repent and move back into society.

Communities of Justice, Communities of Injustice

The Prophet nurtured his followers to be open to those who called them to justice and to give them their rights. It didn't matter how high or low the person's social standing; what mattered was who had transgressed, even unintentionally.

But other communities are nurtured *against* justice, particularly if they always have each other's backs, defending them no matter what. In these communities, if a complaint is raised against one in the "in" group, the others can't hear or see anything bad about them. They do everything in their power to defend the person in their group, without listening to the accuser.

Of course, we should never stab our friends in the back. But instead of immediately and passionately leaping to a friend's defense, we should realize that everyone—even those we love—makes mistakes. We might say, "I don't know my friend to be the sort of person who'd do a thing like that, but perhaps we should bring in an independent judge."

Even if our friend *isn't* guilty, it's important to create an institutional culture in which claims are investigated. Otherwise, claims can be too easily dismissed as "he-said, she-said" when it's really "she-said-and-nobody-listened." In this environment, it becomes difficult for those who are not in power to be heard.

We don't have to say, "I believe her" for every single case. But we must say, as Anita Hill said, "We need a thorough and independent investigation" for every credible accusation.

Being open about these issues and talking about them is a first step. We must learn to be aware that we're all human and that people often take advantage of those who are weak and unprotected.

Bad Judgment and Revenge

Sometimes people start out on the path toward justice, and yet they don't know where the boundaries lie. Like the family of the man who was killed in a passionate fight, those seeking revenge might set out on the path to justice. But then, once justice has been given, they keep going, transgressing the boundaries of others and going from oppressed to oppressor.

Revenge doesn't accept an eye for an eye or sincere repentance and restoration. Rather, when faced with a loss of an eye, it wants to obliterate a whole village.

Bad justices—just like bad lawmakers—often confuse justice and revenge. Look at the Japanese internment camps or the punitive "justice" that followed in the wake of the September 11 attacks. The same goes for many individual sentences. If the sentence is disproportionate, out of step with other sentences for similar crimes, it's likely the judge was thinking not of justice but of revenge.

This is often related to the sort of patriotic, jingoist, in-group thinking in which, instead of being dispassionate, we simply have each other's backs. Judges must have an emotional distance from those they are judging; otherwise, they are not qualified to judge.

No judge is going to be right 100 percent of the time. That's neither possible nor the point. The point is to be open and accountable and to create institutions and communities where we have openness and a regular auditing process, where we have independent judges or mediators who can listen to claims and hear them out. These are systems in which people—even those without much power—get an opportunity to push back and seek out justice.

Toward Reconciliation and Healing

"Or, Who listens to the (soul) distressed when it calls on Him, and Who relieves its suffering, and makes you (mankind) inheritors of the earth? (Can there be another) god besides Allah? Little it is that ye heed!" (Quran 27:62)

There is a narration on the Prophet's cousin Imam Ali ibn Abu Talib, who was fighting an enemy with his sword ready to deal the final blow when the enemy spit in his face. Ali refused to continue the battle as the fight had become personally motivated.

We learn from this incident that whether in battle or in discussion, when conflict or a fight becomes poisoned with personal angst, the wisest thing to do is to ground ourselves and remove the personal angst. When the personal angst is removed, the discussion can continue.

There are many roads in the valley of impotence in the face of adversity, and many lead to loss and perpetual suffering. At times, we find ourselves at a junction where many voices are giving us advice; however, all these voices lead us astray. There is the road of guidance, which is a steep road, but first we must acknowledge that we do not know and seek guidance.

At times, voices that validate our pain and suffering seek to manipulate us in our most vulnerable state when we are hurting and unaware. Voices of guidance, on the other hand, seek to center and ground us so we can see the roads ahead and choose the road to travel with wisdom and reflection. It is for this reason that God guides us to show patience in times of adversity, so we can reflect and follow the road of guidance and not one of the seductive roads of validation or conformity.

I like to emphasize listening but not to validate the one speaking. But if our aim is to guide another or receive guidance, then we must find where we are emotionally, mentally, and spiritually on the map before we can guide each other appropriately. Giving people advice based on conjecture, false assumptions, or projections of our own internal issues can lead to many misunderstandings and much name-calling.

One of God's names is *As Sami*, or the one who listens to all. God doesn't just hear what the lips say but beyond that. He hears our thoughts, our feelings in our hearts, and even our emotions that, at times, we struggle to put in words. Furthermore, the beauty of God is that He listens to us before He asks us to listen to Him.

At times, because we feel heard by God, we assume our feelings and views are then correct, and God is on our side. Yet God listens to all of us, even if we are wrong and misguided. We fail to go beyond being heard by God to listening to God with humility. Hence, to love God is learning to listen to Him.

Many religious people from all faiths, myself included, are very good at speaking to God and speaking for God without His permission. We end up seeing, hearing, and experiencing the false image of faith. But real faith requires us to go beyond our blabber and challenges us to embrace humility and listen to God. Listening to God means finding the courage to ask God, "Am I wrong?" It is when we learn to listen with a will to His call and trust in God that we are guided to see, hear, and experience the reality of faith: hence, to walk in the right way and learn to coexist in peace.

Prophet Muhammad, upon him peace and blessings, was known to have this quality of listening to others compassionately. He was mocked for this quality by his adversaries.

> *Among them are men who abuse the Prophet and say, "He is (all) ear." Say, "He listens to what is best for you: he believes in Allah, has faith in the Believers, and is a Mercy to those of you who believe." But those who abuse the Messenger will have a grievous penalty.*
>
> —Quran 9:61

As we engage in discussion on racial bias or Islamophobia, it is important that we take a moment to challenge ourselves to listen to the other but also and more importantly to turn to God and ask Him, "Am I wrong?" then listen to God. The road ahead is a challenging one, given our experiences, but we have the potential to rise to the challenge.

The suffering that is a result of trauma, if not addressed, can spill over and affect family members as well as the community and society. Now we can take our journals and reflect on the stories of the Prophets as we reflect on their lives and journey to God.

Your Commands Are Just

> *Oh Allah, I am Your servant, the son of Your servant, the son of your maid-servant, and entirely at Your service. You hold me by my forelock. Your Decree is what controls me, and Your Commands to me are just. I beseech You by every one of Your Names, those which You use to refer to Yourself, or have revealed in Your Book, or have taught to any one of Your creation, or have chosen to keep hidden with You in the Unseen, to make the Quran the springtime of my heart, the light of my eyes, the departure of my grief, and the vanishing of my affliction and my sorrow.*
>
> —Ahmad and Ibn Hibban

We must overcome our human weakness and refuse to allow anyone to sow discord or lies against God in our hearts and minds. God is *Al Aziz* and it is not befitting for people to enter His Heaven while their hearts are not purified. When Satan attempted to sow discord between humanity and God, God expelled him. This is a manifestation of His Love and Protection for us. He is *Al Waali*, The Protecting Friend.

However, God's admonitions and warnings to us about Satan were ineffective. The enmity between humans is packed with lessons on what not to do. Therefore, we should strive to have solid and unwavering faith in God and not be swayed by false narratives or delusions. We should also remember to approach God with humility and awe, recognizing His Infinite Glory and Mercy. None of us would want to be around people who readily believe rumors and can be pulled into a sedition campaign against us. Don't ask God what we, as humans, would not accept for ourselves or our loved ones. Again, He is *Dhul Jalali wal Ikram*, The Lord of Majesty and Generosity.

Acceptance or *Reda*, which is contentment, should not be confused with fatalism. The former prevents the trial from worsening and promotes healing, and the latter breeds indifference to human suffering. Imam al-Sha'rawi shared something profound:

> God wants the whole community to taste peace and security. If there is a repenting person and the latter who is not repenting. The latter will make the life of the former miserable. However, Allah wants all people to repent, so they benefit from each other. If there are only some repenting people, they will suffer from those who are not. Therefore, Allah said pass your knowledge to others, because you do not benefit from your knowledge unless you do so.

To understand the insight of Imam al-Sha'rawi, it helps to reflect on the following passage in the Quran, Chapter 4, Verses 105–114:

> *We have sent down to thee the Book in truth, that thou mightest judge between men, as guided by Allah: so be not (used) as an advocate by those who betray their trust; But seek the forgiveness of Allah; for Allah is Oft-forgiving, Most Merciful.*
>
> *Contend not on behalf of such as betray their own souls; for Allah loveth not one given to perfidy and crime: They may hide (Their crimes) from men, but they cannot hide (Them) from Allah, seeing that He is in their midst when they plot by night, in words that He cannot approve: And Allah Doth compass round all that they do.*
>
> *Ah! These are the sort of men on whose behalf ye may contend in this world; but who will contend with Allah on their behalf on the Day of Judgment, or who will carry their affairs through?*
>
> *If any one does evil or wrongs his own soul but afterwards seeks Allah's forgiveness, he will find Allah Oft-forgiving, Most Merciful. And if anyone earns sin. he earns it against His own soul: for Allah is full of knowledge and wisdom.*
>
> *But if any one earns a fault or a sin and throws it onto one that is innocent, He carries (on himself) (Both) a falsehood and a flagrant sin. But for the Grace of Allah to thee and his Mercy, a party of them would certainly have plotted to lead thee astray. But (in fact) they will only Lead their own souls astray, and to thee, they can do no harm in the least.*
>
> *For Allah hath sent down to thee the Book and wisdom and taught thee what thou Knewest not (before): And great is the Grace of Allah unto thee.*
>
> *In most of their secret talks, there is no good: But if one*

> *exhorts to a deed of charity or justice or conciliation between men, (Secrecy is permissible): To him who does this, seeking the good pleasure of Allah, We shall soon give a reward of the highest (value).*

This will allow us to refine our character and coexist. How? Some know their faults and own them and work on them. Others do not and, hence, do not see others in truth; instead, they project onto others their reality, become fixated with another's personal life, and try to live through them because their life is empty.

They say remembrance of God repels Satan. We worry about human beings engaging in brainwashing, and we should. Likewise, Satan engages in spiritual attacks nonstop on our hearts in the spiritual world. Why? He wants to prevent us from turning to God and repenting or seeking guidance.

God heard the inner reality of Satan as he was climbing the road of nearness to God, praying with the angels. God created a situation. Instead of telling us what is in Satan's mind and heart, God asked Satan why he refused to obey God. Satan responded, revealing his inner reality: blame and projection.

Satan revealed that he was worshipping God out of ego, not receiving virtue or *fadilah* from God. He was full of himself, not faith or virtue from God. And he refused to receive faith or virtue. Whereas Adam, upon him peace, turned to God and repented (emptied himself) to receive.

God does not benefit by our turning to Him, nor is He harmed by our refusal to turn to Him. We benefit. Our constricted hearts expand with the spiritual lights of faith showered upon us with the gates of heaven open.

Trials and tribulations are inevitable. Some face trials that would make others lose their minds. By connecting to those who are manifesting their faith and perseverance, we can learn from them how to face our little trials and help others.

As Adam, upon him peace, modeled healthy remorse to Satan, such individuals model to us how to process our own trials to prevent a trial in the temporal world from becoming a trial of faith or the eternal world.

Hence, we need to be very careful when promoting healthy remorse or repentance to God via shaming tactics. This can add salt to the wound.

Healthy remorse and turning to God benefit us tremendously. I amplify the voices of people suffering in Palestine as they display their faith to the world in the face of cruelty, injustice, and trials.

It is not an "it could be a worse moment" but a "this is what faith looks like in the face of trials and tribulations" moment. It is also an opportunity to reach out and help them, through whatever we have in our power.

Beyond Shame, Violence, and Terror

> *It has been said that the essence of courage is not never having fear, but overcoming that fear when you have it. In many ways, the struggle of din [adhering to values of your faith] is the same. If it was always so easy for us to 'stay in it' then there wouldn't be much value in it. The key is to struggle with yourself, and surrender even when you don't feel like it, and when it doesn't come easy.*
>
> —Dr. Abdul Lateef Krauss Abdullah

Faith, as I've said before, is about accepting ourselves as humans and turning to God to help us grow, heal, and be nurtured. This isn't possible if we feel ashamed of who we are, of our core identities.

Oppressors—who are often themselves suffering from unacknowledged shame—don't fight us just physically but also psychologically.

The path to faith and healing is the path to knowing yourself. The more you know yourself, the harder it is for you to be recruited against another person.

Where Does Shame Come From?

Every group or society relies on its members getting along. Being a member of a community entails being concerned about the well-being of those around you. We need people to feel at ease and trusting of one another, and we do this by developing social norms.

These social norms contribute to a shared understanding of what is and is not acceptable behavior, as well as a framework for resolving conflicts and maintaining social order within the group or society. Respecting personal space, using polite language, and adhering to laws and regulations are examples of social norms. Finally, these norms contribute to forming a sense of community and developing positive relationships among individuals within a group or society. When social norms are violated, shame comes into play.

Shame is a powerful emotion that can lead to feelings of worthlessness and self-doubt, making it difficult for individuals to move past their mistakes and take positive action toward change. In some cases, their culture and identity are shamed as a whole. But they can also be told about the social norm violation respectfully and invitingly. It is crucial to approach the situation with empathy and understanding, acknowledging the impact of shame on a person's mental health and well-being. By creating a safe space for them to express their emotions, we can help them repair the violation and regain their confidence.

The key thing: the language you use to express social norms or manners—which should ideally make us more comfortable with one another—should foster invitation instead of control. If you use control, even if your aims are positive, eventually, you will face resistance.

The Quran says we must "invite to the way of your Lord," not shame to the way of your Lord.

When we are invited to something, we feel special. We feel a sense of control and empowerment, and we feel respected. There are certainly times in a social group when a person crosses boundaries, and this person must be pushed back, and they should feel remorse. But shame shouldn't be used as a tool to batter people and control them, to make them try to force their identities into something more comfortable to the dominant group.

We could also use shame—insulting the person's ethnicity, throwing jabs at the food of their culture, suggesting they are *less*. This creates a wound and feelings of worthlessness. If a person doesn't find a witness to their shame, it can also be very dangerous.

What to Do with Our Shame?

It is important to find a witness to our shame, someone who can hear and see that this shaming was unwarranted, someone to take it from us. If we have a witness, then we can step away from the abuse and understand it was wrong.

If there's no one else around, we must connect to God as the witness. One of the ways to connect to God is by using His name.

If you do not have a witness, you turn to God with His beautiful names, bring His presence to mind, and have him bear witness. This way, you don't feel alone, and you feel His comfort.

We can see this in the story of Joseph. When his brothers threw him in the well, he had no witness but God. Joseph was bewildered and shocked to find himself at the bottom of the well and even more so when his brothers returned and sold him for a small price. But he managed to turn this wound over to God, knowing that he would one day tell his story.

While we do not know of the internal states of the prophets, we can benefit spiritually from reflecting on the story of Joseph, upon him peace, who had no protector other than God through most of his life journey. We can find hope in our own struggles and know that one day, as Joseph, upon him peace, was elevated to a position of power and proven innocent, we will likewise find such victory with God.

In the Quran, after Joseph's brothers threw him in the well, God sent a message internally to his heart:

> *So they did take him away, and they all agreed to throw him down to the bottom of the well: and We put into his heart (this Message): "Of a surety thou shalt (one day) tell them the truth of this their affair while they know (thee) not."*

It was God's plan that the care of his father was cut off from him, and his brothers turned against him to open a secret door within his heart to God.

When you are innocent, a trial befalls you, and you are alone, God *Al Waali*, is very near to your heart. This message from the Divine overpowers and buffers the pain of trauma, which can destroy someone within if they are disconnected from God and face the same trial.

If we don't have a witness to the shaming we undergo—among family or from the wider culture—all we have left is our own wounded ego. We can turn to other people for protection, we can turn to God, or, if we don't, we end up turning to our own ego. Unfortunately, the ego's defense is pride, and that's what it will turn to. In order to restore one's pride after suffering from shame, the easiest way out is to harm others to make ourselves feel bigger.

That's how the ego, unchecked, responds to shame or oppression or humiliation.

If you turn to God as your witness, on the other hand, you will absorb the light from God, instead of the darkness from a controlling or xenophobic culture. In many controlling cultures, there is an obsession with being powerful in the eyes of others and wanting people to fear you more than you want them to respect you.

The psychologist James Gilligan uses the language of disease to talk about shame, calling it a "psychological pathogen" spread by "social, economic, and cultural vectors." In Gilligan's view, shame is the primary cause of violence, with the core purpose of violence being to "diminish the intensity of shame and replace it as far as possible with its opposite, pride."

In order to stop the spread of this disease, we must do two things. We must heal as individual cases, and we must inoculate through our faith.

The Shaming of Muslims

One form of social-control shaming has been the humiliation of Muslims in an attempt to get us to transform into something "more American," more comfortable, and more familiar.

This is likely a transferred shame, a shame that is spreading because it is rooted in other, older shames, a way to regain pride. But it is also rooted in *guroor*, one of the prime drivers of Islamophobia. Some scholars sight that the more *guroor* a person has, the more harm comes out of this person.

Guroor is a belief in one's moral superiority over another. It is a hidden desire to deny the "other" a right to exist unless they accept this moral superiority of the "us," visible both in the belief systems of ISIS supporters and Anders Breivik. This stance of moral superiority—whether about clothing choices, food, gender relations, or other behaviors—is itself toxic.

But just as we shouldn't shame the oppressed, little good comes of shaming the oppressor, even when it feels therapeutic. We must, like Moses with Pharaoh, invite and remind the oppressor of their better self. We must remind them of their values and invite them to God.

Moses didn't go to Pharaoh to shame or humiliate him but to remind him of his values. Pharaoh didn't listen—there is no guarantee of that—and an oppressor who won't listen must be forced back within their boundaries.

You can't be in denial that there are people you have to fight. But it can't be your first resort, and it can't be based on emotion. And shaming only creates more shame, a greater need for the facade of greatness.

Whenever someone doesn't heal from shame, they may not be conscious of it, but they're going to further spread it. They might not be the main architect of *guroor*, of superiority; they might just allow it to flow past them. But shame begets more shame. Instead, we must accept our humanity and our limitations, and we must turn to God.

Nonjudgment versus Hatred

The best way to nurture oneself to be nonjudgmental is to repent often. Being nonjudgmental is not an act or words. There is a difference between being nonjudgmental and self-hatred or hatred of others. Self-hatred or hatred of others associates the sin with the person or oneself and defines the person or oneself by that sin, whereas being nonjudgmental associates the sin with the human condition and recognizes that everyone is a recipient of the Divine breath. And that Divine breath is precious and sacred.

Think of repentance as self-love. On the Day of Judgment, we will be asked, *"What seduced you from your Generous Lord?"* It is an important question because repentance allows us to receive God's blessings, which He is showering upon us. The more we repent, the more we can receive from Him.

The book *Prayers for Forgiveness*, by Hasan al-Basri has seventy prayers and is an excellent start. I add the word *protection* to each prayer as God knows us and our weaknesses and blind spots best. Here are examples:

> *O Allah, I seek Your forgiveness [and protection] for every sin that Your pen recorded and Your knowledge encompassed—every one that I have committed and that I am to commit until the end of my life. I seek Your forgiveness for all my sins: the first and the last, the intentional and the unintentional, the few and the many; the minor and the major, the subtle and the noticeable, the past and the recent, the secret and the open and public—and all those I am to commit throughout my life.*
>
> *O Allah (God), I seek Your forgiveness [and protection] for every sin that You recorded against me because of my self-conceit, or ostentation, or desire for attention, or*

> *malice, or rancor, or treachery, or pride, or exultancy, or intemperate mirth, or obstinacy, or envy, or insolence, or ungratefulness, or fervor for other than Your sake, or bigotry, or acquiescence to sin, or blind hope, or extreme avarice, or generous spending for sin, or oppression, or unwarranted cunning, or theft, or lying, or backbiting, or idle amusement, or fruitless talk, or calumny, or useless play, or any such activity that by doing it sins are reaped and in pursuing it there is destruction and grief.*

Why Do We Heal?

> *Some He hath guided: Others have (by their choice) deserved the loss of their way; in that they took the evil ones, in preference to Allah, for their friends and protectors, and think that they receive guidance.*
>
> —Quran 7:30

I'd like to encourage us not only to value healing but also to look forward to healing. And in so doing, I'll bring together the narratives of psychological healing and faith, which dovetail in important ways.

No one enters life without experiencing some sort of oppression and transgression of their boundaries: mental, physical, social. This comes in different ways and different degrees, but we are all wounded by transgressions, even if we are at the top of the social ladder. If you're a White American, for instance, and you're not learning anything about oppression, you're not going to be aware that you're absorbing it.

As human beings, we at times, and to various degrees, will absorb the dark light of oppression. If we're not conscious and mindful, then we will absorb the darkness of the social realities that surround us. God is constantly showering people with blessings upon blessings, but if our mirrors become too clouded, then we will not be able to reflect these blessings.

By this, I don't mean the material blessings that appeal to someone with a strong-man complex. These are not the blessings of popularity, crowd size, or money. They are the blessings of being able to do the right thing, of being able to help others, of having mercy and compassion.

The possibility of healing creates a choice for each of us. If you don't heal, if you don't apologize, if you don't repent, you may still acquire the material blessings of our world. But you will grow increasingly afraid of vulnerability, of being honest with yourself, and you will miss the world's real blessings and connections.

The fact that we've absorbed the dark light of the world around us doesn't mean we're bad! It only means that we're human beings. This will happen every day if we're not conscious, if we're not studying the reality of the oppressor and rejecting all the macro- and micro-oppressions to which we're being invited.

Moses and Joseph

The Prophet Joseph, upon him peace, experienced multiple oppressions from his siblings and a paternal aunt. In the case of the prophets, they were divinely protected. So when they faced oppression, they immediately entrusted it to God, and they did not absorb its darkness. Still, their actions were instructive.

Muhammad, upon him peace and blessings, was nurtured by the stories of the other prophets. We can connect to the same stories that were used to nurture him, and, in reading about his life, we can see how he dealt with oppression.

The prophets came to help us to heal. It wasn't just the oppressed who ran after Muhammad; it was people of ethics, people of privilege who followed their values. Following the prophets and learning their stories can give us a blueprint of how to deal with life's difficult issues. Studying the Prophet's life helped me understand that he nurtured people and gave them both a voice and choice. That's what healing through servitude is about.

We also saw this struggle in Moses, who had a hatred of oppression. And even though he saw all the privilege around him in Pharaoh's home, Moses didn't develop a love for the material world. When he couldn't take Pharaoh's world any longer, God helped guide him out to a place of exile, where he could cleanse himself and heal.

Sometimes, when we're being oppressed, we develop a love for what the oppressor has. Healing—asking forgiveness, repenting—will help protect us from this love-hate relationship that otherwise will foster in us what we hated in our oppressors.

Early Americans, for instance, were running from oppression when they first came to the Americas, and yet they were usually not mindful enough to see they projected that same oppression on the people they met on the new shores. If you experience oppression or live around it, you will probably absorb the reality of the oppressor to a greater or lesser degree.

Healing means recognizing that's what's happened to you. It's acknowledging your reality, acknowledging the hurt. According to Islamic Law, the worst oppression is *kufr*—rejecting Allah and or ingratitude for His favors, which is internal self-oppression. *Kufr* is the cause of every other kind of oppression. No oppressor can cease oppressing others till he stops oppressing himself, and no oppressed party can rise above their circumstance to heal till they likewise stop oppressing themselves. Both children of Israel and Al Fira'wn or the Pharaoh had the wrong attitude toward Moses, who was above them both while they oppressed themselves.

Harm and Self-Harm

Again, it's important to acknowledge that everyone is harmed in different ways. The clearest harm comes to those who are marginalized or othered or who are the invisible classes of our world. But all of us are harmed in this system.

When you harm others, you have done not only an injustice to those you've harmed but also an injustice to yourself. From a faith perspective, you're going to be held accountable to every single person you've harmed.

But even from a psychological perspective, harming others without repenting gives us a skewed image of ourselves. Someone with a strong-man complex who can't apologize, was never pushed back inside their boundaries, and was constantly rewarded for every transgression will develop a very dark image of the world and will be increasingly unable to deal with others and especially unable to process criticism. Every time punishment comes, it will take them by surprise, because they are neither mindful nor conscious of God.

Without Becoming the Oppressor

If, on the other hand, you're the persecuted, then part of your healing is absolutely to fight injustice. But you must fight it in such a way that you don't seize what the oppressor had and *become* the oppressor.

For the well-being of society, we cannot continue to go after every person who has wronged us. At some point, someone has to lead and say, "I will end the cycle."

When there is a war, we count the dead, but we don't count the psychologically damaged. It takes generations for healing to take place, and forgiveness has to be a process of choice.

Muhammad, upon him peace and blessings, was at first rejected and chased with stones when he spoke about God and justice. Any ordinary human would have become enraged. But when he was squeezed to the very depths of his soul, what came out of him? His heart was filled with magnanimity and love.

If you're seeking materialism, then you'll tolerate harming others. But is that really what you want? It's important to ask what

Make sure, once you have won the thing you seek, that it's something you wanted. If you get it, do you win?

Can't We Be Good People without Healing?

Yes, you can do good actions, whether or not you heal. But unless you cleanse your internal mirror, that mirror will repel the blessings that come to you. So you want to heal, not just for yourself but for the people around you.

If you remain wounded, there is always the danger of transferring your wound to others. You may not be aware of it because so much happens on a subconscious level, but you may be transferring your wound onto someone else.

You certainly don't have to spend your whole life and all your time in healing! The idea is not to gain a level of perfection but to cultivate a sense of vulnerability and to embrace your humanity.

Moses, when he left Pharaoh, was divinely protected from transference. Instead of seeking to recreate the oppressions of Pharaoh in his new life, he took work as a shepherd. He took a humble position and was, most importantly, mindful of God and mindful of those who were in a weaker position than he was.

Healing Communities

Healing is not just an individual matter. For hundreds of years, Palestinians—both Christian and Muslim—have used a community healing process called *sulha*.

But we can create healing communities wherever we are by linking the concerns of different groups together and including others who aren't exactly like us but who have also experienced oppression.

To have faith in God is to see things with God's eyes. It doesn't matter what the strongman says, you need to have faith that there are good people in the community, and this also helps protect you from absorbing the light of the oppressor. The oppressor wants you to believe that everyone's like him. "I have a large crowd," he says. "My poll numbers are the highest." People with a strong-man complex reject vulnerability and human limitations: they pretend to be invulnerable, and they put up walls.

But you know, by seeing with your heart, that there are good people around. Just as you don't reject yourself, you don't reject that there are still good people out there.

We'll never reach utopia, either personally or as a community, because that's not what human beings are or what they do. But peace and community healing are commitments to a process of reconciliation through all the trials and tribulations God places before us to purify and beautify our hearts with faith "and to Him will ye be all brought back." (Quran 36:83)

Knowledge and high positions do not prevent one from lying and scheming to harm others. Rather, they make one more responsible and accountable before God. An ignorant person can possibly be forgiven, where a knowledgeable abuser is confessing their arrogance when sinning.

There is healing in the Quran for such people. I recall someone said if you are falsely imprisoned or your child is taken away from you, to keep reading the story of Joseph and, with your heart, direct the supplications within the chapter to God.

I know of cases in which those imprisoned falsely kept reading the story of Joseph as a healing and strength, and God opened the closed doors for them.

I know of a story of a mother who was worried about her son and would read this chapter, praying to God to answer her prayer. She had not heard from him for over a year. One morning as she was reading it, someone knocked on the door, and her son stood there when she opened it. She cried in happiness.

As we amplify people's suffering, remind those suffering to turn to God with their needs and help them experience and witness

Al Waali or the Protecting Friend. Tell them to read Chapter 12 of the Holy Quran or Yusuf (Joseph).

We are witnessing, after hundreds of years of people promoting lies, that the truth eventually rises like the sun. It is a waste of time to collude against others and project our sins onto them. On the Day of Judgment, everyone is going to know.

Let the war in Iraq be a moment of reflection, not just for Americans but for everyone. How many were convinced Iraq had weapons of mass destruction? How many had PhDs and high-profile positions? Now the truth has risen, and it is evident and clear that Iraq never had weapons of mass destruction.

Ghuroor, Muslim Women, and Shutting Down Grief

When most people talk about American Muslims and the chilling events that took place in New York City, in Washington, DC, and in planes above the US on September 11, 2001, they're looking at it through one lens: Did American Muslims condemn those attacks? Or did they not condemn the attacks?

Most recently, public figures posed this question in a different way about Representative Ilhan Omar: Is she reverent enough about what happened on 9/11, or is she insufficiently reverent?

For anyone who has met Representative Omar, the ways in which she is being portrayed in the US media—as an angry, attacking firebrand—must be surprising. I have met Ilhan Omar several times. She is a petite woman and a calm public speaker who is not at all intimidating. She is good natured, always smiling, dignified, and approachable. She frequently talks about how she thanks God that she came to the US and that she recognizes the opportunities it has opened up for herself and her children. She has worked diligently within the system in order to improve things for Americans.

And yet public discourse has repeatedly looked down on Representative Omar, who, because of her hijab, is the most visibly Muslim woman in the US Congress. It has painted her as an angry, hateful outsider who is attacking America.

But staying silent isn't an option either. Ghazala Khan—the mother of US Army Captain Humayun Khan, who was killed in 2004 in the Iraq War—is another visibly Muslim woman who took the public stage at the 2016 Democratic National Convention. Ghazala, who was a mother, a community volunteer, and worked in a fabric store, was derided by Donald Trump as a silent Muslim woman, unable to speak, oppressed, and in need of liberation.

The Denial of Grief

When people look down on Muslim women, they often do so with *ghuroor*, or a feeling of moral superiority. This is the same moral superiority that Satan felt toward Adam, and Satan could accept Adam only if Adam agreed that Satan was his better. Satan wanted Adam silenced—the only voice those who practice *ghuroor* want from others is the voice of gratitude and veneration. Pharaoh could accept those who said he was great but not those who also wanted their rights.

When we look at the stories of both Representative Omar and of Ghazala Khan, we certainly see *ghuroor*. We see them painted as either "irrationally angry Muslim woman" or "silent Muslim woman in need of a savior." We see people questioning whether Omar sufficiently condemned the 9/11 attacks, whether she was reverent enough in speaking about them. What we don't see is an understanding of their grief.

What we fail to see when we look only at the lens of whether Muslims condemned or didn't condemn terrorist attacks is that 9/11 affected *everyone* across the US. Muslims were also robbed of their feeling of security; they were also victims in the attacks; they also grieved for their neighbors and country. But their ability to grieve has often been snatched from them.

This needn't be so. A whole nation can be allowed to grieve together. The recent terrorist attacks in New Zealand targeted Muslims. And yet the Muslims of New Zealand did not blame all Christians for the attacks, and they welcomed other New Zealanders to express and process grief alongside them. They acknowledged and recognized their fellow New Zealanders and shared their grief communally.

When we rob people of their right to grieve a disaster, either public or private—as Ilhan Omar and Ghazala Khan have both been robbed—then we're also robbing them of a part of their humanity. Ghazala Khan said she didn't speak at the 2016 Democratic Convention and stood silently on stage because she was overwhelmed by grief for her lost son. Representative Ilhan Omar was among the cosponsors of a bill to reauthorize the 9/11 Victim Compensation Fund. She moved to the US at age eleven and became a citizen of the US at age seventeen. She was just eighteen during the 9/11 attacks.

This is not only true of Muslim women, of course. Recently, Dr. Mohammad Abu-Salha testified before the US Congress about the Islamophobically motivated assassination of his two daughters and son-in-law. His daughters Razan and Yusor were fatally shot along with Yusor's husband Deah Barakat, in February 2015. But instead of being allowed the space to grieve as he told his story, he was pushed to explain and defend Islam.

Manufacturing Evidence

Part of *ghuroor* is when a group looks for every possible shred of evidence to support their claim to moral superiority. Every instance when Muslims have committed violence, every tweet, and every word is combed over and framed as evidence that Muslim women are morally inferior beings. In this context, any list of Muslim women's accomplishments can be easily brushed aside.

This doesn't affect only Representative Omar but also Muslim children across the US. My own daughter, for instance, was called a terrorist at school. When the Oklahoma bombing happened, the justice department initially sought a "Middle-Eastern" suspect.

For too long, Muslims have been pressured to feel guilty about the horrific attacks that happened on September 11, 2001, as well as other attacks that have been perpetrated by Muslims around the world. We have been asked to explain and apologize for a crime that took us by surprise just as it did our friends and neighbors.

What gets lost in all this is Muslims' *grief* about 9/11 and other attacks. We, too, need to work through our sorrow, our fear, and our sense of loss.

Why We Shouldn't Normalize Suicide

Given the very high rates of suicide, which continue to rise despite all the intelligence and expertise of mental health professionals, we can interpret God's words as teaching us that this particular door needs to be shut as a possible solution.

One of the reasons I've refrained from mentioning the suicides of famous people is that, by talking about them, we are in danger of normalizing suicide. When famous people—especially those known to be good people—commit suicide, this sends a message to those among us dealing with depression and distress: suicide is an acceptable way to solve our problems.

Most faiths speak of painful punishments for people who take their own lives. At times, people misunderstand or misinterpret when God closes a door. Some are understandably confused by how a compassionate God could punish people who are in pain.

Yet suicide does not affect just the person who takes their life but also everyone around them. A recent suicide in our family caused my own daughter to have sleep problems and nightmares. In fact, this was not the first teen suicide in our extended family, which heightened my concern. Teenagers often go through mood swings and depressions as they transition to adulthood. Yet it becomes worrisome if suicide seems like a possible resolution to these temporary pains.

Statistics show that suicide rates are on the rise across the US. Many people who commit suicide do not necessarily have severe mental health issues but may be depressed and anxious. When we normalize suicide, we send a message that resorting to such means is a normal response to pain and distress.

Thus the message we send is this: Facing distress or problems? Consider suicide, and you will find instant relief.

These words let people know that we shouldn't deceive ourselves into thinking that this is a solution, because it is not, and we must look for and consider other solutions. Why people commit suicide and how God might deal with them is for God to decide. For us, we need to make this solution socially unacceptable, not via shame and blame, but by helping people realize that we do not know that exiting the world by suicide brings peace. Consider the possibility that it could bring further perpetual pain and punishment, not because God lacks compassion or mercy but simply because He is All-Knowing and Wise.

We shouldn't shame or blame people who commit suicide. But neither should we normalize suicide. That door needs to be shut.

We must be brutally honest with ourselves and others and consider the possibility that, by stepping through that door of suicide or homicide, we will face yet more pain.

Now Consider Other Solutions for Relief

What about Anthony Bourdain's death? He never reduced people to objects, images, single stories, or stereotypes so I will treat him the way he treated others. Bourdain is best known for his culinary writings and television presentations, along with several books on food, cooking, and travel adventures. On June 8, 2018, Bourdain died by suicide.

He saw human beings, and I see a human being. He was an empath and a compassionate man, a friend of Palestine, and one of the very best anti-imperialist white Americans I know. Beyond that are parts unknown and not my business to pry into. My condolences to his loved ones. Likewise, train yourself to respect people's privacy.

Limiting Liberty

A few years back, I was invited to be on a panel called Limiting Liberty: The Recurring Collision of Free Speech and Religion. The idea behind it was that religion is the enemy of free speech. We have convinced ourselves that Muslims use religion to limit our free speech, particularly when someone criticizes Prophet Muhammad, upon him peace and blessings, and Islam.

Yet how many know the story of Prophet Muhammad, upon him peace and blessings? And how many know the story of Islam from Muslims who believe strongly in him and in the teachings, he brought to us and practiced?

While convincing ourselves that Islam is an enemy of free speech, we have also convinced ourselves that, as a nation, we believe in free speech and uphold people's right to it. Many across the world seeking democracy claim the same, at least until a rebel movement rises against them. Then we often see similar attempts to silence rebel movements, which fight back, demanding not to be silenced.

We have to ask ourselves, "Are we really promoting free speech?" At times, we convince ourselves we are promoting freedom or free speech, when in reality, we are promoting freedom and free speech only for those who appeal to our ego.

During the Limiting Liberty panel discussion, a pro-Israeli speaker stepped forward. He had been invited to the panel in order to defend the Israeli bombing of Gaza and to bolster the image of the Israeli soldier, and there were a number of protesters who opposed his inclusion.

An oppressor always worries about their image, and part of burnishing one's image means silencing others who might tarnish it. After silencing Palestinian voices at the UN and elsewhere by fearmongering about "Hamas" in order to prevent anyone from wanting to listen to the Palestinians, Israeli officials had the audacity to cry "free speech" when protesters made it difficult for this speaker to be heard at the University of Minnesota.

In a PBS video titled *Why We Shouldn't Forget That US Presidents Owned Slaves*, Clint Smith says, "Oppression doesn't disappear just because you decided not to teach us that chapter. If you only hear one side of the story, at some point, you have to question who the writer is."

The narrative of the oppressed has been missing—silenced. It needs not only to be heard but also to be allowed a considerable platform.

I end with a quote by Dr. Umar Faruq Abd-Allah. While the quote was directed at Muslims, it is applicable to all who cite their religion or Constitution, their values, their First Amendment, their Bill of Rights, or other enshrined creed.

"You've got to be able to defend your faith," said Dr. Umar Faruq Abd-Allah. "From whom: Your ego with all its doubts, its misgivings, its complications."

Historically, we silence people because the truth they speak might expose us or make us question our own truth. We silence others because we fear being wrong or the villain, because we are ignorant of the arguments of our faith and values, or because our argument is very weak and does not hold up under investigation.

If July 4 is a celebration of freedom, then let us celebrate it by amplifying the voices of those who were and are silenced and oppressed. Allow their stories to be heard. Give them space on popular platforms, not just protesting in the streets.

We need panels titled Limiting Liberty: The Recurring Collision of Free Speech and Egoism or Limiting Liberty: Free Speech for Some.

Allahu Akbar: We Love Life

> *"To every people is a term appointed: when their term is reached, not an hour can they cause delay, nor (an hour) can they advance (it in anticipation)" (Quran 7:34)*

I want to take time to discuss the phrase *Allahu Akbar*, which has been misused by those plotting murder but is also used by billions of Muslims throughout their daily lives. We begin each prayer with the phrase *Allahu Akbar*. But what does it mean, and how do we interpret these words in our lives?

I shared something about the phrase *Allahu Akbar* earlier this year in light of recent events. There was a video of a baby found alive in Syria after a bombing caused the collapse of a building. I watched the video in Arabic: Syrian men looking for people alive under the rubble of a bombed building. I listened to the tone and watched the facial expressions.

You can see in the video the happiness that comes with the nonstop usage of *Allahu Akbar* at the discovery of a child found alive after a building collapse. That's because *Allahu Akbar*, or "God is greater," shows a great love of life. I share the thoughts that came to my mind.

The first thing I noticed was the number of times people in the video shouted *"Allahu Akbar,"* which means "God is Greater." In this case, it means God is greater than our imagination, our thoughts, our expectations, our feelings, or our understanding. In the video, it expresses joy, amazement, bewilderment, and other feelings that are hard to put into words. These are all feelings that came after a period of hopelessness, when people found a child alive under the rubble, underneath a collapsed building.

We join them and say loudly *"Allahu Akbar!"*

Second, you'll hear the phrase *"Sali ala an-Nabi"* which means, roughly, "Send prayers to Prophet Muhammad, upon him peace and blessings." It's used in this case for people to calm each other as they are overwhelmed with joy and excitement at finding the child.

Third, you'll find that, beyond the words, the men's faces are filled with astonishing joy. They have exerted tremendous effort and worked together, using their bare hands, to dig in the ground and rescue this child.

Fourth, you'll see the love and celebration as they welcome the child and bring the child out from underneath the rubble. They are hugging the child, cleaning the child's face, comforting the child, and showing genuine love and compassion for this small life.

When we enter the world unintentionally, we may not be conscious that we become like sponges. Just as this child was buried under the rubble, our true being can become disconnected, buried underneath everything we absorb, without consciously and deliberately knowing what to filter out.

Genuine faith sleeps under all that rubble. It helps us focus and recognize that God is greater than what we see and hear and understand. Layer by layer, we can dig out our souls. By reconnecting to God, to ourselves, and to each other, we welcome and celebrate the child within each of us.

The mission of Prophet Muhammad, upon him peace and blessings, was to help us achieve that excavation. In this video, the men calm each other down by showering prayers upon him, thus reminding each other to be gentle as they dig and pull the child from underneath the rubble.

These words of prayers on the Prophet are a soothing reminder, and they help the men stay steady so the child is not pulled out roughly, causing injuries to the tiny body.

The final scene is truly amazing, with childlike expressions of joy present on all the men's faces. As they dug and rescued the child, it was almost as though they had rescued themselves and reconnected to their childlike souls. (Miracle Survival: Baby Buried Alive, Rescued from Rubble in Syria)

Faith Has a Strong Argument

Many people are familiar with the laws of Islam without knowing the religion's spiritual core. Although I, too, have wanted to hold on to the particularities of laws, I believe it is essential to first understand the spiritual dimension to truly begin to understand Islam. I encourage people who are interested to study and seek knowledge on Islam, and their fears and concerns will be clarified, layer by layer, over time.

Yemen is primarily known in the US for being on the list of "banned" countries where visa holders and, in some cases, green card holders suddenly found they could not enter the United States. Also, we associate Yemen with drone attacks that have taken the lives of civilians, for extremist Anwar al-Awlaki, and for the dire state of Yemeni citizens.

Even when I visited in 2007, before the current war, Yemen was a very poor country yet rich with history, conviction, and kindness. Although members of my family urged me not to travel, the biggest problem was the summer's powerful heat and how early taxi drivers want to be. At one point, I asked whether it was safe to walk home at midnight and was told, laughingly, that "nothing ever happens" in Tarim.

I took classes on living as a minority in Western societies; coming to terms with our identities as Muslim American, Muslim British, or Muslim Australian; and accepting both sides of the equation. Although there are extremists and warmongers in Yemen, there are also peacemakers and thinkers.

What Is Coexistence?

The idea of coexistence is not just living together in the same space, tolerating one another. Coexistence means having healthy relationships within healthy boundaries. In a space of coexistence, everyone can share, everyone can benefit from all groups, and everyone gives and takes. In a state of coexistence, no one need be obsessed with their safety. Where groups coexist, all can feel protected and secure, and positive relationships can be established both individually and between groups.

When I got to Yemen to learn what they could teach about coexistence, I was initially skeptical but felt humbled that they were preaching and practicing the message they had projected publicly.

Among the things some teachers said was that we should focus on dialogues to foster understanding, not debates. "Stay away from debates and respectfully disagree," some told us. "Your aim is to benefit [your society] and not dominate or control people."

Some encouraged us to work to connect to our community, including our neighbors, and told us that in every group, there are people who will connect in a positive way. Just as we don't want others to stereotype all Muslims, we also shouldn't stereotype all politicians or all journalists. We shouldn't cast any group as bad but instead work to strengthen relationships with all these parts of our societies.

The same is true for charitable programs and organizations: "We work with good people on good programs and projects and aid them on common grounds."

Watch Ourselves, Positively

Teachers suggested we should always monitor our intentions, which should be to aid others and not to seek power or convince others we are right. We should focus on our principles, they said, not on results. We should never find ourselves in the position of trying to drag people into our religion. We can invite, certainly, but that's different from shaming, manipulating, or attempting to control others.

This is one of the reasons journaling is good: it helps us take a step back from our actions and motives.

When talking about Islam, the teachers said we should understand that "guiding is for God," and we should be very careful of transgressing the boundaries of others.

Another reason journaling helps is that we can watch our perceptions of other groups. One teacher told us that even if we disagree with others, we should absolutely not look down on them. "Monitor yourself to see if you are looking down on others," he said. "If an arrogant thought comes into your heart, try to expel it. See the people before you as good."

Being a Good Citizen

One teacher also emphasized that there's no contradiction between being a good Muslim and a good citizen in Western countries. Some laws will not agree with the Quran: for instance, the Jim Crow laws in the American South. "But we have a means to work with the legal system to address those," they said.

They recognized that some in the West believe that Muslims are planning to take over and said these Westerners include both those who see Islam as the enemy and those who are full of misunderstandings. Outreach should focus not on fighting the former group but on dialoguing with the latter.

All a Muslim should want, they said, is to coexist in harmony. If Muslims' beliefs are healthy and positive, then they will spread naturally to benefit others.

Some Muslims, they said, are calling for a Caliphate. "Where? What are you thinking? Where are you getting these thoughts?" they asked. These people, they said, are not living well with their own selves, their families, and their communities. "Start the Caliphate with yourself."

"Outreach," they said, "should be based on servitude to God and not power or control," adding that "it is amazing that some Muslims are asking to establish Shariah as though they are rightly guided Caliphs themselves."

They didn't deny that, when someone is violently threatened, they need to defend themselves. "But those that wage a war of words and pictures should be fought with words, thoughts, and pictures."

They emphasized that Islam was not established as a religion in the seat of power and that Islam seeks to conquer hearts, not bodies. "Someone who believes that Islam will not spread except if it rules is accusing Islam of being weak in argument," they said.

True Dialogue

Some of those speaking about Islam in the West, they said, use the "scream and yell" approach instead of "teach and nurture." Yet a sign of one's spiritual essence is to be involved in the affairs of their society, helping those who need it.

There are those who say "softness and kindness" won't work, but that is the methodology of the prophets, peace be upon them.

In creating a real dialogue, it's also critically important to understand the other person, to really *listen* to what they're saying.

"If you are truly seeking to understand the person before you," they said, "then it's a good dialogue. If your heart is present in the dialogue, then this is good. If it's all emotions and anger, then this doesn't stir any understanding or benefit."

They added that trying to dominate others in an argument isn't a service to one's country either, but a form of power seeking. "If the dialogue is one of the ego, or 'I am better than you,' this is not a good dialogue. It's like politicians debating for leadership rather than serving their country."

Honest discussions

I advocate a holistic approach toward life. By holistic, I mean that when we talk about everything from medicine to education, we include a view of all aspects of ourselves as people, including our spiritual selves. If we engage only one layer and neglect or encourage people to divorce other parts of who they are, we don't allow for people to fully express themselves, which leads to all kinds of social ills and hardships in our communities.

Honest discussions on faith allow us to holistically challenge the voices of extremism that flourish on the internet. This is also an important step if we are going to build a strong foundation for coexistence.

If faith remains a topic people can shut down and treat superficially without understanding nuances and being engaged respectfully, then we cannot respond to accusations against it meaningfully. I grew from the many mistakes I made online and in person when communicating my feelings. Through this dialogue, I was challenged many, many times to search for aspects of my faith that, had they remained unchallenged in a meaningful way, would never have allowed me to come to a greater understanding of some or shed other views that I now feel were very much in error.

Quite a few accuse Muslims and Islam of trying to take over America and say that Muslims say one thing but secretly plan another. People who have a hatred and fear of Islam (such as Dutch MP Geert Wilders) are asked to brief our elected representatives in Congress in closed hearings and forums. Muslims cannot engage in a debate framed in a way that limits their ability to respond and engage in meaningful dialogue beyond polemics.

For example, Muslim communities were accused of attempting to impose Sharia law in their neighborhoods, prompting protests and backlash from non-Muslims. Despite their repeated denials and emphasis on their commitment to American values, the community leaders were met with suspicion and hostility. This demonstrates how stereotypes and preconceived notions about Muslims can lead to unfounded accusations and prevent constructive dialogue.

That Muslims have a fair opportunity to engage in the affairs of the country, as every rightful citizen should, is seen as a threat. The suggestion that Muslims would take over the US, as if the country is some small island nation, is ludicrous. It also denies the fact that Muslims are, and since the 1580s have been, an integral part of the social fabric of our nation. However, as a Muslim, I question how is it that I and my Muslim brothers and sisters can alleviate these suspicions and concerns while finding space to practice our faith openly without being seen as a threat.

Seeking the truth about what a faith teaches is not threatened by respectful, honest, and meaningful dialogue.

What's unsettling is that the level of intolerance that is acceptable to the public seems to be rising. For example, once, while I was giving a presentation to social workers in Duluth about interacting effectively with Muslims, one person yelled to the crowd that I was brainwashing the audience. If Muslims are using brainwashing techniques, then I challenge people to put our "brainwashing" to the test. Find out why we are saying what we are saying. Engage Muslims openly and honestly in the public square and present your findings in a platform that allows Muslims to respond fairly and alleviate these concerns.

If you believe Islam promotes hatred and violence, find out what elements cause you to believe that and find reliable sources that can help you understand the Muslim perspective.

Truth cannot manifest itself in polemical and superficial debates that are disrespectful in nature where fearmongers and hatemongers mate, breed, and aid each other. These arguments need to be sorted out in a respectful and civil manner in the public square and given the platform to face the criticism and accusations against it.

Let us use the following questions, taken from *The Practical Guide to Critical Thinking* by Greg R. Haskins, when reading articles on Islam:

1. Is there any ambiguity, vagueness, or obscurity that hinders my full understanding of the argument?
2. Is the language excessively emotional or manipulative?
3. Have I separated the reasoning (evidence) and relevant assumptions/facts from background information, examples, and irrelevant information?
4. Have I determined which assumptions are warranted versus unwarranted?
5. Can I list the reasons (evidence) for the argument and any sub-arguments?

6. Have I evaluated the truth, relevance, fairness, completeness, significance, and sufficiency of the reasons (evidence) to support the conclusion?
7. Do I need further information to make a reasonable judgment on the argument, because of omissions or other reasons? (Haskins)

Let's call for raising the level of discourse we have about faith in the public sphere.

Everything We Have Is Borrowed

We may be in a state of plenty and privilege, or we may be in a state of privation. But either way, everything we have is borrowed, not owned, and might be recalled at any time.

The prophets' stories teach us this repeatedly: Jacob has a great deal, but then he loses Joseph and Benjamin, as well as his status in the family. After this, for a long time, Jacob has to deal not only with physical suffering and the loss of his beloved sons, but also with the mockery and ridicule of his other sons. Just so, we humans sometimes have plenty, and sometimes we suffer trials.

How can we understand this? And how can we continue to have a good opinion of God when we're going through trials?

Part of my understanding comes through Dr. Ramadan al-Bouti and his analysis of an aphorism from Ibn Ata Allah: "My God, I am poor in my wealth, so how can I not be poor in my deprivation of wealth?"

Even when Ibn Ata Allah was wealthy, he was poor. How is that? He might have approached God surrounded by many children and in good health, respected in his community and secure in his wealth, or he might have approached God in one of the many human states of affliction. But either way, in either state, he would be poor before God. As Ibn Ata Allah said, "I'm a scholar in the eyes of people, but I am ignorant in the eyes of God, who sees Ibn Ata Allah bare of all these trusts."

In the first state, we might think we *own* what we have. But can we prevent it from being taken away? A wealthy person can easily lose their wealth and a powerful one their influence. Just so, a knowledgeable or social person could have a stroke, and their ability to access their knowledge and to communicate can be taken away. We are only holding things in the moment that are not ours. They belong to God, and we are only the trustee, designated to watch over our trusts.

Just so, we also might be poor but rich in the trusts God has placed in our hands. These trusts, borrowed from God, are to benefit both ourselves and others, and we must accept that not only are these trusts transient—they can come and go—but we are also fallible.

We are not All-Knowing or All-Seeing. We may have a trust of intelligence, but it is a fallible intelligence, a gift and a trust we must keep in good repair for as long as we have it, as we go on our constant revolutions through life, like walking around the Kaaba, sometimes in a state of plenty and sometimes of privation.

Prophets Are Guiding Lights for How We Can Act in Trials and Tribulations

What does hope mean?

Sometimes, when we think about *hope*, we think it means a particular result or waiting for one particular thing. Hope is, instead, having a good opinion of God and believing that, whatever the outcome is, it's for the best.

It may not seem that, for Jacob, losing his son could ever be the best outcome. And Joseph is separated from his father and put in prison. But all this is preparing him to become a leader.

It was hard for Jacob to be hit like this, but in both states—in plenty and in privation—he relied on God.

Those who believe they are responsible for everything they have—Pharaoh, Qarun, or Nimrod—will be shocked when they find these things can be taken away. Nimrod, who thought his powers put him on top of the world, died when a small insect went up his nose.

Satan's Hope, Satan's Plenty

Satan is the prototype of one who thought, *I have this because I'm so wonderful, because I'm so clever, because I worked so hard.* Satan was also obsessed with one state, and he hoped only for one result: power. While Adam sought repentance and connection, Satan was more interested in controlling others.

When Satan was brought down, he asked for power until Judgment Day. This power was all that concerned him, and he was given it. Because Satan had this disconnect, he could never become connected with God; he no longer had the gift of privation, of self-recognition. Because Satan didn't understand them as gifts, he could only look down on those who were deprived.

We often don't appreciate something until we lose it, so Satan was now deprived of true appreciation.

When Satan appeared before God, he didn't remember that he was ignorant, and what he knows, God had taught him. Although it was Satan who was ungrateful, he projected this onto humanity and said it was humankind that was ungrateful.

Yet it was Satan who was ungrateful. He was showered with blessings but unable to see himself for who he was. He said, "I prayed, I fasted, and yet *you* made me sin." Instead of recognizing his weakness, he projected his weakness onto God. Satan attributed all good to himself—he worked hard, he prayed, he deserved what he had—and then blamed God for making him sin.

Adam, on the other hand, recognized his weakness.

Satan was so furious at this he wanted to prove God wrong. "Give me power until Judgment Day," Satan said, "and I will show you how wrong you are about Adam."

Satan can try as he likes, but he has failed to recognize who he really is and is now in a permanently deluded state. Meanwhile Adam and the children of Adam continue turning and turning. Through that state of eternal change, we are prepared to receive. We can always turn to God as Adam did, saying, "I am weak; I don't understand; help me."

Like Satan, Adam was also pushed out of heaven. But Adam understood what he was losing. "If you do not forgive us and have mercy on us," Adam said, "then it is we who will be the losers."

While Satan thought everything he had belonged to himself, Adam recognized that it all came from God and that the wheel would keep turning and turning.

On the Difference between Possession and Love

Each Valentine's Day, many celebrate by giving flowers or chocolate to their loved ones. This day helps blur the lines between love and romance.

Romance, which can be addictive and unhealthy, often means making a person the center of your thoughts and feelings. In English culture, we have Romeo and Juliet; among Arabs, there is the story of

Layla and Qays, or "Majnun Layla." Such love is obsessive, delusional, and blinding.

If the person does not share our feelings, we might stalk them. Natural jealousy can turn into violent rage. The object of one's "love" becomes just that: an object, someone to control and possess.

Many of the murders that occur around the globe come from this sort of rejected passion. My local grocery store faced just such a shooting: a man shot two people, then himself, because he felt rejected by his romantic interest.

Love is different. Real love is not blind. Instead, it is a comforting and nurturing light. Its nature is pure and essentially selfless. We read of many examples of God bestowing His Love onto the Prophets. For instance, the wife of the Pharaoh, Asiya, felt a pure love for Moses, and she both protected and nurtured him.

> *Throw (the child) into the chest, and throw (the chest) into the river: the river will cast him up on the bank, and he will be taken up by one who is an enemy to Me and an enemy to him': But I cast (the garment of) love over thee from Me: and (this) in order that thou mayest be reared under Mine eye.*
>
> —Quran 20:39

Prophet Muhammad, upon him peace and blessings, was also granted protective love. He found it in Khadijah, who helped make him independent financially and supported him with her social influence and wealth.

For Zakariya, Jacob, and Abraham—upon them peace—there were sons like John the Baptist, Joseph, Isaac, and Ishmael to comfort their souls in their old age and to be compassionate and kind to them.

There are many more cases, but in all of these, the love was pure and comforted the soul, helping ease the hardships of life and its various struggles.

Love Is Not Possessive

Hwaa Irfan, in refuting the logic of possessiveness, said, "Our sense of love becomes reduced to lust and cupidity. From the limitless love of Allah and His creations we descend to the limited love of hearts and arrows. Arrows pierce the limited, but not the limitless." And Dr. 'Abd. Lateef Krauss Abdullah wrote that

> *The answer of what is love is one that is very important. The images that our media feeds us everyday aim to present a notion of love that is often more lust than love. True love requires peace—it requires a peaceful heart because real love is love of Allah, which, when achieved, allows one to love truly and completely. The projection and need for romantic love, however, is based more on the desires of our incomplete selves.*

Other Kinds of Love

But there are more than just personal loves. There is also, for instance, the love of the poor. Prophet Muhammad, upon him peace and blessings, used to ask God to grant him the love of the poor, the sick, and those in need so that he could be used as a source of comfort and kindness for them. Such love is also a gift from God.

There's also a love of God, a love of good deeds, and a love of people who love God. One of the *hadith* says:

> *O Allah, I ask You to grant me the performance of good deeds, abandonment of bad ones, and love of the poor; and (I ask You) that You forgive me and have mercy upon me; and if You intend to try a people, cause me to die without being tested; and I ask You for Your love, and the love of those who love you, and the love of actions which draw me closer to Your love.*

Beyond these loves, there is also the love of people who are different. Prophet Abraham was asked to leave his wife Hajar and their son in a Meccan desert. He prayed to God, asking God to place His love in the hearts of the people of that land so that they would be protected and comforted instead of alone.

> *Our Lord! Verily I have settled (a part) of my offspring in a valley without cultivation near Your Sacred House, in order, Our Lord! that they may establish prayer. . . . [T]herefore, make the hearts of some people yearn towards them, and provide them with fruits so that they may be grateful.*

A Love for Nonhumans Too

We can see love all around us as we watch the sun rise or set or the moonrise. We can rejoice lovingly in the singing of birds, flowers blooming, and the laughter of children, reminding us of hope and innocence. However you spend today, you should embrace the love around you. If you are alone or lonely, then seek the various gifts and manifestations of love from God to comfort your soul or be a comfort for others.

Sticking Around Isn't Everything

Although in romance, staying together with one's beloved is the focus, in love, "just sticking around" isn't the best way to judge the success of any relationship.

If harassment is involved, then it is often healthy to walk away. Also, according to Islamic teachings, two people can love each other yet not be suitable for marriage. God might also will that they not be together.

The Strong Rope

Say, "Shall we invoke instead of Allah that which neither benefits us nor harms us and be turned back on our heels after Allah has guided us? [We would then be] like one whom the devils enticed [to wander] upon the earth confused, [while] he has companions inviting him to guidance, [calling], 'Come to us.'" Say, "Indeed, the guidance of Allah is the [only] guidance; and we have been commanded to surrender to the Lord of the worlds." (Quran 6:71)

Prayer is one of the main methods we have of discovering both ourselves and God. The Prophet, upon him peace and blessings, was able to pray continuously. In so doing, he was always in a condition of God-conscious conversation. This continuous conversation with God was the engine of his faith. Indeed, Muhammad has said that "Prayer is the brain of worship."

If we don't pray, our souls can become disconnected from God, which often causes alienation and depression. It's important to make it a habit to always pray and, thus, always be in a conversation with God. It should become so ingrained that, whatever trial we're undergoing, we don't feel alone.

If we are in a constant conversation with God, then we'll have a soul connection that can help us sustain ourselves, no matter what life brings.

The purpose of prayer is to bring us closer to Allah, our creator. An engineer uses tools to fix his machine; however, in prayer, God, who created us, restores us without an operation.

We witnessed the global campaign when a Moroccan boy, Rayan, fell into a well, bringing hearts and minds to pray for his well-being. Likewise, prayer unites Muslims in purpose across the globe to pray and remember God.

Prayer is the means that God uses to unite us five times a day on purpose. Every time we pray, we unite with all Muslims across the globe in mission and purpose.

The nature of the world is such that we all need to empty ourselves from time to time. It is part of the human condition. God gives us many opportunities to empty ourselves and receive the spiritual light of His many blessings or *fadilah* throughout the day and year. As you learn more about yourself, memorize the supplications in the Quran or by the Prophet Muhammad, upon him peace and blessings, that relate to or address your need.

What caused Satan to be misled was that he continued to try to arrive at the answers to his questions on his own and through his own rationalization. It is in the mind that the *nafs* or ego does its work. It is in the mind that all the whisperings and confusion occur.

Remorse targets the heart, the purification of the heart, whereas guilt and shame target the mind. People who are full of shame and guilt use shame and guilt to control others. People who are full of spiritual light or the fruits of repentance remind us of God's Greatness, His Most Beautiful Names, and our journey back to Him. They want us to turn to God and receive the blessings as they did, not control us.

In Chapter 18, Verse 57 of the Holy Quran: "And who doth more wrong than one who is reminded of the Signs of his Lord, but turns away from them, forgetting the (deeds) which his hands have sent forth?"

Sometimes the only evidence people will accept is wrath or punishment from God meeting them face-to-face.

We must turn to God for guidance. This is not a one-time event. And, in doing so, ask the learned in our community—i.e., the scholars—to help us understand these topics. Do *not* turn to the learned without turning to God for guidance and protection. When we rationalize everything on our own without a sound foundation of knowledge, getting a little bit of knowledge here and there from different websites and videos does not compare to having real knowledge from learned scholars.

Choose the eyes you want to nurture you: ego, people, or God?

In the Quran, Chapter 36, Verses 59 through 62 read:

> *And O ye in sin! Get ye apart this Day! Did I not enjoin on you, O ye Children of Adam, that ye should not worship Satan; for that he was to you an enemy avowed? And that ye should worship Me, (for that) this was the Straight Way? But he did lead a great multitude of you astray. Did ye not, then, understand?*

In the commentary by Shaykh al-Sha'rawi, he taught that Adam, upon him peace, did not sin by violating the sacred law but by listening to Satan and taking him as an adviser. Adam, upon him peace, was warned that he was an avowed enemy and to stay away from him. The imam continued that Satan promised to sit on the *siratul mustaqeem* or the straight path. That is who he was interested in—the worshippers on the straight path.

He was not interested in those who were lost unless they tried to repent and return, but the practicing believers. In his deviousness, he even reminded Adam, upon him peace, of the sacred law but manipulated and deceived him.

As we journey in life, we must be aware of and vigilant about staying on the straight path. And if we slip, to immediately repent like Adam, upon him peace, did. The scholar continued that for this reason, when we begin any act of worship, we seek refuge in God from Satan.

If we purify our soul or bring our ego to surrender, Satan will be waiting at the act of worship to throw thoughts of perversion into it. This also includes reading the Quran and even having relations with our spouse. Our surrendered ego will hang up. How? Focus on remembrance of God, not Satan's tricks.

Ongoing Conversation with God

When you're sad, you don't want to bottle up your feelings. There is no prize for seeming to be perfect all the time. We also don't want to encourage others to bottle up their feelings. All people feel negative, angry, or moody sometimes. There are times when we want to bring these feelings to a therapist who can help us work through our thoughts and thought processes.

But in addition to seeing a counselor—if we feel we need it—we should also reflect on the prayers the Prophet taught us. However, choosing a counselor who shares your values and beliefs is advisable. Seek help from God every day in selecting a counselor and overseeing the counseling process.

We pray to purify ourselves according to Islamic teachings, to achieve a particular end result, as well as to improve our thinking and polish our hearts. Over time, an ongoing conversation with God—constant supplication, constant connection, and constant self-awareness—can help us approach our lives in a healthier way.

Through constant prayer, we rewire our brains to better process sadness, pain, and harm.

In effect, as Shaykh Qays Arthur explained, "While God cannot be compelled, He is pleased and angered, and prayer is about attaining His pleasure without which improving one's nature is not possible."

But Can We Pray for God to Help Us?

Yes, we can pray for God to help us. When we pray, we go through many of the same movements day after day.

In addition to these core prayers, there are other optional prayers. During the time when we're in prostration, we can also make supplications for ourselves. The important part is not to supplicate in an accusatory manner. We must supplicate in a way that leaves us open and receptive.

If we pray in an accusatory, complaining way, this reinforces a perception that our life is lacking in some way, that we didn't get our "fair share."

*Praying **to** Create a Soul Connection with God*

People can be faithful and believe in God and yet not have a soul connection with Him. The brothers of the prophet Joseph, upon him peace, were religious. And yet they didn't have a deep connection with God. They had faith but not the God consciousness that Joseph had—and it was this connection with God that helped Joseph deal with the trauma his family inflicted on him.

When we pray continually, we can feel the presence of God. Sometimes we read about the trials other people have faced, and we think, *I could never withstand that.* Yet if we are connected with God, we can hold firm in the face of many things.

There are different prayers that help us approach different needs. If we tend to get angered easily, we can search for prayers that deal with anger. But we shouldn't be trying to achieve a state of perfection as none of us are ever going to achieve that. Instead, we need to keep exerting effort to work through our thoughts and repent our errors.

What Kind of Praying?

Prophet Muhammad, upon him peace and blessings, left us the words of many supplications. At times, when we make them, we focus on the end result instead of the journey of praying. It's important to ask ourselves questions about our praying.

- What is being asked for?
- What words are being used?
- What thoughts and feelings are expressed?

For instance, a person could be praying to get married again. But if they pray as though they are lacking, in a way focused primarily on complaining to God, then they are not doing themselves any good. This person may not have learned anything from their past relationships. Perhaps they will fall right back into a bad relationship.

Instead, it's important to pray openly, leaving it up to God to answer the prayer in whatever way He sees fit.

If we want something—like good grades or enough money to live on—we should put in the effort and exert ourselves but leave it to God to answer our prayers. When Hajar prayed, she told God how much she needed water. But she wasn't accusatory. She also exerted herself to the utmost as she prayed for God's help. While she prayed, she was also trusting in God's wisdom and keeping a positive attitude.

Indeed, the best prayers are not pleas or requests but prayers of gratitude. These stay the same whether we are in good times or bad. The Prophet Muhammad, upon him peace and blessings, would pray to God, saying, "I ask You ... to make my speech truthful while angry or pleased, and to have the same aim in poverty and in riches."

Regardless with what state you're in—better or worse—you should be focused on treating God as God. That doesn't mean you can't ask God for something. But it shouldn't be framed as though you're petulant or complaining.

In Chapter 19 of the Quran, Maryam says, "[A]nd never have I been in my supplication to You, my Lord, complaining in an accusatory manner."

Hwaa Irfan, a woman I admire, once wrote that life wasn't just about getting married, buying things, driving oneself hard, and ruining one's health. Nor was life about "Always doing something to feel that one exists; this leads to leaving one's soul behind." Instead, she wrote, "The soul needs attention through prayer and periods of reflection and inspiration." In essence, prayer is a way of helping us stay in balance with life.

If we don't stay in balance, and our souls are not receiving any attention, it becomes easy to fall into depression. This isn't because of a lack of faith. Instead, it's because we are not giving our souls enough attention. Just as a person can let their health go, they can also let their soul go by neglecting to give it proper attention, by not being present during their prayers.

Then do ye remember Me

> *Then do ye remember Me; I will remember you. Be grateful to Me, and reject not Faith. (Quran 2:152)*

This is from the teachings of Shaykh al-Sha'rawi: We said that the remembrance of Allah must follow the believer's every breath throughout this life. Because there is no life for a man without God's sustenance all over this life and no existence or identity but that extended from God. So, if he wants to continue to have a happy life, he needs to remember who gifted him with this life.

And in our materialistic life, we can realize that clearly in the machine that possesses no innate energy or power, but its energy is derived from another source. As an example, when we drive a car, before the car starts moving, power is needed to run the car.

The battery is the source of energy. This energy is derived from the innate chemical nature of the materials constituting the battery. This electrochemical characteristic of the battery material is natural and inherent in this material and is the creation of Allah Most High. Hence, all materialistic movement in this universe is based on inherent mechanisms or natural processes of God's creation. This logic applies all the way.

Therefore, all types of life sustenance are from God, Most High. Should a man want this to last, he must keep God's remembrance.

Hence, any time you intend to start any action, you should start seeking compliance of all natural resources in the name of God. It is God who avails all to you, not your power or capability. In other words, the world can break you if God gives it permission. Your power or capability over such matters is delusion.

When a human being receives God's blessings, they should say, "Praise be to Allah" or *"Alhamdulillah."* When disaster strikes, they should say, "To Allah we belong and to Allah we shall return."

Hence, the believer must always remember Allah to connect with the power and energy of Allah, the sustainer of all so that this life continues to be blessed.

Otherwise, if they forget God and focus on the materialistic world, they will win the material but not God's blessing. In the eternal life to come, only God's blessings will prevail and light the way over the bridge. Only God's blessings will last and benefit them, not the material world.

"Remember Me; I will remember you. Be grateful to Me, and reject not Faith." So Allah's Most High remembrance to you is conditional on your remembering Him. So the key to the relationship with God is in the hands of the believer.

If the servant wants to get closer to Allah, they have the key, the knowledge, and if they choose to be locked away from His Mercy, they can choose that for as long as they want. God will wait for the servant until an appointed time or until the servant gives up, in which case, the heart is sealed.

So it is impossible for one who has the key to turn to God and still be searching for Him. God said if you come crawling, He will come walking.

> "Be grateful to Me, and reject not Faith." Thank God for His gifts, and don't disbelieve in the giver. Enjoy His gifts and remember Him always.

Ramadan: Month of Self-Restraint

> The Prophet Muhammad, upon him peace and blessings, once said: "When the month of Ramadan begins, the gates of the heaven are opened; the gates of Hell-fire are closed, and the devils are chained"
>
> —Sahih Bukhari 1800

We always focus on the part of the *hadith* that mentions that the devils are chained. All or most sermons mention that part. We overlook the first part of the *hadith*, the most important part that mentions that the heavens are opened.

The fourth pillar of Islam is *sawm*, or fasting, in the month of Ramadan. Fasting is also practiced in many other religions and is mentioned in the Torah, the Bible, and Hindu scriptures. Observant Christians fast during Lent by giving up a particular food. Hindus fast on certain days of the week or holidays, and for Jews, the most important day of fasting is Yom Kippur.

Ramadan is the ninth month in the Islamic calendar. Because Ramadan follows the lunar calendar, it rotates through the seasons, moving back around eleven days each year.

Muslims fast from dawn to sunset, abstaining from food and drink during this time. The fast aims to weaken the physical desire or self and allow for the purification of the soul. It's a process of spiritual purification and strengthening of willpower to carry us through the year. Muslims break their fast with dates and water, followed by the evening prayer and dinner.

Faith: Between Hope and Fear

Ramadan is an opportunity to do practice self-restraint together as a community, an opportunity to learn the mechanisms of compassion, responsibility, self-sacrifice, and mercy. We do not build community as perfect people. We build as people knowing we must engage in *jihad an-nafs* (struggle with the self).

We begin with nurturing, love, hope, and commitment, seeking forgiveness and mercy, and we are taught to end the month with nurturing fear of God, as we beg God to save us from the hellfire.

Those who are sick or unable to fast, such as the elderly, pregnant or nursing women, travelers, and children, are exempt from fasting. However, they participate in the spiritual part of Ramadan, rejuvenating their faith and growing closer to God through extra worship, feeding the poor, charity, and other good deeds.

During Ramadan, it is customary for families to attend the local mosque after breaking fast for special nightly prayers called *taraweeh*.

A Month of Blessings

Prophet Muhammad, upon him peace and blessings, taught Muslims:

> *Ramadan has come to you. (It is) a month of blessing, in which God covers you with blessing, for He sends down Mercy, decreases sins and answers prayers. In it, God looks at your competition (in good deeds), and boasts about you to His angels. So show God goodness from*

> *yourselves, for the unfortunate one is he who is deprived in (this month) of the mercy of God, the Mighty, the Exalted.*

Muslims are reminded to embrace this opportunity and receive the blessed month of Ramadan with gratitude, repentance, sincerity, steadfastness, and fervor.

Prophet Muhammad, upon him peace and blessings, addressed his companions on the day before Ramadan began, saying,

> *Oh people! A great month has come over you; a blessed month; a month in which is a night better than a thousand months; month in which God has made it compulsory upon you to fast by day, and voluntary to pray by night. Whoever draws nearer (to God) by performing any of the (optional) good deeds in (this month) shall receive the same reward as performing an obligatory deed at any other time, and whoever discharges an obligatory deed in (this month) shall receive the reward of performing seventy obligations at any other time. It is the month of patience, and the reward of patience is Heaven.*

A Month of Mercy, Forgiveness, and Salvation

For the first ten days of the month, the emphasis is on seeking mercy. For the second ten, there is an emphasis on seeking forgiveness and the final ten, salvation.

Many view Ramadan as a boot camp for Muslims, where everyone strives to purify the soul together. Teachers will remind Muslims that God should also see from us on the first night of Ramadan sincere remorse and genuine repentance from all the wrong actions of our lives up to that point.

A Month of Charity

Muslims believe that Ramadan is also the month of charity and generosity and a month in which a believer's sustenance is increased. It is also the month that helps and trains Muslims to be compassionate toward those less fortunate. Prophet Muhammad, upon him peace and blessings, used to be at his most generous in Ramadan.

A Month of Prayers

Muslims are taught to make the intention to perform extra acts of devotion and worship therein, including additional midnight prayer (*qiyam*) and end of night prayer (*tahajjud*) and abundant charity to the poor and needy. The last ten days of Ramadan for the aspiring souls is a time of seclusion (*i'tikaf*) wherein Muslims spend the entire night at the mosque in prayer and worship till dawn. This Ramadan, we are invited to make all of it a time of seclusion with God. Check on your family members and remember them in your prayers.

High Intentions and Set Goals

Ramadan trains you and gives you the support, but the acts of worship are encouraged throughout your life. If you make your intention for this Ramadan and every Ramadan until your last moment, act upon it now, and never make it to another Ramadan, you get the reward for every Ramadan you intended as though you did the act of worship.

Makeup Fasts

There are medical and other reasons that allow one not to fast in Ramadan. However, if these reasons or conditions are lifted, the fasts in Ramadan need to be made up.

Help the Poor

Helping the oppressed and feeding the poor are emphasized in Ramadan. However, we do not need to wait until Ramadan. There are many opportunities here and overseas to reach out to organizations or people in person and offer aid.

It is hard to read the stories every day, and you wonder when it will end. Let us use whatever we can to reach out in support and aid. Let us ask God to grant us wisdom on how to bring an end to the bloodshed.

What seduced you from your Most Generous Lord? Make high intentions now, and act with the power and gifts you have. In summary, if you turn to God seeking guidance, He will facilitate the path of guidance for you. If you turn away, He will facilitate the path of misguidance for you.

Why We Have *Zakat*

All of us are both oppressed and privileged in different ways. The Quran mentions two groups: those made weak (*mustadh'afin*) and the haughty (*mustakbirin*). A privileged person is not necessarily one of the haughty.

For the ways in which we are privileged, and for all the gifts we have, our healing means reaching out to people who are persecuted and people who need us. The Prophet Muhammad, upon him peace and blessings, brought together people who were privileged and people who were persecuted. They met not as master and servant or helper and helpee, but at a common point, at equity. He had them meet as brothers and sisters.

Where we have gifts, we must share what we have with others, listen, and understand how others have been abused and hurt. This is the core reason we have *zakat*, or alms, which Shaykh Qays Arthur explains:

> *Zakat is about the rich acknowledging that they, "their" property, and the poor all belong to Allah who has decreed that a portion of the property He gave to them belongs to the poor and is to be surrendered to them failing which punishment (in this and the next world) is due.*

Sadaqah, or charity, is a purification not just of your wealth, but of every gift you have, including your knowledge and compassion. The way you cleanse it is by sharing.

Why cleanse it? If we all followed God's laws and commands all the time, there wouldn't be a persecuted group in the world! But somewhere along the line, hands were shaken, deals were made, and persecuted groups were created in the divides.

You may not have signed the crooked contract, but perhaps you indirectly benefited from it. So when you reach out and give back to those who have less, this is their due.

Service, Servitude, and the Process of Healing

Service and *servitude* may sound similar but are, in fact, different stops along a path to faithful healing. Yet despite their differences, they are both important expressions of love and parts of a healing process.

Service is an excellent start in healing ourselves and our communities. Ultimately, faith is not about service but *servitude.* Still, we cannot reach servitude—by which I mean engaging in acts for which there is no appreciation, acknowledgment, or reward, except from God—without going through service.

When we do service, we're doing good. Yet the good we do is tinged by the expectation of getting something out of it for ourselves. There's nothing wrong with that! Certainly, it's a necessary step along our path. But eventually, we want to move away from reward-focused service. When we're on the *service* side of the service-servitude spectrum, we avoid certain projects, setting them aside because they're not rewarded or don't feel good.

When we stretch ourselves toward servitude, that's what God wants us to do. There may be no reward. Indeed, there are some types of important community work for which there is no reward, either emotionally or tangibly. These acts of servitude might include dealing with difficult people. But servitude is about being humble and doing what needs to be done to help others and make your community a better place.

Moses demonstrated servitude as he was in one of his most difficult moments of exile.

Moses, upon him peace, left Egypt as a fugitive. He went for days without food, his feet bleeding, his body exhausted as he arrived in the land of Midian. He was homeless, penniless, and near starvation. He saw two women who had an elderly father struggling to tend and water their sheep.

Moses, upon him peace, saw these two vulnerable women and used his gifts to aid them without asking for anything in return. Even though his situation was difficult, he did nothing to take advantage of them or promote himself as their protector. Instead, he offered his God-given gifts and then returned to the shade of the tree.

He remained homeless, penniless.

In this moment of great need, Moses turned to God and prayed, but this prayer was not just words on his lips. It was holistic, a whole way of living his life. He strove and struggled to the point of exhaustion, then offered his gifts to the vulnerable without asking for anything in return. Only then did he ask God for help.

Closer to our own time, although it is not appropriate to vouch for any person's sincerity and servitude to God without any earthly benefits, we can appreciate Martin Luther King Jr.'s struggle to fight oppression as he paid the price of his life.

Service is still good! If someone asks you to come to an event, and there's something in it for you, but the event is positive, then there's no reason to decline. Service can make you feel good while, for instance, the servitude of caring for the sick is uncomfortable.

Servitude is a hard road as it is for Allah alone. As we begin engaging in acts of service, we have to go slowly and stay in balance: sometimes reaching purification of our intentions and aims and sometimes returning to service. We also need to be wary of those seeking to abuse others by using the language of servitude. Some use religious texts to get others to do menial tasks that they won't do themselves. No one should pressure us into acts of service or servitude; it must be a choice we make to serve God and seek our reward with God.

Service and Careerism

Sometimes, over time, service can turn into a career. You might do it for money; you might charge speaker fees. Sometimes you might find yourself benefiting more than you're giving.

The allure of opportunity is one of the drawbacks of service. Yet you must go through service in order to reach servitude. As we serve, we can challenge ourselves not just to do acts to get an immediate reward.

But servitude does have a different sort of benefit. Through servitude, we can discover our strengths and pockets of wisdom as well as developing new strength.

Servitude also helps us feel our way to the real meaning of empathy, mercy, and compassion. Before I experienced servitude, I believed in very strict laws: one strike and you're out. But through acts of servitude, I learned to listen and to hear the lessons from people's struggles. Servitude increased my capacity both to repent and to repair harm from my actions.

Servitude helps us discover our ability to apologize and repent, which are among our most important gifts. When we're doing acts of servitude, we have to remember not to get self-righteous: God and the world don't owe us anything. We're acting to benefit humanity but with humility and an openness to where we might be mistaken.

Remember Your Roots

> *Truly, We have honoured the children of Adam. We carry them on the land and the sea, and have made provision of good things for them [to eat], and have preferred them above many of those whom We created with a marked preferment.*
>
> —Quran 17:70

1. The first words Adam spoke upon him peace were "Alhamdulillah."

2. The story begins with a Divine Plan, a gift of the Divine Breath, and Adam responds with gratitude to that gift.

3. The angels bore witness to that gratitude since they responded to Adam with "Yar Hamuka Allah," or "May God have mercy upon you."

4. Finding utopia will not protect us from the human condition, just as Satan being in the company of angels did not protect him from disobedience. Hence, accept who you are.

5. The angels modeled to Satan how to respond in the face of a Divine command that does not make sense. Instead of debating God's knowledge, they said: "Glory to Thee, of knowledge We have none, save what Thou Hast taught us: In truth it is Thou Who art perfect in knowledge and wisdom."

6. Satan refused to follow the angels, and tried to debate God's knowledge, then blamed God.

7. Satan tried to turn God against human beings. God expelled him from heaven, with no chance of return.

8. We said: "O Adam! dwell thou and thy wife in the Garden; and eat of the bountiful things therein as (where and when) ye will; but approach not this tree, or ye run into harm and transgression."

9. Satan tried to mislead Adam, upon him peace, bringing him into harm and transgression.

10. Adam, upon him peace, modeled to Satan how to respond when you disobey God.

11. Adam, upon him peace, accepted his humanity and coming down to earth, but not losing his relationship with God.

12. God said Satan is His enemy, however, humankind are His servants. The world is the abode of trials and tribulations, not a utopia.

13. If we value our relationship with God, we accept where He stationed us, earth. He is closer to us than our jugular vein. We are here to purify ourselves from listening to lies about God.

14. Satan was not willing to accept that he was bound by error. He was willing to lose God but not his station of privilege and high rank or utopia.

15. Satan prayed for time to prove God wrong and Adam ungrateful. God accepted his prayer.

16. Adam prayed for mercy and forgiveness. God accepted his prayer.

17. God will answer your prayer, so be careful what you pray for, as it might lead you to heaven or hell. What you seek, you will find. Acceptance of your prayer does not imply God is with you.

18. Through His Messengers and books, God sent us guidance on how to return, the gift of faith and what genuine love of God is.

19. Love Is Deeper Than Words

In Chapter 5, Verse 5 of the Holy Quran, God, al Ghani, free of want or need, the Majestic and Exalted says:

> O ye who believe! if any from among you turn back from his Faith, soon will Allah produce a people whom He will love as they will love Him, lowly with the believers, mighty against the rejecters, fighting in the way of Allah, and never afraid of the reproaches of such as find fault. That is the grace of Allah, which He will bestow on whom He pleaseth. And Allah encompasseth all, and He knoweth all things.

God does not need this love. He has many angels and beings in the heavens and earth and sea who submit to His glory. Loving God is a gift that we should seek and nurture within our souls since that will guard and purify our hearts from being misled ever again.

Final Reflections

The author of the Quran is undoubtedly the Most Merciful God and not any human being. The Prophet Muhammad, upon him peace and blessings, was solely the final Messenger who transmitted these teachings to the people. It is crystal clear that these teachings were Divinely imparted to the Prophet through Angel Gabriel.

It is important to note that Allah Almighty is the Teacher of this discourse, rather than Prophet Muhammad, upon him peace and blessings. The Quran begins with the Names of God: Ar-Rahman and Ar-Rahim, emphasizing that the revelation of the Quran sent for the guidance of mankind is a manifestation of Allah's Mercy and Grace.

God is Most Kind and Most Merciful to His creation. The Quran was sent down to provide the necessary knowledge for proper guidance and conduct, ensuring success and well-being in the afterlife. Those who seek wisdom will no longer be lost in the dark as they will find the path to righteousness.

As the Creator of humanity, Allah has taken on the crucial role of guiding us through life by sharing knowledge of what is right and wrong, good and evil, lawful and unlawful. This is a testament to Allah's unparalleled wisdom, justice, and mercy. With utmost confidence, Allah promises to always lead His servants toward the right path, even when crooked ways exist, as eloquently expressed in many chapters of the Quran.

Rest assured that God will always be able to reach us, whether in this life or the afterlife. He has complete control over both realms.

In this world and the Hereafter, we are under His sovereignty, whether we follow the way shown in the Quran, or not. If we adopt error, we will not harm God but only ourselves, and if we adopt the right way, we will not do any benefit to God but will do good only to ourselves. Our disobedience cannot cause any decrease in His sovereignty, and our obedience cannot cause any increase in it.

He alone is the Master of both worlds. If we seek the world, He alone can grant it; and if we seek the well-being of the Hereafter, He alone has the power to bestow it too.

Indeed, those who put forth the effort to attain their goals in this life will receive the rewards they deserve from God. Similarly, those who strive towards earning blessings in the afterlife can be confident that God will bestow these blessings upon them without any doubt.

Study the Quranic Arguments

At times, it is observed that some speakers make use of inappropriate metaphors, such as cheesecake or vase, to advocate for the Quran or God. This can be perceived as lacking morals or needing more knowledge, intelligence, and judgment. Moreover, they often address the audience accusatory and confrontationally, using the word "you."

However, God taught us how to argue with others. Go through the Quran and look for the word - "Qul," translated as "Say".

Prophet Muhammad, upon him peace and blessings, is learning from God how to effectively respond to various arguments presented by others.

Have you studied the arguments of the Quran? Do you respond as the Quran nurtures Muslims to respond by affirming your choice?

Here are some examples:

> *Thus do We explain the signs in detail: that the way of the sinners may be shown up.*
>
> *Say: "I am forbidden to worship those - others than Allah - whom ye call upon."*
>
> *Say: "I will not follow your wain desires: If I did, I would stray from the path, and be not of the company of those who receive guidance."*
>
> *Say: "For me, I (work) on a clear sign from my Lord, but ye reject Him. What ye would see hastened, is not in my power. The command rests with none but Allah: He declares the truth, and He is the best of judges."*
>
> *Say: "If what ye would see hastened were in my power, the matter would be settled at once between you and me. But Allah knoweth best those who do wrong."*
>
> —Quran 6:55-58

And...

> *But when Our Clear Signs are rehearsed unto them, those*

> *who rest not their hope on their meeting with Us,*
>
> *Say: "Bring us a reading other than this, or change this,"*
>
> *Say: "It is not for me, of my own accord, to change it: I follow naught but what is revealed unto me: if I were to disobey my Lord, I should myself fear the penalty of a Great Day (to come)."*
>
> —Quran 10:15

Notice, in most cases the emphasis on *I* instead of *You*. Avoid foolish celebrity influencers and preachers seeking fame and praise, and reflect on the Quran and the arguments used, teaching Muslims how to best respond.

References

al-Bukhari, Ṣahih. "Hadith on Tahajjud: Allah descends in the last third of the night." n.d. 1145.

An-Nabulsi, Dr. Rateb. *Al Aziz*. n.d. <https://knowingallah.com/en/articles/al-aziz/>.

Badri, Malik. *Contemplation An Islamic Psychospiritual Study*. Herndon, Virginia: Cambridge University Press, 2000.

Barakat, Farris. *Reddit*. 17 January 2016. https://www.reddit.com/r/islam/comments/41g6v0/pretty_emotional_message_from_farris_barakat/.

"Behaviorism vs Cognitivism." 4 September 2020. <https://youtu.be/hSAIv1O2P9o>.

Fava, Marta. "How much of the Ocean has been explored?" *Intergovernmental Oceanographic Commission of UNESCO*. 9 May 2022. <https://oceanliteracy.unesco.org/ocean-exploration/>.

Ghabra, Omar. *The Cowardice of Bill Maher's Anti-Muslim Bigotry*. 23 October 2014. https://www.thenation.com/article/archive/cowardice-bill-mahers-anti-muslim-bigotry/.

Harris, Sarah Ann. "Richard Dawkins Continues To Criticise 'Clock Boy' Ahmed Mohamed." *Huffington Post*. 24 11 2015. <https://www.huffingtonpost.co.uk/2015/11/24/richard-dawkins-criticise-clock-boy-ahmed-mohamed_n_8637652.html>.

Haskins, Greg. *A Practical Guide to Critical Thinking: Essential Steps for Developing Sound Reasoning and Arguments while Overcoming Hindrances to Rational Thinking*. Independently published, 2016.

Hays, Tom. *Lurid testimony wraps up in case against self-help guru*. 14 June 2019. https://apnews.com/article/ny-state-wire-new-york-us-news-trials-keith-raniere-10ac73ad4cf647fda507eedcfd847b03.

J. Wesley Boyd M.D., Ph.D. "The Dangers of Countering Violent Extremism (CVE) Programs." *Psychology Today*. 19 July 2016.

⟨https://www.psychologytoday.com/intl/blog/almost-addicted/201607/the-dangers-countering-violent-extremism-cve-programs⟩.

Mahmoud, Dr Mostafa. "The MIracle of Sounds." *Science and Faith*. 11 November 2012. ⟨https://youtu.be/PDTc_KqJp1k⟩.

Mahmoud, Dr. Mostafa. "Language and Communication of Animals." *Science and Faith*. 11 November 2012. ⟨https://youtu.be/s1yi6kaR44M⟩.

"Miracle Survival: Baby Buried Alive, Rescued from Rubble in Syria." *Nour Media Center*. Aleppo, 24 January 2014. YouTube. ⟨https://www.youtube.com/watch?v=sRWJv8h9HxA⟩.

Muslim, Sahih. "Hadith on Justice: The just at the right hand of the Merciful." *1827*. n.d.

Odelya Gertel Kraybill Ph.D. *Trauma Processing: When and When Not?* 11 April 2018. Website. ⟨https://www.psychologytoday.com/us/blog/expressive-trauma-integration/201804/trauma-processing-when-and-when-not⟩.

Reuben, Brother. *Atheist Islam-Hater converts to Islam! Funny yet AMAZING story!* YouTube. 2 November 2011. https://www.youtube.com/watch?v=9xhZ00xnHIA&t=480s. ⟨https://www.youtube.com/watch?v=9xhZ00xnHIA&t=480s⟩.

reviewer, Customer. *Amazon*. 29 August 2017. https://www.amazon.com/gp/customer-reviews/R19OF6EY7HER1P/ref=cm_cr_getr_d_rvw_ttl?ie=UTF8&ASIN=1400034728.

Tompa, Dr Rachel. "Why is the human brain so difficult to understand? We asked 4 neuroscientists." *Allen Institute*. 21 April 2022. ⟨https://alleninstitute.org/what-we-do/brain-science/news-press/articles/why-human-brain-so-difficult-understand-we-asked-4-neuroscientists⟩.

"Tony Robbins' Hot Coal Ritual Goes Horribly Wrong." *Inside Edition*. 24 June 2016. ⟨www.youtube.com/watch?v=LfYtHbmI-NI.⟩.

Acknowledgments

First and foremost, Ar Rashid, Allah the Righteous Teacher who ordains righteousness to all His creatures. He has taught us *bayyan* (speech and intelligence), and beautified faith in our hearts, and sent us Messengers with books of guidance to return us back to Him.

To Prophet Muhammad, upon him peace and blessings, his family, his companions, and their followers, who without their sacrifices we would not know how to be Muslims.

To all the Prophets and Messengers of God, whose stories were used to nurture Prophet Muhammad, upon him peace and blessings, and are a source of benefit for us today.

To the Tabi'een or successors of the companions of Prophet Muhammad, upon him peace and blessings, and the beautiful teachers who have exerted their efforts to learn the religion and teach it, with generosity pass it down to later generations until it reached us and benefitted and was a source of inspiration while writing this book.

Special thanks and appreciation to Shaykh Muhammad Metwalli al-Sha'rawi and Dr. Muhammad Said Ramadan al Bouti, Dr. Rateb an-Nabulsi, and Dr. Umar Faruq Abd-Allah whose online teachings made this book possible.

Dr. Malik Badri and Dr. Mostafa Mahmoud, whose writings on contemplation, science, and religion pushed Muslims, including myself to look at these concepts with the light of faith from the Quran.

Hwaa Irfan, whose patience and forbearance helped me to see things differently. Dr. Abdul Lateef Krauss Abdullah, whose wisdom was inspirational as he responded to people in need of help.

My mother, Amenah Abdel Jawwad Wazwaz and my daughter, Maryam Laid, who were my companions in this journey.

My father, Mohamed Abdur Rahman Wazwaz and all my grandparents, who watched the loss and theft of their homeland, then endured an illegal brutal occupation.

About the Author

Fadwa Wazwaz was born into a family of 10 children in Jerusalem, Palestine. A mother of one daughter, she is a Palestinian Muslim American who was raised in Chicago, Illinois, who began her college years at Knoxville, Tennessee, and who graduated from the University of Minnesota. She has used her time in Minnesota to help build and strengthen the United States' Muslim communities, as well as those communities' ties to other marginalized groups.

She co-founded an educational outreach organization, through which she gave talks to local groups, dispelling negative stereotypes about Islam and Muslims. She has also been trained in Restorative Justice at the Center for Spirituality and Healing and has given workshops to social workers on how to work effectively with youth and Muslim patients. In 2003, she was a community columnist for the Pioneer Press. In 2006, she helped start up a civil rights organization, through which she mentored young leaders.

From 2008 to 2009, she was a policy fellow at the University of Minnesota's Humphrey Institute of Public Affairs, and, in 2009, she started as a blogger for the Star Tribune and worked on helping Minnesotans understand Islam and Muslims. Also in 2009, she and her siblings began a new journey, taking care of their mother, who had suffered a major stroke.

In 2015, she formally began work on her books, bringing together writings from over the past twenty years. In 2020, she published *God Intervenes Between A Person and Their Heart*.

The book, *Love Is Deeper Than Words*, continues on the *Key Lessons from The Prophets*. Wazwaz is a social commentator on issues that affect Muslim communities, Palestinian affairs, faith and values, coexistence, and ethics. She currently blogs at EngageMN.com.

www.ingramcontent.com/pod-product-compliance
Lightning Source LLC
Chambersburg PA
CBHW071949070526
44583CB00015B/1124